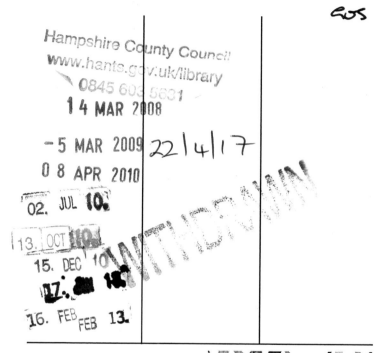
Get **more** out of libraries

Please return or renew this item by the last date shown.
You can renew online at **www.hants.gov.uk/library**
Or by phoning **0845 603 5631**

 Hampshire
County Council

D1342745

C014254310

Human Being to
Human Bomb

Human Being to Human Bomb

Inside the Mind of a Terrorist

Dr Russell Razzaque

ICON BOOKS

Published in the UK in 2008 by
Icon Books Ltd, The Old Dairy,
Brook Road, Thriplow,
Cambridge SG8 7RG
email: info@iconbooks.co.uk
www.iconbooks.co.uk

Sold in the UK, Europe, South Africa and Asia
by Faber & Faber Ltd, 3 Queen Square,
London WC1N 3AU
or their agents

Distributed in the UK, Europe, South Africa and Asia
by TBS Ltd, TBS Distribution Centre, Colchester Road,
Frating Green, Colchester CO7 7DW

This edition published in Australia in 2008
by Allen & Unwin Pty Ltd,
PO Box 8500, 83 Alexander Street,
Crows Nest, NSW 2065

Distributed in Canada by
Penguin Books Canada,
90 Eglinton Avenue East, Suite 700,
Toronto, Ontario M4P 2YE

ISBN 978-1840468-62-5

Typesetting in 11.5pt Plantin by Marie Doherty

Printed and bound in the UK by
Clays of Bungay

Contents

Russell Razzaque is a Muslim and Consultant Psychiatrist in East London where, over the last decade, he has established counselling, leisure, outreach and recreational projects for young Muslims locally. His media appearances are numerous, including the *Independent*, the *Telegraph* and regularly on Sky News.

1

My Escape From The Storm

'Cast not yourselves to perdition with your own hands, and
do good [to others]; surely Allah loves the doers of good.'
—Koran, verse 2:195

An Islam of peace, contemplation, humanity and charity is
what I had been brought up with my whole life. My parents
prayed five times a day, they ate halal food and they
remembered Allah in everything they did. We'd look forward to celebrating Eid each year, and even the fast that
preceded it. I learnt some Arabic through a teacher that my
parents would bring in every week, and I read the Koran.
Religion was a major part of our upbringing, and this was
very different, I found as I grew up, to the outside world
around us. My friends at school were mostly very different
to me, with contrasting lifestyles and home environments to
mine. I felt, however, that I was managing to navigate these
two very different worlds reasonably well. Until, that is, I
left home. Then the cotton wool identity I had constructed
around myself started to unravel.

LONDON, SEPTEMBER 1989. Just like everyone else, I had spent the whole of 'Freshers' Week' hunting for friends around the campus in Aldgate. The very experience of leaving home and going to university was more of a culture shock than I ever imagined it could be. My first friends were other young students who were as fazed as I was by the completely unfamiliar surroundings of a university student union. Before long we had coalesced into a small group of young Muslims and a bond began to develop between us. We were the only people on site who did not drink alcohol, none of us had any experience of pubs, bars or clubs or even girlfriends, we had never danced in a disco, indeed we had seldom survived two days without a curry.

Clinging together like lost children in a shopping mall, we followed each other around the clubs and society stalls on recruitment day. Despite the colourful decor and the enthusiastic senior students behind them, the vast majority of stalls were almost empty, with more students manning than actually visiting them.

Walking into the smaller of the two halls, we were suddenly taken aback. Like ET seeing his mother ship arrive, we looked across the room at the sizeable throng of Asian men and women congregating and chatting around one of the stalls. This had to be home.

Other than the Arabic writing, the slim goatee beards, and the head scarves worn by a few of the women, there didn't appear to be anything obviously Islamic about the stall itself – it looked contemporary by any standard, and so did the people standing behind and around it. This wasn't what I expected from an Islamic Society, and certainly not from Islamic scholars, which is what – as we will see later – some of these men actually claimed to be. Joss sticks, prayer mats, rosary beads and Korans were the characteristics of my religion, but these guys had none of those things. They had a few leaflets and pamphlets and some wonderful food, a book or two and some CDs. They wore jeans and they spoke our language. They were a jolly bunch, too. They cracked jokes and asked us what we were doing later in the evening. Despite a multitude of invitations, none of us had any real plans and, if truth be told, we were slightly afraid of the social structure the student body had placed around us: from 'Toga and Tequila' night to 'Drink a yard of ale' competitions, the evenings seemed to be almost entirely alcohol-based. The more conservative faculty-arranged social events in the daytime, such as 'cheese and wine with the Dean', did not seem terribly far removed to us either.

The Islamic Society, however, served us home-cooked curry in their first Freshers' get-together. The atmosphere was friendly and relaxed. Men and women mixed and we got to know one another. I remember that medics and dentists were evenly divided, but there were also a couple of non-students who were introduced to us as 'very important people' – no more. They too, however, seemed friendly enough. We talked about football, our families back home and how we were finding our first days at university. All the time, however, and unbeknown to us, they were sounding us out – separating the wheat from the chaff. The only sign of religion was a couple of posters on the walls and pamphlets regarding forthcoming meetings and rallies. They seemed to have the word 'Khilafah' all over them – a word I had never heard before. We were encouraged to attend, and most of us there – since for us, this was the only show in town – were only too happy to sign up.

The advertised meeting seemed, on arrival, to be more of a study circle, and this time the tone was altogether more serious. In my childhood, I was taught that the Five Pillars of Islam were: prayers, donation to charity, pilgrimage at least once in a lifetime, fasting, and the declaration of belief. However, rather than discussing the religion in terms of fulfilling these five pillars and exploring them in a more spiritual sense, they were almost completely downplayed. Muslims, they told me, had a greater duty to Allah. There were, apparently, 'hidden pillars' of Islam too. At the time, I had no idea as to the significance of these notions but, come 9/11 and the subsequent attacks in London – in that very neighbourhood – on 7/7, it would become all too painfully clear to me.

The VIP speaker, who had attended the Freshers' social the previous week, introduced himself as Farid Qasim. He was a coordinator for Hizb-Ut-Tahrir, an organisation I had never heard of before that moment. He talked to us about the difficulties of settling into a new life away from home, about how alien the world around us inevitably felt, and about how, for many of us, this would likely be tinged with the experience of racism – more subtle than overt – at the hands of our fellow students, those same people currently drinking themselves silly across the road. This struck a chord with all of us. I looked around the room and it was obvious that a bond was quickly being forged. What I did not realise, however, was that this was a bond that, for many, would endure a lifetime, sometimes even altering the trajectory of that lifetime in previously unimaginable ways. Once he had our full attention and clearly growing respect, he pivoted to the wider issue of the plight of Muslims, just like us, in the rest of the world. He spoke with passion about how our brothers and sisters were being killed in Bosnia, Chechnya, Kashmir, Afghanistan and Palestine. All of this, he said, was inevitable, given the differences in culture, philosophy and attitude. The ultimate manifestation of this difference – as shown by actions in these war zones – was a desire on the part of non-Muslims to always keep us suppressed: it was in their blood.

Our global predicament as Muslims was perfectly tied in to our personal predicaments as Muslim students in a strange, unfamiliar university setting.

Next came the historical context. There was a time when the world was a very different place. A time when Muslims were not oppressed, but lived freely; and not just as equals, but as members of a super-power of their own. This was prior to 1924, when we Muslims were afforded respect and power. This was when, we were told, the Muslim *ummah* (community) existed as a unified body with a large territory across the planet under the leadership of one Khilafah. There was that word.

Khilafah (also known as Caliph) was the name given to the leader of the Muslim world, and the territory ruled by him was known as the Caliphate. The first Khilafah was the Prophet Mohammed himself, who established a system of spirituality-based governance for the lands which, during his time, had converted to Islam. This was indeed a period of unity for the Muslim ummah, but immediately upon the Prophet's death in AD 632 tensions started to arise, most pointedly over the succession. Many believe that the Prophet, during his life, had stated that he wanted his son-in-law and close confidant, Ali ibn Abi Talib, to succeed him. It is uncertain to what extent he had made this clear, as his death came suddenly, after only a two-week illness. A state of confusion then reigned for weeks, while a series of consultations between elder statesmen took place. The result was the proclamation of another of the Prophet's close companions, Abu Bakr, as Caliph. Not all easily submitted to his rule, and in the struggle, Mohammed's own daughter Fatima – the wife of Ali ibn Abi Talib – died. She was pregnant at the time. This was effectively the start of the Shia/Sunni split in Islam. The first four official Caliphs were all formerly close companions of the Prophet, and from AD 661 dynastic succession became the norm with the founding of the Umayyad dynasty. They were, however, overthrown by another dynasty, the Abbasaids, who claimed a closer bloodline to the Prophet, in AD 750. The final dynasty was the Ottomans, whose last Caliphs appeared more preoccupied with expanding their harems than with governing their people (proof of this can be found in Topkapi Palace, Istanbul – the seat of nearly 400 years of Ottoman rule – over a quarter of which was set aside to house all the women of the harem).

The Caliphate, therefore, was far from a single undivided state authority, undefeated and unchallenged like a slab of concrete through time all the way up to its downfall in 1924. Nor was the Khilafah always the best example of the Prophet's piety and humility at all times, either. The whole notion was, and is, a myth; but sitting in this Hizb-Ut-Tahrir study circle, hearing of the concept of Khilafah for the first time, I, like everyone else in the room, had no idea about any of this history. To us it was painted colourfully as a 'golden age' in Islamic history, when Muslims were protected and maintained in peace, harmony, security and comfort at all times, and the Muslim Empire ruled the world. It was only through a return to this age that Muslims could stand proud once again. And, almost hiding away from the mainstream student union crowd that night, in our own little haven, standing proud is just what we wanted to do. This had to be our goal, both on a personal and geopolitical level. This was the hidden pillar of Islam.

Our duty was to fight for the re-establishment of the rule of Allah, not the rule of man. Fighting for the Caliphate was the primary duty of every Muslim, regardless of their age, sex, capacity or country of residence. No details were filled in as to exactly what was involved in this struggle, in a practical sense, but that it needed to be established was not left in any doubt. I must have heard the word Khilafah over 40 times on that day, and by the end of the evening the concept had become imprinted in my mind forever.

The idea possessed the allure of an all-encompassing utopian vision. It promised to banish injustice and inequity for good and, in its place, restore righteousness and perfection. Some of my friends seemed so drawn to it that, although our course began swinging into full intensity – which is, as any first-year medical student will tell you, pretty heavy going – they began to skip classes. Their focus seemed to be on the Islamic Society and, beyond that, the wider activities of Hizb-Ut-Tahrir. I would sometimes see them on the streets fly-posting the 'Khilafah' posters that virtually seemed to blanket Tower Hamlets at the time. The meetings I attended became more and more anti-non-Muslim, something I found difficult to accept, given my increasing friendships with people of all backgrounds from my year group. At their meetings, however, their arguments seemed almost compelling for a moment. 'Why are we here?' one of my closest friends at the time – Naseem Ghoni – a fellow first-year student of Bangladeshi origin, would ask me. It was a rhetorical question. The response: 'To serve Allah and only to serve Allah.' Having accepted that statement, I would then be coaxed down a path, the ultimate conclusion of which was always that it was my duty to fight for an Islamic state here and now, just as much as it was his. I never joined him, however, in his activities, though he and other friends who joined Hizb became increasingly elusive. I often wondered what they were up to, and only recently, in Ed Husain's excellent book *The Islamist*, did I find the answer. Farid Qasim had turned Naseem into a major recruiter for Hizb. He toured universities and colleges up and down the country talking about the hidden pillars of our religion and the impending glory of the Caliphate that awaited us all.

I attended one or two more meetings and began to notice the regular use of another word I had not heard before, 'kuf'. This was short for *kufr*, or infidel. It was a derogatory term to describe non-Muslims, akin to the word 'Paki' as used by British racists. The culture they were propagating saw non-Muslims as beneath them – less than human. That was enough for me. From then on I stayed away from that crowd. My old friends, however, still tried their best to continue their relationship with me and consequently to limit my socialisation with 'kufs'. It was as if they saw me as salvageable.

I got to the point where I actually began to hide from them. Seeing them at the door, I would sit quietly in my room or even crouch behind a sofa to avoid being seen. I decided to learn more about my religion on my own, without having to wear the distorting lenses that my former friends appeared to be wearing. I went back and read the Koran in English – unlike the Arabic version that I, like most of my contemporaries, had read during childhood and only half understood. There are, I found, 49 mentions of the word 'peace' in the Koran, and 83 of the word 'love'. Whole sections of the book are dedicated to diplomacy, respect for other faiths, humanitarian acts and charity.

'And make not God, because of your swearing [by Him], an obstacle to your doing good and guarding [against evil] and making peace between men.'

(Koran, verse 2:224)

'If you give alms openly, it is well, and if you hide it and give it to the poor, it is better for you.'

(Koran, verse 2:271)

'Surely those who believe, and those who are Jews, and the Christians, and the Sabians, whoever believes in God and the Last day and does good, they shall have their reward from their Lord, and there is no fear for them, nor shall they grieve.'

(Koran, verse 2:62)

The more I read, the more I knew they were wrong and so the more determinedly I hid. They were not easy to shake off, but eventually they disappeared. I remember the last time I saw Naseem was towards the end of our degree, in the fourth year. We were both in a placement on an obstetric ward, waiting for the ten babies that every medical student was required to deliver before qualifying. We walked together onto the labour ward, where almost every child was Bangladeshi, and so every baby a Muslim. I commented to him about this huge Bangladeshi birth rate, and he turned to me with the broadest of grins: 'You see man. It's coming! It's coming!' It was as if he was possessed.

A couple of the students who were active in the Hizb, I remember, dropped out of the course and some off the radar screen altogether. I used to wonder what would become of them and the ideology they so tirelessly proselytised.

It would take another ten years for me to find out.

BIRMINGHAM, SEPTEMBER 2001. It was my first rest period for over 30 hours. Being a junior doctor I was used to working in a state of chronic fatigue, still managing to remain alert for important decisions – just. The first rest period after such a long and busy stretch always felt like a deep inhalation after being submerged in water for too long. Having worked in hospital medicine for six years by that time, I had become used to making the most of these moments and slowly phasing out – but not too much – so that if my bleep went off I could always hear it. The television was playing at the other end of the common room and I was barely conscious of it as my systems turned to standby.

My slow wind-down was suddenly interrupted by a sound – the only other sound I was trained to respond to – screaming. It was emanating loudly from the television. I sat up, and there I saw the second plane fly into the World Trade Center.

I was filled, like most of the rest of the world, with horror and disgust, but for me the disgust was multiplied by the subsequent revelation that this had been done by other Muslims and in the name of our religion. For nearly everyone, at that moment, the world seemed to turn on its head – and fear seemed to spread across the globe, including to areas far away from New York. The wall of a newsagents' shop round the corner from my home had new graffiti across it: 'Muslims you're a long way from home.'

Studying the news coverage, I stumbled across an article in a British newspaper exposing the ideology of Al Qaeda.

The article described the motivation behind Al Qaeda's actions: namely, the establishment of an Islamic state. They wanted such an entity to unite Muslims all over the world under the leadership of a single ruler – the Khilafah.

Later TV coverage revealed that the 9/11 bombers all met at university in Hamburg. Possible recruitment pathways into Al Qaeda were then discussed, with university campuses, particularly in Western Europe, singled out as key hubs.

A chill went down my spine as I was struck by the clear resonances with my early university years. This pernicious ideology had spread across the globe, from the Islamic Societies of Western universities to the mountains of Afghanistan, and it had spurred young men to the most horrific acts of barbarity and suicide.

Like everyone else, I wanted to do something to help. As a psychiatrist who had personally gained glimpses of this dark world, I knew there was something I could do. I started to apply my professional knowledge of development, personality and cognitive psychology to an analysis of the individual suicide bombers as I trawled the papers to research their backgrounds. I began to see parallels between their personalities and those of some of the people I had met in my early university years who seemed so easily sucked into the utopian ideology which had ultimately had the opposite effect on me. As the personality type began to take shape, I started contemplating a means of prediction and detection, so that perhaps in the future those vulnerable to following this pathway might be detected early on. I knew that this would one day be the focus of a book I intended to write crystallising my findings.

At the same time I started to discern a form of 'conveyor belt' that took such pre-existing personality types and virtually manufactured them into human bombs at the other end. The more I read, the more I became convinced that such conveyor belts were in operation all over the UK, and indeed Europe. But I always hoped against hope that I was wrong. Four years later, I realised I was not.

———

LONDON, JULY 2005. The inevitable had happened. London was hit, and one of the bombs was in the same place where I had my first encounters with extremist Islam – Aldgate. The first footage focused on the carnage: the deaths and the destruction. Then came the questions. Who could do this? Why? And where did they come from? I knew exactly who they were – young Muslim men, brought up in the UK, just like me. I followed the coverage closely and observed the public reaction. As their identities and backgrounds were released, a previously unimagined horror descended across Britain.

The Prime Minister, nevertheless, stood in a united front with Muslim organisations and declared an instant consensus that the atrocities were the acts of a few lone extremists with no base in the wider Muslim community and no belief that had any resonance with any kind of Islamic or British youth movements. They were far-out, lunatics, fringe elements that had nothing to do with anyone else, and so no one was to blame. Spokespeople for the government and Islamic organisations became too easily comfortable with this picture. So much so, that after the second wave of attempted bombings on 21 July, this official line remained unchanged.

An official inquiry into the atrocity was denied. A palpable fear of the notion that foreign policy, or more specifically, the war in Iraq, had played into the hands of extremist recruiters blinded the government and prevented them from exploring more deeply the malaise beneath the events of that day. Sixteen months earlier, the Spanish government had gone even further, denying that Islamic extremism had anything to do with the Madrid bombings at all, preferring instead to initially pin the blame on Basque separatists.

All of this served to avoid the real challenge facing the world – to look within, for that is where the answer lies: within our own society, our own culture, our own treatment of ethnic minorities at home and foreign powers abroad and, most of all, within ourselves. That is where the spiral of hate begins, and that is where this book will look.

As a second-generation Western Muslim myself, I have found my own experience a good starting point. The dichotomy of being a Muslim in a non-Muslim society is one I have observed in others as well as in myself my whole life. Through my work in youth and community organisations as well as in my professional work as a psychiatrist, I have examined in detail the various outcomes of this inner struggle, and how society – on a local, national and international level – influences that.

The book starts by cataloguing, in detail, the individual stories of each of the leaders of 9/11 and 7/7. Looking back to their earliest days of childhood, we trace their developing minds and observe how they evolved over time – what affected them and how they affected others. By laying out these stories in parallel, we will see the common themes in their journeys and set the scene for the deeper exploration that follows.

Psychoanalysts describe a person's unconscious as the invisible elephant that carries them around. It is only by shining a torch upon what lies underneath each of our visible behaviours that we can truly begin to understand who we are and why we do what we do. Having stripped away the layers of conscious thought and action, we now delve deeper into the bombers' underlying motives – aspects of their psyches that they were unaware of themselves. Through this exploration, the shifting forces beneath each stage of transformation will be brought out into the open, as we follow their inner journeys from birth to violent, self-inflicted death.

In the next chapter we see how aspects of this inner transformation resonate across the board in those men who were the founders of modern extremist Islam. The notions of *jihad* that they developed acted almost as a form of antidote to the psychological turmoil each of these men faced in their childhood years. We explore the ideology and see how the very turmoil that gave birth to it is the same turmoil that encompassed each new generation of followers when they first encountered and then embraced it. This is why it has propagated so infectiously across the world – across languages, cultures and generations.

We go on to learn why it is that the venom of the Islamists is directed almost exclusively towards the West – particularly the US and the UK. This is no accident. In the last half-century, the extent to which these nations have suppressed and manipulated the populations of the Middle East and neighbouring oil-rich countries, when looked at in its entirety, is staggering. It is this cycle of self-interest that has driven these repressed populations towards extremes, and no analysis of the issue of modern Islamic extremism can be complete without a proper examination of this precipitating factor.

In the final chapter I sum up the various causes into a single overarching formula. A variety of strategies to combat this transformation, at a number of levels, are described. Central to these strategies for combating extremism is a tool that can be used, as I had envisaged all those years ago, to detect those who have a pre-existing vulnerability to following a path of extremism, by dint of their underlying personality traits.

The 'Ideological Extremism Vulnerability Scale' represents a major development in the battle against extremist terrorism. It is a 55-question test which is designed from an amalgam of several well-established personality tests. The targeted application of such a test, within a framework of supportive government policy towards disenfranchised Muslim youth, has the potential to slow down, and then finally halt, this conveyor belt.

I will outline a series of solutions that will help divert those detected away from this path. In my work in inner London I have seen many projects designed for Muslim youth that have been very successful in promoting such engagement on many levels – art, sport, film, politics, music, fashion – developing a whole synthesis of Western Muslim culture that young people can gravitate towards without feelings of dissonance. The ultimate goal is to foster a culture that young Muslims can feel at home in, one which demonstrates that there is no contradiction between being Muslim and being British, European, American or anything else.

This is the real war on terror. As Mother Teresa once said: 'Inner peace is the path to World peace.'

2

The Conveyor Belt

'I don't remember the Al Qaeda cells as being something that we were told we needed to do something about.'
—Condoleezza Rice, 8 April 2004

LONDON, 7 JULY 2005, 8:59AM. Hasib Hussain wandered through Boots, the chemists. He was sweating and carried a heavy rucksack on his back. He left the shop and looked around, wondering what he should do next. As he walked on, the instructions he was given years ago came back to him:

'Purify your heart and cleanse it of stains. Forget and be oblivious to that thing called the world. For the time for playing has passed and the time has arrived for rendezvous with the Truth. How much of our lives we have wasted! Shall we not take advantage of these hours to offer up acts of nearness to God and obedience?

'Let your breast be filled with gladness for there is nothing between you and your wedding but mere seconds. Thereby will begin a happy and contented life and immortal blessing with the prophets, the true ones and righteous martyrs. They are the best of companions ...'

17

He walked for almost half a mile, then decided to call his friends.

There was no answer.

He dialled again and again. Still no answer. Hundreds of people start rushing out of King's Cross station, bloody and screaming.

He knows what that means.

He pauses a moment, as if in suspended animation, and thinks back to the first time he met his 'crew' – Shehzad, Mohammed and Germaine.

IT WAS A SMALL GYM IN HARDY STREET – not purpose-built – recently set up with new equipment in the basement of a mosque in Beeston, Leeds. It was frequented by Hasib Hussain, Shehzad Tanweer and Mohammed Sidique Khan, and it was where they were first likely to have met in early 2000. It is certainly where Mohammed Sidique Khan met a lot of young men to whom he became a mentor. He visited a number of gyms where he subsequently established 'study circles' around Islam. He had set up the Hardy Street gym himself, specifically for this purpose.

Born on 20 October 1974, Mohammed Sidique Khan was one of six siblings. His father, Tika, was a factory labourer who moved to Britain from Pakistan in the early sixties with his wife, Mamida. The family was raised in Beeston, then moved to Dewsbury, West Yorkshire, in 2005. Tika was a busy man, having to work hard to feed his large family. It is likely that none of his children got much of his attention. Mohammed spent much of his time outside the home.

In the late seventies, Beeston was a predominantly white area, as was Mohammed's school – Matthew Murray Comprehensive School. Virtually all of Mohammed's friends were white, and he soon began referring to himself as 'Sid' to his friends (after his middle name, Sidique). One of his closest friends, Ian Barrett, remembers him hardly mixing at all with local Muslims, or behaving like them in any respect. 'The other Pakistani lads would have to go to the mosque because their families would say "You're going to mosque." But Sid did not go', says Ian. 'He did not seem interested in Islam and I don't ever remember him mentioning religion.'

Whenever there was conflict between white and Asian youths in the school, Sid was conspicuous by his absence from any of it. 'If it wasn't for the colour of his skin, he would have been [seen as exclusively] English', says Ian. 'I just thought of him as a Beeston lad – and that's what he was – a Beeston lad, born and bred.' He was widely liked among white classmates and, more than anything, remembered for his charm with the girls, neat hairstyles and sensible jumpers.

As we shall see later, contrary to popular belief, Khan's secular leanings and initial steps towards integration with non-Muslims is the more typical profile of an Islamic extremist. Very few of them spring from religious backgrounds and most of them show few, if any, signs of religiosity in their early years.

His parents approached him with an arranged marriage proposal in the traditional Muslim fashion and he rejected it. Instead he dated and later married a fellow student at Dewsbury College, Hasina Patel – an Indian Muslim. By this stage a gulf must have evolved between Mohammed and his parents. Not only did they not know about his relationship with his future wife, but they assumed he would agree to their own choice. Rejecting their selection in this way would have caused a major conflict within the family and left Mohammed's parents feeling humiliated within the local Muslim community.

Mohammed and his parents drifted further apart, leading him, after marriage, to move out of their home. It is usual in working-class Muslim families for the son's wife to move in with his parents' family, but Mohammed and Hasina did the opposite – they moved in with her mother instead. Such a move would have been frowned upon in many quarters of the Muslim community.

Farida Patel, Mohammed's mother-in-law, was a much-respected bilingual teacher and community volunteer. She was honoured in the highest echelons of British society for her good works – once travelling-to Buckingham Palace for a ceremony of recognition. It seems that his mother-in-law's civic-minded personality started to rub off on to the young adult Mohammed, as he began to follow in her footsteps. He got a job as a teaching assistant at Hillside Primary School, helping immigrant children settle into the system. He quickly earned a reputation for outstanding commitment, working regularly beyond the call of duty. The head teacher of the school, Sarah Balfour, said: 'He was great with the children and they loved him – he did so much for them – helping and supporting them and running extra clubs and activities.'

It is clear, at this stage in his life, that he was devoted to his job and increasingly to the multicultural community in which he felt more and more at home. Several years into his teaching career, he was asked to help with a community drugs project, designing an anti-drugs leaflet for local children. The project leader, Mohammed Choudry, recalls a discussion around whether or not the British flag should be placed on the leaflet, when Mohammed interjected forcefully: 'The British flag must be part of it, I was born here and I am proud to be British.'

But not everyone agreed with his stance. And sooner or later – as it had been to every other first- or second-generation non-white immigrant before him – that feeling would be communicated to him. Whether it was an overt attack, a rejection, a slight, or unfair treatment, a different realisation ultimately descended upon him. The feeling of not quite fitting in is one that hits all immigrants – in every generation – at one time or another.

Separated from his parents and wider aspects of his culture, a flame of identity anxiety began to flicker within Mohammed: Who was he really, and where did he fit in?

So he turned to his religion.

Increasingly Islamic undertones began to enter his conversation, and his circle of friends started to narrow. He continued working diligently in his job, however, and his behaviour seemed to change little to the outside world, although he started to take on more and more extra-curricular work.

He began attending mosques regularly and found himself gravitating towards younger hard-liners, and soon began attending study circles. They would talk about the stricter, more political interpretations of Islam – the Islam that saw Muslims as the victims of the world – a philosophy that interpreted every societal failing and every injustice through the lens of a global anti-Muslim conspiracy. They studied works of the more fundamentalist scholars and learnt from one another's collections, then fanned out to community centres and local gyms to recruit others. The base of this growing fundamentalist hard core was the Iqra

21

Islamic bookshop, which, together with the Hardy Street gym and the Leeds Community School, became a Bermuda Triangle of radicalisation for Muslim youth in the area – where many trespassed and some would be lost forever. Even the police became aware of it (though little was done about it at the time), when a 42-year-old computer programmer by the name of Martin Gilbertson walked into the local Holbeck police station saying he had material and names of people he wanted to report to anti-terrorist officers.

Gilbertson had been hired by the Iqra bookshop circle to work on flash media and video presentations for them. One was called 'War on Terror: Hidden Agenda'. 'They would give me material you would never see on television – horrific stuff from Iraq ... Afghanistan and the Middle East – and there I was, editing terrible pictures of what the Americans and Israelis had done to children ... If these pictures can make me cry, what effect are they going to have on some impressionable Muslim youth?' says Gilbertson. They would watch these videos in secluded locations. 'There were back rooms at the bookshop, and access was by invitation only, and, apart from two colleagues of mine, I never saw a non-Muslim inside these rooms. They consisted of a downstairs internet suite with four PCs linked to the web by broadband, a first-floor prayer room and storage room for a women's group that met there every Sunday afternoon.' There they were free to pontificate upon their own radical world-view at the darkest fringes of Islam. 'The talk around me ... was about Jihad, Jewish conspiracy, how the Holocaust was a fake, the "Great Satan" America – and Britain's alliance with the Satanic USA. Bush's word "Crusade" triggered them off – triggered off their ranting about the "Jihad", and we used it in the presentations – very effectively, I would add.'

Mohammed Khan was someone he often bumped into there. 'He wasn't the ranting type; what he seemed to want was kudos within the group, and among people on the street outside. Khan's way was to be a "cool dude"; it was all about kudos in the Muslim community.'

As well as Khan, another increasingly regular attender of the circles was Shehzad Tanweer.

Like Mohammed, Shehzad was not particularly religious in his earlier years, and instead spent much of his time in snooker clubs and on cricket pitches. Known as 'Khakha' to his friends, he was someone who took everything he did very seriously. He rejected most local snooker clubs for the more organised Northern Club which had a regular coach in attendance. In cricket, he batted for the 'Shaan B' team in the Quaide Azam Yorkshire League. Another parallel with Mohammed was that he also had parents who were very busy. Shehzad's father opened one of the earliest halal slaughterhouses in the area – a pioneering and full-time business – and later a fish and chip shop. Shehzad, therefore, threw his attention into sport and enjoyed every aspect of it – so much so that, at eighteen, he won a place at Leeds Metropolitan University to study Sports Science.

During time off he would spend much of his day in local gyms, keeping fit and boxing – a sport he became increasingly passionate about, and through which he met sparring partner Hasib Hussain.

Six foot two, in his teenage years Hasib went to Matthew Murray – the same school as Mohammed Khan, although much later, being thirteen years his junior. Mohammed was ideally placed to act as mentor to Hasib, who began smoking weed and getting into scuffles with local white youths early on in secondary school. His disillusionment appears to have come a lot earlier – he came across as a big, angry young man, who later channelled his energy into boxing and, ultimately, religion.

Although he went on to further education, his heart clearly was not in it. He studied at Thomas Derby College, where he began to turn up wearing robes and Islamic clothing. Noticing his son turning to religion, his father became more than a little perturbed at the direction his beliefs were taking. 'Is it Islam or another religion?' he once asked.

From 2000, Hasib, Shehzad and Mohammed began to meet regularly, talking about their own more and more extreme version of Islam whenever they got the chance – eventually forming their own more exclusive study circle around the gym and bookshop together. Each person's disillusionment added to that of the others as they compounded their sense of alienation from the rest of society and railed in increasing anger against it. Others would be allowed into their select group, but they stayed only if they could talk the talk. One such person was Germaine Lindsay.

Like the others, Germaine was never religious in his younger years; in fact he was not a Muslim at all. Again, he went through a trajectory of integration into the society he believed was his home, and then turned. He went to Rawthorpe High School in Huddersfield and was described by classmates as academically bright but also a good sprinter and interested in sport. 'He did weights and took that weight gain stuff. He was into boxing and was always practising flying kicks.' He seemed content after he left school in his job as a carpet-fitter in Huddersfield, and seemed to have no quarrels with the wider world. On 9/11, when watching the footage of the falling towers on TV, he cried with his mother.

Within a year of that, however, things had changed.

He converted to Islam, and neighbours and friends began to notice a difference – not that he had many close friends in the first place. 'He was always a bit of a loner', said one local man. However, after his conversion 'he used to pray with all the other Asians'. By then he was already married to Samantha Lewthwaite, whom he persuaded to convert to Islam as well as his mother. Despite not being a particularly sociable family, the conversion was noticeable to locals. 'He started growing a beard and wearing a Muslim cap', said one, while other neighbours complained: 'He played Koranic CDs loudly all day.'

The one area of his life that remained consistent was his interest in martial arts and physical fitness, and so he frequented local gyms on a regular basis. This is where he met the others. With his increasing interest in Islam, and retreat from the world around him, he became quickly hooked into their world. Their developing philosophy complemented his increasingly agitated state.

Each of them had started by finding sport as a means of discharging their frustrations and anxieties, and then transferred that aggression into religion. The gym was therefore a natural meeting place, and others of like mind also drifted in and out. Their regular gym, in Hardy Street, soon became known to local youths as the 'Al Qaeda gym' and, over time, only those who were sympathetic to their growing militancy attended.

Other similar extremist hubs were forming around the world at the same time. As we will see later, this sequestration from the outside community is a key step in the conveyor belt. People radicalise in groups, never alone. They need to bounce off each other's prejudices and anger in a kind of venomous synergism to travel further. Groups which develop a hard-core membership begin to grow a life of their own – sending their attenders down a trail of ultimate self-destruction.

This is a trail that was first blazed by four men in Frankfurt in the late nineties. It was their example that every single emerging cell has followed – and still follows – since they went to their deaths on 11 September 2001.

THE LIFE STORIES OF THE LEADERS OF THE 9/11 BOMBERS – Mohammed Atta (Amir), Ramzi Bin Al-Shibh (Omar), Ziad Jarrah, and Marwan Al-Shehi – read as definitive case-studies of the Islamist extremist, especially that of the man who ultimately led them – Mohammed Atta: robotic in his demeanour, obsessional in his personality and, once his cause was found, unflinching in his determination.

It was in the remote Egyptian delta province of Kafr El-Sheik that Mohammed Atta – known as Amir – was born in 1968. His parents had an arranged marriage when his mother was fourteen and his father was already practising as a lawyer with degrees in civil as well as Islamic (Shariah) law. Marriage at this age was not uncommon in these parts and, as the daughter of a wealthy trading and farming family, Amir's mother provided a route to fast-track social advancement for his father. The couple had two daughters and later, a son – Mohammed Amir Atta – named after his father.

Village life in Egypt is very open, with strong bonds between kin; however, even after the children arrived, Mohammed senior remained a private man, aloof from his and his in-laws' families. A serious and stubborn character, he was rigid in his views and very set in his ways. He was also an ambitious man – single-minded and intensely goal-orientated. He was not a religious man, but had big plans for his future, which is why he moved to Cairo in 1978. According to his sister-in-law Fateh, 'he wanted to be famous'.

He bought a large flat in the city, giving the children plenty of space – but only physical space. There was no room for social or emotional outlets of any kind. Amir's maternal aunt described it as 'a house of study. No playing, no entertainment. Just study.' Terry McDermott, in his book *Perfect Soldiers: The 9/11 Hijackers – Who They Were, Why They Did It*, describes the scene:

> The children weren't allowed to play outside the apartment. Young Amir's room looked out the back of the building, over rooftops into a tangle of wires and adjacent windows. Neighbours said he used his window for clandestine conversations with local boys. That was playtime. On the rare occasions they were allowed to watch television, said a cousin, Amir would leave the room whenever belly dancing programs – staples of Egyptian broadcasting – came on.
>
> 'Amir's friends would sit on the corner there chewing pistachios, spitting out shells. Not Amir. There was no hanging around, no friends, very strict rules,' said a neighbour … Another neighbour said the walk to elementary school – a mere 100 metres away – had been timed, and if the children took longer than the allotted few minutes to get home they would be called to account. And another neighbour said they sometimes

heard the father shouting at the children. 'No one ever shouted back,' he said.

The father himself was unapologetic about his lack of sociability. 'We are people who keep to ourselves,' he said. 'We don't mix a lot with people and we are all successful.'

Amir certainly had a lot to live up to academically. After studying at the prestigious University of Cairo, one sister, Azza, became a cardiologist and the other, Mona, went on to become a professor of zoology. These were the standards Amir was expected to meet and was constantly pushed towards by his father. Amir eventually gained entry to Cairo University and excelled in his first year, being selected, after his foundation year, to specialise in engineering. The best students, which included Amir, in the engineering faculty were awarded a place to study architecture, but it was in this field that Amir's academic star began to wane. He continued to excel at the more analytical fact-based subjects, but in the creative and artistic areas he fell significantly behind. This was clearly not a side of his brain he was able to draw from – and given the weight of such subjects in his architecture course, his overall marks were low. Amir's, as we shall see later, is a good example of the mode of thinking developed by would-be suicide bombers during their childhood. It is one that favours fact- and science-based learning and is very poor at more subjective, debatable or artistic subjects.

He did not take this very well. A friend said that he was 'so like a child that one time something happened where he did not get the grade he wanted, and he pouted. Somebody said to him, "You're acting like a child", then he got very

very angry, proving the point. He really was like a child. Spoiled.'

His father drove him to and from university every day. He also insisted that his son enrol in an English class at the American University of Cairo. Mohammed senior's ambitions for his son were clearly secular, and he always steered him clear of political Islam. He was a supporter of the secular government and identified with its cultural values.

Amir graduated in the middle of his class. This is unlikely to have pleased his father, who insisted that he go on to study further – at least until he had earned the title 'Doctor' before his name, as both his sisters had done. He was persuaded to seek places in postgraduate centres abroad and to learn German, for which he took language classes at the Goethe Institute.

His father's pressure was relentless. 'My son is a very sensitive man: he is soft and was extremely attached to his mother', said Mohammed senior. 'I almost tricked him into going to Germany, otherwise he never wanted to leave Egypt ... But by pure coincidence, a friend of mine had visitors from Germany, two high school teachers in Hamburg. I invited them to dinner and Mohammed was the king of the evening because he spoke German fluently.'

In his father's eyes, Amir was always in need of absolute direction. Of course he had no idea where the path he was pushing him down would lead, but he was keen for him to have some education abroad, and that evening proved to be a turning-point.

Two weeks later, Amir was in Hamburg.

By now Amir had grown into almost the perfect receptacle for the ideology that was to drive him to his heinous death. All the ingredients were present in abundance during his childhood, as we will soon recognise: his father raised a secular household, though was himself at all times stern, aloof, rigid and almost completely devoid of affection. Amir was left without a fully developed sense of self, of who he was or how or where he fitted in. He gained a mode of thinking that was able to work only in black-and-white, all-or-nothing terms, so his judgements would tend to fall into one of two categories: right and wrong, good and evil. A concrete-minded, almost robotic, deeply insecure character, uncomfortable in his own skin, with little sense of his own place in the world – this was the man who landed in Hamburg in 1992. He was highly vulnerable at this point (and he would have scored highly in any test of vulnerability administered to him any time since his arrival in Hamburg), but it would take an encounter with a virulent ideology at exactly the right moment to turn this vulnerability into something more sinister.

He was given accommodation by the two teachers whom he met in Cairo and who allowed him to stay rent-free at their home. His first reaction on arrival in this alien country was to turn to religion. His religious practices soon went beyond anything his father or family had ever observed: he prayed five times a day, at a mosque whenever possible, observed a strict halal diet and avoided any socialisation with non-Muslims, particularly women. He made his objection to Western women's clothing very clear – shrinking from anyone wearing a short skirt or sleeveless blouse. He was clearly uneasy in the bars, clubs, restaurants and cosmopolitan, open culture of Hamburg.

His host family was keen to be supportive at this time of adjustment and, as a favour, during a trip to Cairo, they had his visa upgraded from tourist to student status, which he required for his studies. Instead of expressing gratitude, however, he exploded: 'I am grown up now! I can take care of myself!' 'He said a lot', his host said. 'I am abroad now: I am grown up now. I can decide on my own!'

The first day he arrived for college, however, things went from bad to worse. He turned up for the postgraduate architecture programme at the Hamburg University of Applied Sciences to find that he had been, in fact, denied admission. The university said the programme was full. His father was outraged, alleging racism, and Amir threatened legal action. The university quickly relented, admitting him to the course for the 1992 autumn term.

Two weeks into his studies there, however, he left for a new course in urban planning at the Technical University of Hamburg-Harburg (TUHH). Being a more analytical, fact-based course, Amir was far better suited it.

Through his turmoils, his hosts made constant attempts to reach him, but his then-Muslim landlady felt there was 'always a wall between him and the family'. She debated the Koran and the Bible with him, arguing that the roots of both religions were the same, but she ended up increasingly perturbed by the closed-mindedness of his views; and when her daughter visited, a whole new layer of anger seemed to erupt. She was a single mother who would arrive with her child and, although he played lovingly with the child, Amir never missed an opportunity to scowl at her mother for her supposed moral laxity. When she turned up he would often leave the room in a huff.

In the spring of 1993, by mutual agreement, he moved out.

His next abode was a two-bedroom university-subsidised apartment that he had to share with another student. His first flatmate was a slightly anxious young Asian student with whom Amir quickly ran into difficulties. Amir only rarely cleaned his dishes or the bathroom, he left his food uncovered in the fridge, sometimes for weeks, and would rarely take on any chores. He wore the same clothes most of the time and saw food preparation as a cumbersome chore – so much so that most days he would simply mash up a pile of boiled potatoes and shovel them into his mouth with a fork, leaving most of it behind so he could return to it – without reheating – again and again for a week or more. 'This is boring', he would say. 'Eating is boring.'

But more than house-training and hygiene, it was his personality that drove the flatmate out and quickly began to bear down on the next student who was housed in his place. The second flatmate was chosen specifically by the house manager for his laid-back attitude to life, and at first he began to make an effort to connect with Amir. Once he invited him along to watch a film with him. It was Disney's *The Jungle Book*. On arrival in the theatre Amir was instantly uncomfortable, soon writhing in his seat with agitation. 'Chaos, chaos!' he would mutter to himself repeatedly – the chattering, the giggling, the sound of eating and the general unruliness – he couldn't bear it. On his way home Amir remained completely mute, and when he entered the flat he went straight to his bedroom and slammed the door behind him.

He seemed to have no friends and was never seen laughing. 'He was reluctant to any joy', the flatmate said. He kept his own bedroom neat and tidy, and whenever he ventured out of it he said little or nothing – not even a greeting. The flatmate's girlfriend – a frequent visitor – found him even more difficult to deal with: he never even looked her in the eye. She persuaded her boyfriend to put up a nude picture on the bathroom wall and eventually Amir asked for its removal. She then replaced it with a photo of the Muppet character, Miss Piggy – wearing a negligee.

Meanwhile, at university, Amir was also found to be quiet and reluctant to engage at first. He would not enter discussions quickly, but instead listened and would then come back a week later with a comment on the matter. It was hard to draw him on any subject – even outside the classroom, he always appeared to consider his comments carefully, never the first one to speak. He seemed to have a very thick filter through which he passed everything before issuing an opinion.

Interestingly, however, he displayed a marked deference towards his superiors and teachers who knew their subject area well. This is a trait I have personally observed in those vulnerable to extremism. At university, those who gravitated towards the further extremes of the Islamic Society tended to skip lectures, but if there was a teacher they admired, they would always attend, listen intently and often speak of him in hallowed tones afterwards. The yearning for guidance, for a lead – a father figure – to help fill the ever-growing void within was almost palpable. This easy transition into idealisation, we will see later on, is a key characteristic of those vulnerable to extremism, and it was very evident in Amir. Classmates described his attitude as 'respect bordering awe', and a professor referred to him as 'beeindruckt und beeindruckbar', meaning impressed and impressionable.

A similar impression was gained by his employers at Plankontor – an urban planning firm where he worked part-time. He was an efficient and industrious worker, often going beyond the call of duty in his work. He earned the nickname 'Kleinteilig' – which meant that he paid precise attention to detail without necessarily seeing the broader picture. One of the firm's partners, Jorg Lewin, said: 'I think he embodied the idea of drawing. I am the drawer. I draw.' He was 100 per cent focused and dedicated in his work and always respectful and accepting to his employers – never once stepping out of line or offering even comments or suggestions that he considered beyond his station.

Though generally well-regarded by a firm with a liberal internationalist outlook, Amir never joined the company's social activities, always declined invitations to lunch and never went on the firm's holiday trips.

In the summer of 1995, however, he won a grant to go to Cairo and study the Egyptian government's plans for development of an old section of the city, known as Islamic City. On arrival with two other students, however, Amir and his colleagues were instantly taken aback by the way in which the government was displacing the indigenous population to make way for a totally new environment. The young students challenged the Egyptian bureaucracy, while, at the same time, Amir began making inquiries about possible employment and a future in the Egyptian civil service. What he found was a system riddled with nepotism and corruption. During his stay, his criticism of the government intensified and broadened day by day. A spark of anger seemed to have been ignited within him as he railed more and more passionately against the leadership of his country.

After the five-week trip, the other two students returned to Hamburg but Amir, after spending some time visiting his family, travelled to perform the pilgrimage – Hajj – in Mecca.

On his return, his classmates found him to be – if it were possible – even more introverted. But at the same time this virtual recluse seemed to be budding another dimension to his personality. This different side to Amir was discovered suddenly one day when fellow student Volker Hauth passed a mosque in which Amir was praying. What he saw was a self-confident, proud young man leading the congregation in prayer. He was animated, socially adept – talking to anyone and everyone there, smiling – even playful. Hauth was astonished. Amir was a man who had appeared to speak only when necessary and who never appeared to enjoy anything; yet here he was, 'like a fish in water'.

He frequented mosques increasingly as his dedication to Islam took over more and more of his life. He grew a beard and eventually settled on his favourite mosque – one which he began to attend on a regular basis, a mosque that would change his life forever, as well as that of countless other young Muslim men – Al Quds.

Al Quds was founded by Moroccans and still had a significant Moroccan contingent in attendance by the time of Amir's arrival. However, by then it had become well known for a more sinister reason altogether. It was the most hardline, extremist mosque in Germany and it attracted militant Islamists from far away. Some young men would even enrol in the nearby university to be able to attend there regularly, while moderate local Muslim families would dissuade their children from ever setting foot in it.

The message was uncompromising, yet for those who responded there was an embrace. One of the main preachers there was a Moroccan man – Mohammed Fazazi. A commanding presence at six foot three, and part of a rising tide of militant Islam spreading around the globe, his version of Islam involved the killing of unbelievers as an obligation to Allah. 'Who participates in the war against Islam is an infidel on a war footing, that shall be killed, no matter if it's a man, a woman or a child', he would say. 'The jihad for God's cause is hard for the infidels because our religion has ordered us to cut their throats and that we kill their heirs is a hard thing ... God the merciful has created the hell for the infidels as he created the paradise for the believers too.'

He would blast this message out to the worshippers, and those to whom it appealed returned – those who were appalled by it never did. Social circles developed out of this congregation, and before long, through regular attendance, Amir found himself centrally involved in the activities of the mosque. He began teaching classes there increasingly frequently, which were as much about politics as religious education. He would talk about the plight of the Palestinians and downtrodden Muslims in Chechnya, Afghanistan and around the world, and stir up a sense of injustice in his pupils. He was, however, also harsh with them in terms of following a prescribed set of rules, and would not tolerate long hair – certainly not ponytails – jewellery, music or headphones. All of that was the work of the devil, and they were there to follow Allah strictly and to the word. Women were forbidden from attending at all times. He led his own group on Friday and Sunday evenings and co-led another group on Tuesdays and Thursdays.

His religious teaching would not, however, stop at his classes. He would continue giving instruction on prayer to the students of the university on their way to and from the mosque.

'Don't cut corners when you pray', Amir would tell fellow student Malkat every day. 'Pray the last three of four prayers separately, not en bloc. Also, usually you pray the duty prayer, a special prayer, and you also praise Allah with a third prayer, which is not a duty.' He would rarely stop. Eventually, Malkat started to leave the mosque early to avoid Amir, whom he started referring to as the ayatollah.

Amir became so engrossed with the mosque that he wasn't seen at his course for the next two years. If he wasn't in the mosque, then his friends from the mosque would be visiting him in his flat. They were, of course, all men – mainly young – and from a variety of backgrounds: North Africans, Gulf Arabs, Syrians, Germans and even Indonesians. Usually there was not a word of interaction between them and Amir's flatmates. He never even introduced them. He often helped the newcomers to organise themselves, find accommodation and navigate their way round the university and local bureaucracy.

The network broadened and soon another man began to run parallel classes at the mosque, a man who grew to become Amir's best friend – Ramzi Bin Al-Shibh – or Omar to his friends.

Omar arrived in Germany in August 1995 and handed the immigration authorities a note: 'Dear sirs, with this application I ask you for political asylum. Your sincerely, Ramzi Omar.'

He was sent to Lübeck to make his application and given accommodation at a refugee centre there while he awaited a judgement. In his case he stated that he was an economics student from Sudan, where he was arrested after anti-government demonstrations. In fact he was not from Sudan at all, but from the Yemen.

Omar's father had been a busy merchant who died in 1987, after which his elder brother, Ahmed, took over his upbringing. Omar was a gregarious child, often mischievous yet always the centre of his mother's affection – a relationship that Ahmed was often envious of. None of his family, again, was particularly religious, and it was only Omar who, in his teenage years, began attending the local mosque. This was a time when militancy in Islam was growing around the world and countries like the Yemen were endorsing the Muslim mujahideen rebellion against the Soviet Union.

Omar's brother was busy trying to raise his own family as well as his father's, and also working as an analyst at an economic research institute, so although he was effectively Omar's male guardian, the necessary closeness was lacking. Omar worked as a messenger boy in the meantime, but began planning his escape to a new life in the West. 'He was always one of those guys talking about studying in Europe or the US', said Ahmed. 'He saved money for years. He wanted to improve himself. He was very ambitious and forward-looking. We couldn't afford the expense of sending him.' So he worked hard, raised the money and eventually set off for Germany where – compared to other countries – he thought he'd have a better chance of securing a visa.

However, he was initially met with rejection when his asylum claim was denied on the grounds of implausibility. He appealed, and during the process was sent to stay in a camp near the town of Kummerfeld. He was registered as a resident there for over two years but in fact hardly spent any time there at all. He was determined to find a way to stay in Germany in case his appeal failed (which eventually it did), and so he sought numerous jobs – sometimes two at a time – and earned money to travel and meet people, explore avenues and eventually secure a student visa. On his journeys he stayed with a variety of people who were happy to help a fellow asylum-seeker. Through them he was introduced to and attended a number of mosques, becoming more and more drawn to his religion as the host society of the country he came to join seemed to be reject-ing him.

Eventually he arrived at Al Quds mosque. There he began to develop a sense of common cause. It was there that he met Amir, and a deep friendship quickly developed. By winter 1995 they had grown so close that Omar was spending more and more of his time in Amir's flat.

Though at times inseparable, Omar and Amir were different in many ways in terms of their outer persona. Where Amir was a cold, withdrawn man of few words and no laughter, Omar seemed to be outwardly playful, almost carefree – although in comparison to Amir it was not hard to appear that way, and some who met him described him as hectoring and unpleasant. Nevertheless, the two came across as a contrasting double act and began touring local mosques and meeting young Muslim men in the area. They shared a common determination to explore the furthest reaches of their religion, and the more they explored the hungrier they seemed to get. They organised study circles around Koranic texts and heard tapes of sermons from obscure scholars with more and more extreme interpretations of Islam. They found men from local mosques with a similar drive whom they got to know and then invited to their discussion groups. As time went on, their whole waking day became one giant discussion group – dissecting, analysing, interpreting and expanding. A German investigator described the scene: 'They are not talking about daily life stuff, such a buying cars – they buy cars, but they don't talk about it, they talk about religion most of the time … these people are just living for their religion, meaning for them that they just live now for their life after death, the paradise. They want to live obeying God so they can enter paradise. Everything else doesn't matter.'

Over three years, dozens of men drifted in and out of Omar and Amir's group. One of those who stayed was Ziad

Jarrah. Again, outwardly, there was no obvious militancy about Ziad – his early life, his family or his background. He was a Lebanese man from a well-off family in Beirut. His father was a middle-ranking civil servant and his family drove round in Mercedes Benz cars. They owned an apartment in town as well as a second home in the country. While Ziad was very much a city boy, his father preferred the country, so he spent most of his early years apart from his father. Ziad attended a private Christian school and appeared to be more interested in girls than school work. Again, there was virtually no sign of religion in the household. Men drank whisky in the evening and women wore short skirts around town and bikinis at the beach.

When he left school, Ziad was given a choice of two places abroad to study. One was in Canada and the other Greifswald, Germany – both places where the family had relatives. He chose Germany.

Soon after his arrival he met dental student Aysel Sengun – an attractive daughter of Turkish immigrants to southern Germany. She had already been in university for a semester and had a boyfriend, but it seems Ziad's charms won her over and they soon began seeing each other regularly. She helped him learn German and they would go out on the town together, although they were both quickly disappointed to learn that Greifswald was no modern metropolis like the cities they had come from. It was altogether smaller and more parochial, many of its styles and fashions almost seemed to be stuck in a time warp, and there was also a neo-Nazi skinhead element in town. For someone who had looked forward to experiencing the modernity and openness of Western society – a society he had longed to join – this environment must have come as a culture shock to him, and the racism as a body-blow.

Ziad began to turn inward, away from Greifswald society, and soon he found a particularly attractive alternative to turn to. Abdulrachman Al-Makhadi was a classmate of Aysel and a self-styled Islamic enforcer on the campus. He led prayers in the neighbourhood mosque – which the locals would refer to as 'the box' – and there he would preach a harsh version of Islam between prayers, often keeping people behind until the early hours of the morning. He was also known to hold collections for the Palestinian terrorist group Hamas. He had immigrated from Yemen and lived near the campus with his wife and children, studying in name only. He visited Hamburg regularly, where he found a growing collection of fellow-travellers.

In early 1997, Ziad is reported to have told Aysel that he was 'dissatisfied with his life up till now', that he wanted to make his mark and 'did not want to leave earth in a natural way'. After returning from a trip back home in winter, he no longer seemed to be the laid-back playboy of old, becoming altogether more serious. His cousin noticed him reading the radical Islamist publication *Al Jihad*.

His new lifestyle caused immediate friction with Aysel, who wanted to find out more about what was going on inside her boyfriend's head, but he was not forthcoming. They had very different communication styles and there was a new layer developing within Ziad that she was finding impossible to reach.

Almost all suicide bombers manage to successfully hide their transformation from those around them. Ziad was the rare exception. His relationship with Aysel allows us to gain a great deal of insight into his growing deviation, but at the same time, as we shall see, it was also the reason why the others in his group grew increasingly concerned about his ability to follow through the mission, and perhaps ultimately why, by what would have been their standards, he failed. Of them all, he was probably the most rescueable, but at the time no one could have imagined where his journey would ultimately lead.

After finishing his German classes, Ziad applied to study dentistry, like Aysel, at Greifswald; but he also applied for biochemistry there as well, and aeronautical engineering at Hamburg, in addition to several other medical schools in western Germany. He was accepted to several courses in the end, but lied to Aysel and said it was only the aeronautical engineering course in Hamburg that had accepted him. Somehow – almost certainly through Makhadi – Ziad had learnt of the burgeoning community in Hamburg and set his sights on moving there. Within days he was a regular at Al Quds mosque.

He travelled back to Greifswald most weekends to see Aysel, but increasingly his time during the week was spent with Omar and Amir and their inner circle. They would sit at the back on the right side of the main prayer room, where they could be found at every prayer session. As the network expanded, more new faces emerged. Then one day appeared a man who was instantly a hit with the group. With his background steeped in the religion, he would take their knowledge of radical Islam to new levels, raising their sights to what only recently would have been considered unthinkable. He was Marwan Al-Shehi.

Although from the oil-rich United Arab Emirates, Shehi – as he was known to most – came from a relatively modest background. His father was a muezzin – that is, he issued the call to prayer from the mosque. A devout Muslim with strict views, he dictated his son's upbringing with a degree of rigidity that ensured he did not stray from his prescribed path. He took him to the mosque regularly, and Shehi would stand in for him when his father was away.

He joined the army after school and from there was awarded a scholarship to study in Bonn, Germany. Though he had no academic interests, Shehi went to class on a regular basis and remained committed throughout. He was deliberately inflexible when it came to his religious practices, much to the chagrin of fellow Arab students who followed more of a 'when in Rome' philosophy. Then his father died in the spring of 1997. This was a major and sudden blow to Shehi, given his father's influence on his life thus far. He made a request for leave on compassionate grounds, but the army denied him. After a short while he left anyway, returning to find that he had been failed in his course, which he had to retake the next year. This time his religious devotion intensified. He was cold and aloof with the family he lived with, and even started refusing visits to McDonald's because he had heard they used pork fat to make their french fries.

He attended the local mosque regularly and began to mix in radical circles which attracted him, like a magnet, towards Hamburg. Then, in the winter of 1997, he managed to secure a transfer there. Like Amir, Omar and Ziad before him, he fitted into the environment 'like a fish in water'. He immediately relaxed among his new friends and, coming from a more hard-line Islamic background than any of the others, he was quickly deferred to for his greater knowledge of jihad and martyrdom. He enjoyed every minute with the group – humming jihad songs as he ate and entertaining the others with Arabic fairy tales. When it came to his religious beliefs, however, he was deadly serious and possessed no doubt in his mind about them. The point in their beliefs that the others were reaching through study and networking was the point where Shehi had been since he was a child. His arrival on the scene at this time served to cement the notions they had been incubating and provided them with confirmation that they were on the right path.

Amir and Omar had very different teaching styles. Amir's was very rigid, which often put people off. Every session would start with a reading from the Koran by a member of the group, then comments on the passage by another, followed by reading of some statements from the Prophet, and then Amir himself would speak on the subject. Only after that was a wider discussion allowed to ensue – until then the rest were required to remain silent. What put people off just as much as the rules was Amir's almost completely robotic behaviour, which broke only if and when he became angry. He never laughed. When asked why this was, he would respond: 'How can you laugh when people are dying in Palestine?' Once he told a fellow worshipper: 'Joy kills the heart.'

Amir had to vacate his student accommodation that summer and so moved into a flat in a suburb called Wilhelmsburg. Only this time, the gang came with him. It gradually developed into almost a parallel universe in which they spent all their time, with few links to the outside world. Through interviews with neighbours, Terry McDermott has managed to shed some light into what it was like:

There was almost a feral quality to their activities. They were seldom seen outside and when they were they were moving in a pack. Inside they kept the blinds drawn shut night and day. They had no furniture, only mattresses. They piled their clothes in a corner of the living room floor. They spread newspapers on the floor in place of a tablecloth and ate their meals sitting there. There was no telephone or, apart from the lights [and television], electrical devices of any kind. The men talked long into the night most nights and disappeared all day most days, says Helga Link, a downstairs neighbour. Link lived directly beneath their apartment and could hear every footfall on the hardwood floors. She never once heard a radio or a television or a single note of music – just soft stockinged footsteps and the voices of men talking.

Their main bridge to the outside world was Omar, who acted as a kind of recruiter/ambassador for the group. His active nature meant he was out a lot of the time, but he was always dedicated and focused, visiting mosques and networking with young Muslims, inviting some of the more like-minded ones back to the flat and establishing useful links with others. He always kept a mobile phone and a note pad in his pocket, and continued around an almost constant circuit during the day – including the university campus, student homes and other study circles. He would travel up and down Germany, as if on a mission, but always returned to the flat.

Though superficially fluid, with a few people coming and going, the inner sanctum of the group remained solid – Omar, Amir, Shehi and Ziad. They became closer and closer until it almost seemed that they started to blend into each other, sharing everything from cars to bank accounts, eating together, cleaning together, staying together most nights, praying together five times a day – even holding hands as they did. They would talk, sometimes all night, about their beliefs and also about conspiracy theories. They believed Monica Lewinsky to be an agent of Mossad – Israeli intelligence. They would watch battlefield videos together and sing songs about martyrdom. Increasingly preoccupied with the notion of martyrdom, Omar would say: 'It is the highest thing to die for the jihad. The mujahideen die peacefully. They die with a smile on their lips, their dead bodies are soft, while the bodies of the killed infidels are stiff.'

Later in 1998, they moved from the flat in Wilhelmsburg to a larger one in Harburg – Marienstrasse 54. It had three bedrooms, a full kitchen, was cleaner and had been recently refurbished. They referred to it as 'Dar Al Ansar' – the house of followers. Their landlord remembers them as ideal tenants – they paid on time, were never noisy, and they looked to him like philosophy students: always pensive and preoccupied. Streams of men would come and go all the time, eat a simple evening meal, and talk of jihad through the night.

A consistent dynamic began to evolve. Amir was the one who set the rules, and his talk was more about politics. He saw giant conspiracy theories everywhere in the world, at the base of which were always the Jews and Americans – he believed that Jews ran America and this was all part of a giant war against Islam. Omar, on the other hand, made more of an emotive appeal based on the religion and the obligations that flowed from it to fulfil their duties to Allah. He gave them a sense of purpose. He played them jihad songs and showed them propaganda videos about Chechnya, Bosnia and Kosovo, telling them that their obligation was to go to these places where Islam was under attack and fight as holy warriors. Ultimately, however, 'One has to do something about America', he said.

Meanwhile, clarion calls for jihadis were going off everywhere that year. Osama Bin Laden released a statement, issuing his most public and explicit fatwa on the United

States, and a couple of months later the US embassies in Kenya and Tanzania were attacked with truck bombs, causing the slaughter of hundreds.

At the same time, Omar, Amir and their group seemed to be preparing themselves for something. They were feeling a call to jihad. Though the shape and form of their role was, as yet, undetermined, they were nevertheless focused on being ready to leave and fight at any time. Some of them began physical fitness training, others tidied up personal affairs – assigned powers of attorney and handed over bank accounts to friends. They rushed to give up or finish their courses.

After a whole year of absence, Amir returned to his course to complete it. His tutor asked him why he had been away, and Amir told him he had had problems 'in the family at home … Please understand, I don't want to talk about it.' And that was that. He then plunged back into working on his final thesis. Six months later, in the spring of 1999, he submitted a 152-page manuscript with an inscription praising Allah on the front page. It was a work of urban analysis on the design of contemporary cities, and one of the issues he considered was how to accommodate women in the home all the time instead of working. His tutor assigned another professor to work with Amir to polish the thesis – she was female. He worked side by side with her, at the same table, for six weeks until he could continue no longer. Complaining that he could not bear to be in such close proximity to her, he terminated the sessions. He finished off the thesis himself and was awarded high marks for his final submission.

Problems around the issue of women would often crop up for the group. Omar would occasionally be caught taking a sneaky look at a woman on the street and then grin in embarrassment when frowned upon by the others – there were even rumours that he entered into a relationship with a woman on one of his tours. But it was Ziad Jarrah for whom the issue was most vexing. He continued to see Aysel, a westernised woman who went out, socialised and drank alcohol, and all out of wedlock. To try to improve the situation Ziad decided to marry her, and in the spring of 1999 they married at Tabligh mosque – not Al Quds, at Aysel's instance. However, it was a quiet affair – neither family was invited, and it was not even registered with the state. It was almost as if Ziad was trying to hide the event. Aysel herself once said she did not consider it a genuine marriage; however, it was genuine enough for her to ensure that Ziad signed a contract specifying that Aysel should be allow to continue her studies.

Soon after the wedding, Ziad's visits to her quickly tailed off, ultimately becoming rare events, with contact in between visits also waning. Within weeks they had broken up, but, as they had many times before, they made up again soon after. When they were together their notes to each other would ooze with intimacy and affection, with Ziad writing long-drawn-out goodbyeeeeeeeeeeeeeeeeeeeeeeeees at the end of his e-mails and Aysel writing: 'It's me again. How is my darling? All I can say is I miss you very very much. Meow. I want to cuddle. I love you.'

Ziad then tried to renege on his agreement regarding her medical studies, trying again to talk her out of a career, and it was only after the intervention, at Aysel's request, of the imam who married them that Ziad reluctantly dropped it. By late summer, however, they had split up again. He never let her into the Marienstrasse flat, saying it was a place women could not visit, and when she came to Hamburg to see him he would often leave her at a rented flat alone while he stayed at Marienstrasse. Aysel always knew that it was not another woman that was keeping him away – it was the mosque, the boys, religion and jihad.

'He spoke about religion in general and tried to convert me step by step', she said, 'his opinion about the jihad, the holy war, I was afraid because of that. That was the reason I spoke to friends about it, to learn more about jihad. And I also felt at that time that I wasn't the centre of Ziad's life anymore. It was faith and religion. He started to visit me less. Because of me being afraid I did not mention the issue of jihad anymore. I couldn't and did not want to understand and I couldn't hear of it anymore.'

Then Aysel became pregnant. After some consideration she had an abortion. 'I don't want to be left behind with children because my husband moved into a fanatic war', she told a friend. She told him afterwards: 'I had to think about our baby today. I am sorry about everything I did to you.' Their yo-yo relationship continued. Sometimes he would be out of touch for days, and when that happened she would phone round everyone she knew who he mixed with, once even trawling through one of his phone bills, calling every number on it looking for him. As days passed, she felt him slip away more and more. In a note she wrote:

Again you haven't been reachable. I left a message for you to call me back. Since you haven't done so, I assume you haven't been at home at all. I couldn't sleep last night and I thought for a long long time. What is love for you? ... I want to tell you what is love for me: To take the other as he is, to share everything with him you have (mentally and physically, materially, in all areas of life) to do something for the other you wouldn't do for yourself, to be there for the other (especially in bad times) ... I just want to ask you one thing: Be honest to me, and don't just say it, if you don't mean it with all you believe and if you think I would change my mind about jihad ... Think carefully about it, if you can't give me that promise, it is better to forget about our marriage even though it would hurt a lot ... In love, Aysel.

It wasn't just Aysel that Ziad was moving away from, however – it was his family too. They saw less and less of him, and reports went back to Lebanon that his studies were waning and he was spending more and more of his time in mosques. They sent people to talk to him and once threatened to stop his allowance. Another time he was told that his father had suffered a heart attack in the hope that he would visit home. He did not.

The allure of the group was proving irresistible to Ziad. By now they had found the extremist teachings of Abu Qatada – a London-based Palestinian cleric who was increasingly popular as a spiritual leader within radical circles. In his videos he talked of the obligation under Islam to put right the world currently run by infidels. It was a Muslim's duty to do whatever was necessary to remove the infidel from power, and to do this he implored Muslims to kill the infidels' children, capture their women and destroy their homes. It was God's will that they die. This corresponded well with Omar and Amir's view of the universe. 'Paradise', they would tell their friends, 'is overshadowed with swords.' They called Qatada regularly, scrutinised and pored over every word he uttered.

In Qatada, the men found a perfect subject for their idealisation. He was telling them what they wanted to hear, only taking it several steps further. Again, the void was being filled, but this time it was moving beyond ideology into the realms of personal goals and plans. Although in subsequent investigations into suicide bombings the figure of an Al Qaeda/terrorist mentor has often been an elusive one, this idealised character is always an essential component of the process of radicalisation.

Evidence of the strengthening bond and hardening ideology growing within the group came about at a public gathering in October when a frequent visitor to the flat, Said Bahaji, decided to get married. The ceremony was, of course, held at Al Quds. It was a male-only ceremony, with any women packed away behind a cream curtain in one corner of the room. Virtually nothing about it resembled a wedding, and towards the end Omar stood and gave a speech. 'We are now in school, like in Arabic lessons', he said. 'In the end we will all have a test. In this test some will pass and others won't.' He apologised for bringing politics into it, then continued: 'The problem of Jerusalem is the problem of the Muslim nation, the beloved nation. To talk about that does not harm this wedding, quite the contrary. Every Muslim has the aim to free the Islamic soil from the tyrants and oppressors.' Jerusalem, he concluded, would one day be swept 'by a wave of fire and blood'. He then handed the microphone to Shehi, who led a chorus of jihad songs. One went:

I came to this life
Which is only a short elusive pleasure
A journey through, a battle
I became fire and light, a melody and fragrance.
Until I lived a generation
Which I spend watching you through the light
My eyes are full of light
Mine are the virgins in paradise

I sing like an angel
That you are the light of my eyes
These gardens smell sweet
And their smell is my wound
He is the spirit
I have been visited by the prophets
And my brothers are martyrs.

One person conspicuous by his absence from the proceedings was Amir. He had gone to visit his family in Egypt. His parents had split up over the arrangements for his sister's wedding. His mother's family had chosen a suitor – a heart surgeon – who was not to Mohammed senior's liking. His mother's health was deteriorating (she had diabetes) and Amir spent more of his time with her. He said that he wanted to stay to look after her, but she would have none of it. She told him she was at one with his father, who had issued strict instructions that Amir had to return to Germany to continue his studies – he had to earn the word 'Doctor' before his name.

This final command – another rejection – from his father agitated Amir further, and this was evident on his return to Hamburg. He was now more impatient than ever. The group would punctuate their discourse with sudden shouts of 'Our Way!', to which others would shout back 'Jihad!' The atmosphere was increasingly frenzied – Shehi spoke longingly of paradise: the peace, the joy, sitting beneath a lone shade tree on the banks of a river of honey, and of course the virgins.

In early October Ziad wrote himself a note: 'The morning will come. The victors will come, will come. We swear to beat you. The Earth will shake beneath your feet.' And later he wrote: 'I came to you with men who love death just as you love life … The mujahideen give their money for the weapons, food, and journeys to win and to die for Allah's cause, but the unhappy ones will be killed. Oh the smell of paradise is rising.' He asked Aysel to help him pack some belongings he had in a nearby flat in Hamburg. She was scared and suspected something terrible might be afoot, but he reassured her that he was going to Lebanon to visit his parents. She knew he wasn't.

That same month, Shehi withdrew $7,000 from his bank account to pay for air tickets.

They left separately so as not to raise suspicion. First Shehi, then Amir and Ziad and then finally Omar.

They seemed to vanish from Hamburg into thin air. The next time they were seen was in Karachi.

THIS SAME DISAPPEARING ACT HAS BEEN PERFORMED REPEATEDLY in the years since by hardening Muslim youth around the world, undergoing ever-deeper stages of transformation. Back in Leeds in 2001, Mohammed Khan left his job, family and wife, unexpectedly, to travel to Malaysia. Whatever reason he gave them, it certainly wasn't the truth, which was that he was visiting a Jemaah Islamiah training camp.

Jemaah Islamiah's roots are in the original Darul Islam movement which spread across South-East Asia in the fifties. It was a particularly virulent strand of Islam advocating the overthrow of all governments in the region to establish a pan-national Islamic state there. It instigated a number of armed revolts against several governments, but after a widespread clamp-down it was all but exterminated by the end of the decade. However, an ideologue named

Abu Bakr Bashir continued proselytising the message through a pirate radio station. He managed to garner enough support to establish an Islamic boarding school in Java whose motto was 'Death in the way of Allah is our highest aspiration'. Bashir tried to incite several armed insurrections through this, but was unsuccessful each time and eventually jailed.

After his escape from prison in 1982, he fled to Malaysia where he began to recruit jihadists from that country as well as Indonesia, the Philippines and Singapore under the new banner of 'Jemaah Islamiah'. The main work of Jemaah Islamiah became one of propaganda. Rather than engaging in any armed uprising, the organisation stuck to holding discussions, study groups, pamphleteering and lecturing, and that is the way it would have continued had it not been for the arrival of Riduan Isamuddin – otherwise known as Hambali. Having graduated from one of Al Qaeda's training camps in Afghanistan, Hambali was a fully experienced and trained mujahideen, ready to put his new-found fervour into action. It was not long before Jemaah Islamiah began translating its words into action, and soon they were transformed into an outpost for Al Qaeda, sponsoring operations in the Philippines and surrounding areas. In 2000, it was responsible for a series of multiple church bombings across Indonesia and later spread its targets to government buildings and shopping malls.

During his trip to the Jemaah Islamiah training camps, Mohammed Khan met Hambali and a series of discussions between the men ensued.

Khan returned to England with a new-found vigour and, back in his home town of Leeds, he and Shehzad Tanweer, Hasib Hussain and Germaine Lindsay moved their meetings to a more private venue – the Hamara

Community Centre. Away from the open-plan atmosphere of a gym, they had their own space to which they could escape, removing themselves from what they increasingly saw as the impure, infidel-ridden world around them. The subjects of their conversation remain locked in that room forever. There they returned again and again – talking, debating and plotting until the early hours of the morning.

By day they would make forays out into the community, spreading their brand of Islam. The most effective way they had found to do this – and one that is used by radical Islamist groups throughout the UK – was through drug counselling services. In a town where heroin use was widespread this was an ideal means of recruitment. 'They cleared up the area', a local man said. 'Lads would be taken by the group and put through cold turkey by locking them in a room for five days.' They then took the young men on outings, encouraged physical fitness and fostered a sense of kinship within the group. Though the trips were of an adventure/recreational nature, they would be taken very seriously – Mohammed would help some of the boys out, supporting them any way he could. Shehzad was remembered for taking a paint-balling trip particularly to heart on one occasion, proving an expert marksman with his gun. 'He was approaching it like a proper soldier', said one who attended. However, these trips were available only to their own kind: 'To be invited on one of these outings you had to be part of their religious set … They would not take lads who had become too "westernised" for their liking.' The group grew to a strength of fifteen regulars and became known as 'the Mullah Crew'.

Though spreading their broader message further afield in this way, the mainstay of their activity was in preparing themselves for higher things within the confines of the base they had been constructing at Hamara. Even after the centre closed, they continued to meet there regularly. Neighbours would see the four enter there at all hours and wonder what they could be doing in a now-disused building. Ironically, the likely assumption was drug use.

In 2003, Mohammed Khan made a couple more trips abroad. The first was for a suspected involvement with the first-ever British suicide bombers – Asif Hanif and Omar Shariff. Coming from neighbouring Derby, these two young men were likely to have been introduced to jihadist circles through Hizb-Ut-Tahrir, the supposedly non-violent international Islamic party which, like Jemaah Islamiah, advocates the establishment of a pan-national Islamic state – the Caliphate. Although claiming to be a peaceful movement, it nevertheless demands the overthrow of 'kufr' – infidel – governments around the world to achieve its ends, and in the early nineties it recruited heavily in university campuses, including my own, which I subsequently learnt was one of their central hubs. It was to this very organisation that I lost several friends in my medical school days – see Chapter 1.

Mohammed Khan travelled to Israel on 19 February 2003, and just over a month later Asif Hanif and Omar Shariff attacked Mike's Place, a bar in Tel Aviv, killing themselves and three others. After their deaths, investigators found a stash of Hizb-Ut-Tahrir literature in Omar Shariff's house and his wife testified to his being an active member.

The second trip Khan attempted was to the US, only this time he never made it. Over recent months, the CIA had become aware of a friendship that he had sparked over the internet with a man they had been watching in Northern Virginia by the name of Ahmed Omar Abu Ali. He and Khan would exchange e-mails with ideas for a

string of violent activities, including 'blowing up syna-
gogues on the East Coast'. On studying the case, Dan
Coleman of the CIA declared, in a memo to his colleagues:
'This is a very dangerous character ... we and the Brits
should be all over this guy.'

There is a cloud of uncertainty over what the intelligence services on both sides of the Atlantic then did with
this information, but the action they took was minimal –
perhaps even counterproductive. On the day Khan arrived
in Heathrow to fly to see his friend, he was informed, at the
check-in counter, that he was on a US 'no-fly' list and so
not allowed to travel there. He must have been bemused by
the experience but, perhaps for the first time, alerted to the
fact that somewhere, and on some level, he was being
watched. Any plans he was hatching now had to be executed with a greater sense of urgency.

That occasion was not, however, the last time the intelligence services encountered Khan. MI5 surveillance records
reveal that in February 2004, Khan met up with Omar
Khyam in Crawley, 25 miles south of London. Khyam was
subsequently convicted, in May 2007, of the fertiliser bomb
plot which was thought to have targeted several central
London locations including the Ministry of Sound night-
club. Khan and Khyam were followed as they spent the whole
day together, travelling around town in a white Honda.
They stopped for a meal in a local kebab shop before Khan
dropped Khyam off and headed back home up the M1.

Several months later he travelled to Pakistan to meet
known Al Qaeda fixer Hasan Bhatt. This was followed by a
longer trip back there the following year. This time he took
Shehzad Tanweer with him.

They travelled together to Karachi in November 2004
on Turkish Airlines flight TK1056. From there they took a

train to Lahore, where they stayed in a hotel for a week in the Saddar area. Next they travelled to Faisalabad, and from there it is thought that Khan went on to Rawalpindi and Tanweer to the home of his maternal uncle, Tahir Pervez. Pervez was a landowner in the village of Kottan in Punjab. Shehzad spent several weeks of his three-month visit there, and Pervez was struck by the extent of his nephew's religious devotion: 'He wore a beard and the sel-war kameez [traditional flowing garbs worn by strict Muslims]. If you woke up in the night sometimes he would be praying on his mat.' In the time they spent together his uncle learned a lot about him, and he did not like every-thing he saw. He was very different from the young boy who had visited him in 2002. 'He said Bin Laden was his hero and everything he did was right. He believed that America had made Muslims suffer all over the world. He also used to say about Kashmir that India was committing great atrocities against the Muslims.' His feeling for the Muslims in Kashmir seemed to run deep. 'When his father in England gave him money to buy clothes he would not spend it on himself, but for buying coats for those waging the jihad in Kashmir.'

Shehzad went on to demonstrate a commitment to Kashmir, however, that went beyond words and clothes. It is reported that one of the visits he made on that trip was to meet Osama Nazir, one of the leading activists of radical group Jaish-e-Mohammed.

Jaish-e-Mohammed was formed in 2000 on the release of its leader, Masood Azhar – a notorious militant Islamist – from an Indian prison in exchange for the safe return of 155 hijacked Indian Airlines hostages. Their avowed aim was to unite the whole of Kashmir with Pakistan under the framework, again, of a pan-national Islamic state, and on

13 December 2001 they were held responsible for the terrorist attack on the Indian Parliament in New Delhi.

Shehzad Tanweer travelled extensively during his trip. He would visit a number of Islamic schools – madrashas – stay for a few days, make some contacts and then move on. He seemed to be shopping for militants. Places he travelled to included a madrasha in Mudrike run by banned Sunni group Lashkar-e-Taibi, twenty miles outside Lahore. He is also said to have been sighted at this time in terrorist training camps in Mansehra, a remote area near the Kashmir border, run by Harkat-ul-Mujahedin (meaning 'movement for holy warriors'), who admitted to the kidnapping and beheading of the *Wall Street Journal* reporter Daniel Pearl in February 2002.

Tanweer was visited, while at his uncle's, on numerous occasions by Khan. 'They seemed like great friends', Pervez said. 'They would talk and laugh for long stretches of time together.'

It is likely to have been around this time that their mission began to take shape as a specific plan started emerging. Hasib Hussain also came to Karachi in July of the same year, travelling on flight SV714 from Riyadh. It was a trip they all had to take – a pilgrimage followed by every Western suicide bomber of recent times ...

ARRIVING IN KARACHI FROM GERMANY BACK IN NOVEMBER 1999, Omar, Amir, Ziad and Shehi took domestic flights to Quetta. From there they were instructed to take a taxi to the local Taliban office. Any taxi driver would know where to go, they were told, and indeed that was the case. They had to leave all their belongings at the

Taliban guesthouse before donning local attire, after which they would be transported through the Pakistan/Afghanistan border. This was about as porous a border as anywhere in the world. The checkpoint could easily be driven straight through or around without any problem.

The training base, like a gigantic insect colony, was a sprawling network of up to 50 different camps, layered in a loose hierarchical system – each funded and sponsored by one of a variety of radical Islamic organisations around the world. Some camps specialised in certain forms of warfare, such as urban warfare, sabotage, rocketry and bomb-making. Graduation from one level would lead to the next, providing higher and higher levels of training. The Al Qaeda camps were based in Khalden, near Kandahar.

Each morning would start with dawn prayers, then physical fitness training followed by an hour-long class-room lecture, then prayers, then drills/weaponry training. After an afternoon nap, the cycle would continue until bed time around 8:30pm. Bin Laden would tour the camps giving lectures and encouraging the trainees. A particular poll he would often cite demonstrated that an international survey had shown him to be more popular than the United States – something he was evidently pleased about.

Few men ever got the chance to have a one-to-one with Bin Laden. Not long into their training, however, Omar, Amir, Ziad and Shehi were invited to Bin Laden's flat in Kandahar, and there waiting for them was Bin Laden himself. The men had completed questionnaires upon arrival at the camps, and their demographics, place of residence and background seemed to fit with exactly what Bin Laden had been looking for. The last question on the survey was: 'Are you prepared to commit a martyrdom operation?', to which they had each answered: 'Yes.'

They had talked for months about the glory of being a martyr, about the higher place in paradise afforded to anyone who died in this way, and how the best method to serve Allah was to follow this path. To talk of it, study and sing about it was one thing, however, but to commit to it was another. This was why Bin Laden asked them again, face to face. Were they prepared to accept a mission that would result in their certain deaths? Would they pledge to him their loyalty and their lives?

The answer, of course, was yes.

Bin Laden was now ready to activate the plan he had been working on for the last two years – 'the planes operation'. These men would lead it, but they were not yet allowed to know their roles. After pledging oaths, they were sent back to their camps to await further instructions. From there they would be sent to Karachi to meet the director of the operation, Khaled Sheikh Mohammed. They were kept in the dark at that time deliberately – if they were apprehended on the way, they would have nothing to reveal.

The first World Trade Center bombing was carried out in 1993 by Ramzi Yousef. A worldwide manhunt ensued for two years, at the end of which Yousef was captured at a hotel in Islamabad, Pakistan. As CIA agents flew him into the US, they descended over Manhattan. Removing his blindfold as they passed the twin towers, they told him to look out of the window. He looked for a few moments then turned and said: 'If I had my way, I would have brought them both down.'

What they did not know was that he had already begun to hatch a plan to do just that. The first person he brought the idea to was his uncle, Khaled Sheikh Mohammed – known to the CIA as KSM. Another graduate of the anti-Soviet Afghan jihad along with Bin Laden, Hambali, Ayman Al-Zawahiri, Abdullah Azzam and others (see Chapter 4),

KSM was well connected in the Islamist terrorist world, although he tended to work more as a freelancer like his nephew. On hearing of the outline of the planes operation, however, he knew that the only network big enough to hatch something like this would be Al Qaeda, so he joined forces with Bin Laden in the late nineties, swearing an oath of fealty to him.

The plot itself had evolved through several versions, starting with ten planes, with KSM himself hijacking the tenth, landing it at an airport and making a speech condemning US policy in the Middle East before releasing the women and children passengers. Bin Laden gradually scaled the plan down to four planes. The original scenario involved hijackers seizing control of the aircraft, rather than flying them. Over time, the necessity for actual pilots to maintain maximum control became apparent, and so the hunt started for pilots or men capable of training to be pilots in the US.

KSM met them for the first time in Karachi in December 1999. Amir had already been chosen by Bin Laden to lead the group – his absolutist thinking, single-mindedness and attention to detail made him the perfect candidate. KSM elaborated on the operation they had been chosen to perform. At the end of the meeting they were instructed to return to Germany and obtain visas for the US, where they should enlist in training programmes that would prepare them for flying commercial airliners.

They returned as they had arrived – one by one. Shehi first, stopping at his home in the United Arab Emirates, Ziad and Amir heading back to Germany, and Omar setting off last, staying behind a little longer to record his suicide/martyrdom video.

ON RETURN, THE TRANSFORMING HUMAN BOMB IS OFTEN NOTICEABLY DIFFERENT. He is now a 'soldier'. Mohammed Khan started to subtly overhaul his life after returning home from Karachi in February 2005. He and his wife had moved to a new home in Lees Holm in Dewsbury. By now they had a ten-month-old daughter and his wife was reported to be pregnant again. Instead of stepping up his work to support his growing family, however, he made an unexpected move.

Only four months before, he had supervised a school trip on a tour of the Houses of Parliament with his MP, John Trickett, who was also the partner of Sarah Balfour, the head teacher of his school. He met Hilary Benn, the International Development Secretary, and by all accounts the trip went well. He made no complaints to his employers about his job, and he received none from them about his performance. Nevertheless, in early 2005, he resigned.

At a similar time, Germaine Lindsay met up with Egyptian chemistry student Magdi Mahmoud El-Nashar. It was a chance meeting during prayers in a Leeds mosque, and Lindsay approached him about finding some accommodation. He said his wife and he were looking to move into the area, and El-Nashar was keen to help someone he assumed was a recent convert to the religion. Through his then landlord he located a flat for the couple at 18 Alexander Grove in Burley.

Lindsay had no intention of living there, however, moving instead with his wife – also pregnant with her second child – to a flat in Aylesbury, 30 miles north-west of London, in April 2005. On one visit to the Burley flat he introduced El-Nashar to a man he said was called Mohammed – he later turned out to be Hasib Hussain.

The men did everything they could to uphold the semblance of normality. They would each go to the mosque as usual and continue their community activities with the Mullah Crew. Tanweer would continue to spend time with his family regularly, behaving towards them as he always did. One evening in May, however, while watching a documentary on Muslims in Britain with his parents, he turned to them and said: 'You better get out of here. Everyone's going to hate you.'

Tanweer, Hussain, Khan and Lindsay would visit the Alexander Grove flat with increasing frequency through the spring of 2005. They started to bring with them large containers which they used to store explosives that they had been constructing in the bathroom. The flat had effectively been turned into a bomb factory.

They taped net curtains across all the windows of the flat so no one could look in, but they were unable to prevent the smell and fumes of the chemicals escaping. Neighbours would often wonder what was going on in there, as the leaves of surrounding trees began to die. The men would wear shower caps when working with the chemicals so as not to discolour their hair, but their families, nevertheless, noticed some fading. When asked about it, Tanweer, Hussain, Khan and Lindsay would simply inform them that it came from the chlorine in the local swimming pool.

They had crossed the Rubicon – their words had finally turned into fervent action. They had contemplated it for so long and now they were ready. Their journey to paradise was now well under way.

SHEHI ARRIVED AT NEWARK INTERNATIONAL AIRPORT in New Jersey on 29 May 2000 and Amir followed five days later. They each took a convoluted route through several countries to get to the US, making it harder to trace where they had come from. They had also acquired new passports, claiming to have lost their old ones, so as to erase any record of their Afghanistan visit. Soon after their arrival they enrolled into Huffman Aviation for commercial pilot training on the Florida Gulf coast. Ziad Jarrah had already started classes at another flight school only a couple of hundred feet away. Both schools used Venice Airport for practical sessions. As Ziad had already moved into his own accommodation, Amir and Shehi rented a place together in the nearby town of Nokomis. Again, their landlord was very pleased with his new tenants – they were quiet, frugal and did not even use the air conditioning.

All three of them were diligent students, even taking extra lessons on flight simulators in neighbouring towns. Their fellow students found Shehi and Amir cordial – although sometimes brusque in Amir's case – but never social. The two would be seen together so much that most assumed they must have been related in some way. No one had reason to believe they were other than what they claimed to be – middle managers in computer firms.

Meanwhile they were receiving regular wire transfers from KSM to manage their fees and living expenses. They both sailed through their first exams, earning licences to fly single-engine commercial aircraft by December 2000.

The impression Ziad left with his classmates was, however, altogether different. He made friends with a few of them – taking a trip to the Bahamas with several on one occasion. He even moved in with some of his colleagues at one point, claiming his own flat was unfurnished. Despite his efforts at friendship, however, many found him to have a short fuse. He was occasionally awkward and hostile, and always cocky. He seemed to claim confidence in areas he had no reason to – including flying. One fellow student refused to fly with him, saying he wasn't careful enough in the cockpit.

His relationship with his classmates was, however, the least of his worries. It was the situation with Aysel that was the hardest to handle. Before flying to the US, one day, out of the blue, Ziad suddenly appeared on Aysel's doorstep. She hadn't known if she would ever see him again, and so his arrival brought relief and joy. What's more, the Ziad that turned up this time appeared to be the one she had originally fallen in love with. He had brought her gifts – jewellery, honey, shoes and a skirt – and started to talk to her about long-term plans together, about how he wanted to follow his childhood dream of being a pilot and how together they could lead professional lives and start a family. It was all music to Aysel's ears, but she still did not know where he had been.

'And of course I asked questions. "Where have you been?" And I did not ask it once. I asked it a lot of times. The only answer I got was "Don't ask me." Later he would say "Don't ask me, it's better for you." That sort of irritated me, so I asked, "Why was it better for me?" I would not receive an answer.

'At some point I just told myself, "It's OK," and I was content with the situation. Basically I was happy that he was here and that his *sturm und drang* – that's how I interpreted his time – was over … He came back without a beard and I hoped that he had decided for me.'

Ziad did seem altogether more relaxed about his religion, more moderate, and so together they put the past behind them and started looking for local flight schools. The peace lasted a couple of weeks until one day Aysel came home to find a message on the answering machine from a representative of a flying school in Florida, USA. She was shocked that his old ways of evasion and deceit had returned but, as ever, he had a list of explanations. He said that it was the best training and that he could complete it quicker than anywhere else. Also, the US certifications he would earn were transferable to any other country, widening his employment prospects with airlines around the world, and finally it would enable him to get away from his old friends in Hamburg – the religious ones who had led him so far astray. Aysel accepted this. What she did not know, however, was that those same mysterious friends would be right there with him in the USA.

Once in the US, Ziad would fly back to Germany to see Aysel every couple of months with gifts, and the first time he returned, in October, he took her on a trip to Paris. They ate, drank and took in the sights on a whirlwind weekend. Once she flew to Florida to visit him and he flew her down to the Keys to show her the Boeing simulator he had been training on. With his parents sending at least $2,000 a month, they never wanted for money. 'He was leading a high roller's life', Aysel said. 'Whenever he or I needed money, I just had to call Ziad's parents, just tell them how much. Whenever I called up his parents and they asked how much I needed, they would always send over two or three times as much.'

Ziad's parents were the only family who had even the vaguest idea of what was happening with their son. Amir's parents believed he was studying for a PhD in urban planning, albeit in the US, and Shehi's family seems to have known nothing at all. He used to phone regularly every year during the month of Ramadan but in December 2000, when he failed to call once, his mother grew concerned. She contacted the UAE embassy in Bonn, who made inquiries as to his whereabouts at the Technical University in Harburg. They informed the embassy that they had not seen him for a year and that he had, in fact, been removed from the school's registration rolls altogether. His brother, Mohammed, was then dispatched to find him in Germany, and he and an officer from the embassy spent several days searching Bonn and Hamburg for him. Eventually they ran into Mounir El-Motassadeq, to whom Shehi had signed power of attorney over his bank accounts, and he informed Mohammed that his brother was likely to be in Afghanistan or Chechnya. Mohammed returned home empty-handed. Soon after that, however, Shehi, having heard what was going on in Germany, called home. He told them that he had in fact been transferred to another college and was living in a different part of Hamburg. He explained that things were looking up and his course would soon be complete. That seemed to do the trick – reassuring them enough to prevent any further investigations or expeditions.

Meanwhile, Omar was the only one of the original four who was still actually in Germany, and he was doing everything in his power to get out. His first application for a US visa failed and so he immediately appealed. He appears to have assumed correctly that his application failed on the basis that the embassy saw him as a possible economic migrant and not a genuine student, so to rectify this he arranged for several thousand dollars to be deposited in his Yemeni bank account. His second application, nevertheless, also failed. He made two more attempts, and in the final one wired $2,200 to the flight school where Ziad was training to book a place on the course and use this as evidence toward his student visa application. His desperation comes through in a note he sent the flight training school to inquire about his visa:

TOP URGENT
I wish to inform me by which company did you send me my visa document and which code nr has the mail got.

Please inform me today. It's too important. I'm waiting for.

All applications failed. 'Please acknowledge that we cannot give you a visa', was the American embassy's final communication to him. His part in the plot had collapsed.

He was, however, determined to stay involved. This was not a mission he had any intention of bailing out of – he saw it as his duty. As he had already been acting as something of a go-between for finance, logistical support and communication between KSM (and other Al Qaeda hierarchy) and his friends, he stepped up his work in this area and formalised his role as the official intermediary – just as he had been, in many ways, when he and the boys had first moved in together to the flat in Wilhelmsburg.

As 2001 arrived, the operation stepped up a pace. The group travelled across the length and breadth of the US to scrutinise airport security procedures, familiarise themselves with the general layout, and identify flaws within the system. The small print of the plan was clearly evolving. Amir alone travelled to Oklahoma, Nevada, New Jersey, Virginia, California, Georgia, Massachusetts and Maine.

In late spring the 'muscle hijackers' began to arrive. These were the men who were assigned with the task of seizing the aircraft and controlling and killing the passengers and crew to enable the pilots to do their job. They arrived over a period of two months and Amir received each of them at the airport in person, taking them to their accommodation and starting the briefing right away.

All but one of the men were from Saudi Arabia, and most of their fathers were well-off tradesmen or civil servants with busy lives. 'Several were described as among the best boys – bright, respectful – in their towns', writes Terry McDermott, and in their early lives 'none of them stood out for their religious or political activism.' However, things changed later. 'Many had [been] to University in Riyadh or Jeddah. Three had studied Islamic law. At least one, Ahmed Ibrahim Al-Haznawi, just 21 years old, had memorised the Koran, a sign of deep devotion, much respected by others. One man, Wail Al-Shehri, was a physical education teacher. Shehri had grown depressed, his family said, in late 1999. His father sent him to a local imam for advice. The imam prescribed recitation of Koranic verses to treat the depression. Not long after he and his brother left home for Afghanistan.'

In the Al Qaeda camps, the training for these men centred around physical power-building and hand-to-hand combat. Before they left Afghanistan, many of them recorded videos in which their unflinching certainty, indeed fervent enthusiasm for what they were about to do came through loud and clear. In his recording, Abdul Aziz Al-Omari tells us: 'I am writing this in my full conscience and I am writing this in expectation of the end which is near. An end which is really a beginning. We will get you, we will humiliate you. We will never stop following you … May God reward all those who trained me on this path and were behind this noble act and a special mention should be made of the Mujahid leader, Sheikh Osama Bin Laden, may God protect him. May God accept our deeds.'

They travelled to the US via Dubai in the UAE, where they were met by another nephew of KSM for a final round of training on how to dress and behave in the US. They were also loaded up with bank account details, money and credit cards.

Upon arrival, they enrolled as members of their local gyms and worked out regularly. They also travelled with the pilots on surveillance flights, looking into airline practices and protocols, while the pilots also conducted test flights in light aircraft around target areas.

On 8 July 2001, Amir flew to Spain for a meeting with Omar. He was clearly nervous, making over 74 calls the day before he left. Omar flew directly to Tarragona, the town of their meeting. Amir took a flight to Madrid, then rented a silver Hyundai and drove there. The town was a popular tourist resort on the Mediterranean coast, where hundreds of thousands of European, particularly British, tourists flocked at this time of year, and it was in the midst of them that Amir and Omar met for the last time. The meeting was organised by a well-known Al Qaeda fixer in Spain, Abu Dada, who went on to become one of the orchestrators of the subsequent Madrid bombings.

The main agenda was around the final preparations, but first they had to discuss Ziad Jarrah. He and Amir had fallen out. The two men were never close, and it was in fact Omar who took Ziad under his wing in the first place. Without Omar with him in the US, Ziad had been more of a loose cannon. He was never keen on following Amir, and Amir, with his rigid ways, found him difficult. He had not progressed as well as the others in his flight training, and his relationship with Aysel was a perpetual cause for concern for Amir. He wanted to lose him. Omar had already been forewarned about this and had discussed the matter with KSM, who was displeased at hearing this and not about to sanction any split within the group – it was far too late for that. Omar, in the end, through his relationship with them both, managed to broker a peace.

Omar's main concern, however, was the timing. Bin Laden had made it clear he wanted them to strike very soon. Amir, with his attention to detail, was not keen to go early – he still saw much more to be done. But Bin Laden was insistent. There was too much risk of detection and therefore too much danger in them delaying now. Omar pressed the message home hard.

A few weeks after his return to the US, Amir phoned Omar and keyed into his phone three numbers: '9-1-1'.

In the final days the men moved into position, renting hotel rooms in and around Washington, New Jersey and Boston. Several of them had a few alcoholic drinks at nearby bars on their last night, and some of the Saudi men made calls to look into renting prostitutes for the night but decided they were too expensive.

Ziad Jarrah wrote a final note to Aysel. For once, he did not hold back:

Hello my dear Aysel,

My love, my life. My beloved lady, my heart. You are my life.

First of all I want you to believe truly and really take care that I love you from all my heart. You should not have any doubts about that. I love you and I will always love you until eternity. I don't want you to get sad I live somewhere else where you can't see me and can't hear me, but I will see you and I will know how you are. And I will wait for you until you come to me. Everyone has his time and I will go then. I am guilty about giving you hope about marriage, wedding, children and family. And many other things.

I am what you wish for, but it's sad you must wait until we come back together. I did not escape from you but I did what I was supposed to. You should be very proud of me. It's an honor and you will see the results, and everybody will be happy. I want you to remain very strong as I knew you, but whatever you do, head high, with a goal, never be without goal, always have a goal in front of you and always think, 'what for'.

Remember always who you are and what you are. Keep your head high. The victors never have their heads down!

Hold on to what you have until we see each other again. And then we will live a very nice and eternal life, where there are no problems and no sorrow in castles of gold and silver and, and, and …

I did not leave you alone. Allah is with you and with my parents. If you need anything ask Him for what you need. He is listening and knows what is inside you.

Our prophet said: 'He is a poor man who has no wife and she is a poor woman who has no man.' I will pick you up anyhow and if you marry again do not fear. You know I don't like all men. Think about what you are and who could deserve you.

I hug you and I kiss you on the hands. And I thank you and I say sorry for the very nice, tough five years, which you spent with me. Your patience has a price … God willing, I am your prince and I will pick you up.

See you again!!

Your man always.

Ziad Jarrah

The final day came. Shehi wired his remaining money – $5,400 – to his family in UAE.

As they walked towards their fate, signs of anxiety flickered – if only briefly – across their minds' eye. Ziad made one final call to Aysel on the last morning. His calls were short and abrupt at the best of times but this was particularly so. He told her he loved her three times, then said goodbye. Shehi got into an argument over a parking space as he tried to park his rented white Mitsubishi Mirage in the car park of Logan Airport.

As they approached the terminus their final instructions – written for them by Abdul Aziz Al-Omari – spread like a fire blanket over their anxieties:

1. Vow to accept death, renew admonition, shave the extra hair on the body, perfume yourself, and ritually wash yourself.

2. Know the plan well from every angle. Anticipate the reaction or the resistance of the enemy.

3. Read the Surahs of Repentance and The Spoils. Contemplate their meaning and the bounties God has prepared and established for the martyrs.

4. Remind your base self to listen and obey ... for you will be exposed to decisive turning points wherein listening and obeying is one hundred per cent necessary. Train your base self, make it understand, convince it, and goad it on to this end. 'And obey God and His Messenger, and do not quarrel together, and so lose heart, and your power depart: and be patient: surely God is with the patient.'

5. ... Imploring in prayer for victory and strength and perspicuous triumph, and the easing of our task, and concealment.

6. Much recitation of sacred phrases. Know that the best of dhikr [chant] is reciting the noble Koran. This is the consensus of the people of knowledge or, indeed, of the most learned. It is enough for us that it is the words of the creator of the Heavens and Earth towards Whom you are advancing.

7. Purify your heart and cleanse it of stains. Forget and be oblivious to that thing called the world. For, the time of playing has passed, and the time has arrived for the rendezvous with the eternal Truth. How much of our lives we have wasted! Shall we not take advantage of these hours to offer up acts of nearness [to God] and obedience?

8. Let your breast be filled with gladness for there is nothing between you and your wedding but mere seconds ... Thereby will begin a happy and contented life and immortal blessing with the prophets, the true ones and the righteous martyrs. They are the best of companions. We beseech God for his grace. So seek good omens. For the prophets, may blessings and peace be upon him, who used to love divination about every matter.

9. Then fix your gaze such that, if you fall into tribulations, you will know how to behave, how to stand firm, how to say 'We are, verily, from God and to him we shall return.' Thus you will know that what has befallen you is not because of any error you committed. That you

committed an error was not so that you would face tribulations. That calamity of yours is in fact from God, may he be exalted and glorified – so as to elevate your station and cause your sins to be forgiven. Know that it is only a matter of seconds before it shines forth by the permission of God. The blessed is he who attains the great recompense from God. God says, 'Did you think you would enter paradise when God knows those who strove among you, and knows the patient?'

10. Then recite the words of God, 'You were wishing for death before you encountered it, then you saw it, and are looking for it.' And you wanted it. After then, recite the verse, 'Kam min fi'ah qalilah ghalaba fi'an kathirah bi idhn Allah.' [There are many small groups who are victorious over large and powerful groups with the help of Allah.] And 'In yunsirukum Allah fa la ghalib lakum.' [If Allah helps you, then no one can overcome you.]

11. Bring your base self, as well as your brethren, to remembrance through prayers. And contemplate their meaning ...

12. The jet: suitcase, clothing, knife, tools, identity papers, passport, and all your papers.

13. Inspect your weapon before setting out and before you even begin to set out ...

14. Pull your clothes tightly about you, for this is the way of the pious ancestors (as-salaf as salih), may God be pleased with them. Pull your shoelaces tight and wear tight socks that grip the shoes and do not come out of

them. All of these are means that we have been commanded to adopt. God has hasabna and he is the best of advocates (na'im al wakil).

15. Pray the morning prayers in congregation and reflect on the reward for doing so while you are performing recitation afterwards. Do not go out of your apartment without having performed ablutions. For the angels seek forgiveness for you as long as you have prepared ablutions and they pray on your behalf.

'IF ANYONE THINKS THEY'VE HEARD SCREAMING BEFORE they've never heard that kind of screaming. This was the screaming of ... dying people. It was an unnatural screaming sound', said one survivor who happened to board the London Underground at King's Cross on the morning of 7 July 2005.

'It was a dialogue in my head, of the body just saying: "Rest – go to sleep, close your eyes ...", and the other half saying: "If you close your eyes, Gill, you won't ever open your eyes again"', said Gill Hicks. 'I think the most amount of panic I ever felt was suddenly – does anyone know we're down here?'

Hasib Hussain did. He tried to call his friends one last time and then he must have realised the game was up. It was now or never. He looked around and saw the number 30 bus pulling up. He paused for a second and then boarded it. As the bus pulled away he fiddled nervously with his rucksack.

Shahara Islam was on the bus. At 9:47 as the explosion ripped through the upper deck, collapsing it onto the deck below, she managed to hit the call button of her mobile phone but no words could escape her mouth. 'There was no voice', said her uncle, whom she had dialled. 'Just a commotion in the street. Then it went dead.'

Her father, who was praying in the East London mosque in Aldgate on the day, broke down on hearing the news: 'She was a true Muslim and proud to be so!' As was Mr Bhatti, a British-born Muslim, who walked the streets of London that day with a home-made missing person poster, looking for his fiancée, Benedetta Ciaccia. He joined hundreds, roaming the streets through the night: mothers, fathers, sons, daughters, holding back their tears but losing their hope.

Hasib Hussain's parents called the police to report him missing. He had played cricket the night before and, out of consideration for them, slept on the sofa downstairs, leaving first thing in the morning after saying his prayers. They wanted to know where he was. There was no way he could have been involved in what happened that morning – after all, they thought, he was a good Muslim boy.

3

What Lies Beneath

'The unconscious is the ocean of the unsayable, of what
has been expelled from the land of language.'
—Italo Calvino

IN 1998, PSYCHOLOGIST MARY AINSWORTH SET UP A
TEST called 'The Strange Situation'. It was a way in which
to assess the degree of attachment between a parent and
her infant child.

A child, with its mother, is introduced to an interview
room with a few toys. The child will be left to play in the
mother's presence but the mother will not join in. The
mother will then exit the room, leaving the baby behind.
The baby's reaction to the mother's departure is observed,
and the baby continues to be observed alone in the room as
he/she adjusts to the mother's absence. A few minutes later,
the mother returns and the baby's reaction to this is also
noted.

In most cases the baby shows varying degrees of agitation as the mother leaves – perhaps a little crying – then
gradually settles and turns his/her attention to the toys.

When the mother returns, the child reacts with happiness and smiles.

However, in about 20 to 30 per cent of cases the child will not react. He/she will remain silent both during the mother's departure and on her return. This is called the 'insecure-avoidant' style, and it tends to occur when there has been relatively distant parenting. This is often more common in Asian and Muslim families.

The most important influence in the development of any personality is this initial parental bond. The nature of this relationship is usually very different in Muslim societies and Eastern cultures in general. It is altogether more formal and more hierarchical, with often more distance existing between the parent and child than is usually the case in the West.

The relationship tends to be more goal-orientated in that the emphasis is on producing results – results in school, in behaviour, in Koranic and religious studies, and later in employment, marriage and family. The concept of quality time – spending one-to-one time, playing or just being together for the sake of it – can be uncommon, and so the level of emotional intimacy that develops is limited. There is a reason for this. Outside the West, Muslim families tend to live together as a larger extended family. First-generation immigrants, therefore, will have been accustomed to an upbringing at the hands of numerous guardian-like figures, from grandparents to uncles, aunts and elder cousins and siblings, with the actual parents taking on a more limited parenting role. This is the level of input from the mother and father that they are used to, and this can be then transposed into their own parenting when they have children in the West.

In addition to this, many facets of the parents' culture differ from so many aspects of the culture that the child is learning in the outside world – music, language, food, fashion, even values. Therefore, from a very early age, a distance between the child and parent usually develops.

It must be noted, however, that it is not just in immigrant families that such a distance can develop. Other parenting and lifestyle patterns that involve a marked generational/social gap can result in the formation of a similar dynamic, and therefore psychological issues, for non-immigrant children.

As a result, the environment that is required to nurture a growing personality is lacking and so psychological development becomes impaired. Over time, therefore, instead of evolving more mature thought patterns through this relationship, the child is left behind, still using infantile means of processing the world around him.

This can be especially extreme if the same-sex parent is particularly aloof or inaccessible in those crucial early years. The father is every boy's first role model, and it is this modelling that he relies upon to form the earliest characteristics of his personality as he travels out of the world of childhood. Lack of closeness to such a role model was certainly noticeable in Mohammed Khan's childhood. His father's busy lifestyle, working as a factory labourer to feed his large family of six children, kept him away from the home and the growing children for a lot of the time. Shehzad Tanweer's father, with his pioneering halal slaughterhouse business, was in a similar position, as was the father of Ziad Jarrah, a busy Lebanese civil servant who did not even live in the same house as Ziad, preferring their country home while Ziad and the rest of the family lived in their Beirut flat.

It is not just a physical unavailability that is the problem; the distance is more importantly an emotional one. A father or same-sex guardian who is there all the time but emotionally unavailable will have the same effect. The father of Ramzi Bin Al-Shibh – Omar – died at an early age, after which point his elder brother, Ahmed, became his male guardian. He was also a busy man – raising his own family and his father's simultaneously, as well as working as an analyst at an economic research institute – but there was another important spoiler in his dynamic with Omar. Their mother had displayed an overt favouritism for Omar from his birth, and this was something that Ahmed often commented on. Despite being the one who looked after the family, this favouritism grated with Ahmed, and a degree of jealousy towards Omar was inevitable. As a result, it seems the two were never close, and indeed in many ways Omar appears to have been left to fend for himself, ultimately seeking out a new life alone in Germany.

This lack of an early male bond is a pattern with most of the Western suicide bombers. Almost all of the fathers of the 9/11 muscle hijackers were described as well-off tradesmen or civil servants with busy lives, but the best example of all – as in so many areas – is that of Mohammed Atta: Amir. A man of few words and little affection for anyone, his father was virtually illiterate in the language of emotion. He was himself ambitious, at one point moving to Cairo to pursue his desire to become a famous lawyer, and he pushed that ambition on to his children too. He was demanding, insisting that Amir had to follow his sisters, who became doctors and professors, even timing his children on the way home to make sure they didn't stop to play. The house was described as 'a house of study. No playing, no entertainment. Just study', and so Amir was deprived of emotional involvement with anyone at all – not just his father. Even the very last time he visited his father, Mohammed senior insisted that Amir return to Germany, and not stay in Egypt with his family as Amir had wished. He had to earn the word 'Doctor' before his name.

Just as oxygen deprivation can impair growth or cause damage to the unborn child, so lack of attachment and emotional deprivation can harm the growing infant and stunt his psychological development. He will then be left to inhabit a very different world and see things in a very different light from the way adults do, even as he grows older.

INFANT THINKING

During our first days out of the womb we experience the world only in reference to ourselves. We believe the world literally spins around us.

Freud described the type of thinking that goes on at these early stages as a form of narcissism. If the child is hungry, he will cry and food will appear. If the child is sleepy, he will cry again and the parent will come along and rock him to sleep. Any demand that the child makes is realised immediately, and this produces and perpetuates the feeling of being at the centre of all things. The infant comes to believe that he creates and controls all things.

This is the natural way we assimilate the world around us in infancy. Further work by subsequent analysts who developed a whole field in this area (e.g. Melanie Klein) has given us a broader picture of the way infants think.

The infant begins to develop feelings, and these occur on a very basic 'good'/'bad' level. The world, and everything the baby experiences, is divided into either wholly 'good' or wholly 'bad'. As the child grows, this split thinking and narcissism gradually diminishes over time through what is known as 'reality testing'. Through experiencing the world – holding, needing, asking, interacting, almost in the form of experimentation – the child starts to realise that other people have needs and demands too and that their own demands will have to compete with those of others. To learn how to deal with this, the child will engage in a behaviour that, psychologically, is in essence the defining characteristic of primates: copying. This is a speciality for humans.

In order to copy well, the growing child needs to be able to identify with someone. The identification figure is traditionally a parent and, as the infant grows older and becomes aware of his gender, the same-sex parent is the one on which he starts to focus his copying. Without such a figure, the child's ability to grow emotionally and climb out of the well of infant – good/bad, self-centred – thinking is severely hampered, leaving those underlying constructs at the base of his developing personality.

THE AUTHORITARIAN PERSONALITY

When the parent and child do spend time together, over-strict parenting will mould the personality further in this direction. A strict parent, rather than enabling the child to blossom, can turn him in on himself. Meting out harsh punishments for even the slightest indiscretion or misbehaviour will lead the child to suppress natural drives and tendencies. He will, ultimately, feel ashamed of aggressive and angry thoughts and feelings that are, in reality, natural for a child of this age. As these impulses cannot be made to vanish into thin air, they are instead projected onto others. This refusal to hold and acknowledge his own feelings is, therefore, resolved by pushing them out onto others. He then begins to accuse others of possessing the same – now unwanted – thoughts and drives that exist within him. A judgemental attitude to other people then ensues. As a rule, ethnic, political or religious minorities are the easiest screen for these projections, as they are different and often removed from his own cultural/societal circle. As a result, there are usually fewer social sanctions to fear – and some prejudice may even be socially acceptable.

What then develops was described in 1950 by a psychologist named Theodor Adorno as the 'authoritarian personality'. This is the kind of personality that is more likely to be attracted to right-wing ideologies and extreme religious beliefs. They resort to infant thinking: black and white, good and evil. Adorno outlined a list of characteristics possessed by such personalities:

- Conventionalism: the tendency to accept and obey social conventions and the rules of authority figures; adherence to the traditional and accepted.
- Authoritarian Submission: submission to authorities and authority figures.
- Authoritarian Aggression: an aggressive attitude towards individuals or groups disliked by authorities; particularly those who threaten traditional values.
- Anti-Intraception: rejection of the subjective, imaginative and aesthetic.
- Substitution and Stereotypy: superstition, cliché, categorisation and fatalistic determinism.
- Power and Toughness: identification with those in power, excessive emphasis on socially advocated ego qualities.

- Destructiveness and Cynicism: general hostility, putting others down.
- Projectivity: the tendency to believe in the existence of evil in the world and to project unconscious emotional impulses outwards, e.g. to display exaggerated concerns with respect to sexual activity.

Each of the bombers quickly fell into this default mode of thinking as they grew up and started to experience stress or pain. They saw evil and injustice everywhere; there was no such thing as a mistake or bad luck in the world – it was all part of a grand conspiracy, the cosmic struggle between Islam and the infidel, the non-believer, the Jew. Shortly after 7/7, when associates of the bombers were captured in the West Midlands, England, there was a minor tornado – a rare sight in that part of the world. Omar Bakri Mohammed, leader of the now banned extremist group Al Mujahiroun, declared it to be an act of vengeance by Allah for the arrests.

Again, Amir – Mohammed Atta – is the best example of this type of personality. He was a totally serious man who would listen in awe to his tutors and professors at university, and was described by one as 'beeindruckt und beeindruckbar' – impressed and impressionable. Outside classes he had no time for playful or social activities, aggravating his flatmates, towards whom he would not display even basic social etiquette. He took life so seriously that he was hardly ever seen to laugh. 'How can you laugh when people are dying in Palestine?' he once said. He would scowl openly at those he considered to be immoral, like his landlady's daughter when he first moved to Hamburg. He saw her as living a life of shame and sin for being a single mother, and could never resist making her aware of this whenever he saw her.

Although focused in his study and very successful academically, he lagged behind seriously in the more creative aspects of his architecture course. He had no interest in aesthetics – almost no capacity to appreciate them – and this deficiency was stamped through his whole academic career. In the same way, every one of the bombers earned any academic success mainly in literalist, logic-based subjects, and so tended to study science, mathematics and engineering courses at university. Very few were able to study the arts or the humanities – subjects not so black-and-white and fact-based.

It is not hard to see, therefore, how literally interpreted, scripture-based religion would have an obvious appeal to such personalities. Most of them, however, were not at all religious to start with, coming from families that minimised, sometimes even avoided, their Islamic roots. One of the Madrid bombers, Jamal Ahmidan, shocked his family by attending the mosque so frequently, and his fellow bomber, Omar, was the first in his family to attend one at all. The men in Ziad Jarrah's family regularly drank alcohol, and the women thought nothing of wearing short skirts and bikinis on the beach, while Ziad himself was a regular visitor to the bars and clubs of Lebanon in his younger years. Mohammed Khan stood out in his school for not being like or mixing with the other Muslim boys in the area, and was never seen going to the mosque or to Arabic class or reading the Koran. Mohammed Atta's father made a conscious effort to steer his son away from fundamentalist or strictly observed Islam, preferring instead to guide him towards his own secular outlook – one in keeping with the government and wider Egyptian societal attitude of the time.

Instead of religion, therefore, they all found different things to set their minds to, yet whatever they did, they took very, very seriously. As a form of reaction to the inadequacy they were made to feel as young children – receiving little emotional support while being subjected to high demands and tough comparisons – they tried as young adults to excel at something, so they applied themselves to their chosen field. Mohammed Khan was showered with praise for the work he did in schools. Mohammed Atta's employers at Plankontor found him diligent, industrious and unparalleled in his dedication. He went above and beyond the call of duty. For example, unlike others in his department, he would often visit the sites he was due to draw maps for, to get a feel for the place in advance. Shehzad Tanweer, Hasib Hussain and Germaine Lindsay were so dedicated to bodybuilding and fitness that they were hardly ever seen outside a gym, and Tanweer ended up studying a for a degree in Sports Science. As an estate agent, the leader of the Madrid bombers, Serhane Fakhet, held the record for the highest number of properties sold in one month.

This period of exposure to the outside world is a crucial stage in psychological development. It can facilitate a rapprochement with the parents and serve as a corrective function for the growing mind. Just as it can turn things around, however, it can also push them back and send the young adult further down the wrong path.

FLYING THE NEST

Peer Relationships

By finding a group with which he can identify, the young man will gradually take on elements of a wider-shared identity by association with the group. Research has shown that moral, cultural and value norms tend to more often follow those of a youth's peer group than those of his parents. The peer group, therefore, has a very significant role to play.

The way in which we judge our self-worth is always very much related to how we perceive others are reacting to us. Our self-image is therefore a constant construct of opinions from the outside world. The youth will seek positive or negative reinforcement for his evolving identity from those around him, and this stimulates further change and adaptation.

For young Muslims in the West, however, this natural process of social nourishment is often packaged with another layer of potentially damaging obstacles – particularly for those who are second-generation immigrants. It is difficult for anyone who has not been in the same position to truly comprehend the enormity of the dichotomy with which second-generation Muslim children are faced. Behind the closed doors of a Muslim home is a world that can be as different from mainstream Western culture as that found in any foreign land – despite sitting in the middle of any major Western city. So many issues came to mind, through my own personal experience, when writing this section that I could do justice to it only by producing a list:

Decor: Muslim households will often have pictures of the holy mosque in Mecca in them. The crowds gathering for the pilgrimage is a common image. Arabic writing – usually verses from the Koran – is also common. Any artwork is likely to be more landscape or pattern-based, as traditionally Islamic art does not include portraits. Posters of idols (be they pop stars or actors) are often not permitted – the extent of religiousness of the household will obviously determine this. Some more literalist believers will not allow any artwork to adorn their walls at all.

Leisure: In stricter families, radios, music players, computers and TVs might all be banned, but although this is rare, some people, including some younger Muslims these days, do take the view that any music is *haram* – against God. Other restrictions are more common: for example, in virtually no household with a TV is watching a kiss, let alone anything more passionate, permitted. It was only after I left home, became a doctor and got married that I felt comfortable about not changing the channel every time such a moment arose in front of my parents.

Clothes: Again, this is very dependent on the religiosity of the family. Stricter households will insist on all women wearing burkhas at all times and remaining separate from the men. This is, however, rare in most of the West – as indeed in most practising Muslim families around the world. More common is the saree or selwar kameez in Asian households, and the man would commonly wear a similar selwar or, as in the case of people of my own culture, Bengali, a serong.

Food: Understandably, Eastern food will predominate. In most Asian households nothing else is served. The taste is so rich that first-generation immigrants are virtually unable to find taste in Western food, as a result of which it is seldom made. The nearest I ever got at home was the odd fish finger. Alcohol is, of course, universally absent and meat will generally be halal only.

This entirely different environment is representative of what, underneath, is a very different dynamic. The relationship between parent and child is, as mentioned, far more hierarchical and deferential. Conversation is usually more perfunctory and formal and there is less evidence of a peer-type relationship growing between parent and child, as the child grows older, than would be the case in Western households. Religion is far more pervasive in discourse; for example, one will always mention the name of Allah on greeting, farewell, at the start of each meal, whenever talking about the future, whenever expressing appreciation, whenever expressing dislike, indeed peppered throughout the conversation. This is reflective of the higher priority given to religion and religious education, which is why most Muslim children, at some point in their lives, will take Arabic lessons and start to read the Koran in Arabic. All will be taught to start following their parents in the five daily prayers, to fast during the month of Ramadan and celebrate Eid together.

All in all, therefore, leaving home for university or the wider world for the first time can be just as daunting a scenario as that experienced by anyone entering the country for the first time. And for those young Muslims who do come from abroad, the culture shock can often be beyond anything they had ever expected. Other ethnic groups can usually find common ground with the host community more easily. Hindus can drink alcohol, as can Sikhs and African-Caribbeans. Their social structures are often similar and at least an amalgam Western-ethnic culture exists, in which they can immediately immerse and feel comfortable simultaneously with their background culture and new home. The lack of such an integrated hybrid sub-culture for Muslims is a major contributory factor to the dissonance experienced (which, like the feeling of alienation, can be just as powerful for converts to the religion as for those born into it), and its importance will be emphasised further when discussing solutions in the final chapter.

Amir, Omar and Shehi all showed evidence of some degree of culture shock upon arrival in Germany, withdrawing into themselves and mixing very little with those

around them. This was noticeable to flatmates and colleagues early on, in the case of Amir and Shehi. They each
ultimately found social outlets only in their own ethnic
group – specifically those feeling equally estranged from
the host community – and often, as was the case with Amir,
it was many months before such a grouping was even discovered. Hasib Hussain never seemed able to bridge the
gap between East and West. Getting into fights at school at
an early age, he always seemed to be a fish out of water,
never fully content.

Romantic Relationships

Involvement in the first romantic relationship can often be
a time of bridge-building between parent and child.
However, in many Muslim families the opposite is true. In
conservative Islamic traditions the parents choose the offspring's partner, and romantic engagements, particularly at
a young age, are considered as folly at best and punishable
and sinful at worst.

As these natural impulses develop, a further wedge is
driven between parent and child. In Western societies, as
friends start engaging in such relationships openly, the
Muslim youth begins to feel further alienated. Worst of all,
he will start to feel alienated from himself and his own feelings. Notions of sexual attraction – considered to be wrong
and unacceptable in conservative quarters – are then projected onto others, and sneering disgust towards any display of sexuality, even fashion and the opposite sex in
general, begins to set in. We will see in the next chapter that
this form of repression was a major element in the personalities of the earlier founders of extremist Islam, as it is with
religious extremists and right-wing leaders around the
world, and as it was with Amir in his attitude to anyone

wearing short skirts or low-cut tops in his presence, indeed women in general – even his female professors. This is also, of course, a central facet of the authoritarian personality.

In Amir's early days at university, during a study trip to an excavation site in northern Syria, an interesting event took place. Amir found himself becoming attracted to a woman he met there. She would tease him, calling him the Pharaoh, and he even made tentative advances to her. Though he would confess an attraction to her to his family later on, he quickly terminated contact with her, believing her to be too forward and not sufficiently Islamic. He effectively suppressed his own spark. These energies would, of course, return only to be channelled elsewhere in future.

THE TURNING POINT

For all Muslim youth in the West, a certain amount of westernisation is inevitable. Faced with the contradictory universes they simultaneously inhabit, a degree of 'when in Rome' takes place. A journey then ensues in a westerly direction, and each person ultimately finds their own turf somewhere along the East–West spectrum where they feel most at home. It can take a while – sometimes a whole lifetime – before the final territory is settled on, however. Mohammed Khan was clearly headed for a significantly westernised existence from early on. He was not seen praying or going to the mosque like the other Pakistani boys in his school, and he even became known as a bit of a ladies' man. He rejected his parents' arranged marriage proposals and defined himself as proud to be British. That is, of course, until he – like the others – was stopped in his tracks.

For some, the journey towards the West can be rudely interrupted. In a time of such uncertainty and insecurity, coming up against a major experience of racism or rejection can be instantly destabilising.

Experiences like this tell you you're different, 'not one of us'. For those who had felt that they were, this can be like a bucket of iced water, leaving the young man feeling suddenly awakened from a dream or a delusion. It is not the nature of the experience itself as much as the interpretation of it that is most important. The actual event may be anything from a slight to being ignored, being treated differently in an unexpected way, or an overt verbal or physical attack. Often it takes the form of denial of a goal or an ambition that the young man had, apparently on the basis of race. In Amir's case, it was arriving in Hamburg to discover that the place he had been told he had won in his chosen subject no longer existed as the course was full. It was only after openly complaining that he was the victim of racial discrimination and threatening legal action that he was finally awarded a place. This must have been devastating for him and crucial to the views evolving in his mind about the West. For Omar, the experience was around successive rejections for asylum when he was convinced he had a good case, and for Ziad the experience may well have been an experience of overt racist confrontation, one might speculate, given the rise of neo-Nazi skinheads in the town of Greifswald where he first arrived. This was likely to have been the turning point.

At this time, a rebounding back into the parental bosom is a common and natural reaction. If that bond is not sufficiently developed, however, the youth may feel a sudden lack of the comforting blanket he seeks. After being shut out by the Western world and neglected at home, feelings of abandonment will surface, causing him to retreat further back into himself. The certainties of the old 'black or white', 'all or nothing', 'good or evil' thinking will return with a vengeance.

Now he is at his most vulnerable.

The easiest thing to turn to at this point is religion. It provides hope, comfort and definition, allowing the young man to carve out for himself a unique identity that does not depend on the approval of those by whom he feels rejected. In most cases it also acts as a means of differentiation from the parents – even as a way to attack them. Where the parents had spent their lives practising more moderate versions of Islam, the child brings home an altogether more literalist strain. Being more devoted than they ever were, he can now even feel a sense of superiority over his parents for the first time in his life. Indeed, the deeper he goes into such a brand of Islam, the greater this sense of superiority will grow over more and more people around him. An escalating cycle then develops: he follows more exclusive realms of the religion, leading to greater and greater ego inflation, which in turn leads to pursuing further extremes. As the cycle continues he seeks out the more obscure, fringe elements of the religion, which at the same time are looking for him.

THE TOXIN

Religion, therefore, has provided the youth with certainty in an uncertain world – it has taken away the pain of feelings of inferiority, ambiguity and insecurity, and lent his world structure and meaning. In the guise of this perfect medicine, therefore, arrives the perfect toxin – theocratic Islam.

This ideology is a political one. It sees the conquering of lands for Islam as its ultimate goal. According to those who follow this creed, the goal of every Muslim, as mentioned in earlier chapters, is not only to follow the personal and spiritual guidance of the Koran but also to establish a pan-national Islamic state, known as the Caliphate. The Caliphate, as we have seen, was never really a singular construct in history, nor was it a paragon of ideal Islam across all of its various iterations, but the ideologues would have their recruits believe that it was. They see it as a divinely inspired religious dictatorship in which the ruler – the Khilafah – has absolute power to rule within the framework of an ancient interpretation of Koranic jurisprudence known as Shariah law. A Muslim is not a true Muslim, according to this philosophy, unless he has joined this global struggle – jihad – to establish the Caliphate; and until it has been formed, no Muslim should be allowed to rest or live in peace with infidels, all of whom are seen as obstacles to this divine right. Most Muslim countries are also on the hit list, as they are seen as following an infidel system of government and in tow to non-Muslim interests, particularly those of the 'Great Satan', the US, and its closest allies, the UK and other Western countries. The complete lack of any such system of government as the Caliphate anywhere on the planet, even in almost entirely Muslim-populated countries, does not deter the extremist in his belief that it is a genuine construct and a wholly achievable goal. Osama Bin Laden himself said: 'The jihad will continue until we have an Islamic state.'

Nowhere in the Koran are the words 'Islamic state' or 'Caliphate' to be found. Those who would have us believe that this is a core aspect of Islam are, therefore, forced instead to quote passages that are ambiguous at least and could easily, in fact, be interpreted to mean the opposite. For example: 'O you who believe! obey Allah and obey the

Prophet and those in authority from among you.' (Verse 4:59) Far from urging the formation of a separate Islamic state, as some would argue, this passage could just as easily, in fact more likely, refer to the importance of following the authorities – the government – wherever you are at the time.

The struggle by jihadists around the world is to gain control and/or land for this purist entity. Jemaah Islamiah fights for this in Indonesia, Singapore, the Philippines and neighbouring regions of Asia, while Chechnyan rebels fight for it in Russia, Hamas fights for it in Palestine, and Muslims in the West fight to defeat its chief enemies in their heartlands. Everyone therefore has a role to play, and those who are not part of the struggle are deemed as obstacles to and hence targets of it. The means used are therefore indiscriminate, uncompromising, ruthless and deliberately bloody, and as the cause is so illusory, the battle is almost perpetual.

This central notion of relentless and violent jihad towards this version of utopia is what binds every Islamic extremist around the world and separates them from the mainstream followers of Islam. The coming together of these disparate groupings under one literal roof came about with the help of Western intelligence and funds during the Afghanistan war against Soviet occupation in the eighties. The first physical manifestation of it was the sprawling web of terrorist training camps in the mountains of Afghanistan and, like any cancer, it has since metastasised and spread to cities and towns around the globe, East and West.

As a series of hubs gradually emerged, it was towards these centres that young Muslims, travelling through a curve of increasing militancy, would gravitate. The 'Al Qaeda gym' in the basement of Hardy Street mosque in

Beeston was one such place, as was the Al Quds mosque in Hamburg. 'The box' where Abdulrachman Al-Makhadi preached, and to which Ziad Jarrah was first attracted in Greifswald, was another example; and there are undoubtedly many more around the world today. Each of them provokes a similar reaction in the community around it. Parents steer their children clear of it, youngsters laugh at it, clerics try to ignore it, and – like parents quizzed about a wayward child – a wall of silence descends across the town when asked about it.

There is a warm embrace for all who enter this ideological realm. They are joined in a brotherhood, a community who would literally die for one another. They are above all others. Non-Muslims are dismissed as kufr or infidel, and even Muslims who do not follow the religion their way are included in this category, leaving them – the brotherhood – to claim an elite status.

It is clear how appealing this mindset is to the troubled youth experiencing existential turmoil. The world view fits perfectly with his regressed psychological tendency to black-and-white, all-or-nothing thinking. He is told that he is on the side of absolute good and kufr are on the side of absolute bad. They are evil and he and his new-found friends are righteous. Instead of feeling like an outcast, an inferior – unworthy of their society – he feels the opposite. It is *they* who are not worthy of *his* society. This new framework feeds the narcissism that has resurfaced from infancy to massage the ego. He is now closer to the centre of the universe than he has ever felt since childhood.

Similar 'cures' for the imploding ego have evolved and spread, in one guise or another, throughout history to young, disillusioned and disenfranchised men and women. Examples include Nazism, extreme manifestations of socialist and communist ideology, and a variety of political and religious cults. A once wayward and insecure existence is given structure and meaning. A peer group of like-minded people is attained and the world seems to make sense with 'the brothers' at the top of the pyramid.

Their hatred of the outside world intensifies. For the Islamist, the kufr becomes a repository for every grievance, irritation or anxiety. They deny any fault in themselves or their 'brothers'. They cannot do wrong, for they are the righteous – it is the kufr, it is always the kufr. They watch videos of Muslims being killed and tortured in Afghanistan, Iraq, Guantánamo and Palestine and their anger escalates. The sense of injustice becomes overwhelming. Something must be done.

INCUBATION

People going through this transformation, arriving at the stage of action, start to gravitate towards each other. It is almost as if they can smell one another from far away, until ultimately they coalesce to form cells of dedicated brethren.

Every cell goes through a period of incubation. The 9/11 bombers spent over a year in the small Hamburg flat at Marienstrasse 54, the Madrid bombers spent their time in a cottage on the outskirts of the city, and the 7/7 bombers went almost every day for months to the Hamara Community Centre even after it had been closed down. There are few places where they can really speak their mind, unleash the ferocity of their passion and anger and feel understood, supported, even encouraged. This is why their hideaway becomes so important – it becomes like a tunnel, transporting them to another dimension. Although inhabiting the same geography as their local town, it is as detached and removed from it as any cave in Afghanistan – which is where the very first incubation took place, with Bin Laden, Al-Zawahiri, Azzam, and the first generation of 20th-century mujahideen (holy warriors) locked in attendance.

The initiates spend more and more time there, neglecting work, obligations, friends and family. Amir and Shehi missed their classes at university for long periods of time; Amir's teachers were shocked to see him return over a year later, and Shehi's college de-registered him altogether. Ziad Jarrah, just like Germaine Lindsay and Mohammed Khan, neglected his partner to the extent that their relationship became a perpetual yo-yo of break-ups and reconciliations. Every time Ziad promised he had changed, he would soon go missing again for days, even weeks. His wife could never visit him at the Marienstrasse flat – it was a place where women could not go, he had told her. Despite this secrecy, the trusting Aysel Sengun never suspected Ziad of involvement with another woman. She knew where he was, unlike the wife of Germaine Lindsay, who friends say would often start to worry that her husband was having an affair. In many ways, these men had transferred their libidos on to each other in what Freud would have described as displacement. Instead of expressing their sexuality to their female partners, they would choose to spend that time with their friends, whom they came to see more and more as their real soulmates. They would hold hands during prayer, not at all standard practice in Islam, have tiffs and arguments and then make up with one another, and move in a pack, unable to perform even the smallest tasks without being together.

Spending more and more time in each other's company leads ultimately to de-individuation, in which each identity begins to merge until there is very little left of the individual outside the identity of the group as a whole. They feed off each other's notions, pushing one another's world views inexorably into further and further extremes.

The danger of this kind of environment was demonstrated in 1951 by psychologist Solomon Asch. He conducted an experiment in which he invited a subject into a room, to sit around a table with a group of men and women who the subject was told were volunteers just like him. In reality, the other men and women were Asch's assistants. He presented the group with a series of cards containing several straight lines of various lengths. When asked to identify the longest line, his assistants all stated with conviction that they believed a line that was clearly one of the shortest to be the longest. Asch found that the subject – seated in the middle of his assistants – gave the same wrong answer over a third of the time.

This is an example, in a small way, of peer group pressure and how those around you can influence judgements and even interpretations of reality. Increasingly detached from reality, the incubating cell communes into the small hours of the night, with conversations descending into a whirlpool of passion and hate. The angry and violent impulses that build up within are projected on to their enemies, whom they then hate all the more, sparking off a vicious cycle of projection and reaction.

As they redefine the world around them, death takes on new meaning. In a process known as *cognitive reframing*, notions of life and death become inverted so that life is considered a form of death, from which all humans must escape to experience the real life after death. Such psychological reinvention, contrary to the experience of the reality outside, gradually chips away at the most human trait of all – the fear of death. Their heroes are now the martyrs of old:

songs are sung and poems are read in praise of them. The 9/11 hijackers were singing virtually all day towards the end of their time together in Hamburg.

What was once a perfect means for massaging a bruised ego has now begun to get out of hand as a monster grows within, straining to be unleashed. For talking to turn to planning, what is needed is a network and some direction – a figure of authority whom they trust and who can guide them to the next level.

IDEALISATION

'Whoever enjoins this battle is remitted in entirety all penance in the afterlife for his sins.' With these words Pope Urban incited 60,000 Christians to discard the Sixth Commandment – 'Thou shall not kill' – and, in 1096, to commit the bloodiest slaughter in history against Muslims, in what became known as the Crusades. People were inspired to kill en masse in the name of God with promises of the afterlife.

History is littered with examples of authority figures – respected leaders, popes and presidents – persuading men and women to commit acts of brutality and murder against their fellow man. The success of such a tactic is as much dependent on the status of the leader as it is on the personality of the follower.

In 1963, Yale University psychologist Stanley Milgram conducted an experiment entitled 'The Behavioural Study of Obedience'. He recruited a series of students from the university and informed each of them that in the next room was another student who had volunteered to participate in a memory experiment. The two – 'teacher' and 'learner' – were connected by an audio link, so each could hear the other, and the 'teacher' student had in his room a machine that could pass serially increasing voltages of electricity to the 'learner' student, if he answered any of the questions he was about to be asked incorrectly. In fact the 'learner' students were all actors with no voltage wires attached. Every time the 'learner' answered a question incorrectly, the 'teacher' pressed the button for the next level of voltage. The actor on the other side screamed louder and louder each time he received a shock, yet the 'teacher' continued to pass higher and higher voltages. This continued even after it appeared that the 'learner' may have passed out or even died, as reaction from the other room ceased altogether – not even breathing could be heard.

Despite the increasingly horrific feedback the 'teachers' pressed on, and all because in each case seated next to them was a man in a white coat who they had been told was a scientist. He instructed them to press the button each time and they did. They received a command from the figure of authority and they obeyed.

The findings shocked the world of psychology, and Milgram wrote: 'The extreme willingness of adults to go to almost any lengths on the command of an authority constitutes the fact most urgently demanding explanation.' In subsequent years, he repeated the experiment over a dozen times, each time producing the same result.

Milgram proved unequivocally the enormity of the power that a recognised figure of authority has over those who accept him. It can lead the follower virtually anywhere.

During the Afghan war against the Soviets, Bin Laden was touring the trenches where simple Arab men had come to fight in what they saw as a holy jihad. Two fighters had just arrived in a trench to fight on a 24-hour watch. Bin Laden spent some time with them before leaving them to fight. The following day, when they were due to be relieved, they asked to stay and fight another day. The next day they asked to stay another, and then another. After several days without rest, a commander came and asked them why they were still fighting, and they replied that Bin Laden had told them that, for them, this trench was their gateway to Heaven.

Every suicide bomber has been inspired in the same way. Soon after they had begun their training at the terror camps in Afghanistan, Omar, Amir, Ziad and Shehi were called to meet Bin Laden himself. They had spent countless hours discussing Bin Laden's international terror campaign – watching it, celebrating it, and yearning to join it – and finally they had come face to face with him. It was he who set them on the path to fulfilling his sponsored 'planes operation', and later the baton of direct mentorship was passed to Bin Laden's organiser in the field, Khaled Sheikh Mohammed, and his so-called spiritual ambassador in Europe, Abu Qatada.

Just over eighteen months later, a similar path was travelled by fourteen young men in Morocco preparing to take their place in the annals of martyrdom. They sought guidance from those they considered to be scholars and, somehow, in the middle of the 2001 war with Afghanistan, managed to e-mail the Taliban leader, Mullah Omar, to ask if suicide for the cause of Islam was a sin or an act of martyrdom. He answered that it was the latter, and so on 16 May 2002 the fourteen went to their deaths in the Jewish sections of Casablanca, killing a further 45 innocent people.

It is likely that such incubations are going on all over the world at this very moment, but it is only those who manage to hook up to the wider Al Qaeda/extremist network and gain inspiration, guidance and logistical support who manage to translate ideology into action. It was through his trips to Pakistan and Malaysia that Mohammed Khan managed to tap into this wider network and later bring Shehzad Tanweer and Hasib Hussain with him. Somewhere on one of these excursions the germs for the 7/7 operation were probably planted, leading to months of planning and support before the final act.

The way that men such as Bin Laden ultimately win their authority within these peripheral pockets of Islam is by claiming a special understanding of the message of God. In times gone by, such men would claim to commune directly with God, but for Bin Laden it is a question of interpretation. Via reams of declarations littered with citations of the Koran and associated works and words of the Prophet, known as the Hadith, he and his supporters have worked as a veritable think-tank providing their alternative version of what they claim to be Allah's real message. It is by channelling the power of the God ideal, therefore, that they gain their status of authority. The power of the God ideal is an energy that lies at the heart of every religion – it is based on the desire of followers to realise and commune with their God, a desire that can sometimes become all-consuming and therefore that can be used for the good of mankind as well as for the opposite: violence, hate and destruction.

Freud saw this idealisation as being derived from the residual narcissism that such personalities still carry around from childhood. A proportion of this self-love is broken off and attached to another object. This object may be another person, group, concept, deity or ideal, and once the projection is placed in it, it becomes idealised. Idealisations can take on a particularly intense, sometimes even romantic intensity. James W. Jones in his book *Terror and Transformation* points out how.

> Evangelical Christians regularly sing of the love of Jesus in hymns that shout 'what wondrous love is this', or speak of 'love divine', '[all] loves excelling'. They claim 'how sweet is his love to me' and sing of the 'love that will not let me go'. Evangelicals want to 'tell the story of love' and call for 'more love to thee Christ, more love to thee'. In India worshippers of Kali, like the 19th-century Bengali mystic, Ramakrishna, picture the goddess 'as the perfect erotic object' – naked, with ample breast, and shapely thighs in a seductive pose – and worship her with sensual music and dance and a mantra which contains images of lust, fire and sexual desire.
>
> It is not coincidence that religious devotees write poems, sing songs and use language that often parallels the secular language of romantic love. Deep psychological connections are at work here including the dynamic of idealisation.

This mindset can precipitate experiences of ecstasy:

> Ecstatic experience – whether in the honeymoon suite or the Pentecostal meeting hall – involves more than the release of emotion: it also involves an idealised object. Such ecstasies demand letting go of all inhibitions and giving oneself over to another and to the powerful psychological currents that are thereby set free ... one can only abandon oneself so completely, so unreservedly, to another who is highly idealised.

This reservoir of near-overwhelming emotion acts as the fuel that drives the would-be terrorist to a determination to perpetrate what he fast grows to believe is his duty to his maker. Ultimately, he reaches the point of no return. He becomes impervious to alternative reason – his goal is fixed and his mind is set. This was described by the psychologist Anthony Stahelski in 2004 as the stage of complete 'social psychological conditioning'. The terrorist has passed every step defined by Stahelski as the 'road map' to reaching this point:

1. Depluralisation: stripping away all other group member identities;
2. Self-deindividuation: stripping away each member's personal identity;
3. Other-deindividuation: stripping away the personal identities of enemies;
4. Dehumanisation: identifying enemies as sub-human or non-human;
5. Demonisation: identifying enemies as evil.

Now he is ready to act.

In his final days, the bomber considers himself 'Shaheed', a martyr already. His associates refer to him in this way – sometimes in the past tense – so he begins to feel that he has already died. He has no more life to miss, as in his head he has already left it. This conviction assists him in the last hours, but nothing can completely remove the inevitable final bursts of anxiety as he walks to his certain death.

Shehi had an argument over a parking space in Logan Airport on the morning of 9/11. Having already said good-bye to Aysel in a note the night before, Ziad felt compelled to call her again that morning and tell her three times that he loved her. Hasib Hussain walked through town for a whole half hour before making his final move and boarding the number 30 bus on 7/7. During that time he made numerous calls to the other bombers, even though he knew they were likely already dead. Survivors from the bus saw him nervously fiddle with his rucksack repeatedly before finally detonating it.

As children they feared abandonment, as adolescents they feared rejection, as adults they feared failure. They thought they had overcome it all as they steeled themselves in those final moments. Their transformations were complete; the final drops of their humanity had drained away. They had become slaves in the end, not to a higher cause, but ultimately to themselves and their own original fears.

4

The Pied Piper

'We love death. The West loves life.
That is the big difference between us.'
—Osama Bin Laden, November 2001

SALIM HAD HIGH HOPES FOR OSAMA. Ever since he took over the family business, after their father's death, Salim believed his smart younger brother would one day play a major role in the multinational Bin Laden construction corporation. That's why he had him enrolled into the civil engineering course at the prestigious Abdul Aziz University in Jeddah. What he didn't know, however, was that, instead of civil engineering, the young Osama was dedicating more and more of his time to Islamic studies.

A family member went to visit Osama and noticed that he was praying, listening to tapes and reading Islamic texts virtually the whole day. This was not the Osama of old. The book most frequently on his desk – apart from the Koran – was *Milestones* by Sayyid Qutb, the brother of Mohammed Qutb who was a lecturer at that university. Together with fellow teacher Abdullah Azzam, he preached the ideology of *Milestones* in every class. A small group of students appeared to be gradually becoming hooked. The words sank in deep, capturing their imaginations, slowly stealing their hearts.

The young Osama had found his calling. Sayyid Qutb, the words, the book, the man, were sinking deep into his soul. This was his calling …

No story of the birth and growth of extremist Islam could begin without first looking at the life, character and works of one man – Sayyid Qutb, born 9 October 1906.

Qutb's father, Qutb Ibrahim, was a farmer in the Egyptian village of Musha, about 235 miles south of Cairo. Although his family led a wealthy lifestyle, the income from their farm seemed to dwindle in Qutb junior's early years. As a result, his father's waking hours were increasingly sucked into the farm and eventually he was forced to sell portions of it to pay off their growing debt. Despite his escalating work on the farm, Qutb's father also found time to engage actively in politics, becoming a member of his local branch of the Nationalist Party. He would often host meetings at his home, and always kept abreast of local party developments. In the – albeit limited – time he managed to spend with his son, a strict attitude and forbidding presence seemed to dominate.

In years to come, Qutb would write of his father: 'When I was a young child you imprinted on my senses a fear of the day of judgement.' We see here, therefore, how the aloof yet demanding parenting style leading the child to develop a sense of 'don't-fit-in-ness' at an early age is at the very core of the personality of even the early founders of the evolving ideology of terror.

Qutb's mother was an intense woman who left a major impression on her children. She was the more religious of the two – insisting that all her children read and memorise the Koran at a young age. When Sayyid was ten, she approached him, weeping, the day Ibrahim was forced to sell some of their land. She insisted that Sayyid would soon have to take on the mantle of family bread-winner. In so doing she wedged a further divide between Sayyid and his increasingly embattled father.

The ingredients for an insecure attachment with his father were therefore already in place in the Qutb house-hold early on, and a consequent impairment in the matura-tion of his psyche soon became evident in his schooling.

At that time in Egypt there were two forms of primary school: the modern government 'madrasha' and the more traditional, religious 'kuttab'. Sayyid, after apparently much debate within his family, was sent to a madrasha. He quickly settled in and became proud of the modern madrasha. Due to rumours, however, that the madrashas were planning to drop Koranic studies from their syllabus, Qutb was forced to attend what for him was a much despised kuttab school. Once it became clear that Koranic studies were still to continue in the madrasha, he was able to return to his original school – to his utter relief.

He took part in competitions of Koranic recitation and memorisation between madrasha and kuttab pupils, and was overwhelmed with a sense of pride whenever his school won the contest. So much so, that a couple of years later he would describe his life's ambition as wanting to return to his beloved madrasha and defend it from the 'dirty kuttab' and its children. He appears to have framed the situation in his mind into a clear good versus bad scenario – demonstrating an early black-and-white mindset. He was also clearly uncomfortable in unfamiliar surroundings, not keen to stray too far from what he knew. For this reason his teenage years must have hit him particularly hard. On top of the usual stresses of adolescence, Qutb's family fell on hard times and so he was sent to live with his uncle in Cairo.

He went to university there, and afterwards decided to take up poetry. He saw his role in life – in grandiose terms that were becoming increasingly typical – as the purveyor of a superior imagination shedding light on the complexities of existence for the common man. He earnestly set about this task by trying to understand the nature and meaning of life and what lay beyond. He would make frequent visits to the Valley of the Dead, and one of his poems, 'The Poet in the Valley of the Dead', painted a picture of a young man yearning to learn what the bodies in the valley know. This existential unease was a hallmark of his early poetry. He would often turn to escapism for a way out of turmoil. A large section of his work was love poetry – usually loaded with excessive idealisation for the beloved.

But despite all his searching for meaning, he remained resolutely, in his early days, a secular man without any religious leanings. He followed the nationalist religious sentiment of the day and, indeed, resented those who brought religion into the realms of science and art, devaluing it, in his view, in the process. Few were left in any doubt of his strong views on this once he moved into the area of literary criticism:

Religion … Religion … This is the cry of the feeble and the weak who seeks protection in it whenever the current takes him away … Say it one hundred times for thank God, we are not ones who are terrified by such empty cries … and we studied religion more than you and we understand it more than you.

Standing apart from religion did not, however, stop him from studying it, and in the 1930s he decided to conduct a literary analysis of the Koran. He was captivated by what he saw as its artistic qualities. The black-and-white nature of the prose also appears to have struck a chord with him. 'Heaven and Hell', verse 7:44, was one he quoted from often: 'And the dwellers of the Garden cry unto the dwellers of the Fire. We have found that which our Lord promised us [to be] the Truth. Have ye [too] found that which your Lord promised [to be] the truth? They say: Yea, verily. And a crier in between them crieth: The curse of Allah is on evil-doers.'

His interest at this stage was, nevertheless, purely literary, as he saw himself as essentially an independent secular critic analysing the text. This exercise caused much irritation among the Muslim Brotherhood and other fundamentalist groupings at the time. He became more and more comfortable and vocal in the literary niche he had carved out for himself, and carried the aura of a man stimulated and fulfilled by his work and life. Then things changed. In 1940 his world turned around.

The death of his mother that year shook him deeply. Though his father had died several years before, it was his mother's death that he felt the most. She had helped him in raising his younger brother Mohammed and sisters Hamidah and Aminah, but after her death he felt alone. 'Only today have I felt the heavy burden', he wrote, 'because as long as you lived I was strengthened by you.

But now that you are gone I am alone and weak.' All through his life his mother had been a motivating and guiding influence – encouraging him to believe in himself, even his own greatness. 'Mother who will narrate to me the tales of my childhood in which you portray me as if I were of a unique texture which made me think that I was great and required to live up to this greatness.'

His health also seems to have deteriorated after his parents' death, particularly with the added stresses involved in raising his younger siblings. Stomach, lung and heart ailments were said to have developed around this time, and were gradually exacerbated over the following decades.

The event, more than any other, that seems to have halted him in his tracks, however, was a failed love affair. Soon after his mother died he fell in love. They were subsequently engaged but, for some reason, the relationship did not last. The episode shook him to his core and he never again involved himself with a woman. In the dying days of their liaison he expressed his yearning, as often in the past, through poetry:

Come, our days are about to end,
Come, our breaths are about to cool,
Without hope, no meeting and no date.

So return, here is the nest calling us:
Let us not O, sister destroy it with our hands:
Come let us spend the rest of our lifetime,

Two comrades in good and evil,
Two allies in wealth and poverty.

And then of the grief at their final demise, he wrote:

> O, dream which kindled
> A tumultuous flame burning in my blood,
> Whenever the palm of my hand touches her hand
> Ecstasy touches my heart and my mouth!
>
> Where are you now O, secret of my life?
> Where are you now O, meaning of my existence?
> Where are you now O, the inspiration of my hymn and
>   my prayer?
> Where? In a remote valley of silence.

Not all of his grief was managed so productively. Over time he began to see the relationship itself as wrong, and started to refer to the woman as 'forbidden fruit'. 'O Fate', he once wrote, 'Why did you put her in my way and make her a forbidden fruit? I hear, O Fate, your severe and mocking judgement.'

Increasingly, through this period, he found himself seeking solace in the Koran. It was, for him, a rock of certainty in an ever-changing life. After months of reclusive reading he declared, as if stepping into the light after a long hibernation: 'There is only consolation. There is God [Allah] whose existence has no beginning and for His extension no end. God who is free from all fetters. I love you! I love you because you are "the infinite": the only one in this existence. I love you because you are the only hope for the human heart when it is unable to stand the limits.'

Shortly after, articles by Qutb began to appear in national publications, calling for a new spiritual leadership in his country. He identified the lack of such a leadership as the cause of their political, societal and moral decay. Tied to this was his interpretation of Islamic history. For him, Islam's golden age was the time when the Muslim 'ummah' (community) was ruled by first the Prophet and then the subsequent Khilafah. At this time, Muslims had managed to conquer the Persian and Byzantine empires, accruing lands stretching from China in the east to the Atlantic in the west. This was not, he believed, anything to do with imperialism, but instead a noble pursuit to spread the 'High Idea' of Islam. The bringing of freedom and the liberation of people from tyranny was the duty of Muslims everywhere and the policy of a rightly guided Islamic state.

He began to single out specific aspects of Egyptian society and culture for particular criticism. His first target was the popular music broadcast on Egyptian radio, which he referred to as 'sick singing'. He claimed that such songs corrupted the virtues of men and women who listened to them, and described them as poison running through the veins of society. He proposed a censorship committee to screen out any such lewd or unsophisticated music or cinema. The committee would be composed of educated people well versed in the arts with high standards of taste. This would be enforced by groups which would operate similarly to organisations combating societal evils such as narcotics or disease.

His next target was women, particularly those he found on the beaches of Alexandria in swimsuits. Here his sexual repression came to the fore. Qutb was a man who up to that point, and indeed during his whole life, had experienced no sexual relations with women at all. Taught to be modest at all times and raised under a strict moral code by his assertive parents, he pushed his innate desires down into the deepest recesses of his mind – eventually converting them into demons which he saw as evil in other people.

'Many of these naked bodies lose even the value of the expensive meat. I do not doubt now that clothes are the product of Eve.'

He sneeringly observed the lifestyle on the beaches: 'Here quick friendships thrive: acquainting one with another begins in the forenoon and everything is accomplished by night. Next morning all are dispersed and friendships are terminated as if nothing had happened. Then all begin looking for something new.' His disgust then gradually spread to young people in general. 'Why should they read a serious book when they have cheap magazines and obscene films which flatter their instincts and appeal to the more contemptible part of them?'

The blame, as far as he was concerned, lay squarely with the mass media, who he wished were subject to the same sanctions that their sister organisations endured in Saudi Arabia, as designed by its founders, Abd Al-Wahhab and Abd Al-Aziz ibn Sa'ud. 'Over there in Nejd, poets who flirt with love poetry are whipped. Over here in Egypt they clap for those who guide boys and girls toward immorality and train them on shamelessness. God have mercy on you, O Abd Al-Wahhab! And God favour you, O Abd Al-Aziz ibn Sa'ud. We need only one night and one day in Egypt to whip those fools in the broadcasting service, the cinema studios and in all Egyptian magazines.'

The irony of his own preoccupation with writing love poetry in his earlier years was of course entirely lost on him.

He began to weave these notions together in 1948 when he wrote his first major Islamic book, *Social Justice in Islam*. It began with these words:

To the youngsters whom I see in my fantasy coming to restore this religion anew like when it first began ... fighting for the cause of Allah by killing and getting killed, believing in the bottom of their hearts that the glory belongs to Allah, to his Prophet and to the believers ... To those youngsters whom I do not doubt for a moment will be revived by the spirit of Islam ... in the very near future.

For these words it was banned. Only after the removal of this dedication – thought to be a signal to the already hard-line Muslim Brotherhood – was it allowed to go on sale. In the book he elaborated his version of Islamic history. Whenever Muslim people were allowed to live within the framework of the Islamic state, he believed, they were able to live a just and righteous life. Things went astray the moment that structure collapsed. The historical cause of this collapse was the West. 'The overthrow of Islam', he writes, 'took place only in the present age when Europe conquered the world, and when the dark shadow of colonisation spread over the whole Islamic world, East and West alike ... Europe mustered its forces to extinguish the spirit of Islam, it revived the inheritance of the crusaders' hatred and it employed all the materialistic and intellectual powers at its disposal. With these it sought to break down the internal resistance of the Islamic community and to divorce it gradually over a long period from the teachings and the inheritance of its religious faith.'

In the second half of the book, he described the Islamic system of government and compared it favourably to the existing capitalist and communist systems in the world at the time. 'Both philosophies depend on the preponderance of a materialistic doctrine of life. But while Russia has already become communist, Europe and America are as yet merely going the same way, and will ultimately arrive at the same position, barring the occurrence of any unforeseen happenings.' By lumping them together in this way, he conveniently (for his mind and that of his subsequent followers) colours the world into a state of Islam versus non-Islam. And thus he arrived at his final proposition. 'We are indeed at a crossroads, we may join the march at the tail of the Western caravan which calls itself democracy; if we do so we shall eventually join up with the Eastern caravan which is known to the West as Communism. Or we may return to Islam and make it fully effective in the field of our own spiritual, intellectual, social and economic life. The world ... is today more than ever in need of us to offer it our faith and our social system, our practical and spiritual theory of life.'

By this time he had gone into teaching, and in the mid-1940s he took up a job as a schools inspector at the Ministry of Education. He would enthusiastically write reform proposals requesting more Islamicised schools and teaching programmes. Having worked hard to perfect his proposals, he would present them eagerly to his superiors who would then summarily dismiss every one of them. In the end his extremism disturbed them so much that in 1948 they decided to send him on a scholarship to study the school system in the United States. The idea was that some time in the West would dampen down his intolerance and perhaps even liberalise him a little. The effect was, however, the opposite. It was during his stay in the US that his words began to turn into a determination to act.

His trip coincided with the settling of America's position towards the embryonic state of Israel. America's stance on the Palestinian question enraged him. It was Truman's support for the international committee of inquiry's recommendation that 100,000 Jewish refugees from Europe be immediately admitted to Palestine that particularly disturbed him. He felt that this had revealed the United States' real colours – the action showed no concern for the Palestinian claims to statehood, and instead displaced their citizens. The US must have a 'rotten conscience', he said.

It was on the ship on his way to New York, however, that his first personal memorable event took place. Initially he was struck by the awesome beauty of the oceans surrounding him. He recalled a Koranic passage as he stood on the deck: 'ships that speed through the sea with that which is useful to men, and in the waters which God sends down from the sky, giving life thereby to the earth.'

A Christian missionary was proselytising among the passengers and this annoyed Qutb, who swiftly set up a rival mission arguing for a Muslim prayer area, which he eventually won. He proceeded to lead a series of Nubian seamen in prayer throughout the day – much to the fascination of other passengers. What he remembered the most, however, was a 'drunken semi-naked' Yugoslavian woman who appeared at his door and attempted to seduce him. He claimed this was a sickening affront. The long-suppressed sexual feelings that such a sight must have stirred within this 42-year-old virgin would have been very powerful. The encounter left behind an indelible trace on his memory.

He arrived in New York just before Thanksgiving in November 1949. His immediate impression, as he walked round the city, was that it appeared like a 'vast workshop, noisy and clamorous'. In the days and weeks ahead, though he attended his course regularly, he found difficulty assimilating into American culture – often unwelcoming to men of colour at that time. What conversations he did have, he

felt unstimulated by. 'How much I need someone to talk to
other than [of] money, movie stars and models of cars', he
once wrote to a friend. No aspect of the culture or society
seemed to appeal to him. 'Jazz music was created by the
Negroes to satisfy their primitive inclinations and their
desire in noise on the one hand and to arouse their vital dis-
positions on the other hand', he said; 'the louder the din of
instruments and voices becomes and whizzes in the ears to
an unbearable degree, the more excited the crowds
become.'

As the months passed, homesickness began to set in and
he sought solace, as ever, in poetry:

O, You whose banks are remote,
Here is your beloved lad,
Wandering has become long for him,
When will the stranger return?

When will his steps touch
That dusty surface?
When will he smell its fragrance
Like scented daisy?

Your visions in his eyes
Flutter like dreams,
I wonder if your heart beat with passion for him
Throughout the days

Your passing nights
Are like the genius breeze,
Which changed into scented
And dewy memories

Their fragrance have wings,
Their wishes flutter
In an exhausted world
Embroidered by songs

There where his steps
Are scattered on the road,
They still have life,
They utter the call of the drowned!

O, land restore to you
This lonely stranger,
His love is dedicated to you,
Restore your beloved lad

His biggest problem, however, was – as always – with women. Projecting his agitated desires onto them, he talked in lurid detail of 'thirsty lips, bulging breasts, smooth legs ... The calling eye, the provocative laugh.'

Another area he found fascinating was the church. 'Nobody goes to church as often as the Americans do ... yet no one is as distant as they are from the spiritual aspects of religion.' He saw them competing for worshippers like supermarkets or theatres for customers, referring once to an advertisement for a local church posted on a college dormitory. 'Sunday October 1st, 6pm. Light Dinner; Magic Show; Puzzles; Contests; Entertainment.' Despite his sneering, and perhaps as a result of loneliness, he nevertheless joined a church club; and yet ultimately he ended up being drawn to the same focus he had returned to his whole adult life – sex. It was at a church dance that his volcanic revulsion erupted once again. 'The dancing intensified ... The hall swarmed with legs ... Arms circled arms, lips met lips, chests met chests and the atmosphere was full of love.' The host – the local pastor – dimmed the lights to create a 'romantic dreamy effect', Qutb noted to his horror, while the gramophone played the popular tune 'Baby It's Cold Outside'.

Malise Ruthven, in his book *A Fury For God*, provides a good interpretation of Qutb's reactions:

> Charles Dickens, in his account of one of the last public hangings he witnessed in London, described the ghoulish fascination of the crowd as 'the attraction of repulsion'. Qutb's description of his sexually charged encounters with American women exhibits a similar mixture of fascination and horror. To adapt Dickens' phrase it might be called 'the repulsion of attraction'.

Towards the end of his stay in the US, just before he was due to complete his course, he dropped out. Exams were looming and his refusal to sit them, rather than any academic anxiety, was likely to have been an act of defiance. He refused to be judged by their system.

Meanwhile, in Egypt, Qutb's book had raised his profile among more fundamentalist circles, and the Muslim Brotherhood organisation had begun to take an increasing interest in a man they once regarded as an adversary. On his return to Cairo in August 1950, some of their younger members went to the airport to welcome him.

Soon after his return, he wrote his second book, *The Battle of Islam and Capitalism*. In it he fleshed out his notion of Islam as a rival governing system, superior to all others. It was not, however, in his view, properly applied anywhere. He angrily attacked the then Muslim hierarchy for not addressing the injustices in the world and bringing it, through Islam, back to the path of righteousness.

Having returned from the US in a state of hyperactivity, within a few short months he released his third book, *Islam and Universal Peace*. He saw Islam, and strict adherence to it and God's word, as the sole means to achieving peace on earth. 'God is the supreme legislator and he has no reason to favour an individual or a class as all belong to him equally.' The ultimate goal must be 'when Islamic laws are fully implemented in the political and economic spheres'. This implementation had to be fought for, and the way to do this was through jihad. 'Jihad', Qutb wrote, 'is a means to achieve a universal change by establishing peace of conscience, domestic peace, national peace and international peace.' There was no cause more urgent than this, for 'the most serious injustice is luring people from the worship of God and forcing them to deify those rulers who empower themselves to legalise what God has prohibited and to prohibit what God has allowed.'

Through this discourse, Qutb grew increasingly close to the Muslim Brothers and a mutual admiration and respect began to blossom between them. In the early fifties he became a regular writer for one of their publications. In one of his pieces, in November 1951, he proclaimed that it was they who were the chosen vanguard of Islam, as prophesied by Allah in the Koran, 9:111: 'Lo, Allah hath brought from the believers their lives and their wealth because the garden will be theirs: They shall fight in the way of Allah and shall slay and be slain. It is a promise which is binding in him in the Torah and the Gospel and the Koran. Who fulfilleth his covenant better than Allah?'

In July 1952 a revolution in Egypt brought to power an alliance of rebel army commanders known as 'the Free

Officers' and the Muslim Brothers. Qutb was considered one of the intellectual figureheads of the revolution and was very close to one of its leaders – future President Gamal Abdal Nasser. They would talk for 'more than twelve hours daily' on all manner of topics, primarily 'the issue of transition, its duration and the constitution'.

But within days of winning power, the honeymoon was over. Qutb was not rewarded with the cabinet post he had coveted for so long. 'Sayyid Qutb was extremely angry', according to one insider. 'He considered Abdal Nasser responsible for the loss of his dream in the Ministry of Education which he expected as a reward for supporting the revolution and promoting it.' A formal split between the revolutionary government and the Muslim Brothers followed in January 1954. The administration had begun negotiating with the British over Suez. To the Muslim Brothers this was a betrayal – they wanted jihad, not compromise.

Refusing to allow dissent, the government promptly arrested the Brothers and Qutb. Instead of occupying one of the high offices of state, Sayyid Qutb was sent to jail. His disillusionment sank to new depths. While in jail, he established and maintained links with a wider apparatus of Islamists on the outside. Despite his incarceration, a lot of activity seemed to be going on within this network. It was around this time that Qutb encountered one of the most important thinkers to influence his evolving ideology, Taqiuddin Al-Nabhani. He was part theologian, part psychologist, and he shared Qutb's world-view: that true Muslim thinking, existence and behaviour had been all but extinguished in this infidel-ridden world. He believed that the first stage of the restoration needed to be a battle of ideas. He studied the science of idea formation and became fascinated by the internal workings of the mind, how people reach conclusions, and how concepts and convictions shape emotions and vice versa. He then used this knowledge to incubate a factory of concepts that he designed specifically to capture hearts and minds, which he hoped would then catch on and spread like a virus through time and space. It was Al-Nabhani who formed Hizb-Ut-Tahrir – the same organisation that lives on today, and which I myself encountered in the Islamic Society meetings of my university days. In the early 1950s he wrote numerous books on 'the concepts' of an Islamic state: *The System of Islam*, *The Ruling System in Islam*, *The Economic System in Islam*, *The Social System in Islam*, *The Concepts of Hizb Ut-Tahrir* and *The Islamic State*. It is likely to be no coincidence, therefore, that the next – and last – book that Qutb wrote contained a set of concepts that were written in such a way as to capture the imaginations of generations of Muslims who answered Qutb's call to jihad.

Qutb was released after nearly ten years in jail; but soon after, a conspiracy was unearthed in which the Muslim Brothers had been planning a series of public assassinations including that of President Abdal Nasser. Qutb was rearrested, tried and sentenced to death.

It was in jail that he wrote the final and most infamous of his books – *Milestones*. The book and its philosophy changed the frame of Islamic thinking in innumerable circles for decades to come, and continues to hold influence to the present day. Like a match to a firework, it has lit up the minds of young followers from one generation to the next.

He starts the book with an analysis of civilisation's current position. 'Mankind today is on the brink of a precipice', he tells us, 'not because of the danger of complete annihilation which is hanging over its head – this being just a symptom and not the real disease – but because humanity is devoid of those vital values for its healthy development and real progress.' For him, this lack of vital values in the West is clear. 'The civilisation of the white man has already exhausted its restricted usefulness ... because [it] did not issue from the divine source and origin [but] was established on bases repugnant to the nature of life and human beings ... It is the problem of the hideous schizophrenia which is the common denominator between all the systems prevailing in the white man's world where the Russians, the Americans, the English, the French, the Swiss, the Swedes and all those who follow in their steps whether East or West ... all these stand on the same precarious footing ... At present one hears voices of alarm coming from everywhere warning mankind of its catastrophic end under the white man's civilisation.'

He describes mankind's malaise as 'Jahaliyya' – paganism: 'We may say that any society is a Jahili society that does not dedicate itself to submission to God alone, in its beliefs and ideas, in its observance of worship and its legal regulations.'

The current Muslim world also, in Qutb's eyes, falls into the category of Jahaliyya. Real Islamic civilisation had been long extinct, 'buried under the debris of manmade traditions of several generations ... our whole environment, people's beliefs and ideas, habits and traditions, rules and laws is Jahaliyya even to the extent that what we consider to be Islamic culture, Islamic sources, Islamic philosophy and Islamic thought are also constructs of Jahaliyya.'

Few are immune from this nihilistic vision, and its significance, Qutb warns us, is devastating:

If we look at the sources and foundations of modern modes of living, it becomes clear that the whole world is steeped in Jahaliyya, and all the marvellous material comforts and high level comforts do not diminish [this] ignorance. This Jahaliyya is based on rebellion against the sovereignty of Allah on Earth. It attempts to transfer to man one of the greatest attributes of Allah, namely sovereignty, by making some men lords over others. It does so not in the simple and primitive ways of the ancient Jahaliyya, but in the more subtle form of claiming that the right to create values, to legislate rules of collective behaviour, and to choose a way of life rests with men, without regard to what Allah has prescribed. The result of this rebellion against the authority of Allah is the oppression of his creatures.

Today we are surrounded by Jahaliyya. Its nature is the same as during the first period of Islam, and it is perhaps a little more deeply entrenched.

Muslims have no choice, therefore: they must not only reject, but attack it. A new Islamic vanguard – the torch-bearers of the true Islam – must stand firm to the faith and remain sterilised from the Jahaliyya that lies all about it, while always preparing to engage with and ultimately defeat it.

The Muslims of this vanguard must know the landmarks and the milestones on the road to this goal … [They] ought to be aware of their position vis-à-vis this Jahaliyya, which has struck its stakes throughout the Earth. They must know when to cooperate with others and when to separate from them; what characteristics and qualities they should cultivate … How to address the people of Jahaliyya in the language of Islam; what topics and problems to discuss with them; and where and how to obtain guidance on all these matters. I have written signposts for this vanguard which I consider to be a waiting reality about to be materialised.

It is through jihad that the vanguard must advance. Qutb pours scorn on any notion that the jihad to be enjoined is in any way spiritual or defensive:

> It is a movement to wipe out tyranny and to introduce true freedom to mankind using whatever resources are practically available in a given human situation ... What kind of a man is he who, after listening to the commandments of God and Traditions of the Prophet – peace be upon him – and after reading about the events which occurred during the Islamic Jihad, still thinks that it is a temporary injunction related to transient conditions and that it is concerned only with the defence of the borders ... in the verse giving the permission to fight, God has informed the believers that the life of this world is such that checking one group of people by another is the law of God, so that Earth may be cleansed of corruption ...
>
> The peace of Islam means that *din* [meaning, law of society] be purified for Allah, that all people should obey Allah alone, and every system that permits some people to rule over others be abolished.

Having defined the mission, he then proposes a blueprint for action, turning on its head the way in which the Koran has been read for centuries: in its entirety and in context. Instead he promotes a new form of Koranic interpretation – one based on segmental, selective extractions. He openly argues for a piecemeal approach to the text which, though not comprehensive, would nevertheless serve what he believed to be its primary purpose – the fuelling of the fire of jihad.

The first generation, Qutb tells us,

... did not approach the Koran for the purpose of acquiring culture and information, nor for the purpose of taste or enjoyment. None of them came to the Koran to increase his sum of total knowledge itself or to solve some scientific or legal problem or to remove some defect in his understanding. He rather turned to the Koran to find out what the Almighty Creator had pre-scribed for him and for the community in which he lived, for his life and for the life of the group. He approached it to act on what he heard immediately, as a soldier on the battlefield reads 'Today's Bulletin' so that he knows what is to be done ... At most he would read ten verses, memorise them and then act upon them.

He ends by predicting how the fire of this jihad will spread – from one heart to another, then another, then another:

A man has faith in this belief which emanates from a hidden source and is enlivened by the power of God alone: the existence of the Islamic society virtually begins with the faith of this one man ... This individual, however, receives the revelation not in order merely to turn it on himself, but to carry its spirit too: such is the nature of this belief ... The immense power that has car-ried it into this soul knows with certainty that it will carry it further still ... When three believers have been touched by the faith, this credo means to them 'you are now a society, an independent Islamic society, separate from the Jahaliyya society which does not have faith in this.' From that point onwards the Islamic society will grow apace: three becomes ten, the ten become a hundred, the hundred a thousand, the thousand, twelve thousand. The society has become a movement that will permit no one to stand apart ... The battle is constant, the jihad lasts until the Day of Judgement.

Thus he paints an accurate picture of the troubled youth – reframing the world, and his place in it, in his mind and then finding another to share the vision with, then another, then another. They stand apart from the world. They are the vanguard. What Qutb described was a terrorist cell, and it was this exact model that every one has since followed.

On 29 August 1966, Sayyid Qutb was executed by hanging. The notions he espoused spread almost exactly like the virus he and Al-Nabhani, the theologian-psychologist, had predicted. Indeed, social psychologists have suggested that such viral pathways of propagation are precisely the means by which similar strongly-held beliefs are spread around the world and through time. This is known as *meme theory*. It proposes that, like a virus, an idea – if powerful enough – can attach itself to a vulnerable host. It replicates and spreads, modifying itself in the process, to gradually enable penetration of a wider and wider audience of proselytising followers.

The notion of Jahaliyya has been around since the time of Mohammed. In AD 622 he fled Mecca as a result of pressure from unbelievers who worshipped multiple deities to such an extent that the local economy had become dependent on the sale of idols at the main shrine – the Ka'aba. The date of his departure from Mecca is marked among the most important in Islamic history – indeed, the entire Islamic calendar is dated from that event. He regrouped with his followers for two years and then in AD 624 he returned to take the city. Sura 2:29 in the Koran refers to it: 'Many a small band has, by God's grace, vanquished a mighty army. God is with those who endure with fortitude.'

The strategy, therefore, of separating from Jahaliyya society, in order to regroup, attack and ultimately defeat it, is as old as the religion itself. However, it was only through Qutb's modification of the Jahaliyya notion – applying the term to modern Western culture and peoples – that the idea successfully mutated. Once it had, it was then able to appeal to a new audience: disillusioned, predominantly Western – 20th-century Muslim youth.

The first person to catch it, beyond the initial coterie of the Muslim Brotherhood, was Sayyid Qutb's brother, Mohammed Qutb, who spread the word of his late brother's teachings fervently after his death. One of his first converts was a close family friend – a man who became the second most influential figure in the development and spread of the extremist creed – a charismatic Palestinian by the name of Abdullah Azzam.

———

BORN IN JENIN IN 1941, AZZAM WAS BROUGHT UP in British-occupied Palestine. He graduated from Damascus University in 1966 but his return home after graduation was short-lived. Israel captured the West Bank and Gaza the following year, as a result of which thousands like Azzam were forced to flee. This was a turning point in the lives of many young men in that part of the world. Azzam escaped to Jordan. Once there he signed up for the

Palestinian jihad against Israel. His skills were more in the areas of preaching and propaganda and so he went to the University of Al-Azhar in Cairo, where he studied a master's degree in Shariah law, after which he went on to complete a Ph.D. in Islamic jurisprudence. He spent much of his time in Cairo among local Islamist circles and became a regular visitor to the Qutb household – forging a lasting relationship with Mohammed.

In the late seventies he returned to Amman to teach Islamic law at the University of Jordan. This was precisely the kind of job he had been working up to through his studies thus far – teaching the subject he loved, to the next generation of Muslim youth, in an area that had become dear to him. It was the ideal post. His views, however, clashed with the faculty's secular outlook, and shortly after starting there he was dismissed. Enraged by this rejection, it took him a while to find employment elsewhere, but eventually he found another lecturing job in Saudi Arabia where he was able to join his friend, Mohammed Qutb, at the altogether more welcoming King Abdul Aziz University in Jeddah. It was here that he met the young student Osama Bin Laden, who was a regular attender at his lectures.

After the Soviet invasion of Afghanistan, Azzam moved on. He had found a more urgent calling. He travelled to Pakistan and then to the United States, where he visited no fewer than 26 states in search of funds and volunteers before returning to the front lines on the Pakistan/Afghan border. This degree of movement and the nature of his activity in the US has led to the widespread belief that Azzam was in fact funded by the CIA, who were backing anti-Soviet forces in the war at the time.

For Azzam, the Afghan war possessed an almost a mystical quality. He saw it as part of Allah's grand design – the beginning of the global jihad:

Allah exploded the Jihad on the land of Afghanistan and groups of youth from the Islamic world marched forth to Afghanistan in search of Jihad and martyrdom. Indeed this small band of Arabs, whose number did not exceed a few hundred individuals, changed the tide of the battle from an Islamic battle of one country, to an Islamic World Jihad movement, in which all races participated and all colours, languages and cultures met: yet they were one, their direction was one, their ranks were one, and the goal was one: that the Word of Allah is raised the highest and that this religion is made victorious on Earth.

Azzam became one of the key organisers, motivators and thinkers of the movement in Afghanistan, and during his time at the forefront, he moved the ideology on several steps further.

The Jihad in Afghanistan is the right of every Muslim in order to turn Communism away, and the Afghan jihad has been judged to be *fard* [obligatory] like prayer and fasting which a Muslim is not permitted to neglect ... Jihad is now ... incumbent on all Muslims and will remain so until the Muslims recapture every spot that was Islamic but later fell into the hands of the *kufr*. Jihad has been a fard since the fall of al-Andalus [southern Spain], and will remain so until the other lands that were Muslim are returned to us ... Palestine, Bukhara, Lebanon, Chad, Eritrea, Somalia, the Philippines,

Burma, Southern Yemen, Tashkent and al-Andalus. The duty of Jihad is one of the most important imposed on us by God. He has made it incumbent on us just like prayer, fasting and alms. Such duties are divine obligations. The forbidding of Jihad is kufr which strays from faith.

By adding this element of compulsion to his proselytising, he increased the fervour and energy with which subsequent generations would receive and spread it. The obligation, he claimed, was not to any mild, intellectual or supportive function – it was to direct and deliberate violence:

History does not write its lines except with blood. Glory does not build its lofty edifice except with skulls. Honour and respect cannot be established except on a foundation of cripples and corpses. Empires, distinguished peoples, states and societies cannot be established except with examples of such as these martyrs. By the likes of these martyrs nations are established, convictions are brought to life and ideologies are made victorious ... Indeed those who think that they can challenge reality or change societies, without blood sacrifices and wounds, without pure, innocent souls, do not understand the essence of our religion. They do not understand the method of the best of Messengers (may Allah bless him and grant him peace).

In later proclamations he painted a picture of the afterlife for martyrs – adding an allure that would ultimately prove irresistible to future jihadis.

Indeed the martyr has seven special favours from Allah: all his sins are forgiven at the first spurt of his blood, he sees his place in paradise as his blood is shed (before his soul leaves the body), he tastes the sweetness of *iman* (faith), he is married to 72 of the Beautiful Maidens of Paradise, he is protected from the Punishment of the Grave, he is saved from the Great Terror (on the Day of Judgement), there is placed upon his head a crown of honour, a jewel of which is better than the whole world and everything in it, and he is granted permission to intercede for 70 members of his household to bring them to Paradise and save them from the Hell Fire.

Through Azzam, therefore, the creed underwent a significant transformation. It evolved into a more prolific ideology, enabling it to produce a more powerful pull on those who encountered it in future.

In addition to his motivational and intellectual works, his contribution was also a very practical one. On his arrival in Peshawar, Pakistan, he set up the Beit al-Ansar (House of the Helpers) where volunteers for the Afghan jihad were received and trained before moving on to the front line. It was here that he met Bin Laden again, and this time the two men sparked an instant friendship. Much mutual respect flowed between them and Azzam became very much a mentor to Bin Laden. Together they expanded the Beit al-Ansar and established the Maktab al-Khidamat (the Office of Services), which was a support organisation for the Arab volunteers. Over time it was transformed into a network of recruiters and specialists in a diverse array of skills, from medicine to engineering and bomb-making. This was the forerunner to Al Qaeda.

Bin Laden learned a great deal at Azzam's side – even today, his public utterances are often peppered with Azzam's original phraseology.

On 24 November 1989, Azzam was murdered with his two sons by a car bomb in Peshawar. Suspects for the murder include Mossad, the KGB, the Pakistani ISI and particularly the CIA, for whom – as a once likely partner – Azzam is said to have become too embarrassing a secret.

Profoundly distressed by his friend's demise and what it would mean for the cause, the 32-year-old Bin Laden stepped up to take on Azzam's mantle and began to plan for the internationalisation of the movement. He relocated to Kandahar and started building a number of camps along the border, while widening his network beyond it.

Osama Bin Laden was now at the forefront of the global jihad.

SHEIKH MOHAMMED BIN LADEN WAS A LEGENDARY FIGURE. Born in the Hadramaut region of Yemen, one of the poorest places on earth, he arrived in Saudi Arabia as a young man with little to his name. Within a few years he had built up his own vast construction business, ultimately working his way up to becoming one of the richest men in Saudi Arabia. His company – the Bin Laden Organisation – was the largest employer in the kingdom, and Mohammed was courted, befriended and trusted by kings and princes. The cities of Mecca and Medina are the holiest sites in Islam, and the Saudi royal family regard the stewardship of these locations as the gravest of their responsibilities. In the 1960s the Bin Laden Organisation was awarded the contract to renovate both sites, as King

Abdul Aziz made them his official contractors. The relationship between the two families went deeper than business: they shared friends and confidences and their children went to the same schools.

Though allowed up to four wives in Islam, by the time of his death, Mohammed Bin Laden had amassed 22. He would marry, divorce, and marry again – maintaining officially no more than four wives at any one time. However, as the divorced wives would often continue to be supported by him, he would live with them all together in an impressive compound – complete with Venetian chandeliers and solid gold statues. In addition to the women he formally married were women with whom he established temporary contracts – *serah*. These were like semi-marriages. As Islam forbids intimate relationships outside marriage, Saudi law permits a form of temporary marriage contract that may last hours or years – that way, such relationships remain legitimate within the eyes of the law without involving the formal process or invoking any requisite rights. These semi-wives and any of their children by Mohammed also resided in his compound, as did the children of any wife who was deceased or who chose to leave – they could never leave with their children.

In total he had 54 children, and Osama was his seventeenth. Osama's mother, in many ways, stood out from the rest of the wives. An altogether cosmopolitan younger Syrian woman, Hamida Alia Ghanoum was more likely to be seen in a Chanel suit than an Islamic veil. She remained married to Mohammed Bin Laden until his death, and her son studied and was raised with the remaining Bin Laden boys. The father towered over them all, and each of them looked up to him with awe. He would summon them periodically to his quarters and demand recitations of the

Koran or grill them on any number of subjects. His word was law and no one ever argued with him – not even the King. Once he took one of his sons to see King Faisal. The King asked the boy to sit beside him in a designated space by the throne. Mohammed Bin Laden, however, objected and the boy had to go back and sit beside his father.

As well as having a relatively westernised mother, Osama was also given something of a Western education. He was sent to Al-Thagh, an elite Western-style school in Jeddah, where he learned English. His siblings also became increasingly westernised in their outlooks, choosing to further their education and life experience abroad, in London, Harvard, Egypt and Miami. Osama didn't stand out early on for his religious interest – in fact, if anything he was seen as a conscientious student dedicated to his studies. A teacher at the school described him as 'shy, retiring, gracious and conscientious … very neat and precise'.

In 1967, apparently on the way to marry his 23rd wife, Bin Laden's father died. The man who had cast such an immense shadow over all his sons had left behind an enormous vacuum. A succession struggle ensued between the eldest sons, Salim and Ali. It was only after the intervention of King Faisal that the matter was settled in favour of the older brother, Salim. The biggest turmoil that Mohammed Bin Laden left behind, however, was in the psyches of his offspring.

In the same way that a tree which casts a wide shadow over neighbouring plants can inhibit their growth, so a domineering parent can inhibit that of his children. The Bin Laden case was an extreme one. The Bin Laden children were deprived of emotional nurturing to such an extent that the consequent malaise that set in affected their physical health as well – or at least their own perception of it.

Most of them became nervous individuals, sometimes hypochondriacal and often ill. In her autobiography, *The Veiled Kingdom*, Carmen Bin Laden (the Italian ex-wife of one of the brothers, Yeslam) describes her former husband as 'panicky and fearful ... He was nervous all the time and he had nightmares. He was frightened of everything, especially dying. He had various physical complaints – belly aches, trouble breathing, sudden sweats of panic – that required endless tests but never seemed to amount to anything precise.'

Osama was often reported to need to lie down due to postural blood pressure problems. There are several photos of him receiving shots of insulin – he is thought to suffer from insulin-dependent diabetes and subsequent renal complications stemming from this. An interviewer once reported Bin Laden constantly sipping water and green tea for the entire duration of an interview – likely to be for treatment of his kidneys. In 2002, *Time* magazine reported that 'physicians who analysed photos of Bin Laden determined that he probably suffers from secondary osteoporosis, which is often related to diabetes and kidney trouble'.

On leaving school, he enrolled into the management and economics faculty at the Abdul Aziz University. Once there, he was persuaded by his elder brother Salim to major in civil engineering. However, his interests began to veer increasingly towards the compulsory Islamic studies component of his course. It is there that he encountered the teachings of Sayyid Qutb in the lectures of Abdullah Azzam. As well as the tenets of the creed itself, what Azzam and other Islamists instilled in Bin Laden was the concept of an upcoming noble battle. Their *cause célèbre* at the time was Afghanistan, and many young Arab men were being encouraged by social as well as official circles to travel there and join the jihad against the Godless communists. Indeed, the central focus of the CIA's involvement in the war at the time was the enabling of exactly this kind of recruitment.

For many students of that generation, peers and authority figures alike all conspired to push the youngster towards joining the fight in Afghanistan. It became, as for many, a test of faith. By the time he left university in 1979, Bin Laden had become swept away with the romantic notion of playing a pivotal role in this proud struggle.

By early 1980, he had arrived in Peshawar, his focus entirely on the Afghanistan conflict, and he had come to dedicate himself to it. In the early days he spent most of his time helping out at *Al Jihad*, Abdullah Azzam's pro-war Arabic language newspaper, while staying with Azzam at 61 Syed Jamal al-Din Afghani Road – the guesthouse they were developing together as a transit and support point for newly arriving Arab volunteers: Beit al-Ansar (House of the Helpers). Jason Burke, in his book, *Al Qaeda – The True Story of Radical Islam*, describes how Bin Laden was perceived at the time:

> Journalists in the region began hearing stories of a man known as 'the Good Samaritan' who, it was said, would arrive unannounced at hospitals where wounded Afghan and Arab fighters had been brought. According to the stories, he went from bed to bed handing out cashews to the wounded and carefully noting each man's name and address. Weeks later the man's family would receive a generous cheque … Most say that, at least in the early eighties he was still the quiet shy young man noted by his teachers ten years previously.

Most of the volunteers who were arriving had little or no military experience and so their first training was in rudimentary small arms and basic weapons use as they passed through the various mujahideen camps. The throughput of men grew throughout the eighties and, via this network, Bin Laden began to build a circle of acolytes around him. Burke describes the fledgling group:

> Most were from relatively wealthy backgrounds (otherwise they would have been unable to complete their education) and they included virtually no representatives of the traditional Afghan *ulema* [Muslim citizenry]. They were almost all university educated, mainly in technical faculties … The common features in the background of many of the more senior activists is striking.

A key figure who joined the ranks at that time was Khaled Sheikh Mohammed (KSM). Like each of his brothers, he quickly became a rising force within the network. He was a man whose links with the West and specific plans towards it made him stand out from the beginning. He was to become the mastermind of 'the planes operation'.

There was a large age gap between KSM and the rest of his siblings. In fact, he was the same age as several of his nephews, with whom he attended the same school in Kuwait. The school was very strict – the headmaster was said to prowl the corridors brandishing a bamboo cane. His father died while Khaled Sheikh was still at school, and his much older, strict Muslim brothers took over his parenting. Like those before him, and all those who would follow, his childhood followed the same pattern of the fledgling extremist: aloof guardians with limited contact in an environment dominated by rigid discipline. He was a diligent pupil, and the area he excelled most in was science. A family friend said: 'He was very genius ... From the beginning of his studies it's science. He wanted to go to America for this reason. He wanted to become a doctor [Ph.D.] there.'

His determination to travel to the US set in at an early age. His single-mindedness ultimately paid off in 1984 when he gained admission to Chowan College, a small university institution in North Carolina, where he enrolled in a pre-engineering course. The college accepted a number of Middle Eastern students at the time, and each of them arrived with high expectations. 'We were all excited about going to the States', said one student. 'In high school we had seen all the movies, heard the music. We wondered so much about it.' Their arrival, however, coincided with a time of palpable anti-Muslim feeling in the United States, not long after the Iranian takeover of the US embassy in Tehran. Again, like many immigrants before them, arriving into the wide new world of the West for the first time, they were met with a rude awakening. One that shook their thought processes to the core, prompting the mind down another stage of the conveyor belt.

Local students would refer to them as the 'Abbie Dabbies' and frequently subject them to ridicule and racial harassment. When they left their shoes outside their rooms – in line with Middle Eastern tradition – other students would take them away, leaving the Arab students to find them later floating in a nearby lake. Pranks included filling 55-gallon dustbins with water and leaning them against the Arab students' front door so that, upon opening, their rooms would flood with water. They found little support

from the college authorities either, who, rather than demonstrate sensitivity to their cultural differences, required them
to attend a Christian chapel service once a month.

Their experience turned into a baptism of fire for many
of the young Arab students who, rather than embrace the
new culture they had longed to join for so long, turned
instead to their own religion. Although feeding further the
stereotype they had been cast with, their religious practices
at least rewarded them with a sense of belonging when all
around them they found none. 'They seemed to be praying
all the time', said one student. 'Just chanting like. We never
understood a word of it. Sometimes we'd come home late
on a weekend night, maybe after we'd had a few beers, and
they'd still be praying.'

Khaled Sheikh left Chowan College after a single semester. In summer 1984 he enrolled in the Carolina
Agricultural and Technical State University in Greensboro
to study engineering. The Arab students there seemed to
have reacted to the alienation they had encountered upon
arrival at their new environment in one of two ways: either
they accelerated rapidly towards increasing westernisation
or they immersed themselves ever deeper, like the boys at
Chowan, into their religion. According to one Arab student,
'the students at Greensboro were divided into the mullahs
and the non-mullahs'. The latter would drink alcohol and
go out with American women, and some even drove round
in Mercedes and Porches. The 'mullahs', however, formed
an increasingly hard-core clique and focused their energy
on bringing others back to the fold – while at the same time
remaining sealed off from the rest of the campus. Khaled
Sheikh was a rising member of this community. He would
often, with the others, travel to the airport to meet newly
arriving students and welcome them, luring them into the

fold before they fell prey to the temptations of a Western life.

Arab governments became increasingly aware during this period that, rather than returning home with more liberal and tolerant attitudes after their stay in the United States, the opposite was happening with their young students. 'We had a lot of our students coming back from the United States radicalised.' Said one high official: 'I'm not talking about religious guys going to the United States and coming back fundamentalists. I'm talking about the cool guys.'

One former student explained it: 'Why would they flip religiously? It happens there … When we are there we are vulnerable. That's why we get into groups to protect each other.'

The transformation was certainly noticeable in Khaled Sheikh whenever he returned home to Kuwait. In *Perfect Soldiers*, Terry McDermott relates an eye-opening interview he conducted with a former teacher of Khaled Sheikh:

'When he goes there he sees most Americans don't like Arabs and Islam,' said Dabbous, his high school teacher.

'Why?' I ask him.

'Because of Israel,' he says. 'Most Americans hate Arabs because of this. He's a very normal boy before. Kind, generous, always the smiling kind. After he came back he's a different man. He's very sad. He doesn't speak. He just sits there.'

'Why?' I ask.

'Because of what I am saying about the Americans hating Islam,' he said.

'I talked to him to change his mind to tell him this is just a few Americans. He refused to speak to me about it again. He was set. This was when he was on vacation from school. When Khaled said this I told him we must meet again. He said no. "No, my ideas are very strong. Don't talk with me again about this matter."'

He graduated from college on 18 December 1986 and instead of going back home to Kuwait, he flew straight to Peshawar.

By now the town was teeming with Arab volunteers training and passing through to the border, on to the camps and then to fight in the war. Coordinating the work there was a hard core of men, performing a variety of military and supportive roles. These senior organisers, trainers, financiers, motivators and planners developed into a semi-permanent Arab community residing in the area. This would later formalise into an official leadership council for Al Qaeda, and it included men such as Ayman Al-Zawahiri, Hambali, Azzam and – already somewhat apart from the rest – Bin Laden. 'He had been visiting Peshawar on and off during the mid-1980s', said one man in the area at the time. 'He was also spending a lot of time across the border, fighting in Afghanistan. Zawahiri came [to stay] in 1985. Bin Laden then moved his wife and children to Peshawar in 1986 and lived there until October 1989. During that time he visited Saudi several times a year.'

The group were busy building and expanding their infrastructure. Some of the caves were huge affairs, built in elaborate detail. One of the largest was in the mountains of Khost, four miles in from the border with Pakistan. Jason Burke describes it:

It was a massive complex. Bulldozers and explosives were used to dig seven tunnels into the side of a mountain valley. The tunnels had brick entrances with iron doors and were big enough to shelter a mosque, a garage, an armourer's shop, a small first aid post equipped with American medical equipment including ultrasound apparatus, a radio station, a library with English and local books, a kitchen, a 'hotel' and stores. A generator provided power for the first aid post, mosque and [a] guests' tunnel.

Another similar base was built in Tora Bora, 30 miles south of Jalalabad; another was built in Jaji, and yet another in Khalden – a no man's land between Afghanistan and Pakistan. Bin Laden built one for his own exclusive use, known as Al-Ma'asada – 'The Lion's Den'. This sprawling network was 'the base' after which Al Qaeda was ultimately named. At no point, from their construction all the way up to the American carpet-bombing in 2001, were they ever empty.

Bin Laden regularly visited the fronts along the Pakistan border, handing out food, shoes and coats to the fighters. He would eat modestly with the men during their breaks and sometimes join in direct combat himself. He gradually built up his network of fighters as more and more grew in admiration of him – this would ultimately, in some cases, translate to a formal pledge of loyalty to him.

Bin Laden's direct involvement in the war climaxed at the battle of Jalalabad – fighting alongside the men in a battle in which over 1,000 Afghan fighters were killed. In 1989, however, the Soviets withdrew from Afghanistan and a few months later the puppet regime they left behind in Kabul fell.

Bin Laden and his associates were ecstatic – this was an intoxicating victory for them. Even though they were only a small fraction of the fighting force, with the native Afghans dominating the front lines by far, the Arab and foreign fighters saw this as vindication of their sacrifice, and Bin Laden felt a sense of personal pride in the outcome. They had defeated a superpower. Islam – they believed – had now come of age.

Despite the Soviet withdrawal from Afghanistan, however, would-be fighters continued flowing into Peshawar at a pace – more so now, in fact, than ever. They were coming for a form of freelance jihad training. Jamal Al-Fadl, a young man who travelled to the camps in the early 1990s, provided an eyewitness account of his experience. Born in Sudan, after living for a while in Brooklyn, New York he turned to his religion in his early twenties and ultimately set his mind on joining mujahideen training in Afghanistan. At the age of 26 he travelled to Peshawar, where he spent some time in a guesthouse before travelling to a camp near Khost. There he received basic training with Kalashnikovs and rocket launchers. After this he is said to have moved on to the 'Lion's Den' complex, where he was lectured personally by Bin Laden on his duty to fight in the jihad. From there he went to another camp near Khost, where he was lectured in Islamic jurisprudence and the principles of jihad for two weeks before travelling to a fourth camp for training in administration and then on to a final camp to learn about explosives and bomb-making.

Many of the men who came for training ended up staying on in the area long-term, either because they had married local Afghan women and settled down, or because they were wanted in their own countries where they were likely to face arrest, incarceration or execution upon return. Bin Laden continued to fund an increasing number of guesthouses around Peshawar – three in the city, Beit

Al-Shuhada (House of Martyrs), Beit Al-Salaam (House of Peace) and Beit Al-Momineen (House of the Faithful), and a fourth in a suburb just west of the city.

At the end of 1989, he moved back to Saudi Arabia where, in many quarters, he was rewarded with a hero's welcome. He was seen as a pious and brave mujahid who had lived and fought humbly among the men. His reputation had spread throughout the country and it only grew further when, on his return, he shunned the opulent lifestyle his family afforded him for a barely furnished, modest house in Jeddah. His family, however, were keen for him to settle down and they began to line up a managerial position for him within the Bin Laden group. Like all ex-combatants returning from war, however, he found it diffi-cult to slip back into a civilian life. He prayed and led a pious lifestyle but, all the while, yearned for a means to translate the agitation building up inside him into an active and righteous struggle again – a means to fan the flame that had been lit when he first joined the jihad in Afghanistan.

Then, on 2 August 1989, he found it. Or so he thought.

Saddam Hussein invaded Kuwait. Bin Laden always saw Saddam as a secular, 'hypocrite' president – not even close to his definition of a true Muslim leader. The positioning of Saddam's army on the borders of Saudi soil – the land of the two holiest cities and shrines of Islam – was, in Bin Laden's eyes, unacceptable. He travelled immediately to visit his old family friend, the Crown Prince.

Jason Burke provides an informative description of the scene at the end of the meeting.

Prince Sultan stood up, walked across the sumptuously decorated room and stood next to Osama Bin Laden. He touched Bin Laden on the shoulder and turned to face the guests who had been admitted into the home in Riyadh an hour previously. In his hand he held the five-page document Bin Laden had handed him a few minutes earlier. 'The Bin Laden family have always been loyal friends of our family,' the Crown Prince said emolliently. 'I look forward to many more years of that friendship.' Bin Laden's face was black with anger.

The plan was for a mujahideen force, assembled by Bin Laden, to arrive and defend the Saudi borders. After ten years of building his network, Bin Laden knew he could count on them. They would safeguard the holy cities of Islam, and provide security for the people of the kingdom and tenure for its rulers. This was a win-win situation in Bin Laden's eyes, and he presented it to the Prince with passion and enthusiasm.

The Prince rejected it summarily. Worse still, he awarded the task of protecting the kingdom to the guests who arrived after Bin Laden – the Americans.

Bin Laden was incensed and humiliated by this rejection. To his mind, by such an agreement, the battle had already been lost. It was strictly forbidden within Islam for non-believers to set foot in, let alone be charged with the protection of, Islam's holiest sites. For him and his acolytes, over one-and-a-half millennia of history, since the realisation of Prophet Mohammed's first claim to the holy lands, had been wiped out. They were now under the control of the infidel. It was almost as if this had been their plan all along.

That moment became a turning point for Bin Laden and the wider movement. They had found their cause, and Bin Laden immediately began preparing for it. Sensing the risks he might pose, however, the Prince placed Bin Laden under a form of house arrest at his home in Jeddah. Bin Laden now believed himself to be in a similar position to that of the Prophet Mohammed during the period of Hijra in AD 622 when the authorities of Mecca continued to worship their multiple idols around the Ka'ba (now a holy Muslim site) and rejected Mohammed's teachings outright, leaving him shunned and outcast. Mohammed resolved to fight back, but first he had to flee Mecca.

Bin Laden spoke to his brother, who managed to persuade the interior minister, Ahmed Bin Abdelaziz, that he had to take a brief trip to Peshawar to resolve some outstanding financial matters. On receiving an assurance of his return, the minister released Bin Laden's passport.

The first thing he did on arrival in Peshawar, however, was to write to his brother to apologise for misleading him. He had no intention of returning, and within three months he had established a new base in Sudan's capital, Khartoum.

The regime in Sudan was far more welcoming. Their belief was that by fostering Bin Laden and associated groupings their country would become an alternative power base in the region. Bin Laden set up in a two-storey villa in an affluent suburb of Khartoum. There he met with men from afar all day, and five times a day they would walk to the local mosque en masse for prayers. An increasingly vibrant coterie of the old guard had, in fact, already been building in the area in anticipation of his arrival. Jamal Al-Fadl had been given $250,000 to purchase a farm north of Khartoum as the network became entrenched. Bin Laden had put one man in charge of all the preparation – his now-formal deputy, Ayman Al-Zawahiri.

Zawahiri's parents were both from prominent Egyptian families. His father was a professor of pharmacology, but despite his status, with five children he had to work hard to support his family – not even managing to afford a car. There was no lack of ambition in the family, however, and the young Ayman became known as a studious, introverted and intense character at school. 'Al-Zawahiri's background thus shows many of the elements seen in that of radical political Islamists in Afghanistan, Pakistan and elsewhere', Burke says; 'recent migration from the provinces to the capital, middle-class professional parents, a family full of aspiration and ambition that were unlikely to be fulfilled.'

He studied medicine at the University of Cairo and graduated in 1974 with one of the highest scores of his year. During his studies he had become increasingly drawn to extremist Islamist ideology, and on 23 October 1981 he was arrested for suspected involvement in these circles. Shortly after his incarceration he was visited by Montasser Al-Zayyat – an old friend – who wrote about the occasion in his book *The Road to Al Qaeda – The Story of Bin Laden's Right-Hand Man*:

> He looked very sorrowful. The scars left on his body from the indescribable torture he suffered caused him no more pain, but his heart still ached from it. The torture he suffered was not proportionate to his comparatively minor role … Despite all that he had suffered physically, what was really painful to Zawahiri was that under the pain of torture he was forced to testify against his fellow members in the case. It was a painful memory which was at the root of Zawahiri's suffering, and which prompted him to [eventually] leave Egypt for Saudi Arabia.

On leaving his home country, he worked in a hospital in Jeddah for a couple of years and then in 1987 he flew to Afghanistan. Unlike Khaled Sheikh Mohammed, who often acted outside the group on his own initiatives, Zawahiri remained close to Bin Laden from the outset. Ultimately he became – and still is today, at the time of writing – the man Bin Laden trusts above anyone else to manage the operation if he dies.

While in Sudan, Bin Laden and Zawahiri widened their network by building bridges with a variety of other extremist Islamic groups so that, over time, the various structures began to merge into a virtually seamless web. A degree of central coordination began to take place: men from Egypt were sent to Hizbollah training camps in the Lebanon, while other jihadis were sent via an office in Azerbaijan to fight in Chechnya. Others were said to have been sent to Tajikistan and Bosnia.

By late 1995 the Sudanese authorities began to get cold feet. Their relations with Saudi Arabia plummeted (the Saudis had stripped Bin Laden of his citizenship), Cairo was incensed that Sudan could harbour men known to be involved in plots to murder their own president – including Zawahiri – and the presence of a growing population of fighters from Hamas and Hizbollah badly damaged the country's reputation abroad. The United States declared it as a state sponsor of terror in 1993 and Western oil firms began to withdraw their investments.

Sudan began to make approaches to the Americans. Their price for rapprochement was information on Bin Laden and constant monitoring of the activities of those around him. Bin Laden was no longer welcome in Sudan, and soon he began to realise this. Even here, American influence was capable of reaching him. The impotence of

Islam in the face of this power was becoming painfully clear to him.

On 18 May 1996, Bin Laden, his three wives, three of his ten children and approximately 30 male followers landed, in two planes, at an airstrip in Jalalabad, Afghanistan. 'The sheikh' and his entourage were received on the tarmac by three local warlords who took them to a spacious villa that was once a royal lodge by the river. They were unable to stay there for more than a couple of months, however, as soon strangers started to arrive, showing pictures of Bin Laden and his children to the locals, asking their whereabouts. They decided to move up to the mountains in Tora Bora.

There, in their new base, the path ahead for the wider movement became increasingly clear to the once again growing group. The ideology had been evolving in Bin Laden's head gradually, and on 23 August 1996 he was ready to declare it to the world. In an 8,000-word message, entitled 'A declaration of war against the Americans occupying the land of the two holy places', he proclaimed: 'the greatest infidel military force of the world [the Soviets] was destroyed and the myth of the superpower withered in front of the mujahideen cries of "Allah u akbar."' For him this was a continuation of the crusades – centuries of struggle against the oppressors of Islam – a struggle that, being on the side of righteousness, they were bound to ultimately win.

Their strategy now must be, he believed, to turn to face the real enemy – the 'Crusader-Zionist' alliance that was the architect of all oppression. 'It is a duty on every tribe in the Arab peninsula to fight Jihad and cleanse the land from these occupiers.' He couched it in terms of a defensive struggle – fighting against an illegal invasion – in an attempt to maximise support from those scholars who saw jihad as acceptable only in defensive situations.

It should not be hidden from you that the people of Islam have suffered from aggression, iniquity and injustice imposed on them by the Zionist-Crusaders alliance and their collaborators ... [Muslim] blood was spilled in Palestine and Iraq. The horrifying pictures of the massacre of Qana, in Lebanon, are still fresh in our memory. Massacres in Tajikistan, Burma, Kashmir, Assam, the Philippines ... Ogaden, Somalia, Eritrea, Chechnya and Bosnia-Herzegovina ... send shivers in the body and shake the conscience.

He described the means of attack in his declaration of war as 'fast-moving, light forces that work under complete secrecy'. He called for a young vanguard to emerge to take forward the struggle by becoming martyrs who he promised would go 'to the highest levels of paradise'.

The target was also clear: the USA and her allies. In so doing, he united the various factions of the Islamic extremist movement, with their disparate parochial agendas, under one banner and pointed them all at the same target.

The situation cannot be rectified as the shadow cannot be straightened when its source, the rod, is not straight either, unless the root of the problem is tackled. Hence it is essential to hit the main enemy who divided the ummah into small and little countries and pushed it for the last few decades into a state of confusion.

In the months that followed, he deliberated on his message and the response to it and honed it further. In March 1997, he accepted an interview with Peter Bergen – a US journalist who had worked for CNN and ABC. They met at an undisclosed location in the mountains of the Afghan border. His attitude to the USA was more explicitly venomous:

> The hearts of Muslims are filled with hatred towards the United States of America and the American President. The President has a heart that knows no words. A heart that kills hundreds of children definitely knows no words. Our people in the Arabian Peninsula will send him messages with no words because he does not know any words. If there is a message that I may send through you then it is a message that I address to the mothers of the American troops who came here with their military uniforms, walking proudly up and down our land ... I say that this represents a blatant provocation to over a billion Muslims. To these mothers I say, if they are concerned for their sons, then let them object to the American government's policy.

A few months after this, he had drawn some finalised conclusions and, realising the usefulness of the media in conveying this message, he announced it in an elaborately staged press conference in which he sat flanked by his key lieutenants including Ayman Al-Zawahiri.

Any barriers of humanity or conscience were about to be removed: they were no longer going to distinguish between military and civilian targets.

> Any American who pays taxes to his government is our target because he is helping the American war machine against the Muslim nation ... [They have] compromised our honour and our dignity.

A new high council would now 'coordinate rousing the Muslim nation to carry out the jihad against the Jews and the Crusaders ... Terrorising oppressors and criminals and thieves and robbers is necessary for the safety of people and the protection of their property.'

The press in attendance were left wondering how serious or capable he was. When asked for specifics he promised news of major action soon, as he had to Peter Bergen months earlier. 'You'll see them and hear them in the media, God willing.'

From Qutb's early analysis of 'Jahaliyya' society, through Azzam's prescription for compulsory jihad, on the shoulders of impassioned jihadists like Khaled Sheikh Mohammed and Al-Zawahiri, Bin Laden had taken the ideology to its horrific conclusion. By pointing the finger at every American and their allies and providing justification for any action, no matter how bloody, Bin Laden had effected the final mutation of the extremist Islamic creed, pushing it firmly into the realm of wholesale, indiscriminate mass murder.

Using the mass media, he then sent this call out to the world. Most of those who heard it shrugged it off as the rantings of a madman, but for thousands around the world a flare had been launched. Their own disillusionment resonated with the sentiments coming out of Afghanistan, and like moths to a flame they gravitated towards it.

The camps were more full than ever, and plans for action began to hatch around them. First came the US embassy attacks in Kenya and Tanzania, and then on the USS *Cole*.

The next target had to be big.

5

No Smoke Without Fire

'Terrorism is the price of empire. If you do not wish to pay
the price, you must give up the empire.'
—Pat Buchanan

Extremist Islam was founded upon an anti-Western sentiment from the outset. The degree of this hostility, however,
has wildly inflated over time. The wider the ideology has
spread, throughout the Middle East and Asia, the more
anti-Western it has become. But why?

The sad reality of today's body politick in the West is that
most voters are entirely ignorant as to the possible causes
of this, despite the fact that glaring clues lie widely scattered
throughout the history of the last century and the beginning of the current one. Anti-Western feeling is in fact rife
across the whole of the Middle East and Asia, even among
moderate circles, and rather than incite it, extremist Islam
has been able to simply feed off it.

This widespread feeling is a direct result of the West's
consistent policy towards the region during this time, which
has been to maintain a firm grip on its governments in
order to ensure access to its oil and maintain its economic

superiority. The propping up of dictatorial, undemocratic regimes and the suppression of popular movements has been the hallmark of the West's foreign policy. In stark contrast to public statements promoting human rights, freedom and democracy around the world, the real agenda has been a very different one. Paul Wolfowitz, the recent American Undersecretary of Defence, articulated it frankly: 'In the Middle East and Southwest Asia our overall objective is to remain the predominant outside power in the region and preserve US and Western access to the region's oil.' This well-established policy framework has been carried implicitly by successive administrations, and an illuminating outline of the philosophy underpinning it was laid out by George Kennan, a respected diplomat in charge of long-term planning for the State Department, over 50 years ago:

> We [Americans] have 50 per cent of the world's wealth but only 6.3 per cent of the world's population. This disparity is particularly great between ourselves and the peoples of Asia ... Our real task in the coming period is to devise a pattern of relationships which will permit us to maintain this position of disparity ... To do so we will have to dispense with all sentimentality ... We should cease to talk about vague and, for the Far East, unreal objectives such as human rights, the raising of living standards and democratisation.

Examples of the West's execution of this policy, across a variety of nations, are numerous. However, in understanding the growth of Islamic extremism and the way in which this policy has influenced it, the recent history of four countries in particular is especially worth exploring: Palestine, Iran, Afghanistan and Iraq.

PALESTINE

Before the end of the First World War, Palestine was a part of the Ottoman Empire. In 1917, however, the British defeated the Turkish forces and occupied both Palestine and Syria. Britain had secured the territory by promising the local Arabs independence for a united Arab country covering most of the Arab Middle East, but, at the same time, they promised to create and foster a Jewish national home, which was subsequently laid out in the Balfour Declaration of 1917.

There was resistance to this among some, though not all, of the Arab community, and in a procession in Jerusalem in April 1920, several speakers denounced the Balfour Declaration. They included an imam by the name of Amin Al-Husayni. His words transformed the procession into a violent demonstration, and in the ensuing riots five Jews and four Arabs were killed. Al-Husayni was sentenced to ten years' imprisonment for his part in the riots but he avoided the sentence by fleeing to Damascus.

Then, within less than a year, the British High Commissioner, Herbert Samuel, in an amazing volte-face, decided to pardon Amin Al-Husayni and appoint him Grand Mufti (senior imam) of Jerusalem. This moment was a turning point in the course of the region's history and an indication of the likely thinking of the British administration at the time.

As documented in William Ziff's book, *The Rape of Palestine*, the British Foreign Office was divided into two opposing camps. One camp saw a strong Jewish presence in Palestine as being good for the British Empire, while another group of high-level officials believed that the Jews could become so powerful, if allowed to immigrate in this way, that control would ultimately begin to slip away from the British. Their primary aim was to 'divide and rule'. Ziff writes:

> With conscious design the Administration fostered hostility between Arab and Jew. It directly advised the amazed Arabs of Palestine and Egypt to abstain from any concessions to the Jews. It formed the Moslem-Christian Association and used it as a weapon against the Zionists. It instructed astonished Arab young-bloods to the technique and tenets of modern nationalism, in order to resist Jewish 'pretences'. And in London it contacted reliable anti-Jewish elements to form a liaison which has endured to this day. The Arabs were not only instigated and advised, but supplied with funds, and their arguments ghost-written by Englishmen in high places. They proved a good investment.

Their trump card came with the appointment of Amin Al-Husayni as Grand Mufti. 'Despite the opposition of the Moslem High Council who regarded him as a hoodlum, Al-Husayni was appointed by the British High Commissioner as Grand Mufti of Jerusalem for life.'

He was rewarded with sizeable funds and wielded considerable power. He controlled the Shariah court, the Islamic religious court in Palestine, and appointed all teachers and preachers in the region. Several times when the Mufti was pressed to publish accounts for his funds he refused, and those who asked would either be 'strongly advised' to be still or conspicuously disappear.

Prior to his rise to power, there were active Arab factions supporting cooperation in Palestine between Arabs and Jews. In early 1919 a Treaty of Friendship was signed to provide for 'the closest possible collaboration in the development of the Arab state and the coming Jewish Commonwealth of Palestine'. On 3 March 1919 another Arab leader, Feisal, wrote: 'We wish the Jews a most hearty welcome home.' Husayni, however, was installed to put a stop to this.

It seems, however, that they had gone too far with their choice. Husayni had an agenda of his own. His ambition was to become the leader of Palestine and the spiritual leader of the entire Muslim world. The greatest obstacle to his dream coming true, he believed, was the Jewish presence in Palestine and his policies and pronouncements stepped up to open advocacy of violence towards them.

On 23 August 1929 he falsely accused Jews of defiling and endangering local mosques, including Al-Aqsa. The call went out to the Arab masses: 'Itbakh al-Yahud!' – 'Slaughter the Jews!' For seven days Arab mobs terrorised communities, killing 133 Jews.

As the 1930s arrived, Husayni found an ideological home for his beliefs – one through which he could both shake off his masters and crush his opponents: Nazism.

In 1933, within weeks of Hitler's rise to power in Germany, Husayni sent a telegram to Berlin saying he looked forward to spreading their ideology in the Middle East, especially in Palestine, and offered his services.

On 21 July 1937, Husayni paid a visit to the new German Consul-General, Hans Döhle, in Palestine. He repeated his former support for Germany and 'wanted to know to what extent the Third Reich was prepared to support the Arab movement against the Jews'. He later sent an agent and personal representative to Berlin for discussions with Nazi leaders.

In 1938, Husayni's offer was accepted. From August 1938, Husayni received financial and military assistance and supplies from Nazi Germany and fascist Italy. From Berlin, Husayni would play a significant role in inter-Arab politics.

In 1941, Husayni travelled to Europe, where he met the German Foreign Minister, Joachim von Ribbentrop, and was officially received by Adolf Hitler on 28 November. He asked Hitler for a public declaration that 'recognised and sympathised with the Arab struggles for independence and liberation, and that it would support the elimination of a national Jewish homeland'. Hitler liked what he heard, and there began a close and mutually beneficial relationship between the two men.

In 1943, Husayni organised and recruited Bosnian Muslims into several divisions of the Waffen SS and other units. The largest was the 13th 'Handschar' Division of 21,065 men. When the Red Cross offered to mediate with Adolf Eichmann in a deal involving the freeing of German citizens in exchange for 5,000 Jewish children being sent from Poland to the Theresienstadt concentration camp, Husayni directly intervened with Himmler and the exchange was cancelled.

After Germany lost the war, senior active Nazis were hunted down and tried for war crimes. Husayni, however, got away, but the damage had already been done. Through his leadership and influence in the region, a virulent strain of anti-Semitism had been introduced and propagated widely. Through a misguided policy of 'divide and rule' the area's cultural and religious divisions had been highlighted, leaving it ripe for future inter-ethnic conflict.

On 29 November 1947 the UN General Assembly passed resolution 181 partitioning Palestine into a Jewish state and a neighbouring Arab state. The ingredients for perpetual conflict were now firmly in place, and its effects continue to this day.

IRAN

During the First World War, Persia (the state now known as Iran) was occupied by British and Russian forces. In 1919, Britain attempted to establish a protectorate there; however, in that year a military coup established Reza Khan, a Persian military officer, as dictator and hereditary Shah. During his rule, Reza Shah Pahlavi thwarted the British attempt at control, and pushed to have the country developed. However, during the Second World War, the British were back. They reoccupied the country and forced Reza to abdicate in favour of his son Mohammad Reza Shah Pahlavi. The younger Shah, they realised from the outset, was a man who would be far more sympathetic to their outlook and goals.

Britain's primary goal in Iran involved the Anglo-Iranian Oil Company, which was set up in the early part of the 20th century. It struck the largest oil-well that had ever been found in the world. And for the next half-century, it pumped out hundreds of millions of dollars'-worth of oil from Iran. This was a golden goose that Britain enjoyed to the full, passing on only 16 per cent of the profits to Iran itself. During this time, understandably, nationalist ideas began to spread apace throughout Iran. It was on this wave that a man named Mohammed Mossadegh was carried to power in 1951.

Mossadegh was a tall, European-educated aristocrat whose fiery rhetoric equalled his sharp, forensic intellect. In 1951, *Time* magazine named him Man of the Year. He embraced the great national cause of that period, which was the nationalisation of the Anglo-Iranian Oil Company, but this, of course, set him on a collision course with the West.

On the day he was elected Prime Minister, the Iranian parliament agreed unanimously to proceed with the nationalisation of the oil company. The British responded with disbelief. When it became clear that Mossadegh was serious, they decided to launch an invasion. They drew up plans for seizing the oil refinery and the oil fields but, on hearing the plan, US President Truman reacted furiously. He told the British that under no circumstances would he tolerate a British invasion of Iran. Britain then tried to secure a United Nations resolution demanding that Mossadegh return the oil company. Mossadegh, however, embraced the idea of a UN debate so enthusiastically that he decided to go to New York himself – and he was so impressive that the UN refused to adopt the British motion. Finally, the British decided that they would stage a coup and attempt to overthrow Mossadegh. Mossadegh, however, got wind of the plan and immediately moved to close down the British embassy and send all the British diplomats home, including, among them, all the secret agents who were planning to stage the coup. The British then bided their time until a new man entered the White House. As soon as Dwight Eisenhower was elected President, things began to change. The Truman policy was reversed and Allen W. Dulles, the CIA director, approved $1 million on 4 April 1952 to be used 'in any way that would bring about the fall of Mossadegh'.

Kermit Roosevelt, grandson of Teddy Roosevelt and Near East director for the CIA, then slipped clandestinely into Iran towards the end of July 1953. It took him three weeks to overthrow the government of Mossadegh.

The first thing he did was to bribe a whole swathe of members of parliament, religious leaders, newspaper editors and reporters to begin a very intense campaign against Mossadegh. This campaign saw a wave of denunciatory speeches against Mossadegh from the pulpits, on the streets, and in parliament. Then, Roosevelt bribed street gangs to begin causing chaos across the towns. Finally, he also bribed a number of military officers who would be willing to step in and seize control when the time came.

The growing anarchy climaxed on 19 August 1953, when Roosevelt brought all his mobs together, mobilised all of his military units, had them storm a number of government buildings and then, in a fierce gun-battle at Mossadegh's house, where over a hundred people were killed, forced Mossadegh into hiding. He was later arrested, and the Shah, who had fled in panic at the first sign of trouble a few days earlier, returned in triumph to Tehran.

The Shah immediately set about importing what he saw as Western values from his American and British friends, at the same time as exporting many millions of dollars of oil to them.

In return for US support, the Shah agreed, in 1954, to allow an international consortium of British, American, French and Dutch companies to run the Iranian oil facilities for the next 25 years, with profits shared equally. The international consortium agreed to a 50–50 split of profits with Iran, but would not allow Iran to audit their accounts to confirm that the consortium was reporting profits properly, nor would they allow Iran to have members on their board of directors.

Meanwhile, the Shah had been emboldened by the US-inspired coup and began transforming his government into a ruthless dictatorship as he borrowed titles and customs from the Persian Empire of antiquity.

He also developed a repressive intelligence agency, known as Savak, which helped keep his increasingly embittered political opponents in line. This secret police force was formed under the guidance of the CIA in 1957 and its personnel were trained by Mossad (Israel's secret service) to directly control all facets of political life in Iran. Its main task was to suppress opposition to the Shah's government and keep the people's political and social knowledge to a minimum. Savak quickly became notorious throughout Iran for its brutal methods. An interrogation office was established with a vast array of horrific torture tools and techniques. A censorship office was established to monitor journalists, literary figures and academics throughout the country. It took appropriate measures against those who fell out of the regime's favour.

Universities, trade unions and peasant organisations, among others, were all subjected to intense surveillance by Savak agents and their paid informants. The agency was also active abroad, especially in monitoring Iranian students who publicly opposed the Shah's government. Prohibited books were removed from bookstores and libraries. Interrogation, torture and long-term imprisonment were regularly meted out for reading or possessing any forbidden books. Savak operated its own prisons in Tehran, such as the Qezel-Qalaeh and Evin facilities, and many other suspected places throughout the country as well.

Meanwhile, business with the US was running smoothly. The US gave the Shah a $200 million grant to buy weapons from them. Despite his repressive measures, many in the country spoke out. Chief among them was Ayatollah Rouhollah Khomeini – a fundamentalist Shi'ite Muslim. He declared that the Shah had 'sold our independence'. The Shah sent him into exile in 1965, effectively turning his into a cause célèbre.

As opposition to the Shah's harsh dictatorship grew, support for Khomeini rose. People were looking for a way out, and from the distant shores of Paris, Khomeini seemed to be offering it.

The Shah's government grew increasingly corrupt, as oil revenues flowed to the upper strata of society, leaving exactly the sort of disenchanted underclass that often leads to revolution. At the same time the country began to destabilise and, in 1978, the Shah was stricken with lymphatic cancer.

Sick and faced with mounting unrest and resistance, the Shah finally lost control of the country on 16 January 1979 when 9 million citizens came out in protest onto the streets. Although the Shah was opposed by a broad coalition of forces, it was Khomeini's Shi'ite radicals who seized power, and the Shah fled into exile.

On his triumphant return, Khomeini wasted no time in implementing his religious ideology across government. He removed even the slightest hint of dissent from the corridors of power and soon, for the first time in history, an entire system of government had been captured by hardline Islamic clerics. Through massive clamp-downs on every aspect of life, Khomeini imposed a literal, fundamentalist and virulent form of Islam on his people.

It was the first of its kind the world had seen, but at the same time it became a vision of what could be – a shot in the arm for followers of radical Islam around the globe. By ruthless manipulation and repression, the West had brought about its own demise in the region, giving the Islamists their first scent of victory against what was becoming known as 'The Great Satan'. It would not be their last.

AFGHANISTAN

Afghanistan has historically acted as a kind of buffer state between the Russian/Soviet Empire and its neighbouring external empires, which in the 19th century was the British Empire. Its governments, therefore, changed frequently and in 1978, a coup against the then monarch, King Daud, brought in the government of the People's Democratic Party of Afghanistan (PDPA).

The PDPA, as a pro-communist socialist party, implemented a socialist agenda which included decrees abolishing usury, banning forced marriages, replacing religious and traditional laws with secular and Marxist ones, banning tribal courts, and instituting state recognition of women's rights to vote, and land reform. The PDPA invited the Soviet Union to assist in modernising its economic infrastructure, predominantly its exploration and mining of rare minerals and natural gas. The USSR also sent contractors to build roads, hospitals, schools and water wells; they also trained and equipped the Afghan army.

These reforms were resisted by traditionalist pockets of Islamic fundamentalism around more remote parts of the country. Over time, much to everyone's surprise, this disparate opposition somehow began to grow into a fighting force calling themselves the mujahideen or 'holy Muslim warriors'. Towards the end of the 1970s this force began agitating against the government regularly, and in 1979 the Afghan army became overwhelmed with the number of public disorder incidents. The Soviet Union sent in troops to crush the uprising, and subsequently a pro-Moscow government in Kabul. This was the starting point of the Soviet occupation of Afghanistan.

President Jimmy Carter immediately declared that the invasion was unacceptable and that it jeopardised vital US interests. What he failed to mention, however, was that the US had played a significant role in creating the situation in the first place. They had, in fact, been aiding the mujahideen for many months previously, with precisely the intention of provoking a Soviet response. Former CIA director Robert Gates later admitted in his memoirs that aid to the rebels began in June 1979. In a candid 1998 interview, Zbigniew Brzezinski, Carter's national security adviser, confirmed that US aid to the rebels began before the invasion:

According to the official version of history, CIA aid to the mujahideen began during 1980, that is to say, after the Soviet army invaded Afghanistan [in] December 1979. But the reality, secretly guarded until now, is completely otherwise: indeed, it was July 3, 1979, that President Carter signed the first directive for secret aid to the opponents of the pro-Soviet regime in Kabul. And that very day, I wrote a note to the President in which I explained to him that in my opinion this aid was going to induce a Soviet military intervention ... We didn't push the Russians to intervene, but we knowingly increased the probability that they would ...

That secret operation was an excellent idea. It had the effect of drawing the Russians into the Afghan trap ... The day that the Soviets officially crossed the border, I wrote to President Carter: We now have the opportunity of giving to the USSR its Vietnam War.

The Carter administration was well aware that in backing the mujahideen it was supporting forces with reactionary social goals, but this was outweighed by its own geopolitical interests. In August 1979, a classified State Department report bluntly asserted that 'the United States' larger interest ... would be served by the demise of the Taraki-Amin regime, despite whatever setbacks this might mean for future social and economic reforms in Afghanistan'.

After the Russian invasion in December, US support to the Afghan rebels increased dramatically. Three weeks after Soviet tanks rolled into Kabul, Carter's Secretary of Defence, Harold Brown, was in Beijing arranging for a weapons transfer from the Chinese to the CIA-backed Afghani troops mustered in Pakistan. The Chinese, who were generously compensated for the deal, agreed and even consented to send military advisers. Brown worked out a similar arrangement with Egypt to buy $15 million-worth of weapons. 'The US contacted me', the then Egyptian President Anwar Sadat recalled shortly before his assassination in 1981. 'They told me, "Please open your stores for us so that we can give the Afghans the armaments they need to fight." And I gave them the armaments. The transport of arms to the Afghans started from Cairo on US planes.'

The objective of the intervention, as spelled out by Brzezinski, was to trap the Soviets in a long and costly war designed to drain their resources, just as Vietnam had bled the United States. The high level of civilian casualties that this would certainly entail was considered but set aside. According to one senior official: 'The question here was whether it was morally acceptable that, in order to keep the Soviets off balance, which was the reason for the operation, it was permissible to use other lives for our geopolitical interests.' Carter's CIA director Stansfield Turner answered the question: 'I decided I could live with that.' According to Representative Charles Wilson, a Texas Democrat:

> There were 58,000 dead in Vietnam and we owe the Russians one … I have a slight obsession with it, because of Vietnam. I thought the Soviets ought to get a dose of it … I've been of the opinion that this money was better spent to hurt our adversaries than other money in the Defense Department budget.

To hurt the Russians, the US deliberately chose to give greatest support to the most extreme mujahideen groups. The wider plan, according to author Dilip Hiro, was 'to export a composite ideology of nationalism and Islam to the Muslim-majority Central Asian states and Soviet Republics with a view to destroying the Soviet order'.

With the support of Pakistan's military dictator, General Zia-ul-Haq, the US began recruiting and training both mujahideen fighters from the 3 million Afghan refugees in Pakistan and large numbers of mercenaries from other Islamic countries. Estimates of how much money the US government channelled to the Afghan rebels over the next decade vary, but most sources put the figure between $3 billion and $6 billion, or more. This was the largest covert action programme since the Second World War.

When Ronald Reagan became President, aid to the mujahideen, whom Reagan praised as 'freedom fighters', increased; and in March 1985 the administration issued National Security Decision Directive 166,29, a secret plan to escalate covert action in Afghanistan dramatically: they decided to send an array of US high technology and military expertise to the Afghan battlefield in an effort to hit and demoralise Soviet commanders and soldiers. According to reports from that time, the CIA supplied mujahideen rebels with extensive satellite reconnaissance data of Soviet targets, plans for military operations based on that satellite intelligence, intercepts of Soviet communications, delayed timing devices for C-4 plastic explosives, long-range sniper rifles, a targeting device for mortars that was linked to a US Navy satellite, and wire-guided anti-tank missiles, among other equipment. By 1987, the annual supply of arms had reached 65,000 tons.

As well as training and recruiting Afghan nationals to fight the Soviets, the CIA permitted its Pakistani Intelligence Service (ISI) allies to recruit Muslim extremists from around the world.

Between 1982 and 1992, some 35,000 Muslim radicals from 43 Islamic countries in the Middle East, North and East Africa, Central Asia and the Far East would pass their baptism under fire with the Afghan mujahideen. Most notable among them, of course, were Bin Laden and the entire Al Qaeda hierarchy.

Tens of thousands more foreign Muslim radicals came to study in the hundreds of new madrashas (religious schools) that Zia's military government began to fund in Pakistan and along the Afghan border. There they received theological indoctrination and military training. Thousands of young men – refugees and orphans from the war in

Afghanistan – began attending these madrashas. They were from a generation who had never seen their country at peace. They had no memories of their tribes, their elders, their neighbours or the complex ethnic mix of peoples that made up their villages and their homeland. They admired war because it was the only occupation they could possibly adapt to, and their simple belief in a messianic, puritan Islam which had been drummed into them by simple village mullahs was the only prop they could hold on to and which gave their lives some meaning. The graduates of these schools became known as the Taliban.

After nine years of war, the Russians withdrew from Afghanistan in early 1989. American policy-makers celebrated with champagne, while the country collapsed into virtual anarchy. As the mujahideen rampaged across the war-torn nation, the West abruptly lost interest.

By the mid-1990s, the Taliban had seized control of almost the entire country. Afghanistan was now an unadulterated extremist Islamic theocracy. The perfect haven for its mujahideen allies – Al Qaeda.

IRAQ

During the First World War, British forces seized Baghdad from Ottoman rule in 1917. After the war it became a League of Nations mandate under British control, with the name 'State of Iraq'.

Britain imposed a monarchy on Iraq and defined the country's territorial limits with little account for the aspirations of the different ethnic and religious groups in the area, in particular those of the Kurds to the north. As a result, a major revolt against its policies took place between 1920 and 1922. The British, however, saw it off, reimposing their authority using gas and air attacks on Iraqi civilians.

The monarchy, though managing to remain in power for several decades, over the years found itself increasingly isolated from the public; and successive uprisings could be quashed only by resorting to ever-greater political oppression.

Then, on 14 July 1958, a coup of army officers over-threw the monarchy. This, however, ushered in a further period of instability, and in a subsequent coup in 1963 the Ba'th Party came to power under the leadership of General Ahmad Hasan Al-Bakr. His right-hand man was Saddam Hussein, and after sixteen years of rule, during which Saddam had increasingly become the power behind the throne, Al-Bakr stood down for his obvious successor. Saddam Hussein then assumed the offices of both President and Chairman of the Revolutionary Command Council in 1979.

One of the first things he did was to consolidate his power by uniting the country behind a war with Iran. In this he was supported by the US. Among the people instru-mental in tilting US policy towards Baghdad was Donald Rumsfeld, the subsequent Secretary of Defence under George W. Bush, 2001–06. His December 1983 meeting with Hussein, as a special presidential envoy, paved the way for normalisation of US–Iraqi relations. When Rumsfeld met with Hussein on 20 December, he told the Iraqi leader that Washington was ready for a resumption of full diplo-matic relations. According to a State Department report of the conversation, Iraqi leaders later described themselves as 'extremely pleased' with the Rumsfeld visit, which had 'ele-vated US–Iraqi relations to a new level'.

Declassified documents show that Rumsfeld travelled to Baghdad at a time when Iraq was using chemical weapons on an 'almost daily' basis in defiance of international conventions.

At the time, the administrations of Ronald Reagan and George H.W. Bush authorised the sale to Iraq of numerous items that had both military and civilian applications, including poisonous chemicals and deadly biological viruses, such as anthrax and bubonic plague.

A 1994 investigation by the Senate Banking Committee turned up dozens of biological agents shipped to Iraq during the mid-1980s under licence from the Commerce Department, including various toxins subsequently identified by the Pentagon as a key component of the Iraqi biological warfare programme.

US support for Iraq was enshrined in National Security Decision Directive 114 of 26 November 1983, one of the few important Reagan-era foreign policy decisions that still remain classified. According to former US officials, the directive stated that the United States would do 'whatever was necessary and legal' to prevent Iraq from losing the war with Iran. At the same time, however, as revealed through the Iran–Contra affair, members of the administration were selling arms to Iran. The administration's real agenda was, in fact, to prevent either country winning the war and forming a monopoly through access to both territories' oil.

After eight years of war, claiming the lives of over 1 million people, a ceasefire was declared on 20 August 1988. Far from winding up the supply of US military intelligence to Iraq, after that it actually increased, according to a 1999 book by Richard Francona, *Ally to Adversary: an Eyewitness Account of Iraq's Fall from Grace*.

Documents show that the US policy of cultivating Hussein as a friendly Arab leader continued right up until he invaded Kuwait in August 1990. When the then US ambassador to Baghdad, April Glaspie, met with Hussein on 25 July 1990, a week before the Iraqi attack on Kuwait, she assured him that George H.W. Bush 'wanted better and deeper relations', according to an Iraqi transcript of the conversation. 'President Bush is an intelligent man', the ambassador told Hussein. 'He is not going to declare an economic war against Iraq.'

From that point on, however, Saddam Hussein went from being trusted friend and regional ally to enemy number one. There are plenty of theories as to the cause of Saddam's rapid fall from grace in the eyes of his former backers, resulting ultimately in the invasion of Iraq, his subsequent capture in July 2004 and his execution by hanging on 30 December 2006, but two things are certain. First, it had nothing to do with his use of chemical and biological weapons against his own people or others, given the lack of concern – indeed deliberate ignorance – displayed by the UK and the US at the time it actually happened. Moreover, some of the raw materials for such attacks were actually supplied by the West.

Secondly, it had nothing to do with any links his administration had with Al Qaeda and extremist Islam. It is a proven fact that there were none. Ba'thism and theocratic Islam were diametrically opposed to one another from the start – one is a nationalistic creed that shuns religion and the other is a religious creed that shuns nationalism. Furthermore, there is no record of any contact or even any form of mutual recognition between the two groupings. Weapons of mass destruction and any security threats the regime may have posed have, since the invasion, also proved non-existent. Given past form, it is the economic imperative and the desire for regional strategic dominance that is likely to have been the main driver. Iraq has the world's second-largest proven oil reserves. According to oil industry experts, new exploration will probably raise Iraq's reserves to over 200 billion barrels of high-grade crude, which is extraordinarily cheap to produce.

What started off, however, as a cooked-up· threat to international peace and security, through the very act of the war itself, has now become one.

Exactly two months after the invasion, on 20 May 2003, President Bush declared the end of 'major combat operations'. Less than two months after that, the US chief of military operations in Iraq was forced to acknowledge that they had begun to face a 'classic guerrilla-type campaign' on the ground. Given that the entire Iraqi army and all Iraqi security forces, at the behest of the Pentagon, had been disbanded and sent home with their weapons intact, such a campaign should hardly have come as a surprise, and to some of the American officers on the ground it did not. 'When we arrived in Iraq there was a 400,000 to 500,000-man army and they were disbanded … You don't have any skills except those as a soldier, and you don't have a job and you're being offered $500 to blow up a tank, and you've trained your whole life to do that. What would you do?' said Lt. Col. R. Brown of the 3rd Armoured Cavalry Regiment.

Within days of his defeat, Saddam met his key aides. The insurgency at that time consisted entirely of former Ba'thists, defiant and unwilling to accept defeat. As the war continued, however, this changed.

At the beginning of 2004, nine months after the invasion, the Ba'thists began to run out of money. *Time* magazine's Michael Ware, one of the few journalists who has had regular direct contact with the insurgents, reported: 'Around this time I really started to witness tangible changes within the insurgency, with the Ba'thists beginning to surrender power to the Islamists, particularly the imported foreign Islamists. Ba'thist cells I knew were out there doing shake downs and extortions and whatever else to fund their ops. That is one of the things that gave the Islamists room to step into the breach, throwing in a lot of money.' Soon foreign insurgents began pouring in, radicalised by what they had heard about the war. They came from varying backgrounds, and were often wealthy.

A photo-journalist, Ghaith Abdul Ahad, met a few. 'There's a guy who was connected to the Saudis. He has some people on the Iraqi side of the border who will come to the Syrian side of the border and take a bunch of people, like ten, fifteen, twenty ... take them to the villages on the Iraqi side and from there on to Ramadi, Fallujah or any other town. He only wanted to send Saudis as they would often make good suicide bombers, and each Saudi would arrive with $5,000–$6,000. I've talked to a teacher from Saudi Arabia, I've talked to a Yemeni theology student who had a wife and five kids ... the new generation of mujahideen, this is what Iraq is creating.'

The arrival of these men gave the insurgency a new lease of life and consequently caused three things to happen. First, a set of organisers and strong men emerged from within the group, throwing up a new tranche of Al Qaeda leaders, chief among them Abu Musab Al-Zarqawi. Secondly, the previous Ba'thist insurgents began themselves to convert to the cause of radical Islam, as noticed by Michael Ware. 'The former Ba'thists who I knew suddenly started doing something to me that the Taliban had always done when I was in Afghanistan. Suddenly they started badgering me, "why aren't you a Muslim? why don't you pray? do you believe that Mohammed is the Prophet?", just constantly at me like this and they had never done anything like that before. They actually referred to Osama Bin Laden for the first time ever in our experiences together.'

Finally, what Michael Ware also found was that the local population – even young children – who had previously never had an interest in any form of extremist Islam began to radicalise. He gave the example of a young boy who looked no more than nine or ten. 'I sat and spoke to this kid, he is from Fallujah and his family … was killed in an American strike. This kid is intimately familiar with impro-vised explosive devices, how they're crafted, how they're hidden and how they're triggered. It's in this way that Al Qaeda are one of the main beneficiaries of this war.'

Unlike the war in Afghanistan, which energised the pre-vious generation of Al Qaeda leaders, this war is being con-ducted in the full and constant glare of the 24-hour global news media. As coverage of the war dominates the headlines and bulletins month after month, with civilian deaths mount-ing in their tens of thousands, the anger of increasing num-bers of Muslim youths boils over, feeding the ideology of extremist Islam and converting frustration into a determi-nation to act around the world. A better propaganda gift for the recruiters of extremist Islam could not have been designed.

On 11 March 2004, a series of bombs exploded in Madrid's train station, killing 191 people and injuring over 1,500. It was the largest-ever terrorist attack on mainland Europe. Three days later, a video tape was found in a bin outside Madrid's main mosque. It threatened further attacks if troops were not withdrawn from Iraq.

On 7 July 2005, a further 54 people were killed by sui-cide bombers on London's public transport. Exactly two weeks later, on 21 July, another four bombings were attempted, but this time the attacks failed. Within days, four suspects were arrested. One of them, Hussain Osman, is said to have told his interrogators how he was recruited. 'More than praying we discussed, politics, the war in Iraq … we always had new films of the war in Iraq … more than anything else those in which you could see Iraqi women and children who had been killed by US and UK soldiers … There was a feeling of hatred and a conviction that it was necessary to give a signal – to do something.'

If there is a 'war on terror' being fought today, its outcome, far from defeating it, has been to fuel the spread of extremist Islam around the globe and bring it home to a new generation.

Richard Clarke, who served under both Presidents Clinton and Bush in the National Security Council as the US National Counterterrorism Czar from 2001–03, recalls a defining moment towards the end of his tenure at the White House:

President Bush asked us soon after September 11th for cards or charts of the 'senior Al-Qaeda managers' … He announced his intention to measure progress in the war on terrorism by crossing through the pictures of those caught or killed. I have a disturbing image of him sitting by a warm White House fireplace drawing a dozen red Xs on the faces of the former Al Qaeda board, and soon perhaps Osama Bin Laden … while the new clones of Al Qaeda are working the back alleys and dark warrens of Baghdad, Cairo, Jakarta, Karachi, Detroit and Newark, using the scenes from Iraq to stoke the hatred of America even further, recruiting thousands whose names we will never know, whose faces will never be on President Bush's little charts, not until it is again too late.

6

The Real War on Terror

'The guns and the bombs, the rockets and the warships,
are all symbols of human failure.'
—Lyndon Johnson

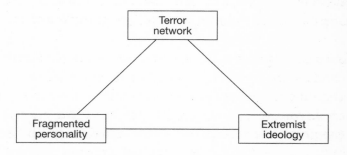

This triangle of causation is an overarching depiction of the driving forces behind Islamic terrorism. Though all three elements are important, each possesses different weights in different situations – usually one corner of the triangle is dominant over the other two in any one scenario. For example, when suicide bombing occurs in war-torn countries like Palestine, Iraq or Afghanistan, the local strength of extremist ideology is the most important driving factor behind the regularity of such actions. In situations such as these, where a country is invaded or attacked or its peoples persecuted, an environment hungry for radical solutions and broad-brush alternatives is created, leaving the field open for extremist Islam to flourish. A robust movement then develops into a broad-based consensus (the election of Hamas to government in the Palestinian Authority provides a recent example of this), making such actions closer to an accepted norm in that society. As a result, other factors such as personality fragmentation are less important – although some degree of each of the three factors will be present in essentially every case.

In the West, personality dissonance is a far more significant factor. Here, the feeling of 'don't-fit-in-ness' is more prominent among immigrant populations. It is well known that levels of suspicion and paranoia are higher among immigrant populations in the West generally, due to the act of immigration itself – as reflected by the higher rate of diagnosed schizophrenia in these communities, in stark contrast to the far lower rates in their countries of origin. From early childhood experiences right through to adult exposure to racism or rejection, the reservoir of unease deep within the psyche leads young Muslims to find comfort in extremist groupings which seem to verify their inner tensions: they are told that this is the way they are supposed to feel, because they are different and have a superior purpose.

There is always, in addition, a network in the background. Just because police and intelligence services do not discover them in every case does not mean that, at least on some level, they do not exist. The links of the 9/11 bombers to the wider Al Qaeda/Bin Laden network are well established, but those of the 7/7 bombers less so. However, both Mohammed Khan's and Shehzad Tanweer's suicide video recordings were joined to a statement by Bin Laden's number two, Ayman Al-Zawahiri, and apparently released by him. Indeed, in Tanweer's video, as if to prove their acquaintance, Al-Zawahiri talked of a young man who 'had a passion for boxing and, although he was from a well-off family, his clothes and appearance did not convey that'. Beyond this, and to a much wider extent, a shadowy, web-based network certainly exists. Although not as public as the formerly bustling camps of Afghanistan, a much more sophisticated network of cyber-propaganda and training sites flourishes in discreet pockets of the world wide web, with a regular following of jihadists watching fully edited MP3 downloads of the latest suicide bombing in Iraq or learning practical bomb-making skills from a Flash presentation. A virtual network has replaced the physical one, and this one is far easier to access and growing much faster.

The real war on terror, therefore, in order to be effective, needs to be fought on several levels – network, ideology and the individual personality.

THE TERROR NETWORK

The physical terror network is the single area that the current war on terror is actually attacking at the moment, with, however, evidently little success. There will always be a population of zealots who are beyond the pale and irreversible in their determination to commit acts of terror in the name of their doctrine. Proper intelligence-gathering about their whereabouts with robust law enforcement and, where called for, military response, will be necessary. However, this needs to be done sensitively, particularly where community policing is concerned. A thorough understanding of the terrorist belief system, mindset and modus operandi is crucial. Recent evidence suggests that this is often lacking, and sometimes badly so. Debacles such as the episode in Forest Gate, London in June 2006, in which the home of two young Muslim men was broken into, one of whom was shot, then arrested, only to be subsequently released with an apology and no charge, are dismal episodes of failure – and not just in terms of the objectives of the mission or resources. The amount of ill-feeling that is then engendered in the local Muslim community is incalculable. In the wake of the Forest Gate case, fear and suspicion of the police rose to such levels that it was hard to find a single member of the community who would agree to volunteer cooperation with the police regarding future actions. Furthermore, any youngsters in the area who may previously have been teetering on the brink of the shady world of extremist Islam would suddenly have felt a further push away from the mainstream, bringing them closer to the arms of the terrorists.

The relationship between the Muslim community and the police does not need to be such a poor one by definition. Local forces need to actively devote time to forging constructive relationships with Muslim community leaders, activists, youth workers and business people. This way, when any terrorist arrest is made or action taken, the police will have immediate links in the local community whom they can approach in order to explain their actions and provide reassurance and an understanding of the circumstances around their decision. It is not enough to release information to the media and assume that everyone will automatically understand. An active effort is required to bridge the local communication divide, and this can be done only via a lengthy process of advanced cultivation. If this is achieved, then local communities will be able to react with greater ease to decisions that are taken and, where necessary, step forward to cooperate. At the end of the day, no peace-loving Muslim (which the vast majority are) has any desire to see another terrorist attack carried out – quite the reverse. If they can be convinced that an action was necessary to prevent such an event, they will support it. The key is in the pre-existing relationship and the subsequent sharing of information. Some signs from recent arrests are emerging to suggest that the latter is being taken more seriously, but there is still a long way to go. It should be a priority for the government, in terms of resource allocation, particularly in the area of long-term relationship cultivation.

Attacking the terrorist infrastructure is as important abroad as it is at home. Destroying Al Qaeda's base in Afghanistan has been an essential front in the fight against the terrorist web, yet, unfortunately, due to the switch in emphasis and resources to Iraq less than eighteen months later, the Taliban have been gradually regaining control ever since.

The folly of Iraq has, therefore, been a misadventure on many levels: not only has it drained resources away from Afghanistan, it has sucked the US and Britain into a state that was formerly not even on the map of extremist Islam. The small Islamist contingent that did exist before the invasion was confined to a remote corner of the country by Saddam Hussein, with whom it was in perpetual conflict. Indeed, with their ideologies diametrically opposed, Saddam had always been the main bulwark against the forces of Islamic fundamentalism in the region. Since his removal, of course, and with the chaos of occupation, those forces are now rampant throughout the nation.

The true priority in foreign policy has, therefore, to be the accurate direction of resources against the real centres of the underlying terrorist web, as opposed to those unrelated and exaggerated threats, the attack on whom, if anything, assists the terrorists in their recruitment. Again, as with actions on the home front, the vast majority of peace-loving Muslims will happily provide support for an attack on a genuine threat. I personally – whether among family or friends or in the wider community work I engage in – find little difficulty in gaining support when I argue for the importance of waging war on terrorists who cruelly tarnish the name of our religion when they use it to justify their heinous acts. It is when a war is being conducted on such a prospectus, falsely, that support cannot be sustained – indeed the reverse, feelings of revulsion and resentment, rise up in its stead. There are, of course, some people who will never support any war on a Muslim land, but that is not the majority. Most people can tell the difference between a war that is necessary in the interests of national and global security and one that is not. The longer the Iraq war drags on, however, the more widespread disillusionment and cynicism with Western governments becomes, and the more people join the former category.

THE EXTREMIST IDEOLOGY: THEOCRATIC ISLAM

While the terrorist network provides the hardware, the strategic web and operational support system that is in the direct business of planning and executing acts of terror, the ideological movement provides its philosophical underpinning. Most people who follow it do nothing by way of actual terrorist planning, but it is from this bedrock of belief that the terrorist well springs. Though the network itself is small, the ideology that feeds it is far more widespread. Its belief, in a nutshell, is that to be a true Muslim means to actively fight for a global Islamic state and to ensure the destruction of kufr (non-Muslim) ways of life.

Followers of this brand of Islam see the world as divided between two opposing poles: Islam, and the unbeliever. Their firm view is that the Muslim world has always been and will always be under attack by the unbeliever. Acts of terrorism, though not necessarily engaged in, are nevertheless condoned or at least excused. This is, however, in sharp contrast to the majority of the world's billion Muslims who see their religion purely as a message of peace, interpret and practise it that way, and condemn in totality all forms of terrorism and violence.

The key policy agenda has therefore to be, first, the differentiation of the two forms of Islam in the eyes of policymakers and the wider non-Muslim community; and second, the active promotion of moderate Islam against its more virulent supremacist form. Such promotion has to be urgently prioritised in today's public policy agenda, and it needs to be conducted via a two-pronged strategy:

1. Politics and Representation

It is widely accepted, including among most politicians, that there is a fundamental disconnection between political leaders and certain pockets of the population, none more so than the Muslim youth population of today, throughout most of Europe and America. After 7/7, for example, the British government called to Downing Street the leaders of the Muslim Council of Britain and associated groups. Unfortunately, groups such as these, though certainly possessing some legitimacy among older first-generation British Muslims, have little or no ties to Britain's younger

second-generation Muslim population. Increased representation for this generation is therefore crucial at this time.

The cancer of extremist Islamic ideology thrives on the
disenfranchisement of young people and, in recruitment
drives, it peddles the notion that young Muslims have no
voice and no place in Western society. This notion needs to
be challenged head-on, and, more than anything else, it is
something that the political establishment can begin to rectify quickly. We need more young Muslim representatives at
every level of politics, with, in Britain, more MPs, ministers
and Cabinet ministers. Currently there are a couple of
second-generation Muslim MPs whose roles are becoming
increasingly important within the community, but in the
rest of Europe and in the US even this level of representation has not been achieved.

Representation outside formal politics is also crucial,
and this can be achieved through engagement with some of
the newer young Islamic groups forming around the world
today. Such groups have sprung up sporadically in the light
of recent terrorist atrocities, almost as a reaction to them, in
order to help define an identity that is expressly Muslim
but, at the same time, implacably opposed to terrorism and
extremism of any kind. A good example of this is the
Muslim Public Affairs Committee in the UK which, after
the protests around the blasphemous depiction of the
Prophet Mohammed in several European newspapers in
early 2006, came out assertively and unambiguously
against the extremist protestors who used the episode as an
excuse to walk the streets of London carrying placards promoting violence and jihad. Other groups include British
Muslims for Secular Democracy – a moderate, active
group whose members range from professionals to journalists and scholars – and Progressive British Muslims.

Groups such as this have a major role to play in winning the hearts and minds of young Muslims and keeping them on a peaceful path. However, without encouragement and the oxygen of publicity, their fight is a tough one. It is, therefore, these organisations – bodies that are taking a direct role in confronting extremism within Islam head-on – that need support from the government. The government has a huge platform on which to place such bodies, enabling their message to propagate, not to mention resources. This would be a far more profitable course of action than lecturing mosque-goers or making an issue out of wearing the veil, for example.

2. Culture

Of equal if not greater importance, in the battle for hearts and minds, is culture. Through the window of film, television, music, literature and fashion, a wider audience can be reached to promote the notion that there is no contradiction between being a Muslim and being British/American/Spanish or a citizen of any Western country. Indeed, at the time of writing, an exciting new synthesis culture is growing around the world, enabling young people to voice both aspects of their joint Muslim and Western identity with pride. Almost a century ago, black culture found a fusion with Western culture in a similar way, which ultimately did not denigrate but rather enhanced its identity. The new phenomenon has been based around a broader Asian culture with, however, more emphasis on Hindu and non-Muslim aspects. It is only recently that young Muslims have been finding their way into a cultural medium that has been growing in momentum and finding mass appeal. Supporting this new movement is in everyone's interest, and so it should be a cornerstone of public policy today. It needs to span across a variety of pursuits:

Film

Several films have been released in 2005–07 which have a plot that centres around Muslim culture. *Yasmin* portrays the life of a young Muslim woman in the north of England, the competing strains of existing within such a dichotomous environment, and in the end how they can be overcome. *Ae Fond Kiss* looks at the community from the perspective of a relationship between a Catholic woman and a young Muslim man. *Love and Hate* uses inter-faith relationships to explore similar ground, and *Brick Lane* looks at lifestyles of the wider Muslim community in the East End of London. Recently, a more exciting wave of cinema has started coming to the fore – this time made by young Muslims about their own communities: one of the most prominent examples of this is *Halal Harry*.

The evolution of this new wave of cinema should be supported through a variety of public bodies. For example, in the UK, the Film Council, the Arts Council and the British Film Institute can make it a priority to promote this genre. This way, the message of a moderate Islamic culture, fully assimilated with Western society, will disseminate and provide young Muslims with an identity and a cultural home. It will also counter the misinformation that leads to Islamophobia, which undoubtedly exists in some pockets of the Western world today.

Television

Programming for television also needs to reflect the growth of this new synthesis culture. Though certain ethnic minority programme interests are catered for in some parts of mainstream television, e.g. Bollywood films, very little second-generation programming is evident. As second-generation Asians are the biggest-spending demographic in the UK and most of Europe today, and Muslim youth is a sizeable proportion of that, one would expect to see more programming specifically designed to relate to the lifestyles and challenges of this particular audience. Though a few soap plotlines is a useful start, what is needed now is more widely-based drama, magazine and other youth programmes made by and for young Muslims. The purpose here, again, is to demonstrate the extent to which this culture is very much a part of the mainstream, rather than the fringe, thereby drawing young Muslims into society rather than making them feel shut out.

Music

Music is perhaps the most popular pursuit of all among second-generation Muslims today. Recording studios around the Western world are full of budding young singers and DJs trying to make their mark. The East End of London alone has numerous studios that are almost exclusively used by the young Bangladeshi population to record their own compositions. It is likely, therefore, that this aspect of the synthesis culture will break through in time on its own; but again, supporting the process through increasing investment into facilities and further improving accessibility would be a step in the right direction, enhancing credibility and removing glass ceilings.

Literature

In this area too, there has been a recent growth, with several best-selling Muslim authors – like Monica Ali – writing about and popularising their own culture. Books by young

Muslims, writing about their own experience of being a Muslim in the West, are both informative and cathartic. They open a window into a world alien to many, and are often written both with frankness and pride. There is no shortage of talent within the young second-generation community, and with a little backing a great deal can be achieved. Some of this creativity is evident in some of the newer magazines too, like *Revival*, a young Muslim youth magazine in the UK which asserts its Britishness as vocally as it asserts its Islamic roots.

Across the entire cultural gamut, therefore, we can see a slow drum-beat of young Muslims finding, describing and asserting their dual identity through creative endeavours. This culture is, however, still in its incubation stages and, as with any movement in its infancy, it will need support to survive and flourish – and the time for this is now.

The growth of this rich, mixed culture will be the most powerful antidote to the extremist ideology that lures young people towards the conveyor belt of terror. It is this inclusiveness that will combat the notions of disenfranchisement that fuel the extremists' propaganda.

If this cultural wave breaks into the mainstream long-term, the most powerful outcome will be a generation of role models, as it is through them that the fusion will perpetuate. When there is a galaxy of Western Muslim presenters, singers, songwriters, actors, directors, authors and also sports stars and other celebrities – with their own styles, mannerisms, fashion and image, while sitting broadly within part of a wider sub-culture – young people will have someone to look up to and also something to aspire to in mainstream society, which is an attractive goal in its own right, but, more importantly, one that is diametrically opposed to any notion of detachment from the host society.

The role of government here is a major one, therefore, and it differs from approaches tried in the past both in the UK and elsewhere. It does not involve forcing a national identity on people, as for example in France, where expressions of ethnicity such as wearing the hijab or head scarf in school are outlawed. Nor does it involve an unfettered multiculturalism in which there is no attempt to synthesise ethnic identities with the host culture. A new approach would see the government providing this fledgling Brit-Muslim sub-culture with a significant boost, one that moves it substantially closer to its counterparts in the black community. Some tentative steps have been made in this direction in recent months by the UK government, but to fully meet the challenge, a deeper, wider commitment is required on a much broader series of fronts.

THE FRAGMENTED PERSONALITY

The pole of causation that has had the least attention in public policy so far is that which lies the deepest – the underlying psyche. Extremist ideologies will always prey on the vulnerable, and unless they can be identified and diverted there will always be a well from which the Islamists can draw. The word 'vulnerable', however, should not be taken to mean those who appear in any way weak, needy or incapable. Superficially there is likely to be no outward sign of a personality in turmoil – in fact, the reverse is often true: the most vulnerable frequently appear to be the most confident, assertive and implacable. It is what is going on inside that needs to be addressed, but first it needs to be detected.

The priority, therefore, has to be in establishing a system whereby young adults who possess personality traits that make them vulnerable to extremist/escapist ideologies can be identified early and supported quickly and comprehensively. This, of course, will have to be essentially the charge of the Muslim community itself, but in doing this it will require support and effective tools from central government. A young Muslim group needs to be established with the remit of visiting and forming links with local mosques up and down the country, befriending and offering support to young men and women. The emphasis has to be on the provision of mentoring for young people, supporting them psychologically and assisting them essentially to find their feet, establish an identity and engage with a wider culture. This will involve career advice and leisure pursuits as well as counselling. Ideally, this work should be geared towards and targeted at those individuals who are most vulnerable to following extremist paths, which raises the question: How can this vulnerability be in any way accurately identified?

Over the years, various psychological rating scales have been developed that measure a wide spectrum of traits relating to personality and psychological disposition. They take the form of questionnaires or interviews that, after completion, are scored and statistically analysed to produce a result indicating the extent to which the interviewee possesses certain psychological characteristics. What would be very useful now, therefore, is a scale that measures vulnerability to extremist ideologies. Such a scale could be administered to target populations in order to divert them before finding their way onto the conveyor belt. At the outset, it is essential to recognise that we are not diagnosing an illness or treating a condition here, we are merely detecting certain tendencies in thinking styles. The test would be conducted within a wider supporting dynamic, where the approach was welcoming and the outcomes met only with encouragement. The dynamic would form part of the wider mentoring network of peers – voluntary and trained – set up to provide outreach support, guidance and a social and leisure outlet for young Muslims.

THE IDEOLOGICAL EXTREMISM VULNERABILITY SCALE

I have contemplated the need for such a scale for many years now. If a scale could be developed that could, in a sensitive atmosphere of mutual trust within local communities, be incorporated into a programme of long-term and comprehensive support, real strides would be made in the most important battleground against terror – the ideological one.

If such a device were properly – and, I repeat, sensitively – deployed, then it might be possible, when combined with other demographic and profiling data, to identify early on – perhaps in the mid to late teens – those with a tendency to perceive the world in such a way that, given the right influences and circumstances, it might lead them down the path of extremism. Those scoring highly who, at the same time, were deemed to have a high chance of encountering extremists by dint of their lifestyle, location, etc. might then be provided with a robust package of support across a variety of areas. It goes without saying that coercion, punishment or compulsion should play no part in such a package. Indeed, the programme provided for such individuals would need to be sufficiently attractive as to recruit people on a voluntary basis. In devising such a package, we should take a leaf out of the extremists' book. We should recall how, in wooing people to their cause prior to 7/7, Shehzad Tanweer and Mohammed Khan's 'Mullah Crew' provided support to their potential recruits across a variety of areas

– from detoxification from drugs to paintballing and white-water rafting trips.

When looking into the possibility of constructing such a scale, I began by searching the literature for any current scales that look at similar areas. One relevant scale for this purpose is Theodor Adorno's F Scale. This scale was based on Adorno's description of the 'authoritarian personality', which has relevance (as discussed previously) to the kind of personality that may be vulnerable to following the Islamic extremist path. Interestingly, soon after its introduction, the F Scale was found not to correlate with a purely authoritarian/right-wing personality very well at all. It was, in fact, found to score highly for those on the far left as well as the far right, suggesting that it is more of a scale for political extremism in a general sense. Beyond this, the F Scale was also found to have a more specific use: it is a good predictor of racist attitudes, and also tends to give some prediction of submission to authority – again, both significant attributes of the would-be Islamic extremist's mode of thinking. Recall the supremacist mentality of the very first extremists I encountered myself, assigning the derogatory label 'kuf' to all non-believers, and also the description of Amir (Mohammed Atta) by his professor as so in awe of some of his teachers that he was 'beeindruckt und beeindruckbar', impressed and impressionable. On its own, however, the F Scale would not be a sufficient measure of vulnerability to extremist Islamic thought. To be more accurate, we need to consider additional aspects of extremist thinking.

Another important scale in this area of personality is Rokeach's D (dogmatism) Scale. In his book *The Open and Closed Mind*, published in 1960, the psychologist Milton Rokeach developed the Dogmatism Scale, describing its purpose as to 'measure individual differences in openness or closedness of belief systems'. He also saw it as a measure of one's 'general intolerance'. All of which, of course, are key ingredients in the mindset of the religious extremist.

The scale that I have been working on, the IEV (Ideological Extremism Vulnerability) scale, is derived from both these scales, with further amendments to eliminate cultural bias and increase its sensitivity to the population it is designed to detect – namely, those who are vulnerable to following the path of Islamic extremism. It is, in its present form, in relatively early stages of development, and it needs to be extensively tested, put through a subsequent robust validation process, and, when used, combined with broader information on the subject's demographic, background, lifestyle, etc. Nevertheless, I put it forward as a template to demonstrate that such a test is possible; indeed, it is several steps along the road to being constructed.

The Scale

The scale takes less than ten minutes to complete and contains 35 questions, each of which must be answered along a scale of 1–6, signifying:

1 Strongly Disagree
2 Mostly Disagree
3 Somewhat Disagree
4 Somewhat Agree
5 Mostly Agree
6 Strongly Agree

1. Obedience and respect for authority are the most important virtues that children should learn.

2. A person who has bad manners, habits, and breeding can hardly expect to get along with decent people.

3. If people would talk less and work more, everybody would be better off.

4. The businessman and the manufacturer are much more important to society than the artist.

5. Science has its place, but there are many important things that can never be understood by the human mind.

6. What the world needs most, more than laws and political programmes, are courageous, tireless, devoted leaders in whom the people can put their faith.

7. What young people need most is strict discipline, rugged determination, and the will to work and fight for justice in the world.

8. An insult to our honour should always be punished.

9. Sex crimes, such as rape and attacks on children, deserve more than mere imprisonment; such criminals ought to be publicly whipped, or worse.

10. Most of our social problems would be solved if we could somehow get rid of immoral, crooked, and feeble-minded people.

11. Nowadays, more and more people are prying into matters that should remain personal and private.

12. People can be divided into two distinct classes: the weak and the strong.

13. Wars and social troubles may someday be ended by an earthquake or flood that will destroy the whole world.

14. No weakness or difficulty can hold us back if we have enough willpower.

15. It is best to use a dictatorship in hard times to keep order and prevent chaos.

16. Most people don't realise how much our lives are controlled by plots hatched in secret places.

17. Human nature being what it is, there will always be war and conflict.

18. Nowadays, when so many different kinds of people move around and mix together so much, a person has to protect himself especially carefully against catching an infection or disease from them.

19. The wild sex life of the old Greeks and Romans was tame compared to some of the goings-on in this country, even in places where people might least expect it.

20. The true God-fearing way of life is disappearing so fast that force may be necessary to preserve it.

21. If people in one's own group are always disagreeing among themselves, that is probably a rather healthy sign.

22. No one has a 'mission in life' that he must accomplish no matter what.

23. It is necessary to be on guard against certain ideas, depending on where they originate from.

24. Truth is so elusive that no one can say when he has it.

25. Man on his own is a helpless and miserable creature.

26. Unfortunately, a good many people with whom I have discussed important social and moral problems don't really understand what's going on.

27. Most people just don't know what's good for them.

28. To compromise with our political opponents is dangerous because it usually leads to the betrayal of our own side.

29. It is annoying to listen to a speaker or teacher who seems unable to make up his mind about what he really believes.

30. For most questions there is only one right answer once a person is able to get all the facts.

31. There is good in everyone.

32. There is something to be appreciated in all forms of art.

33. I usually try to keep a fairly open mind on most issues.

34. It is possible that there are many versions to the 'truth'.
35. People cannot be expected to stick to the same opinions month after month.

Interpretation

In terms of calculating a score: for questions 21, 22, 24 and 31 through to 35, the less the agreement, the higher the score. For all the rest, the higher the agreement, the higher the score.

There are two ways in which the final results from the test can then be interpreted. The first and most notable result will, of course, be based on the total score. In calculating this total we should be left with an idea of the extent of 'extremist-vulnerable' thinking – the higher the total score, the higher the vulnerability to extremism. The score gives us an idea of how judgemental they are, to what extent they are submissive to perceived authority figures, how concrete is their thinking, how superstitious they are, to what extent do they project their unconscious aggression and sexual impulses onto the outside world, etc. If, however, we want a break-down of these individual aspects of the thought process, then we can look at total scores for certain specifically designed clusters of questions. The way in which the clusters are designed and what they mean is listed below:

Questions: 1, 2, 3, 4
Conventionalism: A rigid adherence to conventional values.

Questions: 1, 5, 6
Authoritarian Submission: A submissive, uncritical attitude towards idealised moral authorities.

Questions: 2, 3, 7, 8, 9, 10
Authoritarian Aggression: A tendency to be on the lookout for, and to condemn, reject, and punish people who violate certain conventional values.

Questions: 3, 4, 11, 32
Anti-intraception: Opposition to the subjective, the imaginative and the tender-minded.

Questions: 5, 12, 13
Superstition and Stereotypy: A belief in the mystical nature of fate and a disposition to think in rigid categories.

Questions: 6, 7, 8, 12, 14, 15, 16, 20
Power and 'Toughness': A preoccupation with the dominance–submission, strong–weak, leader–follower dichotomy, plus identification with power figures and an exaggerated assertion of strength and toughness.

Questions: 17, 25, 26, 27, 31
Destructiveness and Cynicism: A generalised hostility and vilification of all things human.

Questions: 11, 13, 16, 18, 19
Projectivity: The disposition to believe that wild and dangerous things go on in the world. This represents the projection outwards of unconscious emotional impulses.

Questions: 9, 19
Sex: Exaggerated concern with sexual 'goings-on'.

Questions: 21–35
Generalised rigidity: Dogmatic thinking.

A crucial next step in the evolution of this test is to calibrate it – i.e., determine what score correlates with what level of 'extremist-vulnerable' thinking. Tests on groups of various backgrounds, including known extremists, will be needed to determine this; but, through this experience, and further adjustments, it should ultimately be possible to ascertain the degree of vulnerability of an adolescent to following the extremist path, based on an overall score and/or the scores of specific clusters, combined with, as mentioned earlier, wider knowledge of an individual's lifestyle, practices, associations etc.

We therefore have some light at the end of this tunnel, a possible path out of our current predicament. It is based first and foremost on a deeper understanding of the terrorist mind: how it grew from an originally unfulfilled sense of self, with flaws exacerbated by events of racism or rejection later in life. How an encounter with a virulent strand of the ideology of extremist Islam at the right time then has the power to blow these wounds wide apart, pushing the transforming convert down an almost inexorable path of increasingly violent notions of the world and the self. And how, eventually, the ideology manages to seep into every crevice of the mind, overwhelming it and finally compelling it to its murderous and bloody end.

Armed with this analysis, we must act to halt the process at every level. We need to provide support with parenting skills and we need to continue the fight against all forms of racism, particularly the more subtle forms which are, nevertheless, capable of devastating effect deep in the unconscious psyche. It must always be remembered that people of this mixed heritage will never feel British alone, nor can they identify solely with their parents' country of origin. This gap needs to be filled, for it is this vacuum upon which the extremists prey. We need to foster the growth of a unique Brit-Muslim culture, one with its own particular identity and flavours that pervade the world of cinema, music, fashion and literature.

At the forefront of this needs to be a properly organised and funded community outreach group. One which visits youth centres, schools, mosques and anywhere else where vulnerable young Muslims may be found. They need to be supported, psychologically and socially, with emphasis on those who may score highly on scales such as the IEV – a test that must be seen first and foremost as a needs assessment, one which opens the door to the provision of a higher-level input, guidance and encouragement.

Underpinning this, of course, will need to be a greater effort, on the part of the government, to encourage a wider rapprochement with the Muslim community. A concerted effort needs to be made to build bridges via the police, for its own sake as well as to assist in more accurate and consensual law enforcement. Crucially, actions abroad need also to be assessed for their genuine benefit in the fight against terrorism. The first duty of any government is to protect its citizens, and if there is any possibility that a foreign action has the capacity to bolster terrorist recruitment beyond any gain that can be achieved by it, then it cannot be justified. This was certainly the case with the Iraq war. It has been a shameful episode in the history of this country. Lessons must be learnt, and must be seen to be learnt, contrition must be expressed and safeguards need to be put in place to prevent such a calamity ever happening again.

At their birth, Mohammed Khan, Shehzad Tanweer, Mohammed Atta, Ziad Jarrah and the others were normal children, like any others, but by the time of their deaths the entirety of their humanity had drained away from them and they died as human bombs.

As I write, there are doubtless countless others out there travelling the same conveyor belt. Merely attacking the organising web or those who have already gone too far is not enough. It needs to be a battle of hearts and minds – and not just those within the Muslim community, but equally those without. It is about how we relate to each other at every level: the international and local as well as the personal and social.

This is the real war on terror. It requires far more global effort than any purely military undertaking. Whether it can be truly engaged remains to be seen; one can only hope that it can.

Bibliography

The Road to Al Qaeda – The Story of Bin Laden's Right-Hand Man, Montasser Al-Zayyat (Pluto, 2002)

Holy War Inc. – Inside The Secret World of Osama Bin Laden, Peter Bergen (Phoenix, 2001)

The Veiled Kingdom: A Unique Insight Into Saudi Society and the Bin Laden Family, Carmen Bin Laden (Virago Press, 2004)

Al Qaeda – The True Story of Radical Islam, Jason Burke (Penguin, 2003)

The Islamist, Ed Husain (Penguin, 2007)

Terror and Transformation: The Ambiguity of Religion in Psychoanalytic Perspective, James W. Jones (Brunner-Routledge, 2002)

Perfect Soldiers: The 9/11 Hijackers – Who They Were, Why They Did It, Terry McDermott (HarperCollins, 2005)

Suicide Bombers: Allah's New Martyrs, Farhad Khosrakhavar, translated by David Macey (Pluto, 2002)

From Secularism to Jihad: Sayyid Qutb and the Foundations of Radical Islamism, Adnan A. Musallam (Praeger, 2005)

A Fury For God: The Islamist Attack on America, Malise Ruthven (Granta, 2002)

Index

Available in October 2009 from Mills & Boon® Special Moments™

THE SINGLE DAD'S VIRGIN WIFE

"Maybe this would be a good time to tell you something," Tricia said, pulling away. "I'm a virgin."

Noah couldn't say anything. Think anything. He was shocked.

"I'm sorry," he finally said. "I don't know what to say." He ran his hand down her hair, but she pulled back, clearly hurt. "Tricia, this isn't the way to lose your virginity. On a couch in my office. We should have thought this through. I seem to lose control when I'm around you."

She looked at him. "I'm sorry, too, Noah. But you don't need to worry," she said, straightening her shoulders. "I won't let it happen again. It'll be back to business for both of us." She smiled in a way that said she was confident, but then faltered a bit.

"Back to business then. That would be best," he said finally. He hoped he had convinced her.

Convincing himself was another matter...

All the characters in this book have no existence outside the imagination of the author, and have no relation whatsoever to anyone bearing the same name or names. They are not even distantly inspired by any individual known or unknown to the author, and all the incidents are pure invention.

First published in Great Britain 2009
Harlequin Mills & Boon Limited,
Eton House, 18-24 Paradise Road, Richmond, Surrey TW9 1SR

The Man Behind the Cop © Janice Kay Johnson 2008
The Single Dad's Virgin Wife © Susan Bova Crosby 2008

ISBN: 978 0 263 87641 3

23-1009

Harlequin Mills & Boon policy is to use papers that are natural, renewable and recyclable products and made from wood grown in sustainable forests. The logging and manufacturing processes conform to the legal environmental regulations of the country of origin.

Printed and bound in Spain
by Litografia Rosés S.A., Barcelona

THE MAN BEHIND THE COP

BY
JANICE KAY JOHNSON

THE SINGLE DAD'S VIRGIN WIFE

BY
SUSAN CROSBY

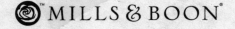

THE MAN BEHIND
THE COP
BY
JANICE KAY JOHNSON

THE SINGLE DAD'S
VIRGIN WIFE
BY
SUSAN CROSBY

MILLS & BOON

THE MAN BEHIND THE COP

BY

JANICE KAY JOHNSON

Janice Kay Johnson is the author of sixty books for adults and children. She has been a finalist for a Romance Writers of America RITA® Award four times for her Superromance novels. A former librarian, she's also worked at a juvenile court with kids involved in the foster care system. She lives north of Seattle, Washington, and is an active volunteer and board member of Purrfect Pals, a no-kill cat shelter.

CHAPTER ONE

"I'M GOING TO LEAVE HIM." Determination was stark on Lenora Escobar's face, but her hands, clenched on the arms of the chair, betrayed her anxiety.

Karin Jorgensen felt a thrill of pleasure, not so much at the statement but at how far this terrorized woman had come to be able to make it. Yet Karin's alarm bells also rang, because the days and weeks after leaving an abusive man were the most dangerous time for any woman.

The two sat facing each other in Karin's office, a comfortable, cluttered space designed to allow children to play and women to feel at home. For almost five years now, Karin had been in practice with a group of psychologists at a clinic called A Woman's Hand, which offered mental health services only to women and children.

She remembered having a vague intention to go into family counseling. By good fortune, an internship here at A Woman's Hand had presented itself while she was in grad school, and she'd never looked back. Women like Lenora were her reward.

Lately, she'd begun to worry that she went way beyond

feeling mere job satisfaction when her clients took charge of their lives. She'd begun to fear they *were* her life. Their triumphs were her triumphs, their defeats her defeats. Because face it—her life outside the clinic was...bland.

Annoyed by the self-analysis, she pulled herself back to the present. *Focus,* she ordered herself. Lenora needed her.

"Are you sure you're ready for this step?" she asked.

Lenora's thin face crumpled with a thousand doubts. "Don't you think I am?"

Karin smiled gently. "I didn't say that. I'm just asking whether *you're* confident you're ready."

Two years almost to the day had passed since Lenora Escobar had come for her first appointment. In her early thirties and raising two young children, she had virtually no self-esteem. Virtually no *self.* She had come, she'd said, because her husband was so unhappy with her. She needed to change.

She'd made only three or four appointments before she disappeared for six months. When she returned, her arm was in a sling and her face was discolored with fading bruises. Even then she made excuses for him. Of course it was wrong for him to hurt her, but... She should have known better than to say this, do that. To wear a dress he didn't like. To let the kids make so much noise when he was tired after work. Only recently had she declared, "I don't want to be afraid anymore. I don't think he'll change."

In Karin's opinion, Roberto Escobar was a class-three abuser, a man as incapable of empathizing with another human being as he was of real love or remorse. Rehabilitation for this kind of offender was impossible. His need to control his wife and children would only escalate; his violence would become more extreme. If she didn't leave him, the odds were very good that eventually he would kill Lenora or one of the children.

Not that leaving him brought her any certainty that she would be safe. He had told her from their wedding night on that he *would* kill her if she ever tried to leave him. Lenora had once confessed she was flattered when he'd first said that. "He was so passionate. He told me I was his whole world."

Now she said, "I know I have to go. I guess I'm scared. I'll have to find a job, even though I've never worked. He'll be so angry…" She shivered. "But I have put a plan in place, like you advised." She talked about the safe house where staff already expected her, about the possessions she'd been sneaking out over the course of several weeks in case she had to go suddenly.

"That took courage," Karin said with approval.

"I was so afraid he'd notice when I had something tucked under my shirt or my purse was bulging! But he never did."

"How did you feel about keeping that kind of secret from him?"

"The truth?" Her face relaxed. "I felt good. Like a kid with a secret from her sister. You know?"

Karin laughed. "I do. Powerful."

"Right! Powerful." Lenora seemed to savor the word.

When had she ever been able to think of herself as powerful? "I've been looking at him and counting off the days. Thursday is payday and he always gives me money for groceries. I've been stowing some away, but a couple hundred more would be nice. So I'm going to leave Friday."

Karin nodded. "Enough for a month's rent would be great."

"But I feel I should tell him I'm going, not just disappear. After fifteen years of marriage, I think it's the least I owe him. If I had somebody there with me…"

Karin straightened in her chair. "You know how dangerous confronting him could be."

Lenora bit her lip. "Yes."

"Why do you feel you 'owe' Roberto?"

Lenora floundered, claiming at first that *owe* probably wasn't the best choice of word.

"Since I've never worked, he has brought home all the money."

"You've talked about how you would have liked to work."

She nodded. "If I'd had a paycheck of my own…"

Karin finished for her. "You would have felt more independent."

Lenora gave a small, painful smile. "He didn't want me to be independent."

Karin waited.

"You don't think I should tell him face-to-face?"

Usually, Karin let clients work their way to their own conclusion, but in this instance she said, "No. I don't think Roberto will let you walk out the door. If you have someone with you, that person will be in danger, as well. And where will the children be? What if he grabs Anna and Enrico and threatens to hurt them?"

Just audibly, Lenora confessed, "I would do anything he asked me to do."

Karin waited again.

"Okay. We'll sneak away," Lenora said.

"I really believe that's smart."

The frail woman said, "He'll come after me."

"Then you have to make sure neither you nor the children are ever vulnerable."

"I wish we could join the witness protection program or something like that."

"Just disappear," Karin said. The ultimate fantasy for a woman in Lenora's position.

Lenora nodded.

"But then you'd never see your aunt and uncle or sister again," Karin pointed out.

"They could come, too."

"Along with your sister's children? And her husband? What about *his* family?"

Lenora's eyes filled with fears and longings. "I know that can't be. But I wish."

"You realize you'll have to stay away from your family and friends for now. He'll be watching them. But if you can stay safe long enough, he'll lose interest."

Lenora agreed but didn't look convinced. And as scared as she had to be right now, who could blame her?

When the hour was over and Karin was walking her

out, Karin asked, "Will you call me once you're at the safe house?"

"Of course I will." In the reception area, furnished like a living room, Lenora hugged her. "Thank you. You've helped me more than you can imagine."

Touched, Karin hugged her back. "Thank *you.*"

Lenora drew back, sniffing. "I can keep coming here, can't I?"

"As long as you're sure he's never known about A Woman's Hand. Remember, you can't do anything predictable," Karin reminded her.

"He's never heard about this place or about you." Lenora sounded sure.

"Great. Then I'll expect you next Tuesday. Oh, and don't forget that Monday evening we're having the first class in the women's self-defense course. It would be really good for you."

They'd talked about this, too—how the course wasn't geared so much to building hand-to-hand combat skills as it was to changing the participants' confidence in themselves and teaching preparedness.

Lenora nodded. "I mentioned it to the director at the safe house, and she said she'd drive me here. She told me I could leave Enrico and Anna there, that someone would watch them, but I think I'd rather bring them. You'll have babysitting here, right?"

"Absolutely." Karin smiled and impulsively hugged her again. "Good luck."

She stood at the door and watched this amazing woman, who had defied her husband's efforts to turn her into nothing, hurry to the bus stop so she could pick up her children and be home before he was, ready to playact for three more days.

Karin seldom prayed—her faith was more bruised than her most damaged client's. But this was one of those moments when she gave wing to a silent wish.

Let her escape safely. Please let her make it.

The blue-and-white metro bus pulled to a stop, and Lenora disappeared inside it. With a sigh, Karin turned from the glass door. She had five minutes to get a cup of coffee before her next appointment, this one a fifty-eight-year-old rape survivor who'd been left for dead in the basement of her apartment building when all she'd done was go down to move her laundry from the washer to the dryer.

In the hall, Karin slowed her step briefly when she heard a woman sobbing, the sound muffled by the closed door to another office. Maybe they should have called the clinic A Woman's Tears, they ran so freely here.

Sometimes she was amazed that of the five women psychologists and counselors in practice here, three were happily married to nice men. She was grateful for the reminder that kind, patient men did exist. They might even be commonplace and not extraordinary at all. In the stories—no, the *tragedies*—that filled her days, men were the monsters, rarely the heroes.

She shook her head, discomfited by her own cynicism. This path she now walked wasn't one she'd set out on because she'd been bruised from an awful childhood or an abusive father. True, her parents had divorced, and she thought that was why she'd aimed to go into family counseling, as if the child inside her still thought she could mend her own family. But her dad was a nice man, not one of the monsters.

She couldn't deny, though, that the years here had changed her, made her look at men and women differently. She dated less and less often, as if she'd lost some capacity to hope. Which was ironic, since she spent her days trying to instill hope in other women.

In the small staff lounge, she took her mug from the cupboard.

Shaking off the inexplicable moment of malaise, she thought again, *Please let Lenora make it. Let this ending be happy.*

"MAN, I WISH *I* could shoot from the free-throw line." Grumbling, the boy snagged the ball that had just dropped, neat as you please, through the hoop.

The net itself was torn, the asphalt playground surface cracked, but playing here felt like going back to the roots of the game to Bruce Walker, who waggled his fingers. "Still my turn."

Trevor bounced the basketball hard at him. "It's not fair."

They argued mildly. The game of horse was as fair as Bruce could make it, handicapping himself so that he shot from much farther out. He pointed out that he was six feet three inches tall and had been All-Southern California in high-school basketball.

"Whereas you," he said, "are twelve years old. You've

developed a dandy layup, and you're quick. One of these days, you'll start growing an inch a week. Kid you not."

"An inch a week!" Trevor thought that was hysterical.

Bruce guessed the idea held appeal for Trevor because it transformed him into a superhero. He was at that awkward age when most boys were physically turning into young adolescents, developing muscles, growing hair. In contrast, Trevor could have been ten years old. He wasn't much over five feet tall, and so skinny even his elbows were knobby. His voice wasn't yet cracking, or even deepening. He wanted to be a man, and didn't even look like an adolescent.

Yeah, tough age.

Bruce, a homicide detective with the Seattle Police Department, had volunteered to be a Big Brother and had been paired with Trevor DeShon a year ago. He'd made the decision to offer his time as a form of payback. A cop had befriended him as a kid, making a huge difference in his life. What went around came around, Bruce figured.

Trev's mother had struggled to keep them in an apartment after Trevor's father was arrested for domestic violence. Her jaw had been wired shut for weeks after that last beating.

His dad had never hit him, Trev said, but that was because his mom always signaled him to go hide when Dad walked in the door drunk and in a bad mood. He'd huddle in his room, listening to his parents scream at each other, and would later get bags of frozen peas or corn to put on his mom's latest shiner.

Bruce didn't want Trevor growing up to be just like his dad, or turning to drugs like his mom. Maybe Bruce, by being a role model, showing Trevor there was a different kind of life out there than what he saw at home and in his rough neighborhood, could change what would otherwise be an inevitable outcome.

What Bruce hadn't expected was to worry about the kid as much as he did.

After the game of horse, they practiced layups and worked on Trevor's defensive moves, after which Bruce let him pick where to go for dinner.

That always meant pizza. Their deal was they both had a salad first so they got their vegetables. Bruce pretended not to notice how much cheese the boy put on his.

They did their best talking while they ate. Tonight, Bruce asked casually, "You heard from your dad lately?"

Trev shrugged. "He called Saturday. Mom wasn't home."

Mom would have hung up on him, Bruce knew. Trevor hadn't seen his father in two years, although the guy had tried to maintain contact, Bruce had to give him that.

"You talked to him?"

"He asked about school 'n stuff. Like you do."

"You tell him about that A in social studies?"

Trevor nodded but also hunched his shoulders. He stabbed at his lettuce with the fork and exclaimed, "Mom and me don't need *him*. I don't know why he keeps calling."

"He's your dad."

Ironic words from him, since he hadn't spoken to his

own father in years and had no intention of ever doing so again. But Trevor didn't share Bruce's feelings toward his father. The boy tried to hide how glad he was that his dad hadn't given up, but it shone on his face sometimes.

"I wish you were," Trevor mumbled.

Bruce felt a jolt of alarm. He'd been careful never to pretend he was a substitute father. He didn't have it in him to be a father of any kind, even a pretend one.

"If you were my dad," Trevor continued, "I could tell everyone my dad has a badge and a gun and they better watch out if they disrespect me."

Thank God. The kid didn't want Bruce as a father; he wanted him for show-and-tell.

Diagnosing the true problem, Bruce asked, "You still having trouble with that guy at the bus stop?"

"Sometimes," the twelve-year-old admitted. "Mostly, I walk real slow so I don't get there until the bus is coming. 'Cuz if the driver sees anything, Jackson gets detention."

Bruce had tried to figure out what he could do to help, but he couldn't walk a middle schooler to the bus stop and threaten a thirteen-year-old kid. A couple of times, he had picked Trevor up at school, making sure to drive his unmarked vehicle, which even an unsophisticated middle schooler would still spot as a squad car. Mostly, his goal was to help Trevor gain the confidence to handle a little shit like Jackson by himself.

He glanced at his watch and said, "I've got to get you home. I'm teaching a self-defense class tonight."

Scrambling out of the booth, Trevor chopped the air. "Like karate and stuff? Wow! I bet you have a black belt."

Bruce appreciated the boy's faith, but he laughed. "No, in my neighborhood how we fought didn't have a fancy name. Anyway, this class is for women. I teach them how to walk down a street and not look like a victim. How to break a hold if someone grabs them." How to fight dirty if things got down to it, but he didn't tell Trevor that. He wasn't going to teach him how to put out an assailant's eye. Jackson might be a bully, but he didn't deserve to be blinded.

Bruce was volunteering his time to teach this class for the same reason he'd signed up to be a Big Brother: his own screwed-up family. If he could help one woman choose not to be a victim the way his own mother was, he didn't begrudge sparing any amount of time. He couldn't change who he was, and he'd long since given up on trying to rescue his mother. But he was bleeding heart enough to still think he could rescue other people.

Trevor lived in White Center, a neighborhood on the south end of Seattle known for high crime and drug use. Bruce had guessed from the beginning that MaryBeth DeShon, the boy's mother, was using. At twenty-eight, she was pathetically young to have a kid Trevor's age. She hadn't finished high school and lacked job skills. Since Bruce had known them, MaryBeth had worked as a waitress, but she was constantly changing jobs. Not by choice, Trevor had admitted. She didn't feel good sometimes, he said, and had to miss work. Bosses weren't understanding. Still, she'd managed to bring in something approaching a living wage, and had food stamps, as well.

Often Bruce didn't see her when he picked up and dropped off Trevor. The last time he had, two weeks ago, she'd looked so bad he'd been shocked. She'd always been thin, but now she was so skinny, pasty and jittery he'd immediately thought, *Crack*. He'd been worrying ever since.

"Your mom—how is she?" he asked now, a few blocks from Trevor's apartment building.

The boy's shoulders jerked. "She's gone a lot. You know?" Trev was trying hard not to sound worried, but his anxiety bled into his voice. His instincts were good. He might not know why he was losing his mother, but he was smart enough to be scared. "She says she's looking for work. Sometimes Mrs. Porter checks on me."

Sometimes? Bruce's hands tightened on the steering wheel. A kid Trevor's age shouldn't habitually be home alone at night, especially not in this neighborhood. But he was twelve, and leaving him without adult supervision wasn't a crime.

Bruce pulled into the apartment parking lot, and noticed that MaryBeth's slot was empty. "Doesn't look like she's home right now," he observed. Although it seemed possible to him that her piece-of-crap car had finally gone to the great wrecking yard in the sky.

Trevor shrugged and reached for the door handle. "I have a key."

"If you get scared, you call me, okay?"

"Yeah. Thanks. I'm okay, though."

Bruce reached out and ruffled Trevor's brown hair.

"You're a great kid. But you are a kid. So call me if you need me."

He was usually in a good mood after a day spent with Trevor, but this time his eyebrows drew together as he walked back to his car after leaving Trevor at the door and waiting to hear the lock click home.

I should have asked if the kitchen was decently stocked, he thought repentantly. MaryBeth sure as hell wasn't eating these days. If she was hardly ever home, would she remember to grocery-shop? Assuming she hadn't traded her food stamps for crack.

He'd call tomorrow, Bruce decided. Check to see if she'd reappeared, satisfy himself that Trev was okay. Frustrating as it was for him, a man used to taking charge, there wasn't much else he could do for the boy.

It bothered him how much he wished there was.

BRUCE HAD PREVIOUSLY driven by A Woman's Hand, the mental health clinic where he was to conduct the self-defense workshop that night. It was in a modern but plain brick building off Madison, the simple sign out front not indicative of the services offered within. He supposed that was because of the clientele, the majority of whom were victims of abuse. A woman cop in the sexual assault unit told him she referred every victim she encountered to A Woman's Hand.

"The counselors there are the best," she'd said simply.

When he arrived, it was already dark, but the building and parking lot were well lit. The small lot was full. Amid all the cars, he noticed the two plain vans, which he guessed were from battered women's shelters. He had to drive a couple of blocks before he found a spot on a residential street to park his car.

When he got back to the clinic, he found the front door locked. Smart. He knocked, and through the glass he saw a woman hurrying to open the door. He allowed himself a brief moment of appreciation. Tall and long-legged, she had a fluid walk that was both athletic and unmistakably feminine. Hair the rich gold of drying cornstalks was bundled up carelessly, escaping strands softening the businesslike effect.

Her expression was suspicious when she unlocked and pushed the door open a scant foot. He took a mental snapshot: great cheekbones, sensual mouth, bump on the bridge of her nose. Around thirty, he guessed. No wedding ring, a surreptitious glance determined.

"May I help you?" she asked.

"I'm Detective Bruce Walker," he said, unclipping his shield from his belt and holding it out for her to see. "I was invited to lead this self-defense workshop."

A tentative smile warmed her face, but she also peered past him in apparent puzzlement. "Welcome. But weren't you to have a partner?"

"Detective Beckstead will be joining us next week. She's the labor coach for her pregnant sister, whose water broke this afternoon."

He'd been hearing about the birthing classes from Molly Beckstead for the past two months. She was un-married, hadn't yet contemplated having a baby herself, and when she was a rookie had been scarred for life, she claimed, by having to assist a woman giving birth in the back seat of a taxicab. All spring, she'd provided weekly reports on the horrors of childbirth, half tongue-in-cheek, half serious, but he'd noticed she sounded more excited than terrified when she'd called to tell him she was meeting her sister at the hospital.

"Ah." The woman relaxed. "That's an excuse if I've ever heard one." She pushed the door farther open to allow him in. "I'm sorry to seem less than welcoming. Some of the women participating tonight are from battered women's shelters, and we always keep in mind the possibility that the men in their lives might be following them."

"I understand. And you are…?"

"Karin Jorgensen. I'm a counselor here at A Woman's Hand."

"You're the one who set this up. Good to meet you." He held out his hand, and they shook. He liked her grip, firm and confident, and the feel of her fine-boned hand in his. In fact, he let go of it reluctantly.

"This way," she said, leading him down the hall. "The women are all here. I hope our space is big enough for the purpose. It's the first time we've done anything like this, and if this venue doesn't work well tonight, we could plan to use a weight room or gym at a school the next time. We're just more comfortable with the security here."

He nodded. "I'm sure it will be fine. For the most part, we won't be doing many throws. With only the four sessions, we can't turn the women into martial artists.

We'll focus more on attitude and on how they can talk their way out of situations."

She stopped at a door, from behind which he heard voices. She lowered her own. "You are aware that most of these women have already been beaten or raped?"

He held her gaze, surprised that her eyes were brown, although her hair was blond. Was it blond from a bottle? His lightning-quick evaluation concluded no. She was the unusual natural blonde who had warm, chocolate-brown eyes.

"I'll be careful not to say anything to make the women feel they've failed in any way."

The smile he got was soft and beautiful. "Thank you." The next moment, she opened the door and gestured for him to precede her into the room.

Heads turned, and Bruce found himself being inspected. Not every woman appeared alarmed, but enough did that Bruce wondered if they'd expected only a woman cop. Ages ranged from late teens to mid fifties or older, their clothing style, from street kid to moneyed chic. But what these women had in common mattered more than their differences.

He was careful to move slowly, to keep his expression pleasant.

Karin Jorgensen introduced him, then stepped back and stood in a near-parade stance, as though to say *I'm watching you.*

Good. He had his eye on her, too.

Bruce smiled and looked from face to face. "My partner, Molly, asked me to apologize for her. Her sister is in labor, and Molly is her labor coach. She plans to be here next week. Tonight, you get just me."

He saw some tense shoulders and facial muscles relax, as if the mention of a woman giving birth and another there to hold her hand somehow reassured them. The support of other women was all that was helping some of his audience, he guessed.

"We'll work on a few self-defense drills toward the end of the session—I don't want you to get numb sitting and listening to me talk," he began. "But we'll focus more on physical self-defense in coming weeks. It'll be easier for me to demonstrate with my partner's help. She's just five feet five inches tall, but she can take me down." He paused to let them absorb that. He was six foot three and solidly built. If a woman ten inches shorter than him could protect herself against him, even be the aggressor, they were definitely interested.

"Most women I know have been raised to believe the men in their lives will protect them," he continued. "That's a man's role. A woman's is to let herself be protected. How can women be expected to defend themselves against men? You're smaller, lighter, finer boned, carry less muscle and are incapable of aggression." He looked around the circle of perhaps twenty women sitting in chairs pushed against the walls of what he guessed was a large conference room. When the silence had stretched long enough, Bruce noted, "That's the stereotype. Here's reality. Throughout nature, mother animals are invariably the fiercest of their kind. Like men, women want to survive. Nature creates all of us with that instinct. You, too, can fight if you have to."

The quiet was absolute. They were hanging on his every word. They wanted to believe him, with a hunger he understood only by context.

"Do you have disadvantages if you're attacked by a guy my size?" He ambled around the room, focusing on one woman at a time, doing his best to maintain an un-threatening posture. "Sure. What I'm here to tell you is that you have advantages, too. You're likely quicker than I am, for one thing. You've got a lower center of gravity. Women are famous for their intuition, for their ability to read mood and intentions. Chances are good you can outthink your attacker. And if you're prepared, you're going to shock him. He won't expect you to fight back. He'll have the surprise of his life."

Murmurs, surprise of their own, but also a gathering sense of possibility: *Maybe he's right. Maybe I can outwit and outfight a man.*

He told them stories of women who'd had an assailant whimpering on the ground by the time they were done.

"The greatest battle you have to fight from here on out," he went on, "is with your own attitude. What you have to do is liberate yourself from every defeatist voice you've ever heard.

"Many of you have already been assaulted." Heads bobbed, and renewed fear seemed to shiver from woman to woman, as if a whisper had made the rounds. "Then I don't have to tell you submission doesn't work." He waited for more nods, these resigned. "I'm here to tell you aggression might. At worst—" he spread his hands "—you'll be injured. But you know what? He was going to hurt you anyway."

Something was coming alive in their faces. They looked at one another, exchanged more nods.

He had them, from the frail Hispanic woman in the corner, to the overweight teenage girl with acne, to the iron-haired woman who could have been his mother had Mom ever had the courage to seek the means to defend herself.

And, he saw, he had pleased Karin Jorgensen, who at last abandoned her military stance by the door and took a seat, prepared to listen and learn, herself.

He didn't let her sit for long, asking her to help him demonstrate. As he showed how an attacker opened himself up the minute he reached out to fumble with clothing or lift a hand to strike, Bruce was pleased by tiny signs that Karin was as aware of him physically as he was of her. Nothing that would catch anyone else's attention—just a quiver of her hand, a touch of warmth in her cheeks, a shyness in her gaze—all were a contrast to the confident woman who'd opened the door to him, prepared to face him down if he'd been anyone but the cop she expected.

She smelled good, he noticed when he grabbed her, although the scent was subtle. Tangy, like lemon. Maybe just a shampoo. Lemon seemed right for her sun-streaked hair.

He wanted to keep her with him, but finally thanked

her and said, "Okay, everyone pair up." Unfortunately, the numbers were odd and she paired herself with an overweight teenager, which left him partnerless.

A fair amount of the next hour and a half was spent with him trying to prepare them to grab their first opportunity to fight back and run. They learned some simple techniques for breaking holds or knocking a weapon from an assailant's hand.

"Next week," he said, concluding, "we'll talk about how to use everyday objects as weapons and shields. Molly will be here to demonstrate more releases, more ways to drop me like a rock." He smiled. "See you then."

Several women came up afterward to talk to him. By the time Bruce looked around for Karin, she had disappeared. When he went out into the hall to find her, he realized that some of the women had brought children. A second room had evidently been dedicated to child care. He spotted her in there, holding a toddler and talking to one of the participants. Karin saw him at the same time, and handed the toddler to the mother, then walked over to him.

"I'll escort you out," she said. "I appreciate you doing this."

They started down the hall, her long-legged stride matching his. "I thought it went well," Bruce commented.

"It was amazing. I saw such…hope." She said the word oddly, with some puzzlement.

Had he surprised her? Given her job, maybe she didn't like men much and didn't think one was capable of inspiring a group of battered women.

Or maybe she'd just been groping for the right word.

He wanted to ask whether she was married or involved, but how could he without making things awkward? And, damn it, he was running out of time—the front door stood just ahead.

"I understand you volunteered for this workshop," Karin said. "That's very generous of you."

They'd reached the door. Opening it for her, he inquired, "Are you making any money for this evening's work?"

He'd surprised her again. She paused, close enough for him to catch another whiff of citrus scent. For a moment she searched his face, as if trying to understand him. "Well…no. But I do work with these women."

"I do, too," he said simply.

She bit her lip. "Oh."

"'Night, Karin," someone called, and she retreated from him, going outside to exchange good-nights with women on their way to their cars.

Maybe just as well, he tried to convince himself as he, too, exited the building. He'd ask around about her. They inhabited a small world, and someone would know whether she was off limits. If nothing else, he'd see her next week.

"Good night," he said, nodding. He'd finally snagged her attention.

"Thank you again," she replied.

Their eyes met and held for a moment that seemed to bring color to her cheeks. Wishful thinking, maybe. He turned away. Even with his back to Karin, he was aware of her speaking to others in the parking lot. The voices, he was glad to hear, were animated.

He kept going, enjoying the cool air and the way the scent of the lilacs was sharper after dark. He liked the night and the sense he had of being invisible. He could see people moving around inside their houses or the flicker of televisions through front windows, but by now not a single car passed him on the street.

He reached his car, now sandwiched between an SUV and a VW Beetle. Not much room to maneuver. He'd be inching out.

His key was in his hand, but he hadn't yet inserted it in the door, when he heard the first terrified scream.

CHAPTER TWO

IT HAPPENED SO FAST.

The parking lot had emptied quickly. Only a van from one of the battered women's shelters remained, the director half sitting on the bumper as she awaited her charge. Satisfied with how the evening had gone, Karin was walking back toward the front door of the clinic when, out of the corner of her eye, she caught movement under a streetlight. She turned to see a dark figure rush toward the lone woman halfway between the building and the van. Oh, God. It was Lenora Escobar. She'd just said good-night to Karin.

"Roberto!"

The distinctly uttered name struck terror in Karin.

His arm lifted. He held a weapon of some kind. Lenora screamed.

The weapon smashed down followed by an indescribably horrible sound. Like a pumpkin being dropped, squishing. Lenora gurgled, then crumpled.

The arm rose and fell a second time, and then Roberto Escobar ran.

During the whole event, Karin hadn't managed two steps forward.

As though time became real once more, Karin and Cecilia, the shelter director, converged on the fallen woman. Karin focused only on her, ignoring the squealing tires from the street.

Should I have run after him? Tried to make out a license-plate number?

But no. There could be no doubt that Lenora's assailant—not her murderer, please not her murderer—was her husband. His vehicle and license-plate number would be on record.

Thank God, Karin thought, dropping to her knees, that Lenora hadn't brought her children tonight. He would have taken them if she had.

Lenora's head lay in a pool of blood. A few feet away was a tire iron. Karin's stomach lurched. Fingerprints... Had Roberto worn gloves? No. He didn't care who knew that he'd killed his wife for the sin of leaving him.

"Cecilia, go back inside and call 911. Or do you have a cell phone?" She sounded almost calm. "Unless... wait." She heard pounding footsteps and swiveled on her heels. "Detective Walker," she said with profound relief—relief she felt not just because he was a cop and he was *here,* but because tonight this particular cop had managed to reassure and inspire a roomful of women who had every reason to be afraid of men.

He was running across the parking lot, holding a cell phone in his hand. Then he was crouching beside her. He spoke urgently into the phone, giving numbers she guessed were code for Battered Wife Down.

He touched Lenora's neck and looked up. "She's alive."

Karin sagged. "Can't we do anything?"

He shook his head. "We don't want to move her. The ambulance is on its way." His gaze, razor sharp, rested on Karin's face. "Did you see what happened?"

"Yes." To Karin's embarrassment, her voice squeaked. So much for calm. She cleared her throat. "It was her husband. She said the name Roberto. She just left him."

"She and her children are staying at the shelter," Cecilia added. "She didn't tell him she was leaving him. I don't know how he found her."

"He had to have followed her tonight." The detective was thinking aloud. "Where are the children? He didn't get them?"

Cecilia was a dumpy, endlessly comforting woman likely in her fifties. Detective Walker hadn't even finished his question before she shook her head. "Lenora's aunt picked them up and took them home for the night. She's to bring them back in the morning."

Karin's heart chilled at his expression. "You don't think…?" Oh, God. If he had the aunt's house staked out…

She'd warned Lenora. "Stay away from friends and family," she'd said.

Focused on Cecilia, Detective Walker asked, "Do you know the woman's name?"

"Yes…um, Lopez. Señora Lopez."

Aunt… Karin groped in her memory. Aunt… "Julia."

"Yes." Cecilia flashed her a grateful look. "Julia Lopez. I have her phone number back at the shelter."

"Call." He held out his cell phone. "We need to send a unit over there. She should know about her niece, anyway."

"Yes. Of course." Cecilia fumbled with the phone but finally dialed.

Karin didn't listen. She stared helplessly at Lenora, who had been so triumphant Friday afternoon because she'd successfully made her getaway. "He never guessed anything," she'd told Karin in amazement. "He gave me money Thursday after he deposited his check. He was even in a good mood."

Now, gazing at Lenora's slack face and blood-matted hair, Karin could only say, "He followed her aunt to the shelter tonight, didn't he?"

At the first wail of a siren, Karin's head came up. She prayed fervently, *Let it be the ambulance for Lenora.*

A second siren played a chorus. Two vehicles arrived in a rush. A Seattle PD car first, flying into the parking lot, then the ambulance, coming from the opposite direction.

The EMTs took over. As Karin stood and backed away to give them room to work, her legs trembled as though she'd run a marathon. And not just her legs. She was shaking all over, she realized. For all the stories she'd heard from brutalized women, she'd never witnessed a rape scene or murder or beating. The experience was quite different in real life.

Cecilia came to her and they hugged, then clung. Karin realized her face was wet with tears.

Bruce Walker was busy issuing orders to two uniformed officers. Their voices were low and urgent; beyond them, in the squad car, the radio crackled.

"We should wait inside," Karin said at last. She needed to sit. "He'll probably want to ask us both some more questions."

Cecilia drew a shuddering breath. "Yes. You're right."

Karin glanced back, to find that Detective Walker was watching them. He gave her a nod, which she interpreted as approval. His air of command was enormously comforting.

Thank God he'd still been within earshot. Imagine how much harder this would be had she been dealing with strangers now, instead.

The gurney vanished into the guts of the aid car, one of the EMTs with it. The other EMT slammed the back doors and raced to the driver's side of the vehicle. They were moving so fast, not wasting a motion. Then once again the siren wailed, and the ambulance roared down the street.

She couldn't stop herself from looking again at the blood slick, dark under the streetlight, and at the tire iron, flung like some obscene kind of cross on the pavement. Then the two women walked into the building, still holding hands.

HE CAME IN sooner than she expected, thank goodness.

Through the glass doors, both women were aware of the blinding white flashes as a photographer worked, a counterpoint to the blue-and-white lights from the squad car. *Why don't they turn them off?* Karin wondered, anger sparking. What *good* did they do?

Once inside, the detective walked straight to them and sank into a chair beside Karin. Turning his body so that he was facing them, he was so close to Karin his knee bumped hers and she could see the bristles on his jaw. Like most dark-haired men, he must need to shave twice a day to keep a smooth jaw. But then, this day had been longer than he could ever have anticipated.

Karin gave her head a shake. Did it matter how well groomed he was? No. Yet she couldn't seem to discipline her thoughts. She *wanted* to think about something, anything, but that awful smash-squish and the sight of Lenora collapsing. Karin had never seen anyone fall like that, with no attempt to regain footing or fling out arms to break the impact. As if Lenora had already been dead, and it didn't matter how she hit.

Detective Walker pulled a small notebook and pen from a pocket inside his leather jacket. With a few succinct questions, he extracted a bald description of events from Cecilia, then Karin.

"Thank the Lord the other women had gone," Cecilia said with a sigh.

"Amen," Karin breathed. Imagine if Olivia, recently raped and still emotionally fragile, had witnessed the brutal assault.

The shelter director asked, "Have you heard anything about the aunt?"

"Not yet."

Was he worried? Karin scrutinized his face. She couldn't be sure—she didn't know him—but thought she saw tiny signs of tension beside his eyes, in muscles bunched in his jaw, in the way he reached up and squeezed his neck, grimacing.

"This was a bad idea," Karin exclaimed. "To bring all these women here like…like sitting ducks! What was I thinking?"

He laid his hand over hers. "No, it was a good idea," he reassured her quietly, those intense eyes refusing to let her look away from him. "Once Roberto knew where his wife was, it was a done deal."

"It's true," Cecilia assured her. "Don't you remember? Just last year, Janine's boyfriend was waiting outside the shelter for her. He shot her, then himself, right there on the sidewalk. It was—" She stopped, sinking her teeth into her lip. "This could just as easily have happened at the shelter. Lenora had to go out eventually."

Karin deliberately relaxed her hands, and he removed his. What was she doing, thinking about herself now? Her guilt could wait. Right now the children mattered; Lenora mattered. Karin was wasting this man's time making him console her, when he should be doing something to catch Roberto.

"Do you know which hospital they took Lenora to?" she asked.

"Harborview. It's tops for trauma." His cell phone rang. "Excuse me."

He stood and walked away, but not outside. Although his back was to them, Karin heard his sharp expletive. Her hand groped Cecilia's.

Still talking, he faced them. His eyes sought out Karin's, and she saw anger in them. It chilled her, and she gripped the director's hand more tightly. He listened, talked and listened some more, never looking away from her.

Finally he ended the call and came back to them. Karin wasn't sure she'd even blinked. She couldn't tear her gaze from this man's.

He dropped into the chair as if exhausted. "He's already been there. The aunt's dead. A neighbor says the uncle works a night shift. We'll be tracking him down next. The kids are gone."

"Oh, no," Karin breathed, although his expression had told her what happened before he'd said a word. Cecilia exclaimed, too.

"I'm heading over there. I'm Homicide. This case—" his voice hardened "—I'm taking personally."

"The children…" Horror seized Karin by the throat. "Does that mean they were in the car? Did they *see* him attack their mother?"

Detective Walker's mouth twisted. "We don't know yet. He had a headstart. He could have gotten there, killed the aunt and snatched the kids after leaving here."

She heard the doubt in his voice. "But…?"

"The officers who found her haven't found a weapon. She was battered in the head. She could be lying on it, or it might be tossed under a bush in the front yard."

Something very close to a sob escaped Karin. "But he might have used the same tire iron."

"Possibly."

"I pray they didn't see," Cecilia whispered. "Enrico and Anna are the nicest, best-behaved children. Their faces shone for their mother."

"Have…have you heard anything?" Karin asked. "About Lenora?"

"Nothing." His hand lifted, as if he intended to touch her again, and then his fingers curled into a fist and he stood. Expression heavy with pity, he said, "There's no need for you to stay."

"I'm going to the hospital." Karin rose to her feet, too, galvanized now by purpose, however little hovering in a hospital waiting room really served. *She* couldn't save Lenora, but somebody should be there, and who else was there until family was located?

Cecilia nodded, rising, as well. "I have to go back to the shelter first and talk to the residents. I don't want them to hear about this from anyone else. I asked staff to wait. I'll join you as soon as I can, Karin."

"Thank you." Karin squeezed Cecilia's hand one more time, then released it. She turned to the detective. "You'll let us know?"

He nodded. "Do you have a cell phone?"

She told him her number and watched him write it down in his small, spiral notebook. And then he inclined his head, said, "Ladies," and left.

Neither woman moved for a minute, both watching through the glass as he crossed the parking lot, spoke to officers still out there, then disappeared into the darkness.

"He's…impressive," Cecilia said at last.

"Yes." Thank goodness Cecilia had no way of knowing how attracted she'd been to him from the moment she'd let him into the clinic. Embarrassed, she cleared her throat. "I hope…" She didn't finish the thought.

Didn't have to. Cecilia nodded and sighed. "What's to become of those poor children?"

"Lenora has a sister in this country. She has children, too. I'm not sure whether they're in the Seattle area." Once they talked to Lenora's uncle, he'd make calls.

Karin shut off lights and locked up. Activity in the parking lot had slowed and the tire iron had apparently been bagged and removed, but a uniformed officer asked that they exit carefully, pulling out so as not to drive over the crime scene. Somebody, Karin saw, was vacuuming around the bloodstain. Trace evidence could make or break a case, she knew, but how would they be able to sift out anything meaningful from the normal debris?

Following her gaze, Cecilia murmured, "What a terrible night," and got into her van.

Karin hit the locks once she was in her car, inserted the key and started the engine, then began to shake again. She was shocked at her reaction. She'd always tended to stay levelheaded in minor emergencies, whereas other people panicked. *Minor,* she thought wryly, *was the operative word.* Bruce Walker had been angry, but utterly controlled, while here she was, falling apart.

She sat in the car for easily two minutes, until her hands were steady when she lifted them. Finally, she was able to back out, and followed the police officer's gestures to reach the street.

At a red light, she checked to make sure her cell phone was on and the battery not exhausted. How long, she wondered, until she heard from Detective Bruce Walker? And why did it seem so important that he not delegate that call?

BRUCE HADN'T TOLD the women that what he most feared was finding Anna and Enrico Escobar dead at their father's hand, next to his body.

Bruce had gone straight to the Lopez home, but on the way he made the necessary calls to get a warrant to go into the Escobar house. If the son of a bitch had intended to take his whole family out, it seemed logical that he'd have gone home with the kids. He might have feared being stopped in the parking lot before he finished the job.

God, Bruce hated domestic abuse cases. Every single one struck too close to home for him.

The woman who now lay dead just inside the front door looked disquietingly like her niece—unfortunately, down to the depressed skull and blood-soaked black hair. Unlike her niece, she had tried to defend herself, though. Her forearm was clearly broken.

Gazing down at her, he thought, *So, Dad, what would you think of this? To keep order in his own house, does a man have the right to kill not just his wife, but her relatives, too?*

Not that his own mother was dead, although she seemed more ghostlike than real to Bruce.

He had barely time for a quick evaluation of the Lopez murder scene before the warrant for a search of the Escobar house came through. Wishing Molly were with him, he snagged a uniformed officer to accompany him to the Escobars'.

They turned off headlights and coasted to a stop at the curb in front of the small place, but the minute Bruce saw that it was dark he knew they'd find it empty. The front door, he discovered after one hard knock, wasn't even locked. No, Escobar hadn't worried about protecting his possessions.

Walking through, Bruce tried to decide whether the place had an air of abandonment because Lenora had moved out with the kids, or Roberto Escobar, too, had departed with no intention of returning.

Near the telephone in the kitchen, a fist-size hole was punched in the wall. Plaster dust littered the otherwise clean countertop. Had Lenora laid the note here, by the phone, telling her husband she'd left him? One of the kitchen chairs was also smashed, and lay in the corner behind the table. Roberto had read the note, thrown a temper tantrum and sworn he'd find his wife and punish her.

It was hard to tell in the small master bedroom whether he'd packed. Lenora hadn't taken all her clothes, and some of his hung in the closet, as well. But Bruce found no coats and, more tellingly, no shaving kit or toothbrush in the bathroom. The tiny bedroom the children had apparently shared looked as though a burglar had ransacked it. Maybe Escobar had been trying to find a few toys and clothes for his kids.

Bruce poked into the single, detached garage and down in the dank, unfinished basement just in case, before finally sealing the property with tape. He'd come back tomorrow, in better light, to see what else he could learn. Right now, he was glad to have found the place deserted. That gave him hope that Escobar intended to run with the children, not murder them out of spite.

But there was no guarantee they wouldn't find the bodies in his car, parked in some alley, or... It was the "or" that stopped Bruce. He hated knowing so little. He couldn't even speculate on where Escobar might go to hide or to commit suicide.

Because he couldn't resist the temptation, Bruce called to let Karin Jorgensen know they hadn't located Escobar and to find out whether she'd gotten any word on the wife's condition.

"She's out of surgery, but in a coma. They...don't sound hopeful."

He wasn't hopeful, either. He'd seen Lenora Escobar's head, and the blood, bone splinters and other tissue on the tire iron. He wondered whether they ought to be hoping she *didn't* survive. He, for one, wouldn't want to wake up at all if it meant living in a vegetative state or anything approaching one. He wasn't sure it would be much better if she woke up clear and present to be told that her aunt had been murdered and her children taken by the violent man Lenora had fled.

"Do me a favor and think back to anything Lenora ever told you that would suggest a place Escobar might go to ground. Does he have family in this country? In Mexico? Did she talk about friends? Hell, I don't suppose they have a summer cabin."

"No, I'm pretty sure they weren't in that economic stratum. Uh..." She sounded muzzy, not surprising given that it was—Bruce glanced at his watch—3:00 a.m. Likely her adrenaline hadn't yet allowed her to curl up in the waiting room and conk out.

"She didn't talk about friends," Karin continued. "I don't think he encouraged them, at least not for her. Maybe not for him, either. He was jealous, of course. He'd imagine any other man would be coveting her, I'm afraid. As for family—his mother used to live with them, but she decided to go back to Mexico last year." Silence suggested Karin was thinking. "Chiapas. That's what Lenora said. Roberto was mad that she went."

"Chiapas." He pinched the bridge of his nose. "So I suppose it's reasonable that he might run for Mexico."

"Maybe. But how would even a mother take the news that he'd killed his wife—*tried* to kill his wife," she corrected herself, a hitch in her voice, "and murdered his wife's aunt?"

"Depends on the mother. I've met some crazy ones."

"You mean, the ones who pay a hit man to knock off the judge or prosecutor?"

"Or a rival cheerleader," he noted dryly.

"Well…yes. But I had the impression Mama had thrown up her hands over Roberto. There was another son, if I remember right, still in Chiapas. But Roberto was the elder, so of course he thought she should stay here."

"What—to babysit and keep a stern eye on his wife?" Bruce loosed a tired sigh. "No sign he's bought airline, Amtrak or bus tickets, and we've got the state patrol here and in Oregon watching for his car. Sounds like it's a beater, though. I doubt he'd make it all the way to the border, never mind damn near to Guatemala. I think you're right about the economic stratum." He paused. "How'd she pay for the sessions with you?"

"Department of Social and Health Services program. When a woman or child needs us, we find funding."

"Ah." He softened his voice. "You should get some sleep, Ms. Jorgensen."

"Karin."

"Karin. The night's not done."

"No." Her breathing told him she hadn't hung up. "I just keep thinking…"

Understanding stabbed him. "You've never been assaulted?"

"No. And now I'm thinking how—how *glib* I must have sounded to women who have. Ugh."

God. Here he'd considered her as a colleague, in a sense, who'd seen it all. Of course she hadn't. She'd only *heard* it all.

"I've been told by people who know that you and your colleagues at A Woman's Hand are the best. I doubt you've been glib."

Even through the phone line, her exhalation sounded ragged. "Thank you for that. And for calling. Oh. Have you talked to Lenora's sister yet?"

"Sorry. I meant to say that first. They're in Walla Walla. Asparagus harvest. No phone—I had to send an officer around. But they're on their way. What is it—a three-, four-hour drive? They should be at the hospital by dawn."

"Thank goodness. When Lenora wakes up…"

An optimist. He'd guessed she would be. He was

well aware that he'd be wasting his breath to suggest she go home and go to bed. She felt responsible, justly or not, and wouldn't let herself off the hook. Lenora wouldn't know Karin was holding vigil, but Karin did, and would think less of herself if she didn't.

There wasn't much more he could do tonight. He'd sent officers out to canvass near neighbors to Julia and Mateo Lopez shortly after the body was found. None had heard a thing. Evidence techs had taken over the house and were still working. He wouldn't get results from the crime lab on exactly whose blood was on the tire iron until tomorrow at best. He knew damn well what the results would be, given that no weapon had been located in or near the Lopez home.

There was a limit to how much he could do before morning to find Escobar's rat hole, either. He'd put out the description of the vehicle and the license number, but not until tomorrow would he be able to access bank records or speak to co-workers and—if any existed—friends. Mateo was so distraught he'd had to be sedated. Bruce hadn't gotten much out of him, not once he'd been told about his wife.

Resisting the temptation to drive to Harborview and keep Karin Jorgensen company in the waiting room, Bruce went home. Tomorrow would be a long day. He'd done what he could tonight to set a manhunt in motion. Now he needed a few hours of downtime.

Funny thing, how he fell asleep picturing Karin Jorgensen. Not with her face distraught, but from earlier in the evening, when she'd still been able to smile.

CHAPTER THREE

BRUCE SLEPT for four hours and awoke Tuesday morning feeling like crap. He grunted at the sight of his face in the mirror and concentrated after that on the path of the electric razor, not on the overall picture. Coffee helped enough that he realized the ring of the telephone had awakened him. He checked voice mail, and found a message from Molly.

"Houston, we have a launch. Baby Elizabeth Molly—yes, named for me—was born at 5:25 this morning. While you were no doubt sleeping, ah, like a baby."

Ha! He grinned.

"Since *I* didn't have an indolent eight hours of beauty sleep," she continued, "I'm taking Fiona and baby home and crashing—Elizabeth Molly permitting—in Fiona's guest room." As an obvious afterthought, she added, "Hope the self-defense workshop went well." Beep.

Oh, if only you knew.

He skipped breakfast, figuring to get something out of the vending machine at the hospital.

Karin had gone home, he found, and was surprised at his disappointment. Instead, the waiting room was filled with Lenora Escobar's extended family. The sister and husband and their brood of five children, and one of the Lopez's four grown children with *his* wife. Lenora, he was told, was still unresponsive in ICU.

He asked to speak privately with Lenora's sister and her husband, and took them to a smaller room likely saved by hospital officials for the grave business of telling family a loved one hadn't made it. Tending to claustrophobia, Bruce left the door open.

Yolanda spoke English well, her husband less so. They switched to Spanish, in which Bruce had become fluent on the job. He'd started with Seattle PD on a beat in a predominantly Hispanic neighborhood, building on his high-school Spanish.

Both told him that they had always thought Roberto was scum. "Pah!" Alvaro Muñoz declared. "You could see the bruises, how frightened she was of him. But she lied to make us believe everything was fine. Only recently…" A lean, mustachioed man, he hesitated, glancing at his wife.

"She told me she was going to leave him. She said so on the phone. She lowered her voice, so I think maybe he was home. She said she'd call when she got to the safe house." She bit her lip in distress. "Did he hear when she told me?"

Bruce shook his head. "Your aunt Julia went to the shelter to pick the kids up. I suspect Roberto was following her."

Yolanda Muñoz was petite like her sister, but pleasantly rounded. Her husband's skin was leathery from the sun, but hers was a soft café au lait. She must stay at home with the children, whatever home might be, given what Bruce gathered was their migrant lifestyle. Grief made her voice tremulous, kept her eyes moist. "You'll find Anna and Enrico?" she demanded. "When Lenora wakes up, how can I tell her *he* has them?"

He offered his automatic response. "We're doing our best. What I'm hoping you can do is tell me everything you know about Roberto. We'll be talking to his co-workers, but what about friends? Hobbies?" Seeing perplexity on their faces, he realized the concept of hobbies was foreign to them, as hard as they worked and as careful as they likely were with every penny they earned. "Ah…did he go fishing? Work on cars?"

Both heads shook in unison. "He didn't like to leave Lenora alone," Yolanda explained. "Even when family was there, so was he. All women in the kitchen, and Roberto. As if he thought we'd talk about him."

Or as if he couldn't let his wife have anything that was hers alone, even the easy relationship with her family.

Bruce continued to ask questions, but they knew frustratingly little. Roberto Escobar worked. Yes, he was a hard worker, they agreed, the praise grudging but fairly given, and he did help keep their place nice. He talked about his mother coming to live with them again. He was angry when she went to live with his brother, instead. Lenora said he called the mother sometimes, but mostly he yelled, so they didn't know if he would take the children to her. Yolanda thought maybe his mother liked Lenora better than her own son. And who could blame her?

Yolanda and her husband rejoined their children and cousins, and Bruce drove to the lumberyard where Escobar had worked. There, he learned little. Co-workers thought Roberto Escobar was surly and humorless, but his supervisor insisted that he was a good worker, and reliable until he'd failed to show up yesterday morning.

"So what if he ignores the other guys here, eats the lunch his wife sends instead of going out with them?" The balding, stringy man shrugged. After a moment, he added, "Maybe you can't tell me why you're looking for him, but... Will he be back to work?"

"I doubt it."

"So I'd better be replacing him." He was resigned, regretting the loss of a good worker but not the man.

Bruce's only glimmer of hope came from the last interview, when the middle-aged cashier said suddenly, "He did used to be friends with that other Mexican who worked here. Guy didn't speak much English. Uh... Pedro or José or one of those common names." She leaned back in her chair and opened the office door a crack. "Pete," she called, "you remember that Mexican used to work here? The one with the fake papers?"

"Yeah, yeah. Garcia."

"Carlos," she said with satisfaction. "Carlos Garcia. That's it. They talked during breaks. 'Course, no one else could understand a word they were saying."

"And this Garcia was the only person you noticed Roberto spending any time with?"

"Yeah, he wasn't a real friendly type. After Pete fired Carlos—and he about had to, once he found out his green card was fake—Roberto went back to sitting by himself at breaks. Couple months ago, we all went in together to buy flowers when Toby's wife died, but not Roberto. He was the only person working here who didn't contribute." The memory rankled, Bruce could tell.

Bank records next. Turned out the Escobars hadn't had a debit card. Roberto, Bruce learned, had been paid Thursday and deposited his check in the bank on the way home, all but two hundred dollars. No checks had cleared subsequently. Monday morning, Roberto in person had gone into his local branch office and withdrawn the entire amount. He'd also taken a cash advance against his one-and-only credit card—which, Bruce noted, had not had his wife's name on it. The whole added up to about fifteen hundred dollars. Not a lot, but if he had someplace to go where, even temporarily, he didn't have to pay rent, he'd have enough to get by for weeks, if not months.

Yeah, but how to find that place?

Still, the fact that he planned to need money was reassuring.

Uncle Mateo was up to talking this morning, although he broke down and cried every few minutes, his daughter and a daughter-in-law both fussing over him. Bruce hid how uncomfortable the display of raw emotion made him.

Uncle Mateo gave Bruce the names of a few men he thought might have been friends of Roberto's.

Yes, he'd suspected Roberto had hit Lenora sometimes, and since she had no father to speak for her, he had talked to her husband. Shaking his head, he said, "He thought it was his right. As if he were God inside his own house." He shook his head at the blasphemy of it.

God. Yes, that was a nice analogy. *King* was what Bruce's father had called himself. *If a man can't be king in his own castle...* That was one of his favorite lines, just after he backhanded his wife for being lippy—a cardinal sin in the Walker home—or committing any of a number of other sins. Or pulled out the leather belt to use on one of his sons.

As if paralleling Bruce's thoughts, Uncle Mateo begged, "What made him so crazy?"

Bruce wished he had an answer. Was it crazy? he wondered. Or too many years of being unchallenged? What would his own father have done if his wife had taken Bruce, Dan and Roger when they were little boys and fled? If a man was king, didn't he have the power of life and death over his subjects?

Knock it off, he ordered himself. It seemed every time he dealt with a certain form of domestic violence, he leaped like a hamster onto a wheel of useless bewilderment. Why, why, why? the wheel squeaked as it spun and went nowhere.

Damn it, he'd put it all behind him, except at moments like this. He detested this inability to stop himself from going back and attempting to reason out his own family history. He couldn't change the past; why replay it?

Back to see Karin Jorgensen. Lenora Escobar knew more about her husband than anyone, and he guessed that, in turn, she'd confided more in her counselor than she had in anyone else.

He called A Woman's Hand and, after waiting on hold for a couple of minutes, was told Karin would be free in an hour and would expect him. Glancing at his watch, he realized the free time would undoubtedly be her lunch break. He'd offer to feed them both.

The moment the receptionist spotted him, she picked up a phone. Karin came down the hall before he could reach the counter.

He hadn't imagined the tug he'd felt last night, even though exhaustion transformed her face from pretty to… Studying her, he struggled to understand. The only word he could come up with was *beautiful*. Not conventional, fashion-magazine beautiful, but something different: the purity old age or illness could bare when it stripped the illusions away and revealed the strength of bones and the life force beneath.

Bruce was not idiot enough to think she'd be flattered if he told her she looked beautiful like an old lady. And that wasn't exactly what he meant, anyway. It was more like seeing a woman in the morning without makeup for the first time, and realizing the crap she put on her face was not only unnecessary, but it blurred the clean lines.

Not that Bruce had ever thought any such thing upon seeing a woman's first-thing-in-the-morning face, but it seemed possible.

As she neared, Karin searched his eyes anxiously. "Have you heard anything about Lenora? Or found the children?"

He held out a hand, although he felt a surprising urge to hold out his arms, instead. "Last I knew, she's still unconscious. And no, regrettably."

"Oh." She put her hand in his, and seemed not to notice that he didn't shake it, only clasped it. Or perhaps she did because her fingers curled to hold his, as if she was grateful for the contact.

"Why don't we go get lunch," he suggested.

"Oh, that's a good idea. I suppose you don't usually take the time to stop."

"Drive-through at a burger joint is usually the best I do."

She shuddered. "I'm a vegetarian. Um…let me get my purse."

He waited patiently, although he had every intention of paying for the meal.

Every block of the nearby stretch of Madison Street had a choice of trendy bistros and cafés tucked between boutiques, gourmet pet food shops and art galleries. The shopping area was an extension of an area of pricey homes and condos, many with peekaboo views of Lake Washington and the skyline of Bellevue on the other side. The street itself dead-ended at the lake, where city-paid lifeguards presided over the beach in summer.

Bruce let Karin choose a place, and they sat outside on a little brick patio between buildings. Today was cool enough that they were alone out there, which was fine by him.

She ordered a salad, Bruce a heartier sandwich and bowl of soup. Then they sat and looked at each other while the waitress walked away.

"Are you all right?" he asked quietly.

She tried to smile. "A nap would do wonders. But you must have gotten even less sleep."

"I'm used to it. But that's not really what I meant."

"I know." She began to pleat her cloth napkin, her head bent as she appeared to concentrate on an elaborate origami project that wasn't creating anything recognizable to his eyes. "When Roberto hit her with the tire iron, it made an awful sound. I keep hearing…" For a second her fingers clenched instead of folding, then they relaxed and smoothed the damage to the napkin.

Bruce watched, as fascinated by her hands as she was.

"Naturally, I didn't sleep very well." She stole a glance up, her eyes haunted. "I saw him coming. And now I measure distances in my head and think, if I'd run, could I somehow have reached them in time?"

"You might have gotten your skull crushed, too," he said brutally. "Julia Lopez did her best to defend herself. Her forearm was shattered before a second blow hit her head."

"Ohh." Her fingers froze, and she stared at him. "Oh."

The image of her flinging herself between the furious, betrayed husband and the wife he was determined to kill shook Bruce. He tried not to let her see how much.

"There's no way you could have reached her in time anyway. Even if it had been physically possible, you would have had to read his intentions first, and that would have taken critical seconds."

"I should have walked her to the van."

"I repeat—unless you're trained in martial arts, you couldn't have done anything but get hurt."

Her shoulders sagged and the napkin dropped to her lap. "Do you think… Is there any way…?"

"She'll survive?"

Karin bit her lip and nodded.

"Of course it's possible." Why not? People had huge malignant tumors vanish between one ultrasound and the next. They woke from comas after twenty years. Miracles happened. "From what I've read, the brain has amazing recuperative properties. Other parts step in when one section is damaged. Right now, I'm guessing the swelling is what's keeping her in the coma."

Those big brown eyes were fixed on his face as if she were drinking in every word. She nodded. "That's what the doctor said."

"It takes time." He glanced up. "Ah. Here's our food."

They both ate, initially in a silence filled with undercurrents. He studied her surreptitiously, and caught her scrutinizing him, as well. He knew why she interested him so much. The question of the day: Did she see him only as a cop, or had it occurred to her to be intrigued by the man?

He cleared his throat. "I hope you weren't alone last night. Uh…this morning."

"Alone? No, Cecilia did sit with me for a while, and then Lenora's sister came…" Comprehension dawned. "Oh. You mean at home."

Bruce nodded.

"I live alone. I mean, I'm not married, or…"

Was that a blush, or was he imagining things?

"I fell into bed without even brushing my teeth. I was past coherent conversation."

He understood that. "I, ah, live alone, too."

"Oh." Definitely color in her cheeks, and her normally direct look skittered from his.

Well. They'd settled that. It was a start. Although to what he wasn't sure. He kept his relationships with women superficial, and somehow he didn't picture Karin Jorgensen being content with cheap wine when she could have full-bodied.

Great analogy; he was cheap.

No, not cheap—just not a keeper.

Somehow that didn't sound any better.

"The clinic's receptionist said you had questions for me."

He swallowed the bite of food in his mouth. *Clear your head, idiot.* "I want to know every scrap you can remember about Roberto Escobar. I'm hitting dead ends everywhere else I turn. No one liked him. I have a handful of names of men who might have been friends of his, although most people I've interviewed doubt he actually had any friends. If he really doesn't, if he's on his own with two little kids, we'll find him. If he has help, that's going to be tougher."

She set down her fork. "What do you think he'll do if he is on his own?"

"Rent a cheap motel room. Two hundred bucks a week. That kind."

Karin nibbled on her lower lip. "That sounds…bleak."

"It is bleak. Especially since I doubt he's ever done child care for more than a few hours at a time." He hadn't thought to ask anyone. "Is Enrico still in diapers?"

She shook her head. "Lenora was really happy to get him potty trained just…I don't know, six weeks or so ago. Although that isn't very long. Under stress, kids tend to regress."

She wasn't exaggerating. Under enough stress, they regressed by years sometimes. He'd seen a twelve-year-old curling up tightly and sucking her thumb. Having your mother brutally bludgeoned right in front of you… Yeah, that would be cause to lose bladder control.

"He'd be mad," Bruce noted.

"Oh, he'd be mad at them no matter what. Enrico is two. You know what two-year-olds are like."

He didn't, except by reputation.

"And Anna is only four. Well, almost five. They need routine, they need naps, they'll want their favorite toys—" She stopped. "Did he take the time to collect any of their stuff from their aunt and uncle's?"

"After killing Aunt Julia, you mean?" he said dryly. "We assume they had a bag packed for the night, and if so, yes. It's not there. But the ragged, stuffed bunny Uncle Mateo says Anna is passionately attached to was left on the sofa, along with Enrico's blankie. Uncle Mateo predicts major tears."

"Stupid," she pronounced.

"He panicked. Wouldn't you, under the circumstances?"

"Yes, but he'll be sorry." Then she shook her head,

visibly going into psychologist mode. "No, *sorry* isn't in his vocabulary. Not if it means, *Gee, I screwed up.* Everything is someone else's fault. The more he gets frustrated with the children, the more enraged he'll be at Lenora. This is all *her* fault. What's frightening is that without her to deflect him, he'll start turning that rage on Anna and Enrico. That he would anyway is worrying. That's what finally precipitated her decision to leave him. She knew that sooner or later he'd lose his temper with them, not just with her."

The sandwich was settling heavily in Bruce's stomach. He was hearing a professional opinion, professionally delivered. "How soon will that happen?"

"Soon. It probably already has. If he'd attacked just Lenora, I'd think there was a chance that he'd have a period of being…chilled. Justifying it in his own mind, but shaken by what he'd done, too. The fact that he attacked two women, with—what, fifteen minutes, half an hour in between?—suggests that he's even more cold-blooded than I would have guessed. No, he'll have very little patience. His own children are just…possessions to him. Evidence of his virility. Not living, breathing, squalling, traumatized kids. He literally has no ability to empathize."

Bruce swore. He supposed he had hoped Escobar was a man made momentarily insane by what he perceived as his wife's betrayal.

Ah, here we go again. Hamster wheel squeaking. What was true insanity—what was cultural and what was in the blood, a legacy from father to son?

Give me a straightforward murder for profit any day.

In this case, at least, Karin was telling him that Roberto Escobar wasn't momentarily nuts. He was the real thing: a genuine sociopath. One who, unfortunately, was on the run with two preschoolers. Now, *that* was scary.

He mined Karin for every tidbit she could dredge from her memory about her client's husband. His favorite color was red; Lenora had once mentioned looking for a shirt for his birthday. Did it say that the guy loved the color of blood?

"He's five foot eight, not five-ten as it says on his driver's license. Lenora said he lied."

Bruce made a note.

"He snores. But he didn't like it when she slipped out of bed to sleep on the couch or got in bed with one of the kids. So usually she didn't, even if she couldn't sleep."

Snores, he wrote, for no good reason. Unless someone in a cheap motel complained to the manager about a guy who sawed wood on the other side of the wall?

He noted food likes and dislikes, Roberto's opinion about people he worked with, his anger at what in his view was his mother's betrayal.

"Guy wasn't doing well where the women in his family were concerned," Bruce commented.

"No, and Lenora admitted to being inspired by the way his mother just let his words wash over her—like rain running over a boulder, I think is what she said—and kept on with her plans to go home to Mexico. Possibly for the first time, she realized he could be defied."

"I wonder if that was a good part of why he was so angry. Afraid his wife would see a chink in his supremacy?"

"Um…" She pursed her lips and thought about it. "No, I doubt he reasoned it out that well. Or believed Lenora had it in her to defy him in turn. Mostly, he'd have been angry that his mother chose her other son. Although since he's continued to call her, he may be channeling that anger onto his brother, who somehow lured their mother from her duty to her older son."

"In other words, he has a massively egocentric view of the world."

"Oh, entirely," Karin assured him.

They quibbled over the bill, with Bruce winning. He couldn't help noticing how little she'd actually eaten. He suspected she'd picked up her fork from time to time more to be unobtrusive about not eating than out of actual hunger.

While they walked back to the clinic, he called the hospital for an update on Lenora. "No change," he told Karin, pocketing his cell phone.

"I'll sit with her this evening, if they'll let me."

"Don't wear yourself out."

There was a flash of humor in her eyes when she glanced sidelong at him. "And you're not doing the same?"

"It's my job."

"Uh-huh. Don't I remember you saying, 'I'm taking this personally'?"

"It did piss me off that this bastard assaulted his wife damn near under my nose," he admitted.

"Was he watching when you walked away?" she wondered aloud.

"And did he know I was a cop?" He shrugged. "Hard to say. It was certainly luck on his part that Lenora was one of the last out of the building."

"If she hadn't stopped to talk to me…"

"Damn it." He gripped her elbow, stopping on the sidewalk in front of the clinic. "Don't keep trying to blame yourself. Talking to you was important to her."

They were facing each other, standing very close, staring into each other's faces. Her thick, long lashes, dark tipped with gold, were the perfect frame for her warm brown eyes. Without conscious volition, his gaze lowered to her mouth, and to the tiny mole beside it. He couldn't remember ever wanting to kiss a woman as desperately as he did this one. His head might have even dipped, before he saw again how worn and vulnerable she looked right now.

"God," he muttered, let go of her elbow and stepped back.

Her eyes seemed dilated, before a jolt shuddered through her and she blinked. "Oh. Um…" She drew in a deep breath and regained some poise, although he was afraid she'd shatter if car brakes squealed a block away. "Thank you for lunch."

"You're welcome," he said, voice rough. *Will you have dinner with me? Come home with me afterward?*

"Will you call me?" she asked.

For an instant, his hopes soared. Yes, she wanted to have dinner with him; she wanted… And then he crashed and burned. Not what she was asking. Not what she wanted.

Hiding his chagrin, he nodded. "I'll keep you informed."

"Okay." She backed away. "Thank you. Um, goodbye."

"I mean it. Take care of yourself. She may need you later. She doesn't yet."

Just before turning away, Karin said, "I think maybe *I* need her. Or at least to feel needed."

Who was he to tell a psychologist what she really felt or ought to feel?

Resigned, he shrugged and repeated, "I'll call," then went to his car, watching until she disappeared into A Woman's Hand before getting in and starting the engine.

Back to the hunt, before the trail he followed grew cold.

CHAPTER FOUR

THE REST OF THE DAY was more of the same. Bruce mostly left the Lopez house to the crime scene people. His driving interest was in finding Roberto. Clues to where he'd disappeared with the children wouldn't be at the Lopez house.

Instead, Bruce returned to Escobar's own house and walked through it again, trying to soak in details. The entire while he was conscious of the need to be there, but also felt unpleasantly like an intruder. Lenora wasn't dead—not yet, at least. That made the house still a home in a sense, rather than a crime scene.

The place was spotless except for the messes Roberto had made over the weekend—unwashed dishes and the damage left by his fury. Did both Roberto and Lenora believe cleanliness was next to godliness? Or was Lenora such a scrupulous housekeeper because her husband insisted on it?

He'd have to ask Karin what she thought. Not that it probably mattered, except that a cop never knew what insight might later prove relevant.

No, use your own judgment. Karin isn't here. He couldn't be calling her incessantly.

Okay, then. The way soup cans were aligned in kitchen cupboards, shoes were in neat rows by pairs in the closets, unused possessions carefully boxed and labeled on shelves was not the mark of an unwilling housekeeper. Even the kids' bedroom, shared, had to have been clean and well organized before Roberto had ripped clothes from drawers and hangers in impatience.

Bruce found a box of romance novels tucked in the linen closet behind stacks of sheets and pillowcases, where Roberto would likely never have seen it. They were fairly recent ones, with a stamp inside the cover from a nearby used bookstore. So Lenora was still able to dream, and not necessarily about her husband. Did Karin know she read these, or was Lenora secretly embarrassed about this escape? Bruce felt a savage wish that she'd have the chance to dream again.

The fourth or fifth time he speculated on what Karin would think about this habit or that room, he growled. What was wrong with him? He didn't lose confidence in his judgment every time he worked with someone better educated than he was.

No, the problem was, he couldn't get her out of his head. And because she was along for the ride, so to speak, he had this bizarre desire to talk to her. Better yet, for her to talk back.

The realization disturbed him. He was single-minded in the hours and days after a murder. He forgot to eat, or to taste the food if he did remember. He did not— repeat, *did not*—keep thinking about a woman.

As if in defiance, he found himself picturing her.

She'd be nearing the end of her day, maybe in with her last client. He had no trouble seeing how she'd listen with grave interest, her attention wholly and flatteringly on the speaker. His inner eye lingered on the line of her throat, her golden-blond hair bundled heavy at her nape.

What is it with her neck, anyway? Okay, I'll think about her lips, instead. Or her eyes, the color of melted chocolate. No, her lips. Or…both.

"Crap!" Scowling, he stalked out of the house, less than happy to have thoughts of a woman riding him quite so hard. Yeah, it *had* been a while since he'd been in a relationship, so it wasn't surprising he was so hot for this one. But the *combination*—wanting her and wanting to discuss with her everything that passed through his mind—that made him uneasy.

His brooding was interrupted by a call letting him know that the blood on the tire iron did in fact come from two separate individuals, confirmed to be Lenora Escobar and Julia Lopez. Time of death on the aunt further corroborated that she'd died first. So the kids presumably were in the car at the time of their mother's assault. Appalled, Bruce hoped they'd been clutching each other in the back seat, not even watching when their daddy got out. Wouldn't they have screamed or called out if they'd seen their mother?

Maybe they had and no one heard them.

Whether they could see out the window depended on whether they'd been in their car seats and therefore sat tall enough. Bruce shook his head. He'd forgotten to check on where the kids' car seats were. He made a note now.

Neither woman who witnessed the crime had observed the car. Bruce would like to think that meant it wasn't in sight. From previous experience, however, he suspected that their gazes had been riveted on Lenora.

Damn it, he wanted confirmation that Escobar *had* been driving his own vehicle. Yeah, it was missing; yeah, both Cecilia and Karin had identified Lenora's assailant as Roberto from a family photo Mateo Lopez had supplied. But at this point, finding him depended on finding his car. If he'd switched—borrowed a different one, stolen one—God, owned a second one that hadn't yet been registered?—then escape became more possible.

To clear his head, Bruce called Molly, and learned that her new niece was enchanting, adorable and had lungs the size and power of an opera singer's.

"Murder sounds good," she said a little wistfully. "But I promised to stay until Thursday, when Mom is flying in. I *told* her Fiona was the size of a house and I thought the baby would come sooner than next week, but who listens to me?"

The question was clearly rhetorical, so Bruce didn't comment. Molly's mother had found a second career leading groups on tours and was currently in the Ozarks. Since it was a one-woman business, she couldn't abandon her group.

"This is an ugly one," Bruce said, instead. "The bastard was willing to kill two women out of pride. He couldn't let his wife leave him and take his children."

"Hmm. And he grabbed the kids first, you say? Did he

go intending to kill the aunt? Or was he just thinking he had the right to take his children and she'd stand aside?"

"Kill." Bruce didn't have much doubt. "I guess it's conceivable he went to the door first and they argued, but then you'd think the aunt would have locked up in the time it took him to go back to his car, pop the trunk and grab the tire iron. He didn't have to break in, and it's hard to imagine she'd have opened the door to him a second time. The family wasn't fond of Roberto."

"Son of a bitch," she muttered. "Maybe Fiona can find a friend who'd stay with her tomorrow."

"No. Enjoy your niece. Catch up on your sleep. I've pulled in plenty of help."

She snorted. "Catch up on my sleep. Yeah. Right. You should *hear* this kid."

"And someday you, too, will have one of your own," he told her, grinning. "Or two or three… Hey, five or six, you being Catholic and all."

She said something rude that left him laughing as he ended the call.

It was getting on to the dinner hour, perfect for catching people at home, so he tried the addresses for two of the names he'd been given as potential friends of Escobar's. No answer when Bruce knocked at the first, an apartment. At the second, he talked to Ramiro Payeda against the din of half a dozen children squabbling at the table while his wife tried to keep them focused on eating their dinner.

"*Amigos?*" Payeda said doubtfully. Well, he *knew* Escobar, sure. They had worked together previously.

He explained that they'd both moonlighted from their regular jobs with a weekend roofing crew. Roberto had gotten a raise at the lumberyard and quit the second job. Payeda hadn't seen him in at least a year.

Another dead end. Bruce thanked him for his time and left.

It was now eight in the evening. The blue of the sky was taking on deeper tones. Good. Time to recanvass the neighbors up and down the street from A Woman's Hand. Some had either not been home or hadn't answered their doors last night. A second round today had caught a few of those at home, but none who'd heard the squealing tires or noticed a speeding vehicle. This was the perfect time of night to get the last few.

Once again, cars were wedged in every available spot along the street. Street parking was at a premium. Many of these older homes had narrow driveways and single-car, detached garages. He left his own car in the clinic lot, pausing only momentarily where the blood-stain was still evident. He'd noticed when he picked up Karin for lunch how careful she'd been not to look that way as they'd walked out. It would be a long time before she could come to work and not think about what happened. Like the victims she counseled, she would never feel quite as safe again.

Bruce checked his list of who had been interviewed and who hadn't, and went to the first door. The porch light came on, and a gray-haired, paunchy guy opened the door.

Last night? No, he and his wife had had dinner at their daughter's and hadn't gotten home until about eleven. Missed the excitement, although they'd heard about it from neighbors. Sorry.

No answer still at the next place.

At the third on his list, two houses down from A Woman's Hand, a man in his thirties answered the doorbell. He wore a uniform, and raised his brow in surprise when Bruce held out his badge.

"Cop, huh? I work security for Reliant. I'm on the night shift. I was just finishing dinner."

"Sorry to interrupt it," Bruce said. He explained his errand.

The guy was nodding before he finished. "Yeah, this jerk parked right in front of my driveway last night. I went out to go to work, and I could tell I wouldn't be able to get out. I'd gone in to call for a tow truck, when I looked out the window and saw him come running. He jumped in, did a U-turn, bumped over the curb across the street and just missed a parked car—" he nodded that way "—and then was gone."

Bruce flipped open his notebook. "Can you describe the vehicle?"

He could and did. Aging Buick, medium blue, must get shit for mileage, some rust on the right side door, dented front fender.

Without having written down the license plate number, he couldn't have more accurately described Roberto Escobar's car.

He hadn't heard screams. He'd presumably been inside during and immediately after the assault. Also, he admitted with some embarrassment, he'd had his iPod on. Shortly after the car sped away, he'd gone out again and left for work.

Bruce confirmed the time of the incident and had him describe the man he'd seen to the best of his ability. *Bingo.* Bruce took down his name and thanked him. "You've been a big help."

So. At least they now knew they were looking for the right car. That was something. Not enough, but something.

Back in his own car, undecided about his next move, Bruce thumped his fist on the steering wheel. How in hell had someone like Escobar gone so successfully to ground? However cold-blooded he was, he had to have been rattled. And, damn it, he was towing two preschool-age kids along with him!

Short of driving by cheap motels himself, Bruce couldn't think of a single other thing he could do tonight. He hated hitting this moment in an investigation. Ideally, the bastard should be behind bars by now. Failing that accomplishment, Bruce wanted to keep working. He was still on hyperdrive. He detested this sense that every direction he turned he banged into a blank wall.

I could go by the hospital.

Uh-huh. And that served what purpose? He'd have gotten a call if Lenora Escobar had either died or stunned everyone by opening her eyes and asking where she was and what had happened.

It was nine o'clock. Chances were Karin had gone home by now, even if she had indeed spent part of the evening sitting with Lenora.

Still. He could find out, couldn't he? Talking to her might quell this restlessness.

He'd started the car and was driving before he had consciously made a decision.

Any excuse to see Karin Jorgensen again.

KARIN SAT in a dreamlike state, her hand on Lenora's. The beep and hum of monitors were oddly comforting, a mother's "Sh, it's all right" murmur translated to a technological age.

Karin knew better, of course. A steady heartbeat, air pushed in and out of lungs meant nothing if Lenora's brain never regained conscious function.

The swelling was subsiding, doctors said. She wasn't brain dead. There were reflexes.

Karin had to take their word on faith. The hand beneath hers was utterly still. Her monologue awakened no response.

Maybe because she wasn't saying what Lenora needed desperately to hear: *We've found the children. They're fine.* Instead, inspiration at a low ebb, she'd been talking about the weather and how she loved spring.

"I'm turning into a gardener," she said. "Did I ever tell you that? It's funny, because I used to roll my eyes when my mother went outside and spent hours and hours grubbing in the dirt. When I was about fifteen, I'd be embarrassed if I had friends over to our house and Mom would come in sweating and filthy and triumphant because the trillium had appeared. 'They're hard to establish, you know,' she'd say. She showed me the three trilliums that had popped up, and they were these funny little plants on a thin stalk with three leaves at the top. Not what you'd call a thriller." She laughed softly, although given the time and place, there was very little humor in the sound. "But me, I wasn't interested. Until I bought a condo, and every year I filled a few more pots with annuals. I knew I was in trouble when I took a class at a nursery so my flower baskets would be unusual instead of just cheerful, with the usual geraniums or pansies. And then I bought a house, and it was all downhill. It looked so *bare* under the trees in the backyard, and I thought, *Just a few woodland plants.* Then the lawn in front and the single flowering cherry tree weren't that interesting. So I dug out a bed along the fence. I have a white picket fence. Hmm. There must be something psychological in that, do you think?" She paused as if for answer, but didn't need one. Yes, indeedy, there was something psychological in the classic symbol of home: a white picket fence. "Anyway," she continued into the silence that lay beneath the sounds of the hospital, "now I'm digging out two more beds to each side of the front porch. I've gotten hooked on old roses, and I want room for more. The worst part? When I got excited this spring because my trillium had spread in back. I called Mom—she lives in Portland— and begged forgiveness for every time I sneered. Mom just laughed."

Maybe this wasn't the best topic, she thought, disconcerted. Because in the end, her story had been about family and home, and not plants or spring as she'd intended. But maybe it was okay, because she wasn't talking about children, which she did not have, and which to Lenora had been all important.

Karin would have left Roberto the first time he'd hit her. But then, she wasn't poor, uneducated and just delivered of her first baby. She had options Lenora had never had.

Options Karin had wanted so much to give her.

"Should I have encouraged you?" she whispered. "You knew him. I didn't. I just…guessed."

And had been frightened, she reminded herself. She'd had that much sense.

She remembered a wistful voice: *I wish we could join the witness protection program or something like that.*

What had she told Lenora in return? Oh, yes. *Just disappear.*

Was that what Lenora had done, faced with the unbearable? There was more than one way to disappear.

A throat cleared behind her. "Hey."

Startled, she turned.

Detective Bruce Walker stood a few feet from the bed, seeming to fill the cubicle with his broad shoulders and tough presence. His posture was relaxed, his gaze resting thoughtfully on her face.

She felt a flush creep over her cheeks. How long had he been standing there? "Um… Have you been eavesdropping on my inane chatter?"

"I heard something about trillium," he admitted. "And then you whispered."

"The whispering part I should have left out." She squeezed Lenora's hand, which could have belonged to a mannequin. "Lenora shouldn't be worrying, not now. She has to concentrate on getting better."

He nodded and stepped closer to the side of the bed, where he wrapped his hands around the metal railing and said, "Hi, Lenora. Bruce Walker. I'm the guy who taught the self-defense workshop. I'm…feeling pretty bad that I didn't say anything that would have helped you. But you're going to defeat Roberto by opening your eyes and by walking into court to testify against him. You're going to be one of the lucky women who sees your abuser sent to prison for a long time. So long you'll be able to quit worrying about him. Feel safe. Raise your kids. That's the ending we're waiting for, when your head quits hurting the way it does."

Karin stared at him. How did he do that—say the right thing so effortlessly? She'd been tiptoeing all around the assault, not wanting to upset the unconscious woman if she was making sense of any of the words spoken to her. But this cop had in essence told her, *Survive and you win.* What could be a more important message to send?

He lifted his gaze and studied Karin. "It's getting late. Have you been here all evening?"

"Oh, not that long." Almost, but what else was she supposed to do? Go home and watch sitcoms? "Yolanda spent most of the day here. I made her leave. Her husband and kids need her, too."

He nodded acknowledgment. "Why don't you say good-night," he suggested. "I'll buy you a cup of coffee on your way out. Or warm milk—" a smile crinkled his eyes "—depending on how quickly you want to hit the sack."

Her answering smile took more effort than she'd thought she had it in her to make. "Warm milk it is, then." She stood, her knees protesting, and bent to kiss Lenora's thin cheek just above the tube carrying oxygen. "He's right, Lenora. I'd better get some sleep so I can give my best to my clients in the morning. I'll come back tomorrow night. I hope by then you can interrupt me when my stories drag on too long."

She waited just a fraction of a second, unable to quell her human faith that someone who looked so alive must be listening. Then she gave what she knew to be an awkward little nod, picked up her purse and walked out.

She said good-night to the nurses, who smiled and assured her that her company had been important to the patient.

Only if she could hear me.

Once through the swinging doors that separated the hushed ICU from the rest of the hospital, Bruce said, "Trillium?"

She loved his voice. It had gravel in it, not so much as to make him sound like someone who'd had his throat damaged; no, just enough to make her toes curl. As if she was going to walk barefoot across him? Through him?

Beside him?

Now, why did that last thought make her shiver?

"The cafeteria should still be open," he said, taking her arm as if he'd done it a hundred times already and steering her to the left, rather than straight down the corridor. "I doubt a cup of coffee will do more than keep you awake long enough for you to make it safely home."

She suspected he was right. She just hoped sleep didn't elude her tonight, too. "You know your way around the hospital. I suppose the cafeteria here is your home away from home."

"One of 'em," he agreed.

They got coffee. Karin shook her head when he took a cinnamon roll and looked inquiringly at her. He insisted on paying, as he had at lunchtime.

The dining room was deserted except for a clearly weary couple who sat at a table near the window, eating but not conversing, their gazes turned inward. They were numb, she thought. Neither even glanced over when Bruce and Karin scraped chairs back from a table.

"Did you have dinner?" he asked with a frown.

"Dinner?" She had to think. "I went home and changed clothes." She indicated her chinos and sweater. "I stuck some vegetables and cream cheese in a pita. What about you?"

"Uh…" He couldn't answer because he was wolfing down the sticky bun.

"Honestly." She shook her head. "They had salads in that glass case."

"I didn't realize I was so hungry. If you don't mind waiting…?" He sounded sheepish.

She tried to assume a stern expression.

His mouth tilted up, and he went back into the cafeteria.

While he was gone, Karin sipped coffee, grateful

he'd stopped by. He was the one person she wanted most to see and talk to right now. Jerlyn, the mother figure at A Woman's Hand, had stopped her earlier and said quietly, "If you want to talk, day or night, you know where to find me." But Karin hadn't felt any impulse to spill her powerfully suppressed turmoil to Jerlyn, no matter how much she usually valued her input. This time, she would simply have to live with the guilt and second thoughts and, oh, memory of that terrible sound.

But she couldn't deny that she kept trying to spill her anguish to the man who wended his way back between tables with a tray that held a wrapped sub, a salad and, yes, another cinnamon roll. And each time he just nodded, unsurprised, making her realize he'd heard it all before, probably *felt* it all before. And that was why she felt so comfortable with him. His life was like hers in that he would have had no job were it not for other people's tragedies. Only, he saw those tragedies one step closer. The psychological aftereffects were her vocation, the physical his.

Sitting down, he unwrapped the sandwich. "So. Trillium?"

"It's a flower."

"I vaguely knew that. Why did it make your mother laugh?"

Then he'd arrived at the end of her monologue, not the beginning.

So Karin told the silly, but no doubt deeply revealing, story again, and enjoyed his smile at the end.

"You need a T-shirt. 'I'm my mother.'"

She made a face at him. "Are you your father?"

Something closed on his face. Bang! Sealed like a vault. "God, I hope not."

What had his father *done* to make him sound so appalled? Would it be an awful intrusion if she asked?

He swallowed and met her eyes, his face still expressionless, and she had her answer. *Yes.*

So she bit her lip. "I assume you didn't come tonight to tell me you'd found Roberto and the kids."

He grimaced. "No such luck. I do know now that he was still driving his own car when he attacked Lenora. And, uh, that he did use the tire iron on both Julia and Lenora."

She took that in. "Then the children almost had to be in the car."

"Yes, but now I know where he parked it while he assaulted his wife. Anna and Enrico couldn't have seen what happened."

"Oh." Her voice failed, and she whispered, "Thank God."

He was watching her. Seeming satisfied, he said, "Otherwise, I'm stymied. Where the hell is he?"

She shook her head and cradled the coffee cup in her hands.

"I kept thinking about you today." He still appeared relaxed, his long legs outstretched under the table, but there was something not quite happy in his voice.

"In a bad way?"

"Huh? Oh. No. Just wondering what you'd say about

this, how you'd read that. If you can get into his head better than I can."

Absurd to feel disappointed. What else had she thought he meant? That he'd been mooning over her?

"I think," she admitted, "that I get into women's heads better than men's. Which might be why I'm unmarried and, well, unattached." Now, why had she said that? Did she want to sound pathetic? "You have an advantage over me where Roberto's concerned."

At her revelation, his eyes had narrowed, just for a beat. But he let that go. "Maybe, but I have a problem where Roberto's concerned."

"What do you mean?"

"He reminds me unpleasantly of my father, which makes it hard for me to evaluate him dispassionately."

Oh. That was why he'd hated the idea that he might be like his father. Considering how little he'd wanted to talk about it, just a minute earlier, she was left wondering why he'd chosen to bring the subject up now.

She judged that sympathy wasn't what he wanted. So she said only, "To find Roberto, do you have to understand in what ways he might be different from your father?"

He cracked the plastic top from the salad and frowned down at it. "If I know him better, I can take more accurate guesses at what he'd do in any given circumstance. He's smart, or we'd have found him by now."

She nodded. "He thinks more clearly than most of us would under similar stress. Rage and pride are his primary emotions. But Lenora used to talk about how he'd blow up, beat her and then walk away calmly, as if nothing had happened. He'd turn on the TV, tell her to bring him a beer, call his mother. In his view, nothing *had* happened, because he couldn't empathize with her fear or pain."

"So, cold and careful, except when he's in the midst of a rage." He shook his head. "No wonder everybody disliked him."

"I suspect it was the coldness that made them uneasy. We unconsciously look for signals from other people, appropriate responses to what we're saying or doing. He wouldn't be giving them."

Bruce abruptly pushed away the barely touched salad. "Come on. Let's get out of here. You must be beat."

"Gee, thanks."

His gaze flicked to her face, and there was sudden heat in his eyes. "You're the most beautiful exhausted woman I've ever seen."

He might as well have zapped her with a lightning bolt. Her blood heated, and her lower belly cramped with longing. She couldn't look away from that glint in his eyes.

She'd known, of course, that she found him attractive. But she'd been distracted enough not to react sexually. He'd just changed that. Karin wasn't sure how she felt about that. She was unnerved enough to regain a semblance of self-control.

"Thank you again. I guess."

He gave a gruff laugh. "Not the prettiest compliment you've ever heard, is it?"

"Well, no, but…"

"But?"

Neither of them had moved. He hadn't picked up his tray.

"The thought was nice." Not what she'd meant to say, but it would do. How could she ask, *Did you mean it? Do you really think I'm beautiful?*

He nodded, picked up his tray and started for the exit. The subject was apparently closed. She waited while he took care of the tray, then walked beside him down the deserted hall.

"Where's your car?" he asked.

She told him, not bothering to insist she didn't need an escort. For one thing, tonight, she was very glad to have one. For another… *Admit it*. She didn't want to say good-night. She didn't know when she'd see him again.

They were in the parking garage when he said, "If I invited you to dinner, would you say yes?"

Karin hadn't felt a clutch of excitement like this in years. She shouldn't now. She made a point of not dating men who were as steeped in the violent underside of human nature as she was. But she had the oddest flash of revelation. How had she expected to fall in love with someone she couldn't talk to?

She must have been quiet too long, because he continued, "If my invitation makes you uncomfortable, say so. We'll consider the subject closed."

"Yes," she said. "I mean, no. I mean…"

He stopped and faced her. Around them, the garage

was brightly lit, yet somehow shadowy. They were very much alone.

"Yes? Or no?"

"Yes," she whispered. "I'd say yes."

There was that look in his eyes again, the one that seemed to liquefy her. "Good," he murmured. "When we have time…"

Her head bobbed. *Soon, please.*

He touched her cheek, brushing it with his knuckles, so softly a shiver passed down her spine.

"What is it about you?" he said, so quietly she knew the question wasn't meant for her.

But then he let his hand drop. "You should get home before you collapse. Where's the car?"

"Um…there at the end."

Hand gripping her arm, he led her to her Camry, then waited while she fumbled in her purse, found her keys and unlocked the driver's-side door. "You'll be okay?"

"I don't live five minutes from here. You'd better go home and get some sleep, too." A smile came from nowhere, surprising her. "Although you're the sexiest exhausted man I've ever seen."

He laughed, as she'd meant him to.

"Yeah, I think I can sleep now. Thanks."

Thanks for what? she wondered, getting into her car. Listening to him? Persuading him to eat? Or flirting with him?

"Do you want a lift to your car?"

"Nah, I'm not far away."

"Then good night."

"Good night."

By the time she backed out, he was striding off. She was only a little sorry he hadn't kissed her. There would be a better time.

CHAPTER FIVE

BRUCE JACKKNIFED UP in bed, lit numbers on his clock a reproach. Oh, crap! He'd forgotten to call Trevor.

At after one in the morning, it was too late now. Feeling guilty, he lay back down. Damn it, what if MaryBeth hadn't come home in the day and a half since he'd dropped off Trev? What if the cupboards were bare? Who was it Trevor had said checked on him "sometimes"? Mrs. Potter? No, Porter. Mrs. Porter. Would he feel okay about going to her if he didn't have any food?

He could've called me, Bruce reminded himself. He had Bruce's cell phone number.

Question is, would he if he wasn't desperate? Trevor tried very hard to pretend he and his mom were doing fine. He wouldn't want to admit they weren't.

Bruce eventually quieted his restless conscience enough to sleep. But Wednesday morning when he called Trevor, he got no answer. Frowning, he thought about driving over there, except by the time he reached White Center, Trev should be on the school bus.

Later.

Still no change in Lenora's condition when he

phoned the hospital. Bruce set out to find more of the men who might have been friends of Roberto's, with no luck. Midday he had word that a pair of uniformed cops, visiting a run-down motel on a tip that a drug dealer was there, had spotted a car that might be Escobar's. Wrong plates, but the ones on the car had been stolen or borrowed from a red 1972 Chevy pickup. This vehicle was a LeSabre, blue, rusting, dented. They hadn't gotten too close because they'd seen the curtain twitch. Should they move on it?

He had them watch the hotel-room door and wait for him. He drove fast, his adrenaline pumping. It was about time they got lucky. Man, he hoped those kids were okay.

"I don't think he has a gun," he told the young cop who was waiting when he got there. "But let's not count on it."

The cop nodded. He and his partner had extracted the key to the room from the manager, and the partner had stayed in the office to be sure the manager didn't call to warn his tenant.

The two of them walked down the row of rooms, smelling marijuana seeping from one room, hearing a dog scrabbling and whining in another. Most of the cars parked out front were beaters. A couple of the rooms had junk heaped on the sidewalk, people moving in or out or maybe partway and losing interest.

The uniform arranged himself on the opposite side of the door from Bruce, his weapon in his hand. Bruce hammered on the door.

"Police! Open up."

Inside something scrabbled, much like the dog, but this time Bruce sensed the sound was made by a human.

He wasn't giving Escobar long enough to kill the kids. He pounded again, yelling, "Open the door now or we're coming in."

Silence. He had the key in the lock when the door abruptly swung inward under his hand.

A skinny, pasty, pimply kid peered out, looking scared. "Whaddya want? We haven't done anything!"

Shit.

"Open the door wide," Bruce ordered.

It swung open to reveal four other teenagers, ranging at his best guess from thirteen up to maybe seventeen. Runaways. Goddamn it, runaways! Not Escobar.

"Is that your vehicle?" he asked, nodding over his shoulder at the Buick.

"It's mine," one of the girls said defiantly. "What's it to you? I'm not even driving it!"

"Plates are stolen."

"They're from my car," a boy said. "It won't start, and I can't afford to get it fixed."

"And I couldn't afford the tabs," the girl said. "So big deal. What's his and mine is ours."

Goddamn, Bruce thought again. He shook his head. "We're going to have to check you all out. Someone will be wanting to know where you are."

"I won't stay in no shelter!" a scrawny, wild-eyed girl said. "We paid for this place. We got a right."

Depressed, he left them to the custody of the two uniformed officers. Yeah, the kids probably weren't hurting anyone or anything except themselves. The girls would be turning tricks. Hell, maybe the boys, too. And all of them would be buying drugs when they could afford 'em. This at an age when they should be in middle school or high school, maybe working the counter at Burger King weekends for enough bucks to pay to take a girl out or buy the clothes Mom and Dad wouldn't spring for. Seeing kids like these upset him more than almost anything on the job, including dead bodies.

While he was out on this stretch of the Pacific Highway, he checked out a dozen similar motels, driving around back of each to be sure the rusting blue Buick wasn't tucked out of sight.

At three o'clock his cell phone rang. He pulled into the parking lot of a McDonald's and grabbed the phone from his belt.

"Walker."

"Bruce?" The voice was thin and boyish. "It's Trevor."

"Trev. I tried to call you this morning."

"I didn't hear the phone. I left early so I could, like, walk down to a different bus stop."

"Jackson?"

"He punched me yesterday!" The boy sniffed. "But everyone else at the stop said if I told, they'd say I just walked into a street sign."

Bruce ground his teeth. "You can't be the only kid he's bullying."

"I guess not." He sounded…uninterested, and Bruce tensed. If Trev hadn't phoned because of the bully at the bus stop…

"It's Mom!" the boy exclaimed. "She hasn't been home since Sunday."

"Sunday?" he echoed. "Damn it, Trevor, why didn't you say something? Have you had anything to eat?"

"At first there was stuff. And I get a hot lunch at school. So I was okay. Mom's gone sometimes for a day or two, but never this long. I'm scared!" His voice cracked and then rose. "Why hasn't she come home or called or anything?"

"I don't know. You sit tight. I'm on my way."

Obviously crying, the boy snuffled and said, "Right now?"

"Right now. It'll take me about fifteen minutes."

While he drove, he radioed in to find out if MaryBeth DeShon had been picked up and was in jail or detox, or if any unidentified bodies meeting her description had been found this week. "No" was the answer all around. Later, he'd make multiple calls to be sure she hadn't ended up in some other jurisdiction. Not for the first time, he wished the patchwork of cities and counties shared information better.

In the meantime… Damn it, what was he going to do with Trevor? Bruce wished like hell a responsible neighbor lived nearby, or the boy had a good friend with whom he could stay.

He'd no sooner knocked and called, "Trevor, it's me, Bruce," than his Little Brother flung open the door. He'd tried to scrub signs of tears from his face, but it was still blotchy, his eyes puffy.

Bruce stepped in and drew the boy, unresisting, to

him for a hug. No reason he should feel such anguish; the kid was okay.

Against his chest, Trevor repeated, "Mom and me— we're usually okay." He stiffened and stepped away, as if needing to regain his pride.

"I checked with hospitals to make sure she wasn't in an accident." He didn't say *or overdosed.* "She didn't look so good to me the last couple of times I saw her."

Trev's gaze slid from his. "I think maybe she's, I don't know, doing something different. 'Cuz it used to be she just drank and partied. You know. But now she gets real shaky right before she goes out. And…and I think she got fired from her job again last week."

MaryBeth had her shortcomings, but she'd done her damnedest to give her son a better childhood than she'd had. Would she have just walked? Everyone had a breaking point. Maybe she'd reached hers.

"I'm going to have to call Child Protective Services," Bruce said. "So you have someplace safe to stay, just while we hunt for her."

Trevor backed away, his eyes widening. "You mean, like a foster home? Can't I stay with you? I thought… when you said you were coming…"

Bruce shook his head. "You know what kind of hours I work. I'm home only to sleep."

"I can take care of myself!" the boy pleaded. "Mom practically always works nights. I'm real responsible! That's what she says."

Bruce wavered, but only momentarily. He couldn't let himself get pulled two ways, feeling he should be home when he needed to be on the job. Homicide wasn't an eight-to-five gig.

"I believe you're responsible, but you're also twelve years old. You *shouldn't* be home alone a lot, and especially not at night. Your mom has done the best she could. I'm not criticizing her. But right now, you need stability, not another empty apartment."

Trevor backed away from him, his expression of disbelief morphing into anger. "You don't want me, do you? Just say so! Don't lie to me!"

Bruce's bad case of heartburn wouldn't be cured by a gulp of antacid. "If I had a different kind of job, or a wife who's there when I'm not, I'd like nothing better than to take you home with me. But I'm a homicide cop, and right now I'm looking for two kids who may be in danger. I can't let up, Trevor."

"I wish I hadn't called you," the boy said with loathing. "I shoulda just waited for Mom." With one hand he dashed furiously at his tears.

Bruce tried talking to him some more. The boy wouldn't listen. Doing his best to harden his heart, Bruce called CPS and requested a caseworker.

He offered to help Trevor pack while they waited, but the boy said, "I don't want you touching my stuff!" and slammed the bedroom door in Bruce's face.

He stood outside for a minute, rubbing his chest above the burning sensation, second-guessing himself. Did he know anyone who would be good for Trevor? But Molly had the same problem he did, plus she was helping her sister out with the newborn. Other fellow cops were single like him; or they had families, and how could he saddle them with an extra? He imagined how gentle Karin would be with him, but she needed to be with Lenora when she wasn't working.

Shaking his head finally, Bruce turned away from the closed door and wandered the apartment. With an effort, he forced himself to think like a cop. Had Trevor tried to determine whether his mother had packed enough to suggest she'd meant to be gone for more than a day or two?

Not sure if he'd be able to tell, Bruce quietly stepped into her bedroom. It was messy and smelled like unwashed armpits. Mattress on the floor, unmade bed-clothes, sheets stained. Another sheet was nailed up to cover the window. Cheap, pressboard dresser and a few hangers in the closet held what few clothes she owned or had left behind. In one corner, the kind of net hamper designed for dorm rooms was half full of dirty laundry, a bra hanging out. A couple of pairs of scuffed shoes, worn at the heels, were left where she'd kicked them off. He eased open the drawers one by one and found drug paraphernalia in the top one. Surprise, surprise.

No suitcase, but chances were she didn't own one. When she and her son moved, their possessions would go in grocery sacks and cardboard boxes from the state liquor store.

Her cosmetics littered the counter in the bathroom, which was dirty enough to make Bruce disinclined to touch anything. In the cup beside the sink were two toothbrushes, both needing replacement. He nudged open the medicine cabinet and saw a half-used foil packet of birth control pills. *Huh.* No, it didn't appear MaryBeth had intended to be gone long.

He was back out in the living room by the time the doorbell rang. The woman he let in had to be fresh out of college, but maybe that was all to the good. Her zeal wouldn't have been ground down to cynicism yet. She introduced herself as Caroline Connelly and asked how long it had been since Trevor's mother had been home.

Trev emerged from the bedroom while they talked, carrying his bulging book bag and a couple of plastic grocery sacks holding clothes. His face was set and pale, and he refused to look at Bruce.

The social worker introduced herself and gave an upbeat, everything-will-be-great speech that made him hunch his shoulders and stare at the floor. Finally, she said, "Do you have everything you need?"

He shrugged.

"Toothbrush?" Bruce reminded him.

Without a word, Trevor went into the bathroom, then returned a moment later.

"Why don't you set down your stuff and write a note to your mom," she suggested. "We'll tape it up where she can't miss it when she gets home."

Again, Trev complied without deigning to speak to Bruce. He pulled a lined sheet of paper from his pack and wrote on it in big letters: *Mom, when you didn't come home, they took me away to a foster home. You got to call to find out where I am.*

He wrote down the phone number Caroline Connelly gave him, then signed the note *Sorry, Trev.*

At Bruce's suggestion, Trevor called his neighbor, Mrs. Porter, and told her where he was going. Hearing only the one end, Bruce gathered she wasn't surprised.

"You'll actually be going to a receiving home," the social worker told him. "You might like that better, because you'll be with a bunch of other boys."

He stiffened. "Are they my age?"

"Twelve to fifteen."

He gave Bruce one desperate, despairing side glance. A sense of helplessness clawed at Bruce, who knew what torture school had become for Trevor this past year or two because the other boys were maturing physically faster than him. And while in some respect all the kids in the receiving home would be, like Trevor, victims of family dysfunction, many would already have been considerably toughened by their lives. Trevor was childlike and naive in contrast to many of the kids who were in and out of receiving and group homes.

Bruce said nothing until they'd locked the apartment and walked down to the cars, then spoke in an under-tone to the social worker. "I think he'd do better in a foster home with some one-on-one—"

She was shaking her head before he'd gotten halfway through with what he'd wanted to say. "I don't have one available, not for a boy his age."

"But look at him."

She did, and he saw the dismay on her face she'd been trying to hide. But she only shook her head again.

Trevor put his stuff in the back seat, then got into the

front on the passenger side. Bruce laid a hand on the
door before he could slam it.

"We'll find your mom."

He shrugged and ducked his head.

"I'll be in touch."

Trevor didn't say anything. Nor did his head turn
when Caroline backed out and drove away.

Standing there, Bruce felt like scum.

KARIN WANDERED her living room, straightening magazines on the coffee table, fluffing the pillows on the
sofa, refolding a throw before laying it carefully over
the back of a chair. She wasn't, she realized, suffering
from anxious-hostess syndrome so much as she was
trying to keep herself occupied.

What on earth had she been thinking to suggest he
come to her house? It was after nine o'clock. She'd left
Lenora's sister sitting at her bedside, and had been so
grateful simply to be home. She'd kicked off her
shoes, made a cup of coffee and reached for the TV
remote control. She'd wanted to watch something
mindless, something that might make her laugh. But
before she'd hit the power button, her cell phone, still
in her purse, had rung.

"Just wondered how your day went," Bruce had said,
but she heard exhaustion and discouragement in his
voice. "Are you still at the hospital? I might stop by."

"No, I've gone home." Before she knew it, she heard
herself saying, "If you need to talk, you'd be welcome
to come by."

Now, butterflies fluttering in her stomach, she was waiting for her doorbell to ring. She hardly knew him. They hadn't even dated! She never invited men she knew only casually into her home. This was her space, her sanctuary. She'd always believed she could tell as much about a person from seeing the inside of his home as she could if he stripped naked in front of her and babbled his deepest secrets. Every item she chose and how she displayed it, the colors she loved, her appreciation for clutter or simplicity, all spoke of how she saw herself, how she felt about herself. Letting him in the front door was like exposing herself.

The doorbell rang and she jerked. She was being absurd. He wouldn't notice her décor; men didn't. And anyway…she wasn't ashamed of her home or anything it said about her. Having a guy over for a cup of coffee was hardly an act of intimacy.

She opened her door to find he looked as worn as he'd sounded. Alarm squeezed her at the sight of this man, who ordinarily exuded such confidence, wearing discouragement as if it were a cologne.

"What happened?" she asked before she could stop herself. "You didn't find…?"

"Find…? No." He grimaced. "Neither hide nor hair."

She stood back. "Come in. Let me take your jacket." As he shrugged out of it and handed it to her, she was jarred by the sight of his shoulder holster and weapon. The leather straps somehow made his broad shoulders appear even more imposing. "Would you like a cup of coffee?" Her eyes narrowed. "Or have you eaten?"

"Surprisingly…yeah. I wanted to think. I stopped for a burger earlier."

She shook her head in disapproval.

"Coffee would be good."

Karin already had it brewing. She poured him a cup and freshened hers, added sugar and cream per their tastes and led the way back to the living room. Bruce sprawled at one end of her comfortable sofa, while Karin sat more sedately in a buttery-soft leather chair across from him.

"So what happened?" she asked.

"First, how's Lenora?"

"Actually, the doctor was encouraged today. She's getting restless. Jerking, some reflex responses to touch. She even had some facial twitches. I kept imagining she was about to open her mouth and say something." Karin gave a small shudder.

Anna and Enrico. Are they safe? That was what she'd imagined Lenora would ask first. How Karin dreaded answering that question.

"We got momentarily excited today when a patrol unit spotted a car matching the description of Escobar's. It had stolen plates." He grimaced. "When we closed in, we discovered it belonged to a group of runaway teens. They weren't real thrilled to see us."

"Do you think he's still around here?"

He frowned. "Yeah. Yeah, I do. I've been in touch with the FBI in case Escobar has crossed state lines with the kids. Neither they nor any other jurisdiction has picked up even a whisper. Besides, I checked with the hospital this morning. They've had a number of calls about Lenora's status. I'm wondering if he's one of the people calling."

Her eyes widened and her fingers tightened on her mug. "Do you mean… Is she in danger?"

"Probably not now, security is pretty tight in the ICU, but we'll need to be cautious if—when—she walks out of there. He's not going to like that." Bruce shook his head, then rubbed his neck as if it ached. "Unless he has delusions that she'll be sorry about what she did to him and is now longing for him. God knows."

Karin studied the man slouched so low on her sofa it might take a forklift to shift him off it. The lines carving his face were surely deeper than they'd been yesterday. With the stubble on his jaw, his dark hair disheveled, the gun nestled where he could grab it between one heartbeat and the next, he should have appeared dangerous. Instead, she read despondency in his posture, would have sworn she saw something wounded in his eyes. Was it just the frustration? Did he hate being thwarted that much?

"Your partner," she probed. "She's okay? And her sister's baby?"

"Huh?" He lifted his gaze from the mug to her. "Oh. Yeah. Kid's got a set of lungs, according to Molly."

Her mouth curved. "Babies come equipped that way, or so I'm told."

"Yeah, and think how long it takes to potty train 'em. Puppy learns in a week or two."

"And you don't have to send it to college, either."

At last he grinned, his body relaxing slightly.

"What I was *trying* to find out," she said with some exasperation, "is why you look like your puppy just got run over."

His grin, though genuine, had vanished as quickly as it appeared, gone in the blink of an eye. Now he tried to smile, but this effort was an abysmal failure. "That obvious, huh?"

"Mmm, hmm."

"It's this kid I've been spending time with. I signed up to be a Big Brother about a year ago—maybe a little longer now. I spend at least a few hours with Trevor pretty much every week."

She nodded to encourage him to keep talking.

"Trevor is twelve now. He's a great kid. Smart, funny. Life just keeps hitting on him." Bruce's voice was bleak. "He's small for his age, for starters. He has his own personal bully at his bus stop. His dad beat the crap out of his mother, who finally kicked him out two years back. Trev hasn't seen his dad since, although he calls sometimes. His mother tries, but she can barely hang on to a job for a couple of months at a time. I think she's on crack now. She's gone for a couple of days at a time pretty regularly, from what Trev says. But from the sound of it, she's been hurting lately, maybe suffering withdrawal, and she disappeared five or six days ago. She's never been gone that long before. He's scared."

"I should think!" she exclaimed.

"He called me. I called CPS. They sent a caseworker

and took him off to a receiving home." Now the agony was exposed, seeping. His expression suggested pure misery. "Trevor feels betrayed. Turns out he thought I'd take him home with me. And damn it, part of me wanted to. But with my hours, how can I? I might as well leave him completely on his own."

On impulse, she set down her coffee and circled the coffee table to sit beside him, instead, reaching out to grip his hand. He grabbed and held on as if to a lifeline. His face looked even more ravaged close up. However matter-of-fact his description of Trevor's situation and their relationship, he loved this boy, she thought.

"Do you still believe you did the right thing?" she asked. "Even after second-guessing yourself?"

"A couple hundred times?" His mouth twisted. "Yeah. I think so. But when I called, I was picturing him getting sent to a foster home. You know, mom, dad, maybe another kid. Instead he's being thrown into a dormitory-type situation with a bunch of bigger, tougher, meaner boys."

"Can't you find his mother?"

"So far, no cigar. She's probably semicomatose in a crack house somewhere." His shoulders moved in an unhappy shrug. "She may take weeks or months to surface if she's too far gone, and when she does, it may be in the morgue. Crap!" he said explosively. "She's all he has. And, damn it, she's tried!"

"Crack is supposed to be one of the worst addictions."

"Yeah, and I'm guessing she just lost her battle with it. But what's going to happen to Trev now?" He didn't expect a response, she could tell; he knew the answer. "I can't see a happy ending."

She bit her lip before saying tentatively, "Have you considered, if his mother can't be found…?"

His blank stare told her he hadn't.

"Taking him in? I mean, long term?" she suggested.

His grunt held incredulity. "Are you kidding? After the way I grew up? I have no more idea how to be a parent than his father did. Probably less. Parenting 101 in my house—kid gives you lip you backhand him. He breaks curfew? You pull out the leather belt. I have no idea what the responsible alternatives are. No. It's not happening." Subject closed.

Karin wanted to argue. She had never seen him interact with a child, never mind a defiant preadolescent, but she *had* seen him talk to a roomful of wary, wounded women with respect, compassion and blunt honesty that had allowed them to lower their guard. She didn't believe for a minute that Bruce Walker was a man who would ever backhand a child, much less become enraged enough to strike him with a leather belt.

Oh, God. Did he have scars?

That flash of speculation was enough to make her suddenly, exquisitely conscious of his body. Or perhaps of hers. No, the truth was, she'd been conscious of his from the moment she'd opened her door to him. She'd just…tamped down that awareness. She knew her cheeks were flushing, because heat seemed to rush through her veins. She was flushing all over.

Say something. Don't let him notice.

"Have you ever been angry at him?" she asked, almost at random.

"Trevor?" His eyebrows rose. "Mildly irritated."

"Then what makes you think…?"

"As parents, don't we all revert to what we learned at home?"

"We may have that tendency, but we can overcome it. The people who do revert are the ones who aren't self-aware. They just go with instinct. But lots of people who were abused as children turn into fine parents."

There, she congratulated herself. She sounded like the levelheaded therapist she was.

Yes, but she was still holding hands with Bruce. He didn't seem to want to let hers go, and she certainly hadn't made any effort to tug her hand free. Should she? Probably, but…

She sucked in a breath. His thumb had begun to move, making idle circles. She gave a tiny shiver of reaction.

"Thanks," he said huskily.

"For?" Her voice emerged barely above a whisper.

"Seeing hope." He paused, his gaze lingering on her face. His eyes had darkened to near charcoal. "Listening to me."

"It's…the least I could do."

"If you didn't want me to kiss you, it might have been smart if you'd stayed over there." Bruce jerked his head toward the chair.

She swallowed. "I think I must want you to kiss me."

"Good." The gravel in his voice was more pronounced. "Because I need you."

He tugged, and she went unresisting, unable to tear her eyes from his face. From his mouth, hard and yet somehow unbearably sensual.

A kiss. Just a kiss, Karin thought in near panic as his arm closed around her.

But she knew a lie when she told herself one.

CHAPTER SIX

SHE TASTED BETTER than any woman he'd ever kissed. From the minute she'd moved to the couch and taken his hand in hers, he'd thought, *I've got to kiss her. Soon.* And then, *Now.*

The urgency was gut level, stunning him. One minute he was tugging her toward him, the next he was devouring her mouth. The pillow of her lips, the warm dark cavern of her mouth, the slippery, sensuous slide of her tongue on his, ripped away any brain power.

Bruce yanked her on top of him, one hand tangled in the hair on the back of her head, the other rhythmically squeezing her buttock. That quick, he was rock hard against her. He tore his mouth from hers long enough to graze his teeth down her throat and lick the hollow at the base, salty and silky, then groaned and recaptured her lips.

She squirmed, and for a split second pure panic rocked him. She was going to pull away. God. He didn't know if he could bear to let her go.

But all she did was wriggle into a more comfortable position straddling him. The sensation of her thighs squeezing his hips was like a sonic boom, muffling the inner voice that counseled him to slow down. He *couldn't* go slow.

Bruce wrenched her shirt up and fumbled for the catch of her bra, even as she ended the kiss long enough to yank her own shirt over her head. He had a glimpse of her face: lips swollen and damp, hair wild, cheek whisker-burned, eyes riveted to his. And then he lowered his gaze to her breasts, more than a handful, peaked with tight, pink nipples.

He gripped her hips and lifted her so that he could take each breast in turn into his mouth, licking, suckling, tugging. Her back arched and her breath whistled out.

Hunger so primitive it was wordless claimed him. All he knew was that he needed to penetrate her. He had to *claim* her.

He pushed them both sideways, so she sprawled beneath him the length of the sofa. He reared to his knees to pull her pants and panties down with no ceremony. Her legs were gorgeous, long, taut and already wrapping around him. Sleek white belly and— yes!—dark blond curls at the apex of her thighs.

She half sat, and unbuttoned and unzipped his pants. Drawing them down, she gasped, "Do you have a condom?"

He was so crazed he didn't understand for a moment. When he did, he reached for his wallet in his back pocket. Did he have a condom? *Yes.* What would he have done if he hadn't…?

Moving had reminded him that he still wore both a shirt and his shoulder holster. Damn, damn, damn. From long practice he unbuckled the holster and dropped it over the arm of the sofa, yanked the shirt off and lifted himself from her long enough to free himself from the slacks, too.

Condom. He put it on himself with hands that shook, then bent to suckle her breast again. Finally, he kissed her deep and long, even as he found her opening and rammed in with no more finesse than a teenager his first time.

She was slick and tight and he couldn't go slow. He retreated and thrust again, and again, hard and fast. Her fingernails bit into his back and she nipped his neck sharply. Her hips bucked, and he fell with her from the sofa, crashing together onto their sides, never slowing. At one point she rose above him, before he flipped them again, banging against the coffee table, and climaxing as he pounded into her. She was spasming, too, and keening as he groaned.

As the wave washed out again, he collapsed. *The little death.* Yes, he simply could not move, could not form a conscious thought, could only feel satiated and boneless and deeply satisfied.

Awareness returned in micro increments. Pain on his upper arm. From where he hit the table. Or was it the floor? Rough-textured carpet beneath his knee, planted between her legs. His mouth sticking to her neck. *Drool?* That unwelcome realization produced a groan from the depths of his chest, and he rose onto his elbows.

"I'm flattening you."

"Hmm?" She looked, if it was possible, more stunned

than he felt. Maybe it wasn't postcoital bliss; maybe she was suffering from oxygen deprivation. He was a big man.

No place to roll. The coffee table, entirely too solid, blocked them on one side, the sofa on the other. Mumbling, he lifted himself awkwardly from her, then held out a hand.

Karin stared at it, as if unable to decipher the gesture. Then she whispered, "Oh." The next "Oh" emerged as a squeak, and she scrambled backward and to her feet. "Let me get…um…" She fled toward a short hall. A door closed behind her. Would she be coming back out?

Clothes. Bruce glanced around. In her absence, he got dressed, wincing every time he moved his right arm. Looked like a nice bruise was forming there.

As if a flashbulb were exploding in front of his eyes, he kept getting pictures. Ripping her clothes off like some kind of animal. Slamming into her. The crash to the floor. Squeezing her breasts. God. Had he left bruises on *her?*

What in the hell, he wondered, appalled, had happened to him? Should he leave before she reappeared? *If* she reappeared?

No. That would be unforgivable. *Slam, bam, thank you, ma'am.*

No.

With hands that felt clumsy, he picked up her clothing and carefully folded it, making a small pile on the coffee table. He slid the table back so it sat square to the sofa, restored to their places the pillows that had gone flying, then went to get a sponge from the kitchen to mop up the coffee spilled on the table. He was carrying the two mugs back to the kitchen when Karin returned down the hall, wearing sweats. Her hair, he saw with a lightning-quick assessment, was pulled back repressively. Even painfully. She didn't quite meet his eyes.

Without a word, he set the mugs in the sink and faced her. She hovered in the kitchen doorway, arms tightly crossed, her teeth on her lower lip.

After a minute, Bruce said, "I don't know where that came from."

She gave a peculiar laugh. "Me neither."

"I can be gentle. Even patient."

Voice as tightly strung as her body language, she said, "I didn't seem to have any problem with your technique."

At her words, he felt a jolt in his groin. No. She'd given as good as she got, and he hadn't mistaken the seemingly endless way her body had spasmed around his.

So. They'd had raw, even brutal, sex, and now they were both embarrassed. He grunted. *Embarrassed* didn't half cover it. He was shaken to know what he was capable of. What if she'd said *stop!* just before he'd penetrated her? *Could* he have stopped? He didn't know, and hated the not knowing. What separated him, then, from the monsters who had raped those women he'd met at A Woman's Hand?

"I hope, ah, that you don't have any bruises."

Alarm leaped into her eyes. "Especially visible ones."

"Yeah, not so good in your line of work." He braced

his hands on either side of the countertop and couldn't suppress a small wince.

"You're hurt," she said.

"Banged my shoulder."

Her teeth worried her lip again. "Oh."

He cleared his throat. "It was…amazing."

Color, already high in her cheeks, rose. "I've never done anything like that."

"Me neither." But, God help him, he wanted to do it again. Soon. With her. Bruce decided not to tell her that. Next time, he swore, he'd be so damn gentle, so considerate, she'd have to beg him to let go.

Assuming there was a next time.

"Can we have dinner tomorrow night?" he asked. "If something doesn't intervene?"

He was a homicide cop; "something" frequently did intervene.

He saw the hesitation—leading up to refusal—on her face. Oh, yeah, he'd panicked her.

"Just dinner," he coaxed. "If we can have wild sex, surely we can talk over the dinner table."

A parade of emotions crossed her face. No, not a parade, more like the Kentucky Derby, every emotion jostling for space, stretched out at a flat run. He'd have really liked to get a good look at each if only they'd slow down.

Finally, she sighed and dipped her head. "Yes. You're right. Dinner. Say, six?"

He agreed. She walked him to the door, offering no suggestion that he hang around, have a refill of that cup

of coffee that had ended up spilled or—especially—
spend the night. There, they eyed each other for a
minute, their precise relationship uncomfortably ill
defined. Thinking *What the hell,* Bruce stepped closer,
tilted her chin up with one finger and kissed her.

He kept it light, gentle and generally everything their
lovemaking hadn't been. The contact was still enough
to stir something in him. She could become addictive,
he thought, disquieted. The one comfort was that her
mouth softened under his, and she appeared dazed when
he lifted his head and, after clearing his throat, said,
"Good night."

She'd backed inside and was locking up by the time
he left the porch. Bruce got in to his car, started it, then
sat there for a minute, trying to figure out whether this
had been a really shitty day, or one of the best of his life.

TOO MANY OF KARIN'S new clients came to her looking
just like this woman. Unlike many, this one had avoided
a hospital stay. Her nose was plastered, however, after
being broken, and the still-puffy flesh around both her
eyes had progressed from being merely blackened to a
rainbow of sickly colors.

Karin and she had already discussed her history with
other men, and the escalating violence of this relationship.

"Tell me," Karin asked, "does Tyrone hurt you in bed,
too?"

Destiny Malone gave her a grin that was startlingly
wicked, appearing on that battered face. "You kidding,
girl? 'Course he does! But in a good way, you know?"

Karin could count on one hand the times she'd blushed in a counseling session. She prayed the heat in her cheeks this time wasn't visible.

Oh, God, she thought in horror. *Did I ask because I needed to know for* her *sake? Or for mine?*

Had she been trying to figure out whether sex like she'd had with Bruce only happened if the man was violent by nature?

Maybe. But if the answer was yes and he was a brute—what did that say about *her* enthusiastic participation last night? Hadn't she actually *bitten* him? Karin cringed.

"He don't beat me or anything like that. It's just that he's hot for me. He say he can't get enough." Destiny smiled again, with some secret satisfaction. "And a woman, she's got to like that."

Yes. She did. Having a man desperate for her, rather than politely anticipating lovemaking, was an incredible aphrodisiac. Karin had had no idea.

"What if you say no?" she asked. "Does Tyrone accept that?"

Her carefully plucked brows rose in apparent surprise, momentarily widening her eyes. "'Course he does. You think I'd take him back if he *raped* me?"

"Ah… He does hit you," Karin reminded her.

"Yeah, but…but…" She scowled. "That's different."

"How?"

"Well, 'cuz…" She shifted in the seat, crossing her legs, uncrossing them, finally bursting out, "He only hits me when I been asking for it."

"Do you believe you *deserved* this beating?"

"I have this trouble, see." Shame suffused her gaze before she lowered it. "I like to shop."

Karin blinked.

Destiny, it developed, *really* liked to shop. She was pathologically driven to shop, and easily convinced herself that she needed that pair of shoes or that handbag or those jeans. She'd run up all her credit cards, then his. Sometimes she'd take things back, but mostly they went into her closet and often stayed there unworn. It was when she spent money they didn't have that Tyrone lost his temper.

So, okay. There were two problems to deal with: Tyrone's temper and Destiny's compulsive shopping. Karin was hugely relieved to feel herself shifting into professional mode. She'd had absolutely no business relating anything a client told her to herself. Particularly when that something was as intimate as whether she had bruises after sex.

As her day went on, she had trouble concentrating. She kept replaying last night's scene, from the moment she'd sat on the sofa next to him and taken his hand, to that last kiss on the doorstep. Remembering, Karin found herself getting aroused. She was both disconcerted and embarrassed. This wasn't like her! She'd always been the cool, calm, collected one, not so much a participant in life as an observer. She'd never really seen that as a negative; she *liked* maintaining a little distance.

Uh-huh. Forgot to do that last night, didn't you?

The awful thing was, Destiny Malone was right. A woman *did* have to like the feeling of being wanted so desperately. Karin shivered at the memory of his face, taut with urgency.

So, okay, maybe her previous experiences with sex had been a little *too* civilized. Maybe even tepid. Definitely lacking. But it gave her the creeps to think she'd been secretly craving that violent act.

Or…was it a man like Detective Bruce Walker she'd been craving? And what did *that* say about her?

Alone in her office at the end of the day, she squeezed her eyes shut and muttered, "Get a grip."

She just had time to make it home and change from a blazer and slacks to a more casual and comfortable pair of wide-legged pants and a V-necked, silk top before Bruce picked her up.

"News?" she asked before she even had the door all the way open. The question seemed to restore their relationship to a former place, when Lenora was the reason they were speaking at all.

She saw the answer on his face, but he shook his head anyway, lines furrowing his forehead.

"Molly is back, which is a help, but we won't be able to stay full-time on this. Upside is, the FBI is galvanized. Lots of good press if they find the kids, you know. The downside is, they're being their usual jackasses." His eyebrows rose. "Ready?"

Once they were in the car, he said, "Oh, I meant to ask you about the upcoming self-defense workshop. Are we going on with it?"

"I can't decide," she admitted. "I tend to think we should. If anything, what happened to Lenora highlights how much these women need the skills you're teaching."

"Canceling on them might send the message that, see, it's hopeless anyway," he agreed. "We don't want to do that."

They talked about the program a little more, including the question of whether another facility would be safer, but concluded that the moment when the women separated to go to cars was always the point of vulnerability.

"This time Molly will be with me, and we'll stick around until every woman's safely on her way."

Karin nodded, wondering about his partner. In the course of her work, she'd met her share of women cops, but still found them…a puzzle, was perhaps one way to put it. Her end of the business, the healing, was more traditionally feminine. She couldn't imagine stepping into the punitive role, or handling the physicality of it. The tendency was to believe that women who chose to go into law enforcement were mannish, but in her experience that wasn't at all true. They were gutsy; maybe, like the men, they enjoyed the adrenaline rush their work brought. But Karin had met many who were soft-spoken, pretty, feminine, even petite.

"What's Molly like?" she asked.

Bruce glanced from the road ahead at her. "Like?" he asked blankly, his tone one of typical masculine befuddlement.

"Young? Old? Married? Does she have kids?" She waved both hands. "You know."

"Oh. Um… Not old. Twenty-nine, and worrying about turning thirty. Unmarried—one of the reasons she's worried. She's always asking what's wrong with her."

"And you tell her…?" Karin probed.

"Nothing's wrong with her!" He shrugged in further bafflement. "She's always seeing some guy. She's the one who breaks it off."

"Hmm."

He shot her a grin. "Was that a therapist's 'hmm'? Or a mild expression of interest?"

Until now, the conversation had felt…strained. Maybe just in her imagination, but she didn't think so. She thought they'd both been pretending to hold a normal conversation. But all of a sudden her mood lightened. He didn't smile often, this cop, and maybe that was why each time he did she found herself newly fascinated. She loved the way his eyes crinkled, so that sometimes they, rather than his mouth, seemed to be doing the smiling.

She loosened up enough to laugh. "Habit, I'm afraid. Shake me if I start saying 'Tell me how you feel about that.'"

He grinned again, then said with satisfaction, and perhaps a little smugly, "A parking place! Damn, I'm good."

He had reason to be pleased; parking around the Pike Place Market was at a premium, and this spot was right in front of the open-air front. Artisans had their wares laid out on tables or blankets on the ground. Inside, under cover, shoppers could buy fresh-caught salmon or giant geoduck clams, local strawberries or armfuls of flowers.

Seattle's Pike Place Market was famous, having evolved from a simple farmer's market into a tourist draw that still offered the fresh produce, seafood and baked goods that local shoppers sought. Multiple levels of an idiosyncratic wooden structure descended from the foot of Pike Street down a steep bluff to the Puget Sound waterfront below. Several high-end restaurants occupied space in the market, along with art galleries, importers, boutiques and specialty shops of all kinds. The market had spread to blocks around, too, making it a shopping mecca, with kitchen, furniture and gift stores, wine merchants and more galleries.

"We're early," Bruce said. "Shall we wander?"

Releasing her seat belt and reaching eagerly for the door handle, Karin agreed. She couldn't remember the last time she'd come down here. It had been too long.

Doing something so *normal* with Bruce eased the discomfiture she felt even more. She wrinkled her nose at the sight of fish fillets spread over beds of ice but admired tables heaped with produce, some local, like the strawberries, some like ears of early corn trucked over the mountains in the early morning from the sunnier eastern side of the state. She hovered over a table of beautiful handcrafted jewelry, finally buying a pair of earrings. When she turned back around, Bruce handed her a bouquet he'd bought from a nearby flower vendor. Karin inhaled the scent of deep pink roses mixed with the simpler blooms of daisies and sprays of tiny flowers she thought were yarrow.

On impulse, she rose on her toes and kissed him lightly on the mouth. "Thank you. Nobody ever buys me flowers."

Eyes glinting, he said, "Maybe because it's coals to Newcastle. You grow enough."

"Cutting them myself isn't the same."

They had dinner at The Pink Door, a restaurant you almost had to be a local to find, and were lucky enough to be seated out on the trellis-enclosed deck as the sun was just setting. Inside, a trio played music that could have been performed in a Prohibition-era speakeasy. The rustic Italian menu used produce from the market.

Karin and Bruce sipped wine, ate at a leisurely pace, listened to music and talked with surprising ease about movies, books, politics and their jobs. Darkness descended, and tiny lights strung on the trellis lent fairy magic to the night. They were still engrossed in their conversation when the musicians finally put away their instruments and they could hear again the muffled sounds of city traffic.

She told Bruce about her childhood and coaxed stories from him about the tough neighborhood he'd grown up in and about his alienation from his own brothers, who had followed in their father's footsteps.

"Why were you different?" she asked.

Bruce began. "I don't know—" But he stopped. "No, that's not true. Me, I hung out at this community center. Some cops volunteered there. One of them became my idol." He shook his head, a wry smile on his mouth. "He was a great guy. He took me places, even to L.A. Lakers games. He had amazing seats. I couldn't believe how lucky I was. His wife was a really nice woman. I remember the first time I went to their house for dinner, she complained—I think he'd forgotten to pick something up at the store on the way home—and I shrank, waiting for him to wallop her."

He seemed momentarily lost in the past, and finally, Karin prodded, "What did he do?"

Bruce shook his head, his boyish astonishment still there. "He said I'm sorry and kissed her. She laughed and greeted me. The way she smiled at me, as if I was a real person, somebody she could hardly wait to get to know…" He cleared his throat. "I found out later that they couldn't have kids. They did finally adopt, a little girl from Colombia."

Some of the tables out on the deck were now empty, and couples at the others spoke quietly. The sound of a ferry horn was somehow haunting at night.

Very softly, so she didn't disrupt the mood, Karin asked, "Have you stayed in touch with them?"

"I haven't talked to them in a couple of years. I got an invitation to their daughter's wedding last summer and sent a present, but I couldn't get away. It would have been hard to go without…"

"Visiting your parents?"

He grunted agreement but didn't elaborate. After a surprisingly peaceful silence, Bruce stretched. "I suppose we should get going. We both have early mornings ahead."

Back in the car, they weren't three blocks from the Market before Karin realized she'd been kidding herself all night. All the talk about Mideast politics and arthouse films hadn't in the slightest reduced her awareness of his body. Every movement, every flex of his muscles, had her remembering him unclothed. He reached for the gearshift, and she saw his big, capable hand cupping her breast or gripping her hip. She knew the taste of his skin, the timbre of his voice when he was aroused, the rasp of his sandpapery jaw. And she wanted him again.

He told a story about his days as a patrol officer in the Pioneer Square area; she asked a question or two. But it required a huge effort to sound…normal. A minute later, she could hardly remember what he'd said or why she had laughed politely.

He gave up talking, and in the next blocks she felt as if the air in the car had become thick, difficult to breathe.

A moment later, he pulled into her driveway. Turning off the engine, he said, "I'll walk you to your door."

Moment of truth. She wanted him to. She didn't want him to. She knew, of course, that he would kiss her, but not whether she'd risk asking him in.

They got out, Karin cradling the bouquet. The slam of the car doors was as startlingly loud as a gunshot in the sleeping neighborhood. The two walked in silence up to her porch, and Bruce waited while she unlocked and faced him.

After studying her face for a long moment, he smiled so ruefully she knew her panic must be blatant.

Voice a rumble, he asked, "Was the evening so bad?"

Karin laughed, if a little shakily. "No. Of course it wasn't. I had a wonderful time."

"But you haven't decided whether I'm man or beast."

Oh, dear. That was exactly it. Or…was it?

"I think," she admitted, "it's more that I'm wondering what *I* am."

His gaze was all too perceptive. "I see." He cleared his throat. "Here's my suggestion. We slow it down a bit. I kiss you good-night, then go home. Tomorrow I'll call you, and we'll talk about how our day is going, and maybe I'll call again late in the evening, just because I'm going to want to. And then we'll plan dinner again. Uh…if that works for you."

Filled with relief—because he wasn't pushing her? Or was it because he hadn't lost patience with her?— she nodded. "That works. Thank you."

He said something under his breath, which she couldn't quite make out, and then his lips found hers. He kissed her so softly a wondering breath was trapped in her throat. Their mouths brushed, pressed, nibbled. The moment was indescribably sweet. He sucked gently on her lower lip, and that breath escaped in a long sigh.

Bruce lifted his head and looked down at her. After a moment, he raised his hand, grazed his knuckle over her cheek, touched a fingertip to her mouth, then murmured, "Good night," and left her still standing stunned on her doorstep.

He was gone before she could whisper, "Stay."

CHAPTER SEVEN

BRUCE LAY IN BED and frowned at the ceiling. So, okay; he'd managed to kiss Karin gently and with finesse. The kiss had lasted maybe one minute, tops. If it had gone on for one more minute, that finesse would have been history. He'd had to make his escape before he lost control. He wanted her with a clawing need different from anything he'd ever felt before, a need that still had him aroused an hour later.

She got under his skin. If he could lose every remnant of control the way he did when they made love, what would happen if he lost his temper with her?

Unfortunately, he knew. He'd grown up seeing what he could become. With the combination of genes and environment, what he *would* become.

They'd had some great sex. If he had any sense at all, he would be satisfied with that and start running the other way, not woo her with dates. He'd decided long ago he wasn't husband and father material, not unless he wanted to follow in his father's footsteps. And, God—did he *want* to live day in and day out with this edgy feeling of obsession? He didn't like that she was in the back of his mind all the time, that he constantly wondered what she was doing, what she'd think about this, what she'd say about that. And this restless, prickling, violent need for her—that would drive him insane.

Do not walk. Run.

But even before he fell asleep, he knew he wouldn't. Couldn't.

SINCE TREVOR HAD BEEN so uncommunicative, on Friday Bruce called the social worker for an update. He sat in the squad room, his feet on the desk, chair leaning back precariously. Molly was late, having announced her intention to stop at Caffe Ladro for decent coffee on the way in. Bruce had given her his order.

"I just spoke with Trevor's father," Ms. Connelly told him. "Mr. DeShon is back in the Seattle area and eager to have his son. So that's good news."

Anger knifed him, and his chair squealed as he sat upright, his feet hitting the floor. Good news? What the hell was she doing in this job if she was really that naive? Or was she just glad to get one kid out of her hair?

Unclenching his jaw, Bruce said, "You are aware that Trevor's mother had to get a restraining order to keep Mr. DeShon from terrorizing her and Trevor?"

After a small hesitation, the social worker said, "I was informed there'd been allegations of abuse."

"Allegations?" Bruce didn't even try to keep the incredulity out of his voice. "How about multiple hospital visits."

"But I understand that Mr. DeShon never abused his son."

"Because MaryBeth sent Trevor to hide in his bedroom when his dad came home drunk and in a rage. She offered herself as a target to keep her kid safe."

"Mr. DeShon freely admits that he had an alcohol problem, but he has completed a treatment program and attends AA meetings twice a week. According to him— and he says his mentor in AA will confirm—he has been sober for two years now. He also completed an anger-management class. I believe that he was devastated to lose his family, particularly his son. Everyone deserves a second chance."

"Leopards don't change their spots," Bruce said flatly. "Once an abuser, always an abuser."

"According to police reports and his own story, he was always drunk when he hit his wife. If he stays sober…"

He snorted. "What are the chances of that?"

Her voice chilled. "Trevor deserves to have one of his parents. Clearly, that won't be his mother. And frankly, given his age I don't envision a better alternative for him. Do you?"

After a silent litany of swearing, he forced himself to admit she was right. What *was* the alternative? There weren't enough caring foster parents. Odds were high Trev would end up with the other kind, the ones who took kids in for the money paid by the state or who abused the kids in turn. Wade DeShon *had* worked at maintaining contact with his son. If the alleged two years' sobriety wasn't a scam, he deserved some real credit for it.

"Unfortunately, no."

"It's really important that you encourage Trevor to give his father a chance."

That stung. Was he supposed to lie to the boy? But again—he knew what she was getting at, and she was right.

"Okay," Bruce conceded. "But I'll be watching like a hawk. If DeShon screws up once, he's not getting another chance."

"People do make mistakes."

"He's made his. He's used up any possible excuses."

She wasn't thrilled with him by the end of the call, but he didn't care. His gut was churning. Wade DeShon was getting his kid back, and MaryBeth wouldn't be there to stand between them.

Trevor didn't know yet, and Ms. Connelly had warned Bruce off. She wanted to talk to him first herself. He had to respect her insistence.

Instead of hitting the road, Bruce spent most of the day on the phone and the Internet. He was becoming more convinced that Roberto Escobar had left the area. Bruce had laid out a map and calculated distances and routes. If Escobar was smart—and his successful disappearance with the kids suggested he was—he'd make sure he went somewhere he could blend in. In other words, someplace with a substantial Hispanic population. Yakima and Walla Walla qualified, but he'd know that Lenora's sister and husband followed the harvests in eastern Washington. He'd probably have met their friends and the husband's extended family. Roberto would want to avoid them.

Bruce's finger moved down the map, touching on one town after another in Oregon, then on into California. Escobar could vanish in Southern California, but getting there was the problem. Would the car make it? Traveling with two young children and no woman, he might be conspicuous. Where would they sleep and shop and eat on the way?

Bruce made phone calls to every jurisdiction he could think of, extracting promises to check the records of cheap motels, talk to gas station attendants, watch for that blue Buick. When he got hoarse, he turned to e-mail, sending photos and Escobar's license-plate number.

Then he repeated many of the same phone calls he'd made the other day in the hope of locating MaryBeth DeShon. No go. He couldn't believe she'd left the area. No, she wouldn't consciously abandon her son. It could be that her body just hadn't been found yet, or she hadn't been identified. Bruce was still betting on option three, the drug-induced stupor.

Goddamn it, MaryBeth, he thought, *Trevor needs you. Where are you?*

He called Karin midafternoon and had a brief, unsatisfactory conversation with her. No news on my end, he told her. No news on hers. She had only five minutes between clients, and he sensed her distraction. The call was…awkward.

It all added up to a worthless day.

Walking out to their cars at the end, Molly asked, "Is this one getting to you?"

He almost said, *Yeah, she's getting to me,* when he

realized his partner was asking about the case, not Karin. She had no idea he was dating anyone special right now, far less someone intimately involved in the current investigation.

"Ah…I guess so," he admitted. "You know I never like these domestic ones."

She slanted a knowing glance at him. "You seem worse than usual."

"I took it personally."

Her shrug eloquently conveyed her skepticism. *Maybe, but I don't believe that's the whole story.*

He hadn't told her about his talk with the social worker. Now he did, successfully distracting her. She'd hung out with him and Trev a couple of times. Like him, she had trouble believing a slug like DeShon was capable of living up to good intentions, however sincere.

Karin had been evasive when he'd asked if she was busy tonight. He wasn't enthusiastic about the idea of more fast food and an empty house, and stopping by the hospital ostensibly to check up on Lenora would smack of stalking. He phoned the receiving home and got permission, instead, to take Trevor out for pizza and a movie.

A group of boys watched TV in the living room, and the woman who let him in seemed okay. She yelled for Trevor, and when he didn't appear went upstairs to get him. Bruce had the distinct impression she'd had to drag the kid downstairs by his scruff.

"Have a good time," she said, enough sympathy in her voice that he figured Trevor had gotten lucky with this placement.

On the way out to the car, he asked, "You talk to Ms. Connelly?"

The boy gave him a look seething with misery and fear. "She said I have to live with my dad! Mom didn't even like him *calling.*"

Bruce unlocked his car. "That's true. But he's made a lot of effort so he'd get a chance to see you again."

"You sound like *her,*" Trevor said with loathing, and flung himself into the car.

Well. They were off to a good start.

Buckling himself in, Bruce asked, "When's he coming to get you?"

"Tomorrow!" Anguish filled his big brown eyes. "Can't I please stay with you, instead? I'm okay alone! You know I am!"

Hating himself, Bruce shook his head. "I told you why it wouldn't work. Besides, I don't think they'd let me take you now. Parents have first rights. Unless your dad screws up, Ms. Connelly won't consider other options."

"You mean, if he hits me."

Yeah. That was what he meant.

"Or," Bruce added, "doesn't live up to his job as a parent in other ways."

The boy's forehead wrinkled. "Like?"

"He doesn't come home when he promises you he will. Gets drunk a lot. Doesn't make sure you eat right or do your homework."

Trevor hunched and didn't say anything. They were both painfully aware that Bruce could be talking about MaryBeth as much as Wade.

"Pizza?" Bruce asked, starting the car.

Trevor's shoulders jerked.

Pizza it was.

Bruce tried talking to him some more while they ate, suggesting that living with his dad might not be all bad.

"I'm told he has a good job now," he said. "He might have a nice place."

Trevor gave him a look that said more clearly than words that he didn't care. Bruce suspected that indifference wouldn't survive if Dad turned out to own a big-screen TV and a Nintendo. An iPod for Christmas would go a long way toward softening any thirteen-year-old's heart. And Trev would be thirteen by then, officially a teenager.

"Hey, at least you'll be going to a new school. No Jackson at your bus stop."

Trevor's expression lightened. Bruce didn't mention that there were bullies everywhere.

They saw an idiotic action-adventure film that would have bored Bruce into somnolence if he hadn't seen how engaged Trevor was. His mom hadn't often had the money for movies. Bruce had taken Trevor a few times, but had preferred spending their time together playing sports, going places like the science center or talking.

On the drive back to the receiving home, Trevor chattered at first about the movie, only falling silent as they got close. When Bruce pulled up to the curb, the boy turned to him and spoke fast. "Please. Please ask if I can come live with you. You're a cop and everything! I bet they'd say yes." He swallowed. He finished with one soft, hopeless "Please."

God. Bruce's hands flexed on the steering wheel. "I'm sorry."

With a strangled sob, Trevor fumbled for the seat-belt fastening and then the door handle. He flew up the driveway without waiting for Bruce, flung open the door and disappeared inside. Bruce followed more slowly, exchanged a few words with the foster mom, then left.

He got back in to his car and sat there for a long time, feeling like a low form of life. He wanted to believe that it meant something to Trev that he'd come tonight, spent time with him, listened to his unhappiness, but he couldn't believe it. All he'd done was once again let down a boy who'd known a lifetime of letdowns.

Jaw flexed, he thought, By God, if Wade DeShon so much as raised a hand toward Trev…

You'll what? Ride to the rescue? Just like you did this time? his inner voice mocked. *Face it. You can't be trusted any more than his father can.*

Knowing he'd done the right thing was cold comfort.

ON FRIDAY Karin realized that Lenora's coma was becoming noticeably lighter; her hands or legs jerked more, her eyelids fluttered frequently and occasionally she moaned or murmured. A couple of days ago, Karin was still talking as much to herself as to the unresponsive woman in the bed. She would unwind from her day by telling stories from her childhood or recounting snippets she'd read in the newspaper. Now…now she hung on every twitch, felt her anxiety ratchet at every mumble. Were Lenora's eyes about to open? Would *she* be in there? Or only some damaged semblance of herself?

The possibilities covered a wide spectrum. She might never regain consciousness at all. She might begin to have seizures and worsen. She might open her eyes but be severely brain damaged. The likelihood was that she'd have suffered at least some brain damage.

Or she might open her eyes, look around with panic and disorientation and then remember.

Lenora was both praying for and dreading the last possibility.

She gave up at last and went home to her empty house. She never used to think of her house that way. She'd always been glad to be home, comforted by the surroundings she'd created, anticipating the hour she meant to spend in her garden the next morning. Now the emptiness was the first thing that hit her when she walked in the front door. How had that happened?

She knew, but didn't want to think about it.

Her voice-mail box was as empty as the house. She felt a little lurch of disappointment. Hadn't Bruce said he'd call at the end of the day "just because he'd want to"? Had he called and not bothered to leave a message? Or had he been busy and not even thought about her this evening?

Which would she prefer to be the truth?

Karin kept listening for the phone even as she brushed her teeth and got ready for bed, but it never rang. She was dismayed to realize how much she wanted to hear his voice.

He finally did call at lunchtime the next day, other voices audible in the background. She was working her one Saturday a month. "Dinner tonight?"

"Sure." She hesitated, then said, "Why don't I cook."

Moment of silence. "Are you sure you want to after a long day?"

"I made a vegetarian chili last weekend and froze it. I'll warm it up, make a salad, some corn bread…"

"Sold."

They agreed on a time, exchanged a few "no news" remarks and said goodbye. Karin set down the phone, aware of her uneven heartbeat and the flush that seemed to be spreading from her chest out. She knew the cause: it was the way his voice had deepened and become more resonant when she suggested they eat at her place. He thought the invitation meant more than a simple meal. And maybe, Karin admitted to herself, it did. She'd offered on impulse, but knew perfectly well that impulses had roots that plunged deep. She wouldn't have invited him into her home again if she hadn't wanted him here, with all that encompassed.

Karin loved her job, but this was the rare day when she'd had to force herself to listen carefully and give her best. A part of her had pulled away and was giddy with anticipation, like a teenager daydreaming in class.

At home, she had time to change into jeans and a T-shirt and get the corn bread in the oven before she heard the doorbell.

Bruce looked as good as he always did to her. Not just sexy and a little dangerous, but also *solid*. Some of that was physical—he was big and strongly built, and she'd known from the first time she saw him that he would defend not just her but anyone he deemed vulnerable, with his life if necessary. But she knew just as surely that he could be depended on. He wasn't a man who'd ever let anyone down if he could help it.

In the end, that quality meant more than broad shoulders or a smile that jolted her heart.

Like the one he was giving her now. He was drinking in the sight of her face as if he'd been hungering for it. Once again, she could tell he was tired, but his smile changed the deep-carved lines, lessening the weariness and depression she sensed.

"Hey," she said, and rose on tiptoe to meet his quick, hard kiss as if her response was a given. And wasn't it? They'd become lovers, after all, however queasy she still was about that first time.

She hung up his coat and he followed her to the kitchen, where she refused his offer to help, then changed her mind to the extent of letting him uncork the wine and pour them both glasses. He watched her start the chili heating, then begin chopping vegetables for the salad.

They talked about Lenora, and he told her about some of the leads he'd pursued. After newspaper coverage, both the Seattle PD and the FBI had been inundated with tips, none of which had panned out. He'd located another of Roberto's supposed friends, only to be received with surprise.

"Says he hasn't seen Escobar in a year or more," Bruce said.

"And you believed him?"

"Yeah, I do. I had the feeling he hardly remembered the guy." He rubbed a hand over his face. "I was able to confirm that another guy on my list was deported a couple of months ago."

"Do you think…" She bit her lip, hating to articulate her worst fear.

"That they're dead?"

Karin nodded.

"No. If he'd intended to do it, he'd have killed the kids and himself that night. He'd have made it splashy." Bruce grimaced. "Sorry. Bad choice of words. But you get what I mean. He'd have wanted everyone to know. The more I learn about our Roberto, the more convinced I am that he believes he's completely justified in everything he's done. He's undoubtedly angry that his life has been inconvenienced. With no remorse, he has no motive for suicide."

What he didn't say, but they both knew, was that Roberto might well have motive to kill the children.

Be good for your daddy, Karin thought, her heart clenched in fear for Anna and Enrico. *Very, very good.*

Carrying the salad to the table, she asked, "Have you talked to Trevor?"

The boy's name was enough to change Bruce's expression. Apparently his Little Brother was the source of the unhappiness she'd sensed.

He set the wine bottle on the table. "Yeah. God." Anger vibrated in his voice. "The DSHS worker contacted his father. They're convinced, since he completed an anger-management class and alcohol treatment, that he's ready to be a great dad. Never mind that Trevor's scared to death of him."

Karin hesitated, choosing her words with care. This conversation was important; dinner could wait. "You don't believe it's possible he's changed?"

"Do you?" he asked incredulously.

"I don't know him."

"You'd never met Escobar, either."

"But I knew him through his wife's eyes. Her view was more sympathetic than you'd expect. For a long time, she was an apologist. Everything was her fault. He had a right." She waggled her hands. "You know."

"Trevor's mother didn't think Wade had a right. She put up with his abuse as long as she did out of fear of being on her own with a kid. She'd have done anything to protect Trev from his father."

"My point, I guess, is that some people *can* change. There's a wide gulf between someone like Roberto, who is incapable of what we consider normal human emotions or empathy, and someone who lashes out in anger because of depression or despair. Alcohol abuse plays a big part in that. So yes, I do believe some people can change. Why would I be in the profession I am if I didn't?" She held up a hand when she saw his expression. "No, I'm not saying Trevor's father is one of those people. I *don't* know him. But if his dad is genuinely trying, is it possible that Trevor's better off with him than he would be in a foster home?"

Bruce scowled at her. "I can't decide if I like your

relentless determination to be fair-minded and logical, or whether I really hate it."

Her mouth curved. "You must like it, or you wouldn't be here."

"Maybe I'm here because I think you're sexy."

She gave him a saucy smile. "That's okay, too."

She fetched the pot of chili and the bread, and then they sat down. As they ate, Bruce talked some more about Trevor: his unhappiness, how much he must be worrying about his mother, his renewed pleas and obvious feeling of betrayal that Bruce couldn't take him in.

"I felt like scum last night after I dropped him off."

"You should have called me." She flushed. "I mean, unless you had someone else you could talk to."

His focus on her was absolute. "No. I just went home. It was pretty late."

Tilting her head, Karin observed, "You really love him, don't you?"

"Love?" His dark eyebrows rose. "That's a strong word. I don't know that I've 'loved' anyone since I was a kid and still bought into the idea that's how you should feel about your parents."

Karin could only gape. "How can you never have loved anyone? Haven't you been *in* love? What about your friends? Don't you call that love?"

His face, formerly expressive, had become impassive. "I hadn't thought of friendships quite that way, no. There've been women, but nobody that serious. I made up my mind by the time I was ten years old that I wouldn't ever marry. I never wanted to have the right to rule and terrorize and hurt the way my father believed he did."

Never marry? Karin struggled to hide her shock. Did that mean she would be a fool to fall in love with *him?* Or a worse fool if she already had?

Thank goodness her work as a therapist had given her plenty of experience in hiding dismay and, instead, asking reasoned questions.

"You've surely met people since who are in happy marriages, starting with the police officer who was your mentor."

"Yeah, I have. But I'm too much like my father." He paused, turning the wineglass in his hand, his expression bleak. "I look like him. I could *be* him at this age."

"Who you are inside has nothing to do with how you look."

"His genes made me," he said flatly.

Karin shook her head. "No. They're part of you. But if he'd been raised differently, would he have been the same man? What about Enrico? Do you believe he's destined to be like his father, no matter how he grows up?"

She saw that he didn't.

"Or Trevor?" she continued, trying to sound merely persuasive and not desperate. How could he believe something so terrible about himself, discounting the day-to-day proof of what kind of man he really was? "You couldn't feel the way you do about him if you thought he was doomed to be a violent alcoholic."

"For both Trevor and Enrico, their mothers have had

a powerful influence. Mine was a victim. She never protected us kids. Far as she was concerned, he had a right."

Imagining the devastation of the boy he'd been almost broke Karin's heart. What was truly astonishing was how he *had* escaped his father's mold. The tragedy was that he'd done something so extraordinary, yet couldn't recognize he had.

"You are not your father," she repeated, having no idea what else she could say. How often would he have to hear it to believe it?

After a minute, his mouth twisted. "No. I know I'm not. I've spent a lifetime making damn sure I'm not. But I've also been careful to avoid putting myself in a spot where the instinct is to repeat what I heard."

"Parenting."

"Exactly."

"Trevor knows in his heart he can trust you. It's sad that you doubt what he can see so easily."

He just looked at her, and she could tell he wasn't really hearing.

"Hey," he said. "I promised the caseworker I'd pretend to Trevor that this was a great idea, and I did. Wade DeShon will out himself quickly enough if he's still the same drunken son of a bitch. When that happens, he'd damn well better not hurt Trevor."

When. Not if.

Karin found herself hoping quite passionately that Trevor's dad truly had changed. Maybe his redemption would have some impact on Bruce's pigheaded determination to believe the past shaped him.

But she, too, worried that Trevor might end up hurt. Her chest felt tight at the thought of so many children so much at the mercy of parents they ought to be able to trust. Every day, she saw both women and children wounded by someone who had promised to love them.

In her own way, she had as many doubts as Bruce did. She didn't know if she could ever trust in something so fragile, so often shattered. Thinking about the near violence with which Bruce had taken her was enough again to awaken disquiet. Did it mean he had something of his father in him, despite her attempts to persuade him otherwise?

Karin didn't believe it. *Couldn't* believe it. Yet the unease she'd felt about him reawakened.

Man or beast? Wasn't that how he'd posed the question?

Karin was struck by a terrifying realization. She was attracted to both sides of him. She wanted to make love with him again, whichever he was.

What does that say about me?

"Let me help clear the table," he said.

"No." Her voice came out oddly. "Let's not bother right now."

He went very still, his eyes darkening. "After what I said about never marrying, I thought you'd boot me out right after dinner."

"Where did you get the idea *I* want to get married?"

Karin heard herself in astonishment. She did want to love forever; she'd always believed, with all her heart, that someday she would marry, and her marriage would last forever. But however powerful the dream, right now it meant nothing compared with her need to have this man hold her again, become *part* of her again.

His chair rocked as he stood. She wasn't even aware of rising, and yet somehow she and he met at the foot of the table, and kissed as if they had both been starved for each other.

CHAPTER EIGHT

THE SECOND SELF-DEFENSE workshop had a very different tone from the first. Bruce and Molly arrived early and stood, deliberately conspicuous, in positions to intercept anyone entering the parking lot besides the participants. Still, the women all scurried into the clinic, their body language fearful.

Inside, heads bent together, and Karin heard the murmurs.

"Were you still here…?"

"Have they caught him?"

"Someone told me…"

After Karin thanked them all for coming and Bruce had introduced his partner, he had the sense to tell them briefly, gravely, about the assault and about the murder of Lenora's aunt and abduction of Enrico and Anna. He was honest about the lack of progress in finding Roberto, about Lenora's coma, about fears for the children. That honesty seemed to reassure the women in a way that platitudes wouldn't have. Heads nodded, backs straightened, and Karin sensed the renewed determination to learn what he had to teach.

Molly Beckstead might as well have been a college student as a woman who was almost thirty. Her eyes were bright blue, she had a snub nose and dark hair and she couldn't have weighed more than a hundred and fifteen pounds. After being introduced, she apologized for missing the previous week's session and told them about her new niece.

She was still talking when Bruce grabbed her from behind. In a flurry of movements so blindingly fast Karin couldn't separate them, she had him flat on his back, one arm bent at an excruciating angle.

"Pax," he said, and she laughed and let him up.

He climbed to his feet with an exaggerated groan that delighted the participants.

Much of this session was spent with the women paired up, earnestly trying out the releases Bruce and Molly demonstrated.

Watching the women gain confidence as they succeeded in breaking even Bruce's grip filled Karin with triumph and a feeling of achievement. When Tonya, a shy eighteen-year-old who'd been raped, beaten and left for dead, swung around and planted a knee in Bruce's groin, then gasped and clapped her hand over her mouth as he crumpled to his knees, Karin stepped forward. But he mumbled something, Tonya giggled behind her hand, then beamed with shining satisfaction as the others laughed.

Instead of scurrying out the way they'd come, the women departed in a block, marching shoulder to shoulder as they escorted one another to their cars.

Perhaps being guarded by Molly and Bruce made them feel secure, but Karin suspected it was more: at least as a group, they felt courage they'd lost, and she actually had tears burn in her eyes as she watched them wordlessly work together to be sure they all got safely on their way home.

Afterward she went out with Bruce and Molly for coffee, and she had so much fun it was nearly midnight before she could tear herself away. She'd be tired tomorrow, but it was worth it. Molly, she thought, might become a friend, and Karin began to question all her reasons for not socializing with cops. With friends, she'd always preferred to escape the grim stories she heard all day, but laughing at a macabre yet also ludicrous tale Molly told of a man who was determined to rob a convenience store and died from sheer idiocy, it struck her how much she pretended with most people.

I'm a professional, she went out of her way to convey. *My days are like yours.* But her days *weren't* like a dentist's or a nurse's or a computer programmer's. They weren't like anyone else's she knew. Tonight, she'd felt herself relax in a way she usually couldn't. There was a freedom to being able to laugh without shame at a story that would have horrified most people.

Bruce gave her a quick kiss on the cheek when they parted at their cars. Karin saw Molly's startled and then speculative glance, and realized he hadn't told her he and Karin had a relationship. Weren't Molly and Bruce close enough friends to confide in each other? Or did he not consider it that important?

Karin rolled her eyes and fastened her seat belt. She was worse than a lovesick teenager, wondering whether he didn't really like her after all, or whether he was embarrassed to have it known he was dating her.

"You're a grown woman," she muttered, and turned the key in the ignition.

As the week went on, Karin talked to Bruce at least twice a day. They saw each other whenever they could, and it seemed impossible for her to get enough of him. She felt a cramp of longing at the very sight of him, and her body would soften and yearn in a way that should have embarrassed her but somehow didn't. As far as she could tell, he was as insatiable for her; whenever he spotted her, his gaze would find her face with a hungry intensity she understood.

It was scary to feel so much, to be so obsessed, about a man who'd told her bluntly that he'd never as an adult felt love for anyone and that he didn't intend ever to marry. Was what they had now all she could hope for? When she was with him, she thought it might be, but at night after he left and she'd gone to bed alone, she knew she was lying to herself. She wanted to be loved, and by a man as fully committed as she was. She wanted someone who would be beside her at night, across the breakfast table in the morning, not just ready to come when she needed him, but already *here,* part of every day.

With Monday night the exception, she did spend at least a little time every evening at Lenora's hospital bedside. Karin wasn't completely sure what drove her, but guilt was clearly part of the mix. She knew she wasn't really at fault. On one level, at least, she knew. If Roberto hadn't tracked his wife to the safe house— and how else had he found her that evening?—Cecilia was right when she said that the attack had been inevitable. At a different time and place, even more people might have been hurt. What if Cecilia had been walking right beside Lenora, for example?

But Karin finally understood why her patients were so slow to let go of unwarranted guilt. There were too many ways to blame yourself. *If I'd done that, thought of this, planned instead of proceeding thoughtlessly...* She could travel the twisted paths of second thoughts well into the night. Rationally, she was convinced that the assault wasn't her fault, but down deeper, she kept blaming herself.

And as Lenora became more restless day by day, Karin's incipient sense of doom deepened. She dreaded Lenora's waking, and dreaded the possibility that she wouldn't.

She tried talking to Jerlyn, one of the two remaining founders of the clinic. Now in her fifties, Jerlyn might have been an aging hippie, her dark hair graying and invariably worn in a braid wound atop her head, her feet shod in Birkenstocks or Earth Shoes, her skirts from India, the necklaces and long, dangling earrings she liked African or Indonesian. Jerlyn's gentle face hid a sharp mind and a heart filled with compassion.

What was disturbing was how little good the talk did Karin. She'd counseled too many women herself, and she recognized Jerlyn's strategies instantly, understood the tenor of her questions, knew what answers were expected. She found herself feeling sulky and then resistant. She wanted to say, *Can't you talk to me as a friend instead of a therapist?* To see how ingrained that style of relating to people was in a woman she'd viewed as a mentor stung a little. Did she do that to people, too? She remembered Bruce asking once whether her "hmm" was the counselor speaking or the woman, and winced.

Thursday, Bruce called to inform her that he and Molly had "caught" another homicide. The powers-that-be thought the trail was cold on the Escobar investigation. And after all, the FBI was working the abduction of the children, as well.

Her heart sank. "You won't give up?"

"No. I'm just going to have less time to work on finding him." In the background someone spoke to him, and he muffled the phone. A minute later, he was back. "Got to go. But don't worry. Every department from Blaine to San Diego is watching for them. Sooner or later, someone will spot him."

Would they? she questioned bleakly, ending the call. Roberto and the children had seemingly vanished. Bruce's attention wasn't the only one that would be waning. Crimes happened every day. All police departments must be flooded with notices asking them to be on the watch. Inevitably, the most recent notices would be at the forefront of their minds. How easy for a Hispanic man and two small children to pass unnoticed at a season when migrant workers were traveling the West Coast.

She wanted to have faith, but that, too, was waning.

"CAN I GET A HOT DOG, Dad?" Trevor asked.

Both men, one on each side of him, turned their heads, but at the crack of a bat striking the ball looked back toward the field. The baseball shot outside the line, foul, and the momentary excitement in the crowd at SafeCo Field settled back to an anticipatory hum.

It was a nice day, only a few cumulus clouds visible, and the retractable roof of the stadium was open. This was the first Mariners game Bruce had made it to this season, but it wasn't baseball that had drawn him today; the sport on the field could have been curling for all he cared. Damn it, he'd intended to spend his Saturday with Karin. But he couldn't say no to this chance to assess for himself Wade DeShon's fitness to have his son.

Bruce had to admit it was decent of Wade to suggest he join Trevor and him at the game. Or maybe it was just smart. Bruce had no idea what Trevor had said about him, but Wade must be able to guess that Bruce wouldn't be enthusiastic about this father-son reunion.

When he picked them up, he'd been startled by their resemblance, for a moment not sure what to feel. He'd come simmering with hostility, but it was hard to hate a man with Trevor's face.

Bruce had always thought of Trevor as taking after his mother, since they were both brown-haired and slight, but the kid's features and hazel eyes were unquestionably his dad's. His father wasn't a big man, Bruce noticed, but he must be five foot nine or ten, so there was hope for Trev.

The two men had shaken hands warily, feigning cordiality for the twelve-year-old's sake. Trevor was really excited, not seeming to notice the way Bruce assessed Wade, or the way his dad stiffened.

Fortunately, the game had been a good one, tied up in the seventh inning at two runs each.

Now, settling back in his seat, Wade said with mock dismay, "You're hungry already?"

"Yeah!" Trevor claimed.

"A hot dog sounds good," Bruce said. "I'll go out with him. Time to visit the john."

Wade reached for his wallet.

"I'll get it," Bruce said.

The other man's jaw tightened, but after a minute he gave a clipped nod.

"You want us to bring you something?" Bruce asked.

"Ah, hell, if everyone else is having a dog…"

He put in his drink order, too, and Bruce and Trevor stepped over legs to the aisle. Walking up the stairs, Bruce laid a hand on the boy's shoulder. "How's it going with your dad?" he asked.

They'd talked a couple of times on the phone, but Trevor had mostly mumbled, "He's okay."

Now he said again, "He's okay," but with more animation, as if he meant it. "He's being really nice. He told me how bad he feels about what a jerk he was. That's not the word he used, but he said I shouldn't say what he did."

Bruce suppressed a grin. "Probably a good idea."

They used the bathroom, then got in line at the concession stand. Bruce persuaded Trevor to talk about his new school, which he really liked.

The boy scrunched up his face, adding with more typical pessimism, "So far."

Bruce laughed this time, and they carried their tray of drinks and bag of hot dogs back to their seats.

Wade offered to repay him; Bruce declined, even though he was a little embarrassed by the whole thing. It was a pissing contest, he knew damn well. All afternoon, these two adult men had been silently warring over who knew best what Trevor liked or wanted, and who would pay for it. The kid remained oblivious, thank God.

The Mariners pulled one more run out of the hat and won. Trevor admitted to being sick to his stomach by the time they walked out of the stadium to the car.

During the drive home, it seemed as if the conversation was all Wade and Trevor. They talked about a movie they'd rented last night, about homework, about stuff Trevor could do this summer.

Bruce forced himself to put in a word now and again, but got quieter and quieter without either of the other two noticing. His chest felt tight, and he finally identified what was wrong.

He was jealous. Trevor didn't need him anymore.

Didn't *think* he needed him, Bruce corrected himself. Wade had yet to prove himself. Putting on a good front for a few days, a week, was easy. Whether he'd stay such a good guy once the novelty of parenting wore off was another matter. Trevor could be a butt; what kid wasn't sometimes? Would a man whose habit was to express his frustration with his fists be able to respond appropriately?

Bruce would believe it when he saw it.

Yeah, he thought. Trevor would still need him, even if he didn't know it yet.

"Good game," he agreed, letting them out in front of the small, white-frame house in Ballard that was now home to a boy who'd never lived in a real house before. He lightly cuffed Trevor on the shoulder and said, "Talk to you soon," then accepted Wade's hand for a shake.

Their eyes met and held. "You be good to him," Bruce said.

"Count on it," Trevor's father told him.

Real quiet, so the boy didn't hear, Bruce said, "I plan to make sure of it."

Damned if he didn't enjoy the flare of anger he saw on Wade's face, as if in provoking it, he himself had somehow won.

Trevor bounced impatiently on the sidewalk. "Come *on,* Dad!"

Eyes narrowed, Wade murmured, "Watch me," and got out.

Bruce did, as the two walked up to the front door, talking and laughing all the way. His fingers tightened on the steering wheel and his stomach roiled.

Shouldn't have eaten the hot dogs.

At last, he made himself put the car in gear.

Oh, yeah, he'd be watching.

TUESDAY MORNING, Susan put the call through to Karin when she was between patients. "A Yolanda Muñoz," she said.

Karin's heart skipped a beat. Lenora's sister had never phoned her at A Woman's Hand. Something had changed. She pushed the button for line one. "Yolanda?"

The woman's voice was charged with excitement. "Lenora—she's awake! Still confused, but she knows who I am!"

"What does the doctor say?"

"He thinks it's a miracle." She was clearly giddy. "The way they all shook their heads, I knew they thought she would die. But she's made them all wrong."

"Thank God," Karin whispered.

"Yes. I've prayed and prayed. He saved her, because Anna and Enrico need her."

Karin bit her lip so hard she tasted blood. "Have you told her…?"

After a long silence, Yolanda returned a subdued "She hasn't asked yet. It just happened. I left Imelda with her so I could call you."

Imelda was her oldest, a plump, sweet girl of fourteen.

More haltingly, Yolanda said, "I was hoping…I thought, if you were here…"

"I have one more client to see, then I'll leave. I should be there in an hour and a half."

"An hour and a half? That should be all right. The doctor wants to examine her. I won't let her ask until you're here."

Karin wanted with all her heart not to be there when Lenora found out that her husband had murdered her aunt and taken the children. But she wasn't quite coward enough to find an excuse. And it wasn't as if she didn't talk every day with distraught women about the most traumatic of subjects.

Still, this was different. She'd actually seen the attack. It had happened on her watch, so to speak. No matter how hard she'd tried, she hadn't quite convinced herself that she didn't share some blame.

Not sure if anyone else would think to call Bruce, as the investigating officer, immediately, she did.

"I only have a minute," she said when he answered his cell phone. "I just heard from Yolanda Muñoz. Lenora woke up."

"My God. Is she talking?"

"Uh…" Karin reviewed the conversation in her mind. "I don't know. Yolanda said she recognized her, and that the doctor was doing an exam. She said Lenora was still confused."

"Are you going over to the hospital?"

"At five."

"We'll want to interview her as soon as possible. I can't get away yet. Can you phone me once you've seen her?"

She promised she would, and then had Susan send her last client of the day in. Fortunately, Lila Wang didn't require great concentration. A pretty Asian woman who had been emotionally abused by a boyfriend, she was upbeat about a new job, and only slightly apprehensive about the move to San Francisco that it would entail. Karin was able to reassure her that she was ready. The time when Lila had needed her was past, to both their satisfaction, although Karin always felt a pang at this moment, as if she were a parent releasing a child to the world.

She walked Lila out and they hugged, Lila promising to phone once she was settled to let Karin know how she was doing.

The moment the woman was out the door, Karin snatched up her purse, gave a hurried explanation to Jerlyn, who'd emerged from her office, and rushed to her car.

Relatives crowded around Lenora's bed at the hospital. All were in a state of high emotion, exclaiming in Spanish over the top of one another and so fast that Karin, who did speak the language, could barely pick out a few words. On the edge of the crowd, Yolanda was wiping tears from her cheeks.

A nurse, who'd hurried in right in front of Karin, said firmly, "Please! Only two visitors at a time!"

Nobody paid her any attention. Yolanda did spot Karin, though, and her face lit with relief.

"*¡La médica està aquí!*" She flapped her hands and shooed the cluster of children and adults back from the bed, telling them to let Karin through.

Lenora lay against the pillows, face wan, distress seeming to ooze from her, and yet the return of life had changed her features to someone Karin was intensely grateful to recognize.

Tears burning the back of her eyes, she stepped to the edge of the bed and carefully took Lenora's hand. "I'm so glad to see you awake."

The dark eyes examined her, the bewilderment in them heartbreaking. For a moment Karin was certain she didn't recognize her, but at last her forehead crinkled and she murmured, a mere breath of air, "Karin?"

"Yes." Karin swallowed. "We've been so worried about you."

"I don't understand." Her gaze wandered to the nurse, and from face to face in the crowd of relatives Yolanda had herded to the foot of the bed.

"You were hit in the head." She hesitated. "Do you remember?"

Lenora shook her head.

Karin looked an appeal to Lenora's sister, who stayed back but said, "She wants to know where Roberto is."

Oh, Lord. She didn't even remember fleeing to the safe house?

Karin pressed her hand. "You left Roberto," she said bluntly. "You saved money for weeks so you'd have enough to get by for a while."

The dark eyes stared at her without comprehension. "Anna? Enrico?"

Karin drew a deep breath, and made a decision. "They're with Roberto."

"Oh." Something like relief relaxed her face. On some level, she had been anxious about their absence. But it seemed too soon to tell her that her husband was the one who had hurt her and had stolen her children.

"Why don't we let you rest," Karin murmured.

"Yes," she whispered, peering uncertainly again at the faces staring back at her, as if she didn't understand quite who they were or why they were there.

Her uncle was present, Karin saw, out of the corner of her eye, his face heavily lined with grief, but he'd had the sense not to say anything about his wife or Lenora's children. As much as Lenora *did* grasp, she would soon enough wonder about her aunt Julia's absence and why Roberto didn't bring the children to visit her. But tomorrow, Karin thought, was time enough to stun her with the awful events she'd missed.

"You're going to be fine," she said, smiling, her vision blurred with tears. "Don't worry, Lenora. Everything will come back to you. Don't hurry it."

A tiny nod, and it seemed to her that the small dark-haired woman allowed herself to relax. Her eyes drifted shut.

Yolanda turned and fiercely flapped her hands again. The rest of the family dutifully filed out, followed by her and Karin. The nurse remained, her hand on Lenora's wrist as she checked her pulse.

"You don't think we should have told her?" Yolanda demanded the minute they were out in the hall.

"Not yet. You're right. She's still confused. I think it would be better if we let her recover a little before we distress her."

Or had she just taken the coward's way out?

Yolanda looked no more convinced than Karin felt. "What do I say if she asks for the children?"

"I don't believe we should lie to her," Karin said slowly. "When she gets insistent, then we'll have to tell her. For now, you can just say again that they're with Roberto."

Lenora's sister nodded, grudging. "You'll come again, *sí?*"

"*Sí*. First thing in the morning, before I go to work."

"That policeman—he'll want to talk to her, won't he?"

"Yes, but not until Lenora remembers what happened." She hoped; having a police officer loom over her bed, asking questions, would certainly mean that Lenora would have to be offered a far more complete explanation than she'd seemed to want tonight.

"Will you call him? Tell him he would upset her?"

Karin agreed, and left Yolanda to send the rest of the family home. She would remain, she insisted, in case Lenora needed someone familiar.

Karin discovered she had no cell-phone reception in the parking garage, so she drove out and found a spot on the street.

The phone rang barely once, Bruce answering so quickly she knew he'd been waiting for her call.

"How is she?"

She described the visit and admitted how much she hadn't wanted to tell Lenora what had really happened. "Should I have?" she asked, feeling pitiful.

"No." His answer was decisive. "There's no escaping it, but you'll know when the time is right. Why are you questioning yourself? You have good instincts."

"Thank you," Karin said meekly. "How's your new case going?"

He and Molly had squeezed out the time to do the self-defense workshop at A Woman's Hand last night, but both had been obviously distracted. Bruce had given Karin a quick kiss afterward, and had gone.

"We're about to make an arrest. That means I'll be tied up all night with booking and reports." He paused. "I'd rather be with you."

A little shakily, she said, "I'd like to be with you, too. But I'm fine. It's good that you've caught the bad guy."

"I do occasionally." He sounded wry. "This was a drug-dealer turf war. No real victims. I'd rather catch Escobar."

"You will."

"I've got to go."

"Okay." The words *I love you* crowded her tongue, shocking her a little. They had come so close to escaping, as if they were something she said often, as commonly as goodbye.

What would he have said in return? she wondered.

"If I get a minute, I'll call you later," he said.

Pressing End and restoring her cell phone to her purse, Karin asked herself if that was the closest he would ever come to telling her he loved her. It was a way of saying that he cared, she supposed. Cold comfort.

What would happen when she let the words slip, as she inevitably must?

Of course she knew. That would send him running. After all, he'd warned her. He didn't fall in love, and he never intended to marry.

Making no effort to put her car in gear, Karin sat with her head resting back, her eyes closed.

I'm a fool, she thought unhappily. She should tell him and get it over with.

Sooner rather than later.

CHAPTER NINE

BRUCE WALKED into Lenora Escobar's hospital room on Thursday to find Karin was there before him. The curtains rattled as he pushed them aside.

Karin, sitting on the far side of the bed, gave him the quick smile that warmed someplace deep inside him. As always, she was beautiful, her corn-silk hair bundled up carelessly, baring the graceful length of her neck. She wore only gold hoops in her ears and a simple white tee that was almost, but not quite, an off-the-shoulder style. Even her collarbone was sexy to him.

He nodded back, then turned his attention to the other woman. Two days had passed since Lenora had opened her eyes and spoken to her sister. This morning, finally, her questions about her children had become so insistent Yolanda had begged Karin to be the one to tell Lenora the entire story.

"Hi, Lenora. I don't know if you remember me."

With the bed cranked to its highest setting, she sat nearly upright, wearing some kind of pink chenille robe that couldn't be hospital issue. Her head was still wrapped in a stiff white casing, but her face was unmarked by the trauma to the back of her head. He pictured her from that first workshop, a pretty, too-thin woman who'd then had a wealth of dark hair, presumably now shaved off.

She studied him with uncomfortable intensity. "I don't exactly remember, but… Maybe a little. I know your face." She glanced at Karin, then back at him. "Karin told me you led that class."

"Yes." He stood, his hands loosely wrapped around the top bar of the bed railing. "I wish it had done you some good."

She shook her head. "Roberto—he could be so mean. When he used to hit me, I never had time to duck. He was fast." Her hand lifted and jerked, an unnerving mimicry.

"Do you recall leaving him?"

Another shake. "I remember putting money away. I liked looking at him and planning how I was going to take the children and go."

"Karin's told you what Roberto did."

Grief suffused her face. "He killed Aunt Julia. She was like my mother. And…" Her voice faltered. "Anna and Enrico. He has them."

"He killed her to get them."

"He always said he wouldn't let me go." Her voice was duller now; she rolled her head against the pillow to speak to Karin. "You warned me not to tell him I was going. You said if I had someone with me, he'd hurt that person, too."

Surprised, Karin exclaimed, "I said that only a couple of days before you did take the kids and leave him."

Her forehead creased. "Then why don't I remember?"

"It's common," Bruce told her, "for someone who has a head injury like you do to have blocked out everything leading up to the trauma. It may be that part of you does remember. Deep inside, you know that the day you left him was the beginning."

"If I'd stayed…"

"Sooner or later, he was going to hurt you just as bad," Karin said firmly.

"I was afraid…" she whispered.

"That he'd hurt the children, too."

"Yes." She was now frantic, and her gaze swung back to Bruce. "Why can't you find them? He can't take care of Enrico and Anna!"

"I'm hoping you can give us some ideas about where he might have gone."

"I don't know! How can I?"

Karin leaned forward and laid a gentle hand on Lenora's. "You know him, Lenora. Detective Walker just hopes you can tell him about Roberto's friends, maybe places he's been."

"I understand his mother recently returned to Mexico," Bruce said. "Do you think he would take the kids and follow her?"

"I don't know! He was angry at her for going back. And his mother—she'd ask where I am."

"We've contacted police in Chiapas. They've talked to her and to her other son. Roberto's brother," he said in an aside for Karin's benefit, "has promised to phone if they hear from him." The officer with whom Bruce had spoken wasn't sure the mother would betray Roberto, but the brother seemed to be angry with him.

"He always said how much better it was here." Lenora moved fretfully. "I don't think he would want to go back to Mexico."

"Did he ever follow the harvests, like your sister and her family?"

"No. When he first came to this country, Roberto worked building houses. He was always good at building. He could make more money doing that than he could picking apples or asparagus."

When coaxed, she told them that Roberto had stolen into the United States illegally, paying a coyote one thousand dollars to smuggle him inside a truck over the border. Roberto had lived in Los Angeles at first, but he didn't like it there, so he had gotten a ride with other immigrants north. He had stopped in Sacramento, then gone briefly to Idaho before ending up in Seattle, where he got his green card following an amnesty offer.

"He always said he didn't like the other places. But sometimes he threatened to move us. He didn't like how much time I spent talking to Aunt Julia on the phone." Her face crumpled, and she whispered, "Is that why he killed her?"

Bruce wondered, too, picturing that day. Roberto had already hated his wife's aunt, and now the aunt had conspired to help Lenora escape him. She was trying to keep his children from him.

How Roberto thought was still more of a mystery to Bruce than he liked. Although filled with rage, Roberto had no ability to empathize or understand normal human emotions. He could hit his wife, then act as if nothing whatsoever had happened. Hot and cold. Which had he been when he'd murdered Julia Lopez? Fiercely glad to punish her for all the years in which she had, in his mind, encouraged Lenora to defy him? Or essentially oblivious to her existence as a human being? At that moment, had she been no more than an obstacle to him, one that needed eliminating?

"She had Enrico and Anna," Karin said simply. "She would never have let him take them if she could prevent it."

Lenora turned beseeching dark eyes on Karin. "Why was I so foolish? You said I shouldn't go near my family. I remember that. Why did I?"

Again, Karin squeezed her hand. "You wanted what was best for the kids. You told me they missed their aunt Julia and uncle Mateo. Staying close with family mattered. You thought they should know that some things hadn't changed."

"We should have gone away," she said dully. "As far away as we could. We should have gone before he could stop us."

"To leave and not be able to see your family— that's hard," Karin murmured. "You couldn't anticipate what he'd do."

"I always thought he'd kill me." Those eyes were haunted now. "I wanted to save Anna and Enrico. And now he has them."

She was too distraught to recall friends Roberto

might have had, or of any special places he might have talked about. She gave Bruce nothing new to work with. Seeing that he was only upsetting her, he told her to call him if anything occurred to her, and Karin walked with him into the hall.

They paused, out of earshot of the room behind them and the nurses' station ahead. "I'll try again later. When she calms down," Karin said.

"All right. Good. Call me if you come up with anything."

She nodded. "Did you ever find that friend he had at the lumberyard? Carlos?"

"Neither hide nor hair. My guess is, the last name at least was false, and he has new ID now. Stumbling over him may require pure luck."

"I wonder if Lenora will ever remember."

Aware of her distress, he touched her cheek. "It might be better if she doesn't."

"Yes. I suppose." She gave him a ghost of a smile. "Will you be by later?"

"Do you want to have dinner?"

"Mmm… Why don't I make something. I'm not sure I'm in the mood to go out."

"Would you rather I didn't come?"

He was startled when tears brimmed in her eyes just before she rose on tiptoe and kissed him quickly. "I would hate it if you didn't come," she said, her voice both fierce and a little desolate.

Two people emerged from a nearby room, and a nurse approached from the station. Bruce wanted to hold Karin, but after a glance at the other couple, who had begun a low-voiced conclave, he said only, "Then I'll be there."

That seemed to be enough; she nodded, and slipped back into Lenora's room.

He'd have hated it if she'd said tomorrow was fine. Walking away, he tried to figure out how he'd descended to this state, unable to get through a day without seeing her. No matter how good the sex was—and it was incredible—he knew damn well he'd be on her doorstep begging for her to let him in even if she'd taken a vow of celibacy. *She* drew him, body, mind and soul.

The common words people used to describe this powerful need crossed his mind, but he shoved them away. He couldn't deal with the implications. What he felt was an obsession, no more or less than the compulsion that gripped him when he was investigating a murder. At some point, he would be satisfied and ready to move on.

Until then…God help him, he couldn't get enough of her.

THIS SHOULD BE the slow season for murder in Seattle, but this past month Homicide was doing a brisk business for some reason. He and Molly had moved to the top of the list again, and within hours of him talking to Lenora in the hospital were called to a shooting that wasn't a mystery.

Two neighbors had been feuding for years, apparently; the last straw was when the victim let his dog, on the end of the leash, crap right in the middle of the neighbor's lawn, in plain sight of his front windows.

Then he petted the dog and started toward home. Walter Sims grabbed his handgun and roared out the front door, where after an exchange of "words"—described by yet another neighbor as a screaming match—he shot his neighbor of twenty-three years, Arthur Shearin.

After examining the body of the balding man, who had died wearing a worn white undershirt, ancient polyester slacks and bedroom slippers that exposed bony ankles, Molly and Bruce straightened and looked toward Sims, sitting in the back of a squad car. He had the downy white hair of a dandelion. She shook her head. "Wouldn't you think they were old enough to know better?"

Sims was in his late sixties, Shearin seventy-one according to their DMV records. Both were widowed. Maybe if their wives had lived, they'd have injected some sense in their husbands. Although Bruce had his doubts. It sounded as if the two men had reveled in their bitter relationship.

"Any next of kin?" he asked.

The uniform standing nearby said, "Woman two doors down says he has a daughter. She visited about once a week."

Sims had already been read his rights and sat unbowed in the back seat, his eyes ablaze with something like fanaticism when Bruce and Molly spoke with him.

"I had a restraining order against him," he snapped. "I had a right to defend myself when he trespassed."

"Sidewalks are city property," Molly observed. "Did he actually step into your yard?"

They knew from a witness that Shearin hadn't. What he'd done was stand on the sidewalk but allow the dog to go to the far length of the retractable leash to do his business on the velvety swath of lawn.

"I was supposed to turn a blind eye to his never-ending provocations? There's a law against harassment."

Bruce knew better than to think this cantankerous old man would ever feel remorse or even a twinge of self-doubt. Both of them, stubborn and filled with hate, had played their parts in a drama as inevitably tragic as *Othello* or *Hamlet*.

Once again, Bruce and Molly spent their day on booking, arraignment and reports. The worst part was visiting the daughter, once they found her name in a search of the home, to tell her that her only remaining parent had been shot dead by his next-door neighbor.

Finally, on Friday, Bruce was able to follow up on an idea that had come to him. Leaving Molly making phone calls on a cold case they'd never quite given up on, he went back to the lumberyard where Escobar had worked. Upon his arrival, the supervisor hurried from the back, appearing less than thrilled to be visited by the policeman again.

"A picture of Carlos Garcia?" His expression suggested that Bruce was crazy. "We wouldn't have any reason to have something like that."

"I'm hoping you can ask your employees. Someone might have brought a new digital camera into work and snapped pictures for the hell of it."

"Why would they have kept one of some guy who didn't even work here that long?"

"Because he was standing next to someone else?"

He grunted, then raised his voice. "Marge? Can you come here for a minute?"

Marge was the middle-aged cashier who, during Bruce's last visit, had recalled the friendship between the two men.

Entering the office, she said, "Detective Walker. Have you found those children yet?"

The *Seattle Times* had moved on to other stories now, but workers here must have pored over the front-page news about a crime that had awakened public sympathy because of the missing children.

"No, and that's why I'm back. I'd like to find any friends Roberto might have had."

"Didn't we tell you everything we knew about Carlos?" she asked, looking to the supervisor.

He shrugged. "He wants to know if we might have a picture of the guy."

"I think we do," she said, to both their surprise. "Not a very good one, because it was of all of us, but not that long ago I was noticing he was in it."

It turned out to have been taken as part of the business's fiftieth-anniversary celebration. All the employees had been lined up in front of a pile of lumber, a panel truck with the lumberyard name, logo and phone number parked beside them. An eight-by-ten, it had been framed and hung, forgotten and gathering dust, in the office.

Sure enough, when Bruce peered at it, he saw that next to Roberto was another Hispanic man, mustachioed, as well, of a similar age. He was a hand span taller, with a beaklike nose that might make him easily recognizable.

"May I borrow the picture?" Bruce requested. "I'll get it back to you."

"Sure, sure," the supervisor said. He'd stood beside Bruce, peering at it, as well, in some bemusement. "Can't believe I never noticed this, even after you were here asking about Roberto and Carlos."

Bruce went straight to a nearby photo shop, where he explained that he wanted a close-up of the two men only, and was told to come back in an hour. The nearest fast food was Kentucky Fried Chicken, where he ate and brooded.

A hunch was a funny thing. Why was his gut telling him that Carlos Garcia was the key? There were still a couple of other maybe friends of Escobar's whom he hadn't located, but he didn't feel the same urgency about them. He suspected it had something to do with Marge's observations being so astute. By God, if she'd imagined a bond between the two men, Bruce would put money on the fact that one existed. He'd told her today that if she ever wanted a change of career, she ought to apply to the Seattle PD. She'd laughed merrily, but he hadn't been altogether kidding. If more officers were anywhere near as observant as she was, there'd be less crime in the Emerald City.

But Bruce's gut instinct wasn't enough to justify calling on the newspapers to print the picture with an appeal to the public. Carlos Garcia, under any name, was no more than a person of potential interest. Realistically, if they did find him, he'd probably frown in perplexity and say, "Roberto Escobar? *Sí*, I worked with him, but I saw him only at the lumberyard."

Bruce was also reluctant to make Escobar feel cornered. He decided finally to distribute the photo to Hispanic grocery stores, community centers and medical clinics. Sympathy, he thought, would be with Lenora, not her husband. The biggest problem was that illegal immigrants were reluctant to come forward, especially given the recent federal crackdown and multiple deportations. Fear might keep silent people who'd like to help. But it was worth a try; a single call, saying, "I know that man," would make all the difference. And they'd be more likely to talk to him than to any federal agent.

He knocked off for the day without going back to the station because he was taking Trevor out for their usual pizza and maybe, with the lengthening daylight, to shoot some hoops. He hadn't gotten together with him since last week, when they'd gone to the Mariners game. Apparently, Dad was okay with the outing, because Trevor had dropped the phone and, after going off to consult him, had said, "Cool," in answer to the invitation.

After Bruce picked him up, they decided to shoot hoops at the local middle school before going out to eat. During the drive, and as they took turns dribbling the basketball along the paved exterior walkways to the hoops in back of the school, Bruce noticed that the boy was unusually quiet.

Bruce had asked once how things were going, and gotten the usual shrug and, "Okay."

He decided not to push it for now. They played one-on-one and then horse, with Bruce handicapping himself. The kid was developing a hell of an outside shot and not a bad layup, considering his height.

"I think you've suddenly grown," Bruce said. "At least an inch."

"You think?" Trevor asked eagerly.

"Your jeans are short."

They both gazed down at the exposed white sweat socks.

"Cool! Except I look like a geek."

He didn't sound as if he cared, not yet having expressed any interest in girls.

"I doubt your dad will mind buying you a couple of new pairs of jeans," Bruce said mildly.

Trevor's face closed and he shrugged, then began dribbling the ball in place, his head bent and his concentration absolute. He didn't want to talk about his dad.

Or else he did, and felt disloyal.

"You hungry?" Bruce asked.

"Yeah, I guess so."

"Why don't we head on back to the car, then."

The boy nodded and dribbled the way they'd come.

Bruce made a feint and stole the ball. "Hey!" Trevor cried, and raced after him, managing to knock it away. By the time they reached the car, they were both breathless and laughing.

They played some arcade games while they waited for their pizza. Not until they were eating did Bruce say, in a neutral tone, "I'm guessing your dad did something that upset you."

After a quick, startled glance, Trevor hunched his shoulders. "Maybe."

"You want to tell me about it?"

He took a piece of pizza and severed a strand of cheese. He took a bite, apparently not intending to answer at all. Finally, he mumbled, "It wasn't that bad."

Anger tightened in Bruce's chest. "It?"

Trevor poked at a congealing strand of cheese on his plate and said barely audibly, "He kinda got mad."

"At you?"

"I guess so." He spoke down to the plate. "Or maybe at Mom. I'm not sure."

"Mom?" What the hell? Bruce thought. Had Mary-Beth called or appeared and no one had told him?

"I was talking about her, and how much I miss her and stuff. You know?" Trevor risked a glance up. "And he grabbed her picture from me and threw it against the wall." Tears filled his eyes. "The glass broke, and the picture got ripped. And it was my favorite!"

That son of a bitch.

Bruce had remembered the framed photo. It was one of several MaryBeth had hung in the hall at their apartment. Most were Trevor's school pictures, and there were a couple of mother and son together. Bruce remembered one that included Wade, although it showed his back as he tossed a delighted Trevor, maybe five, up in the air. But the one of MaryBeth had been taken by a friend, she'd told Bruce, and in it she was laughing and startlingly pretty, free of the strain of financial worries and drug abuse that had later aged her face. For Trevor, the photo was irreplaceable, and by God he had so little to treasure.

Tamping down his fury, determined not to frighten Trevor, Bruce asked, "Has your dad been drinking?"

Trevor sniffed, swiped at his eyes with the hem of his T-shirt and shook his head. "Uh-uh."

"Did he talk to you about why he broke the picture?"

"He came in after I went to bed and said he was sorry and he'd try to fix it. But I don't think he can."

"He didn't hit you?"

"Uh-uh. He just really scared me. It just made me remember how mad he used to get. That's why Mom didn't want me ever to see him again."

Bruce nodded, but made himself add, "Everyone gets mad sometimes, though. Don't you?"

"I would've liked to punch Jackson."

Bruce half laughed. "Yeah. I know what you mean."

"Did you ever punch anybody?"

"I got in fights a few times back when I was a kid."

"I bet you won, 'cuz you're strong."

"I wasn't then. I got beaten up pretty good when I was a freshman in high school." One of the worst days of his life, and he'd shut out the memory for years. "My father was angry at me because I lost the fight."

Seeing Trevor's interest, he wished he hadn't said that.

"But…you couldn't help it!" the boy protested.

"My father thought being a real man meant using your fists." *Pansy* and *coward* were the mildest things his father had called him.

Clear as day, Bruce recalled sitting at the kitchen

table quailing from his father, who bent over him with a flushed, furious face, yelling, "Haven't I taught you anything? You make me sick, boy."

Having his own father stare at him with disgust, as if he'd proved his worthlessness, had hurt more than his throbbing eye or bloody nose. And yet, even then, inside he'd rebelled. He hadn't had the courage to say, *You didn't teach me to fight. You taught me to get beat up and not cry about it,* but he'd wanted to. Oh, he'd wanted to.

"That's why you don't like my dad," Trevor surprised him by saying. "Right?"

Hole in one. But, remembering his promise to the caseworker, Bruce said, "I don't know your dad well enough yet to like him *or* to dislike him. We both need to give him a chance."

"He scared me," Trevor said again.

"I can tell." Bruce looked him in the eye. "Will you promise to tell me if he does again?"

Trevor hesitated, then nodded.

It wasn't quite a promise, but Bruce sensed it was as close as he'd get. Trevor hadn't been sure tonight whether he should tell Bruce about the incident with his mother's framed photo, and the why wasn't hard to figure out. Trevor might not want to admit it, but he knew in his heart that his mother was gone from his life. In his eyes, Bruce had rejected him. In contrast, his dad not only wanted him—he was being good to him. Of course he felt disloyal complaining about him.

Bruce drove Trevor home and walked him to the front door, managing a civil nod at Wade.

But back in his car, he let his anger swell and even fed it with his memory of some of the things MaryBeth had told him. Trevor hadn't been back with Wade for more than a couple of weeks, and the son of a bitch was already up to his old tricks.

Bruce's fingers curled around the steering wheel, making the plastic creak.

Let that bastard lift his hand to Trevor once—just once—and by God he'd be sorry he was ever born.

That's why you don't like my dad, right?

Yeah, kid, Bruce thought. *That's exactly why I don't like your dad.*

CHAPTER TEN

"You look like something's bothering you," Karin observed.

It was Sunday, and Bruce had stopped by shortly after she'd gotten home from a morning visit to Lenora, who would be in the hospital for some time yet. Karin hadn't expected him, and could tell immediately that something was wrong. But when her heart jumped and she asked if he'd learned anything about Roberto or the children, he shook his head.

"Had another false alarm yesterday. Cop up in Skagit County reported a man who met Escobar's description, heading into a grocery store with two young children. Girl's hair wasn't very well braided, her clothes mismatched. The little boy was sobbing. The guy didn't seem to be an experienced parent." Bruce shrugged. "But it wasn't him."

Karin had been outside when he arrived, intending to work in the garden, and they'd ended up sitting on the porch steps in the sun. Roses and clematis were coming into bloom, their leggy stems disguised by a tumble of perennials. She loved this time of year, but the garden wasn't having its usual soothing effect. She kept seeing Lenora's haunted eyes, and now watched Bruce, wondering what had disturbed him.

He was slow answering her observation that wasn't quite a question. When he did, it was by indirection. "I took Trevor out for pizza last night."

She nodded; she'd known Bruce's plans.

"Wade's true character is coming out. He had a temper tantrum the other day."

"Oh, no," Karin said softly. "That poor boy! What happened?"

"The way I understand it, Wade got jealous because Trevor was talking about his mother too much. Wade grabbed the picture of his mom that Trev was holding and smashed it against the wall. Shattered the glass and damaged the photo. Trevor was pretty freaked."

"He didn't hurt Trevor, though?"

"Not this time." Bruce's tone was flat, anger simmering beneath it.

"Um…are you sure Wade was jealous?"

Incredulous, he turned to stare at her. "What do you mean? What else could it be?"

"Well…" Was this a good idea? Not at all sure, Karin picked her words carefully. "Could he be mad at MaryBeth? That is her name?" She glanced at him for confirmation.

Bruce didn't seem to notice. "*He's* mad at *her?* She protected Trevor with her own body when Wade lived with them, and since then she's scraped to make a living and care for Trevor."

"Didn't he pay child support?"

"When he got himself together enough to offer, she refused his money. She was afraid that if she cashed the son of a bitch's checks, it would give him rights."

In genuine puzzlement, Karin said, "But from what you tell me, the cupboards were bare some of the time! Did she consider that by turning down the child support—child support he was legally required to pay, visitation or no visitation—she was depriving Trevor?"

"You think she should have sacrificed her kid so she didn't have to get food stamps?"

The way he looked at her, with something like contempt, annoyed Karin enough that she ignored her better judgment and insisted on making her point. "I'm saying that if it's true Wade got alcohol treatment and went to anger-management classes, pulled his life together and offered child support, maybe he deserved a chance to maintain some contact with his son. Would he have done any of that if he didn't care?"

"How many chances does a bastard who beats his wife deserve?"

Karin shook her head. "I don't blame MaryBeth for not wanting him back. But that's not the same thing as acknowledging they shared a child."

He snorted. "From what I hear, Wade didn't share a damn thing but sperm. He was a loser. MaryBeth cut her losses and figured Trevor was better off without him."

"But in the end, he did need his dad, didn't he?"

"God! After this latest display, you still think that?"

Karin finally did hesitate. "Bruce, are you listening

to me? I haven't met Wade, and I won't pretend to guess whether he's capable of being the father Trevor deserves. But I do think that MaryBeth let Trevor down, and I can understand why Wade might have gotten angry if Trevor was talking about her as though she walked on water. That wasn't the right way for him to handle the situation. He should have understood how much Trevor must miss his mother, no matter what problems she had. But the fact is, by letting her drug addiction win, she may have done as much damage to Trevor as his dad did with his alcohol addiction."

Abruptly, Bruce rose to his feet, stalked a couple of feet down the walkway and then swung back to face her, his eyes glittering and his body so tense she was reminded of a boxer balancing on the balls of his feet, waiting for his opponent to launch an attack. "Why are you so determined to view him through rose-colored glasses? You were quick enough to condemn Escobar."

"Why are you so quick to condemn Trevor's father?" Karin retorted.

"Quick? I've read the hospital records and police reports after he battered MaryBeth."

She felt as if she'd wandered into a hall of mirrors, except that the distorted images she was seeing were of Bruce rather than herself. Did she know him at all? She sat stiffly, gripping the painted steps as though to orient herself.

"Then you don't believe in reformation."

"I know his type." Voice and expression were unrelenting. "They don't change."

"People can learn to manage their anger…"

He made a rude sound. "Pop psychology. The classes are a joke."

Now *she* was getting mad. "Is everything I do pop psychology, too?"

"I didn't say that."

"You might as well have. What I'm telling *you* is that people who are sufficiently motivated are capable of change."

"And you call shattering the kid's favorite picture of his mother *change?*"

"It might be." She knew she sounded brittle, knew that argument was hopeless, but she couldn't seem to stop herself. "In classes, participants are taught that if their anger is boiling over, as a last resort they should vent it on an object rather than a person. That might have been what Wade was doing. He didn't hurt Trevor. It's not good that he scared him, but—"

"God almighty. Why am I wasting my time talking to you about this? Enjoy your fantasy world, lady." He swung around and walked away.

Stunned, she realized he was leaving, thinking he'd had the last word. He'd dismissed every word she said.

Karin jumped to her feet and chased after him, catching up to him as he reached his car at the curb. "Where are you going?"

He slapped the top of the car and swung back to face her. The metal rang out, making her jump.

"To talk to the son of a bitch and tell him that if he lays one hand on his son, he's got me to answer to."

She lifted her chin and met his furious eyes. "After which, he'll slug you and you'll slug him and then… What? You'll arrest him for assaulting a police officer and be sanctimonious because you were right about him all along?"

He raised his voice, making sure the whole neighborhood heard him. "You spend your days with women who've been raped or had the shit beaten out of them, and you still can't admit there are vicious men out there who shouldn't be allowed within a hundred miles of their families?"

It came to her then in an insight she felt dumb for not having had sooner. "You don't just think *he's* like your father. You think *all* men are."

"Don't psychoanalyze me." He leaned toward her, eyes narrow slits, teeth showing. "I don't have anything to do with this. It's about Wade DeShon, and your naive refusal to believe he's anything but a good man who screwed up once. No, oops. Five or six times. Or was it ten? But he's taken a few classes, so he must be born anew."

His sarcasm, snarled at her from inches away, made her even madder and erased her last semblance of good judgment.

She poked him in the chest. "You know what your problem is? You've been playing at being Trevor's daddy. You *want* Wade to fail so you can dash to the rescue again. But you wouldn't make any real commitment to Trevor the last time, and I'm betting you won't the next time, either." She wound down, thought through what she'd said, then asked simply, "Why wouldn't you?"

"Because I can't be trusted any more than his father can!" he shouted.

They stared at each other, his face suffused with angry color, hers reflecting… She didn't know. Bewilderment? Shock? Certainly some anger, as well.

He'd said before that he hadn't learned to parent, and perhaps that he feared being too much like his father. It was true that child abuse did echo from generation to generation, so he had reason to be nervous. But to truly believe he'd lift his hand against a kid he'd done so much to help…?

Still stunned, she shook her head. "You *aren't* your father."

Without stepping back, he visibly retreated from her, pulling his head and shoulders back, stiffening. "I doubt there's a man alive who can be entirely trusted if pushed far enough. Me, I've had an example of what I can be like. I told you. I'm a carbon copy of my dear dad."

"Appearances don't mean anything!" she cried in frustration.

He shook his head. "I'm not fool enough to find out."

"My God," she whispered. "You really are afraid you'd hurt someone you loved, just because you got mad."

"I'm not going to find out."

The hope she'd hardly known she felt came close then to blinking out. She crossed her arms tightly over her chest in an instinctive effort to protect herself.

"Do you have any idea how big a fool I feel right this minute?" Tears burned in her eyes, but she refused to let them fall. "I didn't listen to you. I thought…I believed… No, I *deluded* myself that you might actually love me. But you can't."

His rigid demeanor shattered, and abruptly, he was shouting again. "Don't you understand? I don't dare!"

Her mouth fell open. It was a moment before she could close it. She swallowed, but her voice still emerged as thin and dry. "*Do* you love me?"

What she saw in his eyes was torment, but he said nothing. He wasn't going to answer her. Couldn't?

Weirdly, perhaps, his silence fed the small, stubborn spark in her chest that hadn't quite died. As if hope had been banked and not quenched, it flared again, the heat giving her courage.

"You're a coward," she accused him. "You've spent an entire lifetime avoiding any emotional commitment because you're afraid."

Muscles flexed in his jaw. "I made a decision…"

"No, you're a coward," she repeated. She took a step forward, crowding him, forcing him back against the side of his car. "You don't have the guts to find out whether you're capable of being a better man than your father. And then you condemn men who at least were willing to try and keep trying."

"Don't compare me with Wade DeShon," he hissed.

"Why not?" Karin hardly understood what drove her, then knew. Instinct. "I *am* comparing you, and right this minute, he looks pretty damn gutsy to me compared with you."

Bruce crowded her right back, so much anger on his

face a sensible woman would have quailed. "I told you not to compare me!"

She stabbed him in the chest again with one finger, hard this time. Her vision seemed hazed. With red? "But I'm doing it anyway," she all but crowed. "Wade DeShon had the guts to love someone, and he has the guts now to say, *I screwed up, but I still love you.* That looks a lot braver to me than opting out of any kind of real relationship because you won't even test yourself to find out whether you're just like your daddy or not!"

His eyes were all but black they were so dilated. "Do you want to find out? Is that what you really want?"

"Yes! That's what I want!" Karin yelled.

And then braced herself.

It was like facing down a volcano. She'd never been so aware of how powerful this man was, how heavy-boned and thick-muscled compared with what felt at this moment like her own frailty. He stared at her with those rage-darkened eyes, the hot blood of fury turning his face deep red.

The haze before Karin's eyes was gone, as if with one blink she'd swept it away. Instead, she now saw him with peculiar clarity. Nothing existed *but* this man, so furious with her, so afraid he would hurt her. Time stretched, thinned, as she waited for him to betray himself and strike her.

But his fingers never curled into a fist. He never raised a hand. He only stared, unblinking, not breathing. And finally, his expression changed. Shock was followed by bewilderment that wrenched her heart, so much did it remind her of a child who'd suddenly seen the world he had believed in transformed into something unrecognizable.

Karin's vision blurred again, but this time with tears she let fall. They rolled, hot, down her cheeks.

She laid one hand on Bruce's hard cheek. He made a muffled, agonized sound and turned his head to press his face into her hand, and she felt dampness. Oh, God. Was he crying, too?

"I'm sorry. I shouldn't have…" Her voice broke.

Yes! her heart sang. *Yes, you should have.*

His shoulders lurched.

Karin took her hand from his face and wrapped her arms around him. He leaned against her, buried his face in her hair and shook.

"Now are you convinced?" she murmured, rocking him and holding him with all her strength. "You didn't, you *couldn't,* hurt me. You never would."

Against her cheek, he said hoarsely, "I always believed… I thought I was *him.*"

"But now you know better." When he didn't answer immediately, she tried to pull back a few inches. "You do, don't you?"

He lifted his head and looked at her, his cheeks unashamedly wet. "Yeah. I think I do."

Her tears ran hotter. She smiled through them. "Will you come inside?"

GOD. He'd probably created a spectacle for the entire neighborhood. Earlier on, when he'd stomped to his car, Bruce had been vaguely conscious of a car passing, of a neighbor kid riding his bike on the sidewalk on the far side of the street. His head had swiveled so he could gawk at the two adults yelling at each other.

But Karin didn't seem to care. Through the tears that rained down her face, she shone. Always beautiful, now she was incandescent. He'd be a fool if he *didn't* love her.

Bruce yanked himself up short. It was too quick to consider labeling some emotion he'd never been able to name. What he should think about was what he'd just learned about himself.

He'd always been aware of a core of anger inside him. No, not just anger; something blacker than that, something that scared even him. A violent, monstrous emotion. It had been there as long as he could remember. He kept it in a closed room inside him, locked down. But locks could be broken, walls splintered. Even as a little boy, when he watched his father hit his mother, Bruce would feel the scary emotion swelling until he didn't think he could keep it contained.

He'd also known his whole life that his ability to control the demon that lived inside him was all that made him different from the father he despised. He'd descend to his father's level if he ever once loosed the violence. Bruce had come close a few times, mostly as a young man. He had dreamed about beating his father bloody, about making him crawl. But never, until today, had he felt those walls crash down, felt the fury swell inside him until he was filled with it, sweated it through his pores, was blinded by it.

And now, finally, he knew. He could feel monstrous emotions and not *be* a monster. All the rage his body could contain hadn't made him want to hurt her. Not even for a fraction of a second had he longed to snap her head back with one blow of his hand. He hadn't thought, *I want to see her on her knees, sobbing how sorry she is.*

And somehow, she'd had faith in the man he really was. She had trusted him.

Humbled to the core, Bruce had been shaking when he held her even as she held him. He felt as if he should be embarrassed to have shed tears, but wasn't. He took her hand, likely crushing her fingers when he gripped hard enough not to lose her, and walked the few feet from the street up her walkway, across the porch and into the house.

The moment the door shut behind them, she flung herself against him and his arms wrapped around her with a force he tried to keep from bruising her. The receding tide of anger left in its wake a desperate need to be so close to this woman she could never deny him. A need to be on top of her. Inside her. He wanted their very cells to be united.

An incoherent sound wrenched from him. He bent his head and captured her mouth. Dimly, he was aware that she was kissing him back as frantically, that she'd risen on tiptoe and wound her arms around his neck and was pressing herself against him, feeling the same need. He fell against the door, then at some point spun her so her back was ground against it. He hoisted her, and her legs wrapped around him. She rode him as he plumbed the depths of her mouth and sucked on her tongue.

Bruce thought he might explode if he didn't feel her skin against his. He had to break off the kiss long enough to tear her shirt over her head. He was talking; he could hear himself, a litany that involved praying, swearing, saying her name as if it were the sweetest word ever formed. She seemed to be laughing or crying—he didn't know which—but she yanked at his clothing with hands as desperate as his.

They didn't get it all off. The sight of her body, long and pale and curvaceous, shredded his last bit of self-control. He lifted her, felt her legs clasp him willingly and drove inside. Arms shaking with the strain, he pushed her back against the door and thrust, over and over and over, a madman, not stopping even when her entire body convulsed around him and she keened. Not stopping until she did it again and he found his own release in a mind-splitting explosion of pleasure so acute it might have been pain. An explosion that did finally empty him, so that his knees began to buckle and he sank with her in slow motion to the hardwood floor.

Bodies still joined, they lay as close together as it was humanly possible to be. Almost numb, he knew only that he didn't want to let her go, that he didn't *care* how hard the floor was or whether he could breathe.

Sensations, irritating and unwelcome, intruded nonetheless. The floor was damn cold under his bare ass. His penis slipped from her, however he willed it to keep them linked. He became aware of a few places that stung. Her nails must have dug into his back and shoulders. He had a memory of her head banging against the door. God. Was she hurt?

Bruce groaned muzzily and raised his own head from the floor enough to allow him to see her face. Her cheek was slack. A lock of hair lay across it and trailed into her mouth. As he watched, she scrunched her face up, as if trying to regain muscle control.

"Are you okay?" It came out as a mumble. Hell, he hadn't been sure he could talk at all.

"Um…" Karin wet her lips. "I think so." She sounded uncertain, but suddenly, she lifted her head so she could see him better. "You?"

"Alive," he allowed.

Anxious eyes searched his. "Do you think we ought to get up?"

"Probably."

They didn't. Her head sagged back to his chest. He managed to make one hand move so he could stroke from her shoulder blades down the length of her spine to the swell of her buttocks. Vertebra to vertebra. Muscles quivered as his hand passed. He felt a stirring in the groin. Could he get aroused again?

Yeah, it seemed he could. But this time the urgency was lacking. He continued to stroke, not moving otherwise. Karin shifted against him finally and said, "I'm too old for the floor."

A laugh rumbled from deep in his chest. It delighted him that he could laugh.

When they finally did get up, man, things hurt. He

felt as if he'd been beaten up. He also saw the shadow of new bruises on her white flesh, but she said something he thought was "Pshaw" when he began an apology, and drew him by his hand into her bedroom.

The bed was a hell of a lot more comfortable than the hardwood floor had been. They lay down and touched, carefully this time, tenderly, as if seeing each other and exploring for the first time. Sex this time was slow and sweet and, yeah, damn it, loving.

But still he shied from the word. He didn't say it and she didn't say it. Maybe it wasn't necessary.

Or maybe, he thought at one point, studying her face, which seemed to him exquisitely shaped, maybe he was still afraid.

A lifetime's conditioning… Not so easily overcome.

Yeah. He was still afraid.

CHAPTER ELEVEN

BRUCE SPOTTED Wade DeShon before Wade noticed him. They'd agreed to meet at Dick's near the Key Arena. Already sitting down, Wade had a drink and a bag in front of him, presumably containing his burger, but he hadn't started eating.

His head turned, and the two men exchanged stares, then brief nods. Bruce got in the too-lengthy line and inched forward. He didn't once glance back.

Why did Wade want to talk to him without Trevor around?

He'd been the one to call Bruce, not the other way around. Since the scene with Karin on Saturday, Bruce had stayed away. He still wasn't sure he bought her theory about Wade, the one that conceded him permission to smash the kid's favorite picture of his mother right in front of him. But Bruce had had to concede that he hadn't been prepared to give Wade any slack at all. And yeah, people screwed up. So maybe he'd jumped to a conclusion.

Which wasn't to say that he trusted the guy any more than ever.

The call, though, had been from out of the blue. Hearing the reason for it was going to be interesting.

He carried his own order to the table and sat facing Wade. Deliberately, in no hurry, he uncapped his coffee and stirred in the creamer, then opened the sack and removed the bag of fries and wrapped burger. Then he looked up.

"So, I'm here."

Wade set down his burger and wiped his hands on a napkin. To his credit, he didn't beat around the bush. "Trevor told me he talked to you about my breaking that picture."

"Yeah. He did."

"I wanted to explain."

Bruce took another bite, chewed slowly. Not until he'd swallowed did he say, "Then explain."

"He kept saying he knew something bad had happened to his mom, because she would have come home otherwise. He said she'd never have left him that way if she could help it."

Bruce hadn't intended to step in this quick, but he said, "I think that's true."

"MaryBeth loved Trevor—I won't deny that. But she wasn't any kind of perfect mother, either."

Speaks the perfect father.

On the heels of the snide judgment, Bruce could imagine Karin pinning him with an exasperated stare. *Listen to him,* she would say.

So he did his best to hide his hostility and kept eating.

"I boozed, but she liked uppers. It made me mad that

she used back when she was pregnant with Trevor. I'm not excusing myself. Not for my drinking, not for hitting her. But our fights weren't all me, either. Trevor doesn't remember that."

Wade would say that, Bruce reflected cynically. But he still kept quiet because he remembered that from the first time he'd met MaryBeth, he'd known she had a problem. Plus, while men did abuse women who never fought back—Bruce's mother was one of those—that wasn't what Trevor had described. He'd told of raging battles between MaryBeth and Wade.

"I have this feeling you've already made up your mind." Wade shrugged, looking defeated but determined, too. "I'm going to say this anyway. I got mad because she let him down so bad. I let him down, too. I know I did. But I saw him crying, and I thought he was doing all right without me, but having his mama just disappear like that... Him having to go to a foster home, and then come live with me when he doesn't even know me anymore... I could see in his eyes how scared and sad he was at that moment, and I lost my temper. I wasn't mad at Trevor. Not even just at MaryBeth. I was mad at myself, too. And I grabbed that picture and threw it before I thought, even though I believed I'd learned better. But I want you to know I wouldn't hurt him. I'd never hurt Trevor."

"Am I supposed to be moved by that little speech?"

Wade stared at him in frustration, then crumpled his wrappers in a little ball and started to stand. "Forget it."

"Sit down." Bruce put some snap in his voice.

After a hesitation, the other man complied.

"Maybe you mean that right now, but what happens the next time you crave a drink?"

Wade held Bruce's gaze, a mask dropping enough to reveal torment. "I crave a drink every day. Sometimes it's all I can stand not to have one. Just one, I tell myself. Only, I know better. So I don't have it. I haven't had one in over two years. If I can resist temptation that guts a man's soul for that long, what makes you think I'd give in to it now, when I finally got my son back?"

Bruce shoved the remnants of his lunch away. Despite himself, this time he *was* moved. Wade had been more eloquent than he would have expected. Karin had been right; Bruce didn't want to be impressed. But he was anyway.

"Why are you telling me all this?" he asked. "Why are we having this conversation?"

Wade looked back at him with a man's version of Trevor's thin, earnest face. "If you don't trust me, Trevor won't, either. At first, I was jealous." His mouth twisted. "But I don't have any right to be. The thing is, my boy admires you. So I guess I'm asking you to support my right to be his father. Let him see that you do."

He was begging, and last week that would have given Bruce satisfaction. He would have enjoyed the acknowledgment that he came first with Trevor. He might even have liked the idea of Wade crawling to him for help with his son.

Suddenly, he felt sick, ashamed of what just a few days ago he would have felt. Trevor wasn't his son. He could have been; if Bruce had been willing to make that commitment, trust himself, he could have been licensed as Trevor's foster father and fought any effort to reunite Trevor with his father. But Karin was on the mark. He hadn't had the guts to admit he loved the boy.

And now, *because* he loved him, he had to admit that Trevor was better off with his father. A kid that age needed to know that his parents, whatever their failings, loved him. That Wade had resisted the temptation to take that drink for more than two long years, even though he wasn't allowed to see his son, was a testament to how much he did love him. He'd kept calling, kept trying even when those calls weren't all that welcome. It was right that he get that second chance to show Trevor how much he mattered to his father.

"Do you want me to talk to him?" Bruce asked.

"Maybe. Or maybe just let him see that you approve of him living with me."

After a moment, Bruce said, "I have a friend who is a psychologist. She's been talking to me about her belief that people can change if they want to bad enough."

Wade was watching him, maybe wondering where this was going, maybe already knowing. "She's right. I've got to believe she is."

"I thought she was wrong. Just recently, I've started to change my mind." He paused. "Trevor didn't want to admit it, but back when you used to call, it meant something to him. He pretended he didn't care, but he did."

Wade lowered his gaze. He rubbed a hand over his face, pressing his thumb and forefinger to his eyes as if to make sure they didn't leak. At last, he cleared his throat. "I appreciate you saying that."

"I'll talk to Trevor." Bruce shifted in his plastic chair. "I hope you don't mind if I keep getting together with him now and again. He's a great kid."

"Of course I don't. You got him through some bad times. I owe you."

They eyed each other a little uneasily, dangerously close to emotions Wade probably didn't welcome any more than Bruce did. Finally, Bruce nodded and finished wadding up his garbage.

Wade thanked him for agreeing to meet and they walked out together. They even shook hands beside Wade's car, sealing their agreement.

We will both make things right for Trevor.

BRUCE REMAINED thoughtful as he spent the remainder of the afternoon dropping off flyers with photos of Carlos Garcia and Roberto Escobar at Hispanic grocery stores in south King County. His fluency in Spanish was handy now. At each stop he talked for a few minutes, reassuring the proprietors that he had no interest in the immigration status of anyone who came forward with information. He wanted only to find the children. He talked about Lenora's heartbreak, drawing a picture of the distraught woman in the hospital bed begging him to find her little ones, of the circle of her family waiting to regather the children into her arms.

The storekeepers all nodded and promised to post his

flyer and point it out to their customers. None cried, "I know that man!"

He'd done the Seattle metropolitan area one day, Snohomish County another day and the agricultural and heavily Hispanic Skagit County on yet another day. His lieutenant was becoming impatient with the time he was expending. As newspaper interest in the search for Anna and Enrico Escobar cooled even further—and therefore pressure from the public and from the politicians—so, too, did Bruce's ability to remain focused on the case.

His last stop of the day was in Kent, at a tiny store where several customers and the proprietor at the checkout were carrying on an animated conversation in Spanish, all gesticulating, until he entered. The moment the bell over the door rang and they saw him, they all fell silent and studied him covertly.

The atmosphere wasn't quite hostile, but almost. One of the men said loudly, "We can't even buy tortillas without showing our papers?"

"I'm not from Immigration," Bruce said, unoffended. He understood the unease in the Hispanic community. Recent immigration raids had angered many. Mothers in the country illegally had been torn from their children born in the U.S.—thus citizens—and deported. "I'm from the Seattle Police Department," he told them. "I'm investigating the murder of Julia Lopez and the attempted murder of Lenora Escobar. I am hunting for Lenora Escobar's young children, taken by her husband."

Their expressions changed. They'd all read about the case, talked about it among themselves.

"This man—why would we here know him?" asked the storekeeper, a short, stout, dark-skinned woman who had to be Mayan.

"We have no idea where he went with the children. It could be this area. I brought a picture of Roberto Escobar. But I'm also looking for the man beside him in the picture." He handed it over to her. "He is a friend of Escobar's. Not a suspect. But he might know where to find Roberto Escobar and the children."

All nodded interestedly and crowded closer to study the flyer. The storekeeper handed it across the old-fashioned counter holding a cash register that was probably an antique. With murmurs and clucking sounds, they passed the piece of paper around. It was greeted with shakes of the head.

No, no, they had never seen those men. What a shame. Those poor children! So the mother had awakened? They hadn't read that in the papers. It was true?

Answering their questions, he caught an interesting reaction out of the corner of his eye. It was from a woman, one of the last to look at the flyer. She composed her face immediately and shook her head like the others. But there'd been something there. Perhaps just niggling recognition, but she'd definitely known something and chosen not to say *I might have seen this man before.*

Question was: Which man had she recognized? Carlos? Or Roberto himself? And how to find out?

He grabbed a bottle of grape Fanta, paid and then stood in the shade outside, guzzling it until the woman emerged from the store with a younger woman—her daughter?—and her groceries.

"Buenos días," he said civilly.

"Buenos días," they chimed in return.

"You're certain you don't know either of those men?" he asked. "That Roberto Escobar… We think he's *loco*. Those two little kids aren't safe with him."

"No, no," the young woman said, and her mother nodded.

"If you should see either, will you call me? My phone number is on the flyer."

Sí, sí. Of course they would. The older woman's gaze evaded his. She hustled her daughter away. They loaded their groceries in the back of an old Chevy and drove off. Bruce jotted down the license number.

When he ran it from his car, he found that it was registered to a Vicente Sanchez at an address on the outskirts of Kent. Bruce debated with himself whether it would be worth following her home and talking to her husband and any other family who lived with them, then decided not to. The woman hadn't seemed secretive so much as unsure. He'd give her time to think about the flyer and why the face had seemed familiar, to imagine how she'd feel if her children or grandchildren were snatched from her.

The odds were good that she'd be calling him.

"Yeah," he muttered, putting his car in gear, "assuming she doesn't get home and realize that Carlos resembles some distant cousin of her husband's, the one who still lives back home in the Dominican Republic, and that's why she thought for a minute she might know him."

Feeling the stirrings of hunger, he detoured to a small Mexican restaurant down the street and had a chicken chimichanga. He left a flyer there, too. The waitress, who had been flirting with him, promised she would hang it prominently by the cash register. *Sí, sí.*

He made it back to Seattle in time to meet Molly at A Woman's Hand to teach their last self-defense workshop. Karin engaged as fully in it as the other women participants did, her expression often fiercely concentrated. He suspected that seeing Lenora brought down with one swing of the tire iron had made her aware of her own vulnerability in a way she never had been. It had occurred to her that she might have to defend herself someday, too.

Three weeks, and no progress at all in finding Roberto Escobar or the children.

After escorting the women safely to their cars, he, Molly and Karin went out again for coffee. He was glad Karin and Molly seemed to like each other so much. He'd had his doubts three years back when Molly, newly promoted, was assigned to him, but she'd proved herself with smarts he'd come to believe complemented his own *because* she was a woman and therefore thought differently. As plainclothes homicide officers, the two of them rarely had to chase suspects or pull a weapon. Her ability to bring down a violent suspect holding a knife on them wasn't often put to the test. But Molly had learned every trick to compensate for her lack of height and muscle bulk. Underestimating her was a mistake.

Friendship had grown between them. She'd hung out with him and Trevor a few times. Trevor's shyness hadn't lasted long with her. Molly wasn't girlie. She ate with gusto, took pride in her belches and employed a wicked elbow on the basketball court.

"Did you ever play basketball?" he asked Karin.

Both women turned their heads to stare at him.

"Uh…sorry. Did I interrupt?"

"Yeah," Molly told him. "Good to know you were hanging on our every word."

"I actually did play varsity in high school," Karin said. "I went to a small school, and we were pretty lousy, but I can dribble the ball and I used to have a pretty decent jump shot. Why?"

"Oh, just thinking." He shrugged. "Molly and I play a little one-on-one sometimes."

"Really?" Karin raised her brows and looked at his partner. "You're short."

Molly's blue eyes narrowed. "Bet I can take you."

Karin laughed. "No fair! I haven't played in fifteen years."

Bruce sipped coffee. "You didn't play in college?"

"Too busy by then. And really…I was no more than okay."

Walking her to her car later, Bruce murmured, "You may stink on the court, but you have other talents."

She rolled her eyes at him. "Gee, thanks. Like guiding people toward understanding their own behaviors?"

"That's what I was talking about," he agreed, straight-faced.

Her elbow in his ribs was damn near as sharp as Molly's.

She unlocked her car door and turned to him. "We didn't get a chance to talk about your meeting with Wade."

"He wants my support."

She processed that. "And does he have it?"

"If he doesn't screw up."

"Ah. Wholehearted, then."

"Damn it," he said with some heat, "I'm trying."

Karin rose on tiptoe and kissed him softly. "I know you are," she murmured.

He caught her to him and deepened the kiss long enough to make it really interesting, and to make him regret that he hadn't planned to go home with her tonight.

But when he let her go, she said meditatively, "I'd love to meet Trevor. What if we do a barbecue or something and invite him and his dad? Maybe Molly, too. Is there anyone else?"

He reacted with surprise and pleasure. He liked the idea of getting her opinion on Wade. Bruce was willing to bet she had x-ray vision that cut through any pretense. "I'd like that."

They discussed days, and agreed he'd call Wade.

"I'll let you know," he said, kissed her again, and reluctantly let her get into her car.

WHEN BRUCE CALLED Karin the next day to inform her that Saturday afternoon would work fine for Wade and Trevor, he told her more about his lunchtime meeting with Trevor's father. After she hung up, Karin found herself hoping that Wade was sincere. Given how angry Bruce had been, how certain he was that Wade was a brute beyond redemption, these were big steps for him. If it turned out badly, if Wade DeShon started drinking or lost his job and took out his frustration on his son, Bruce's tentative faith in the ability of any man to prove himself would collapse.

She was afraid of any new hitches because she'd noticed that despite his breakthrough, he had been very careful not to say the words *I love you*. Karin was trying not to think about the possibility that he *didn't*. That he might be willing to believe he could love a woman someday but she wasn't that woman.

Because the truth was, she had fallen head over heels in love with him. She missed him every minute when they weren't together, was giddy with her love when they were. It was like being tipsy for hours on end. She laughed more than she ever had in her life, was sillier than she'd been at twelve years of age, and had begun to dream about things she hadn't known how desperately she wanted: a huge church wedding, a bulging belly beneath a T-shirt that said Baby On Board, storytimes and family picnics and a vacation to Disneyland. PTA meetings, stolen romance with her husband, dinners out when they discovered all they talked about was their children. Normal stuff. Stuff she'd once assumed she'd have someday, but that in recent years she had almost forgotten she wanted.

But even if Bruce did love her, even if someday he said the words, would he ever want to make a lifetime commitment? Would he trust himself enough to father children? She didn't know, and that scared her. Discovering she'd fallen in love alone would be bleak.

She still went daily that week to see Lenora, who was making good progress. Initially, her speech had been better than her motor skills. Some of that was weakness from the weeks of inactivity, but not all. Like someone who'd had a stroke, much of the damage was one-sided. She'd retained more dexterity on her left side than her right. During visits, she told Karin about the physical therapy and about the things she could do effortlessly and the ones she was having to relearn like a newborn child. The bandage on her head became smaller, exposing scalp with a newborn's peach fuzz of dark hair.

One day she returned from the bathroom, walking with a stiff, awkward gait, climbed into bed with Karin's help and burst into tears.

"Anna loved my hair!" she wailed. "She liked to brush it and put her barrettes in. What would she say?"

"That you're as pretty as that singer with the bald head. Sinéad O'Connor."

She must have heard of her, because she laughed through her tears. "I thought she looked so funny when I saw a picture! A woman's hair should be beautiful."

Karin reached out and wiped away her tears. "I think your hair will be beautiful again. And Anna will brush it again, and style it for you. And Enrico will wonder why girls like to mess with their hair."

Lenora cried some more. Karin moved to the edge of the bed and held her as she wept against Karin's shoulder. Her own cheeks grew damp as she thought about how long it had been since Roberto smashed his wife's head with all that weekend's pent-up rage and stole the children not for their sakes but to prove they were *his*. What if they were never found? How would Lenora live not knowing? Looking for the rest of her life at the faces of other people's children, wondering, hoping, fearing?

Bruce hadn't conceded defeat. But eventually, he would have done everything that was possible. Other mysteries would preoccupy him. Other tragedies, other missing children. Not all *were* found. Karin had counseled women who'd had a child die. That was hard enough, but there had been resolution of a sort. Those mothers had a grave to visit. They might forever ask themselves if they couldn't have done something differently, but at least they knew the end.

Lenora might not. Would she be able to bear living with that uncertainty?

Karin went home depressed. As she got ready for bed, she thought about Trevor, whose mother had disappeared. For all that he knew his mother was a drug addict, it must be hard for him to understand her disappearance. Karin hoped that Wade would be willing to let him talk about his mother sometimes. She'd have to urge Bruce to encourage him to do so, too.

THE WEATHER SATURDAY, blessedly, was nice. Bruce had taken her literally when she suggested a barbecue, and brought his own kettle-type grill. He arrived early and started the coals. Karin was letting him prepare the meat for the grill. She was secretly amused by his expertise in this traditionally manly form of cooking.

Since she neither cooked nor ate meat, he'd promised to handle that whole part of the menu. Everything else would be vegetarian, from the baked beans to the salads.

She'd invited a couple who were good friends of hers, and Molly brought a date who had a boy nearly Trevor's age. Wade and Trevor were the last to arrive, and showed up with a case of soda and several bags of chips. She led them through the house to the back patio.

"Bruce is just putting the meat on," she told them over her shoulder. She peered in the bag Trevor had handed her. "Oh, you brought dip to go with the chips. That looks great."

Bruce grinned at the sight of the boy and held out a free hand for a quick hug. Understandable envy flashed on Wade's face before he veiled it. He had to compete not just with Trevor's memories of his mother, but with a man who'd stood in his place in his son's affections.

Molly greeted Trevor with casual affection and introduced him to the other boy. Bruce introduced Wade to everyone, and soon he and Karin's friend Steve discovered a common interest in old cars. Wade, it developed, was restoring a 1970 Camaro, which filled Steve with envy. They huddled, talking about its wheelbase and track and something about the subframe and structural integrity. Steve's wife rolled her eyes and offered to help Karin bring out the rest of the food.

Karin had only one private moment with Wade,

after they'd eaten, when she caught him standing apart from the others, watching Trevor and the other boy attempt to keep a soccer ball in the air with their knees and heads.

"He seems like a really nice kid," she said, pausing at his side.

He nodded. "Thanks to his mother. And Detective Walker," he added scrupulously.

"Bruce seems to think Trevor's settling in really well with you, though."

His face softened. "Yeah. Better than I expected. We've had some rough patches—" he gave her a sidelong glance, and she could tell he wondered how much she knew "—but he's doing good. Real good."

She bit her lip. "Has Bruce told you I'm a therapist?"

His appraisal was more frank this time. "He said he had a friend who was."

"Well, that was me." Here she went, butting in again. She couldn't seem to help herself. "Um…I'm wondering if I can give you a bit of advice."

Despite new wariness, he inclined his head. "Sure. I'm no expert at being a dad."

"It's not that," she said. "From what I've seen today, you're doing fine. I just have one suggestion. Encourage him to talk about his mother. The worst thing for a child is to have to pretend he never thinks about one of his parents. It happens often, after a divorce. Children do their best to please the parent they depend on. But if they stifle too much, it causes damage."

"Okay," he said after a minute. "I can do that. It used

to bother me, knowing that MaryBeth probably never said a good word about me."

"I imagine that made Trevor feel awfully conflicted, too, because on some level he loved you. It's really hard on a kid to have to betray one of his parents, in a sense, by having to agree that Mommy is mean and he never wants to see her again."

Wade nodded again, more thoughtfully. Then his expression changed, and she knew even without turning that Bruce had come up beside her.

He slipped an arm around her and said, "Has she said, 'Hmm—now, exactly what do you mean by that?' yet?"

Wade tried to hide his laugh in a cough. "Uh, not exactly."

"But close enough," Karin admitted. "I was dispensing advice. Just as bad."

Bruce grinned at her. "Just as long as you didn't say 'Hmm.' That's when you scare me."

"It never passed my lips," she promised.

The two men both laughed now, and she pretended to be offended.

The moment was interrupted by Trevor, who called, "Hey, Dad! Look!"

His father went to watch him head the ball to the other boy. Beside Karin, Bruce said not a word. He had gone completely still, his face expressionless.

As if he felt her scrutiny, he let his arm drop from around her shoulders and he turned and walked back toward the others. She looked after him, her heart aching. Trevor hadn't even glanced at Bruce. He'd been too eager to share his pride and delight at his new accomplishment with his father.

She couldn't summon a single word to say that would help.

CHAPTER TWELVE

BRUCE INHALED the scent of Karin's hair, tickling his chin and nose. They'd made love and were still entwined in bed, her head on his chest. He'd been lying here feeling good, but also… He couldn't identify this unease. There was some kind of struggle going on inside him. As if part of him was panicking, even as the rest was feeling happier than he'd known he could be.

"My mother called today," he heard himself say.

Weird. That wasn't even what he'd been thinking about.

She moved, tilting her head so she could see his face, or at least his chin. "Really?"

"Yeah, she does every now and again."

"You made it sound as if you never talked to your parents."

"Never do to my father."

She was quiet for a minute, probably perplexed. "Did she have news?"

"Dad has cancer."

Now Karin pushed back and lifted onto one elbow, studying him with worry. Her corn-silk hair tumbled over her shoulders and arm. "Is it treatable?"

"He's having chemotherapy, but she admitted the prognosis isn't good. Plus, the treatment is making him really sick."

"Does he want to see you?"

Surprised, Bruce said, "God, no! Why would he? This is not a man who's going to discover his kinder, softer self on his deathbed. Trust me."

"But…what about you? How do you feel about knowing he may be dying?"

Therapist speaking, or woman? He guessed, from the concern on her face, that it was the woman asking. She genuinely imagined he'd be broken up about his old man's possible demise.

"Don't give a damn." He examined his own feelings, and realized that he meant it. "I'm not sure what my mother will do without him, though."

What she *should* do was throw a party. In his opinion champagne was in order. But the reality was, she'd have no idea how to function on her own. She'd never been allowed to make decisions.

"Is she close to your brothers and their wives?"

"My next older brother, Dan, the most. He's not as bad as Roger." Which wasn't saying much.

"Would she move up here?"

Bruce shook his head. "She's got the neighborhood. It's her comfort zone. Plus, my brothers and their wives and children are there."

"So you have nieces and nephews?"

"Yeah, I guess. I mean, I've never met them."

He could see her struggling to process these things he'd never told her.

"You really did cut yourself off, didn't you?" she said at last.

"Oh, yeah. And," he warned, afraid she'd feel a mission, "I won't be trying to span the chasm. But Mom..." Uncomfortable, he admitted, "I felt bad. She sounded lost."

Karin continued to watch him in the penetrating way that undoubtedly worked to extract deep dark confessions from her clients. When she made an observation, she kept it neutral. "You love her."

He felt himself twitching. If it wouldn't have been a dead giveaway to her, he'd have sprung from the bed and paced.

"Yeah, sure. Not enough to fly home to hold her hand at my father's bedside, but...yeah."

"Good," she said simply.

"Why good?"

Karin didn't answer, and that weird pressure in his chest of which he'd been aware earlier returned. Or maybe he just noticed it again. After a minute, she sat up and said, "I need the bathroom," swung her feet to the floor and walked out.

He appreciated the view from behind, even as he attempted to pin down his discomfiture. He loved her body: long legs, firm butt that still gave him a couple of handfuls, small waist, tangle of hair. The view was every bit as fine from the front, too, with that gorgeous face and perfect breasts.

Yeah, but a lot of women had great bodies. If there

wasn't a lot more going on, he wouldn't have risked getting involved. Any woman would be getting ideas by now. He was a little startled to realize he wouldn't have liked it if she wasn't starting to envision a future with him.

You want *her to be in love with you?*

He stared up at the ceiling.

Yeah. Yeah, he did.

He should have been surprised to realize the unthinkable. He didn't want to live without this woman. Without the way she had of looking at him and seeing far more than he'd meant to show. The way she had of understanding and forgiving frailties, of caring passionately, of guarding herself.

He had never in his life had this desire to tell another person everything, to share what was bothering him, what shamed him, what pleased him. Now, not a damn thing happened during the day that he didn't immediately think, *I'll tell Karin.*

Dismay punched him. Or maybe shock. *God.* Was this love? Was that what this shaky feeling meant, this sense he had of standing on a crumbling precipice?

Maybe.

He heard her footsteps in the hall and turned his head, waiting to drink in the first sight of her.

Maybe? Who the hell was he kidding?

But would it last? Would it stand up to the crap life threw at everyone?

And maybe the biggest question: Could he give her what she wanted? He hadn't grown up with any kind of role model for ideal husband and dad. Did he have a chance in hell of being the man he suspected she thought he was?

She came into the room, still gloriously naked. If she was anything but utterly composed as she walked toward him, it didn't show.

"Because I'd like to think you do know how to love," she said, as if there'd been no gap between his earlier question and now. "Maybe for my sake, mostly for yours."

Maybe for my sake meant...that she was admitting she loved him?

He could ask. But then, depending on her answer, he'd have to declare himself. Or not. And then... God, then, the crumbling ground beneath his feet would collapse. And he couldn't fly.

So he said, "Yeah, I thought about asking Mom to move up here. She'll say no, but... I might ask."

Karin's smile blossomed, warm and approving. "Might, huh? Heart of stone."

He held out an arm to welcome her. She stretched out beside him, breasts pressed against him, and kissed his jaw, then nibbled on his earlobe.

"Tough guy," she whispered.

"That's me."

It was the last thing he could find voice to say for a while. Which was maybe a good thing, considering his fear of the words he wanted to say.

MONDAY, BRUCE HAD MANAGED to knock off early and pick up Trevor after school, taking him to a community-center playground to play some one-on-one. He needed distraction from his awareness that it was four weeks to the day since Escobar had smashed in his wife's head, killed Julia Lopez and snatched the children.

Four weeks, and the likelihood of Escobar being found receded by the day.

Shaking his head, Bruce dribbled and shot the basketball.

It bounced off the rim, rattling the playground backboard. Trevor sprang to retrieve it.

Hands still extended for the shot, Bruce glowered at the still-quivering rim. "Well, hell."

"You tell me not to swear." Grinning, Trevor dribbled in a circle around him, his feet dancing.

"New shoes," Bruce said, noticing.

"They're cool, aren't they?"

He glanced down to admire. Bruce deftly swiped the ball and swung away, dribbled twice and shot again.

The ball sprang off the rim again. *Clang.*

Trevor cackled, retrieved it again, then drove right past a dumbfounded Bruce and laid it up. The ball slid through the ragged net with barely a whisper.

Bruce shook his head. "Showing me up, are you?"

"I beat Dad at horse yesterday." Trevor gave him a nervous glance. "'Course, he's not as good as you."

"Who is?" Bruce said with mock egoism. He grinned. "Did your dad play high-school ball?"

"Yeah, but he says he wasn't a star or anything."

"You sure he wasn't letting you win?"

Trevor shook his head. "He's out of practice. But it was fun."

"Glad to hear it." Bruce scooped up the ball from where it lay on the asphalt playground and considered how to handle this.

I guess I'm asking you to support my right to be his father.

So little to ask. So much.

"I'm glad he's got time just to hang with you."

"He's been spending a *lot* of time with me," Trevor said with new eagerness, as if given permission to express it. "I heard him on the phone last weekend. Some friend wanted him to go do something. He said, 'I've got my boy living with me now, you know. We have plans.' Only, we didn't really have plans. I mean, not like anything important. We just went to the mall to get me shoes and stuff."

"That's big plans," Bruce said gravely. "You're going to spend that much money you've got to consider it important."

"They cost a bunch." Trevor looked down at his shoes in awe. "I never had *anything* that cost so much before."

Bruce dribbled the ball idly, by instinct. It slapped the asphalt and returned to his hand, the beat rhythmic.

"It sounds like your dad's being good to you."

"He's not anything like I remember." Trevor hesitated. "Could Mom have been wrong about him?"

Bruce held a lightning internal debate, then chose honesty. "No. You remember them fighting, right? Your dad really drunk. Your mom's face all swollen and bruised."

"Both her eyes were black this one time." Trevor's

face screwed up with the remembering. His voice was slow, reluctant. He didn't want this amazing father he had now to be the same man who'd hurt his mother. "So how come he's so nice now?"

Bruce finally palmed the basketball and held it under his arm. "People can change. Mostly, though, I imagine his drinking was the problem. Some people don't handle alcohol very well. It lowers your inhibitions." Noting Trevor's confusion, he said, "When you're drunk, you act on what you're feeling. You're real happy, or real depressed, or real angry. So a drunk person tends to be jovial, or weepy, or violent. From what your mother told me, your dad tended to be angry and violent."

Trevor nodded.

"And then, it may be that your mother and father were having problems that weren't all one-sided. You know she used drugs."

There was a discernible pause before Trevor gave a short, unhappy nod.

"Your dad wasn't always happy about that. And the stuff she was using changed *her* personality, so she probably said and did things she wouldn't have otherwise." And that was enough on that subject, Bruce decided, watching the boy's face. "The good part is, your mother took action and asked him to leave. And your dad loved you enough to realize he had to deal with his problems."

"Is that why he quit drinking? Me?"

"That's what he says. And I don't know any reason not to believe him. Do you?"

A sharp breeze was coming off the sound. Trevor shivered. "No."

"It might be that now you're seeing the man your father would have been if he had never started drinking," Bruce said. "Or maybe not. Maybe he's a better man *because* he feels bad about those years. We learn from our mistakes."

Trevor was silent again for a minute. He appeared very young at this moment, skinny and vulnerable, the boy who'd been victimized every day at the bus stop, who'd huddled in an empty apartment scraping for enough to eat while he waited for his mother to come home.

Bruce's chest hurt suddenly, and he knew he loved this kid. Knew he'd have been a good father if he had had the guts to take him home.

What hurt now was realizing his insight was way too late out of the starting gate. Trevor's biological father was doing a good job, too, and he loved Trevor. Like he'd said, he had a right.

"I miss Mom sometimes," Trevor said in a small voice.

"Of course you do." Bruce stepped forward and wrapped an arm around the boy.

For a moment, he leaned against Bruce. Then, with a sniff, he straightened. "I keep thinking she wouldn't like me being with Dad."

So that was what was bothering him. He thought he was betraying his mom by loving his father.

Bruce shook his head. "One thing you've got to remember is that way back, when they first met and got married and decided to have you, she loved him. What she got to hating was the guy who drank too much and was mad all the time. Letting go of that hate was hard. She had trouble believing your dad had really changed. But I think she'd be really glad to know he actually has, and that you're safe and loved. She loved you more than anything herself, and she'd want whatever is best for you."

Trevor swiped at his face and half turned away, embarrassed to be caught crying. "She's dead, isn't she?" he mumbled.

"I suspect so." Or caught in the purgatory between life and death that was a crack addict's final months. "She wouldn't have stayed away otherwise."

The twelve-year-old nodded, his face bleak but his expression showing that he was also comforted by his faith that nothing but death would have made his mother abandon him.

"You'll keep coming to see me, right?" he asked.

Bruce smiled and squeezed his shoulder, hiding his own grief. Trevor wouldn't need him for much longer. "Are you kidding? Of course I will."

"Okay," the boy said, relaxing at the reassurance, the promise that Bruce wouldn't let go until he was ready.

"You hungry?"

"Yeah!"

They started walking toward the car, the ball still tucked under Bruce's arm. "Pizza?"

Trevor cast him a scornful look. "We always have pizza."

"You might've just had it."

"I never get tired of pizza. It's my favorite food.

Except, Dad makes really great tacos. He doesn't say I have to put tomatoes or anything on them. I like to just have the meat and cheese and sour cream. But he doesn't buy those hard tortillas, like Mom did."

"The ones that are always stale."

"Yeah! Dad gets these corn ones that are fresh from some little store, and he heats them up, and then he…"

Bruce listened to him rhapsodize about his father's culinary genius, followed by his father's exemplary taste in movies and clothes and pretty much everything else, and felt that ache under his own breastbone.

This was the crummy part of loving someone: the having to let go.

TUESDAY, BRUCE AND KARIN had lunch, as they'd taken to doing regularly at one of the half-dozen cafés near A Woman's Hand. They were sitting at a sidewalk table under a green, leafy tree, talking about the latest imbroglio involving the police chief and the city council, when his cell phone rang.

He glanced at the screen—253 area code, meaning south of Seattle down through Tacoma. He didn't recognize the number, but excused himself and answered.

"Detective Walker."

The spate of apologetic Spanish required him to shift gears.

"Señora Sanchez?" For a moment he didn't recognize the name. Then it clicked. Vicente Sanchez, the owner of the vehicle when Bruce ran the license plates. This was the woman from the Kent grocery store, the one who'd showed a flicker of recognition when she saw the photo on his flyer.

"I wasn't sure," she was telling him. "I asked my sister to go look at the picture, too, because she is better with faces than I am. She says the tall man in your picture is Carlos Jimenez."

Satisfaction filled him. So, even though Carlos had used a fake last name at the lumberyard, he'd stuck with his given name. People on the run often did.

Karin was watching him, her gaze arrested by his expression.

"And how do you know this Carlos Jimenez?" he asked.

Carlos lived in a trailer a couple of miles from them, Señora Sanchez informed him. Bruce gathered from her disdain that his was a run-down place, not that nice, perhaps trashy. She'd heard he was away, that he'd worked the strawberry fields earlier and might be picking blueberries down in Oregon now. She only knew him a little—which was why she hadn't been sure that day.

"Can you tell me how to find Señor Jimenez's place?" He kept his voice easy. "Perhaps he's there after all."

"I asked other people," Señora Sanchez said. "They say someone else is living there right now. A man who isn't very friendly."

He sat up, his elbow jostling his coffee cup. Karin snatched it before it could go over. Bruce hardly noticed.

"Have children been seen there, too? Did this person notice?"

"She thought she saw a little girl in the window. When she told me that, I decided I should tell you. For poor Señora Escobar's sake."

"You did the right thing," he reassured her. "If the man isn't Roberto Escobar, there's no harm done. Like I told you, I don't care about papers."

After further nudging on his part, she told him where Jimenez's shabby trailer was. He thanked her several times, and was finally able to end the call.

Karin had been waiting, lips parted. "You learned something."

"The woman saw my flyer and recognized Roberto's friend. But the friend is away, and someone is staying at his trailer."

"You think it's Roberto."

"Don't get too excited," he warned her. "False leads are a hell of a lot more common than good ones."

"But *you're* excited," she observed.

She knew him too well.

"I've got a feeling," Bruce admitted. "But my gut's been wrong before. I'll check out the place this afternoon."

"Will you call me? Immediately? I want to be with Lenora if you find them."

"I promise," he said. He would have anyway. She'd been with him every step of the way on this one. She deserved no less.

They'd both lost interest in lingering. He paid and they walked back to the clinic, where they parted. Using his cell phone, Bruce let Molly know where he was going.

Señora Sanchez's directions took him to a rural part of the Auburn Valley. He'd never been in this particular area before, and was a little surprised at how run-down most of the houses were. The prosperity that had sent real-estate values skyrocketing in most of King County hadn't reached this far south of the city yet. To each side of the road, fences sagged, yards were filled with disemboweled cars and trucks set up on cinder blocks, the paint on houses peeled, and mailboxes were dented and listing on semirotted posts.

He passed the Sanchez home, and noted that although it was modest, this yard was tidy and someone had encased the mailbox in a steel barrel to protect it from the baseball bats teenage vandals liked to use when cruising rural roads.

Go one mile farther, she'd instructed him, and turn at the purple house. Which was indeed an eye-popping purple. The owners were also fond of plastic garden decor, from a wishing well to multiple deer, rabbit and gnome statues.

A quarter of a mile farther, he found the dirt road that she'd described to the left. A row of mailboxes at the corner told him that there were eight inhabited properties down this road. He could drive partway.

These houses and trailers were scattered far apart, each set on an acre or more. A couple had pastures containing spavined horses or a few goats. A cloud of dust plumed behind his car, although he drove slowly. He could see the dead end of the road ahead when he made the decision to pull to a wide bit of shoulder and walk.

Feeling conspicuous, he hoped like hell no one—and especially Roberto Escobar—happened to drive by right now. Maybe he should have left his car out at the main road.

Yeah, and then he'd have had to walk farther. No one who spotted him would mistake him for anything but a cop.

Three driveways split at the end of the road. Jimenez's was the one that led to the left. Bruce took advantage of a stand of scraggly alder trees and vine maples and left the gravel road, trespassing over someone's land. He moved slowly between the narrow trees, carefully, pausing to listen. The hair on the back of his neck had begun to prickle. He kept having flashbacks to army reconnaissance missions.

On the edge of the small woods, he found a towering mass of blackberries, thorny and impassable. Sucking his hand and swearing, he backtracked until he found an opening that allowed him to look across a grassy field studded with more, leggier blackberry vines to the single-wide mobile home Señora Sanchez had described. Indeed, it appeared barely habitable, set up on blocks, like the rusting hulks of cars and trucks that also made the property unsightly.

From here, he couldn't see whether any vehicle that still had wheels was parked beside the trailer. He wished he routinely carried binoculars. He set his phone to vibrate rather than ring. Then, using the cover provided by the derelicts in the yard, Bruce bent low and trotted through the grass, crouching finally behind an ancient tractor.

He inched to peer around it, and gave a feral grin when he saw the dented blue Buick. Goddamn. Escobar *was* here. He hoped like hell the children were, as well.

Bruce settled in for what might be a long wait. He had plenty of practice at stakeouts. He let his mind free-float while he crouched, scarcely blinking as he watched the trailer. He remembered Lenora, frail and wary, in that first self-defense workshop, then the sight of her crumpled body in the parking lot. Her still figure in the hospital bed, chest rising and falling but no other sign of life. Karin sitting beside the bed, talking about gardening and mothers and the happenings outside the walls of the hospital, amused and vibrant and thoughtful. Most of all, he envisioned Lenora Escobar once she'd awakened, her huge, haunted, dark eyes brimming with tears.

Oh, yeah. He could sit here for the next two days if he had to.

But it wasn't more than an hour later that he heard a child crying, then a man's angry voice, too muffled for words to be distinguishable. Another voice—a girl's? It, too, rose to a wail. A door slammed. Something crashed inside, and the first sobs abruptly cut off. The second, shriller, ones hung in the air an instant longer, like an echo, then fell silent, as well.

Bruce saw a shadow move inside, a figure passing back and forth in front of one of the windows. The pace seemed quick and agitated.

Not enjoying single parenthood, Roberto?

Time passed. Bruce waited. At last, the front door—

or was it the only exit? he'd have to check—opened. A man stood on the top step, scanning the yard, his gaze narrowed and suspicious. Had a neighbor called, mentioning the strange vehicle parked beside the road?

But after a moment Roberto pulled a pack of cigarettes from his shirt pocket and lit up. Relaxing infinitesimally, Bruce realized suspicion was Roberto Escobar's constant companion these days.

"Papa?" a small voice called from the open door behind him.

He turned and snarled something, then swung back to face the yard. The child didn't ask again.

Movement at one of the windows caught Bruce's attention. A child's face appeared. As Señora Sanchez's friend had said, a little girl's. She must be standing on something to peek out. In that glimpse, Bruce read desolation.

Anna Escobar, at least, still lived. Bruce guessed the first cry must have been the little boy's. From the sequence of cries, he thought Anna must be doing a nearly-five-year-old's best to protect her younger brother, or at least to deflect their father's rage. She had learned, perhaps, from watching her mother.

At last Roberto went back inside. Eyes on the single-wide, Bruce pulled out his cell phone and made the calls that would bring out a SWAT team. He faded back to the stand of trees and made his way in a large circle around the trailer, which had no other door. Then he walked rapidly to his car. Not until he was out on the main road and had chosen a driveway that looked rarely used, where he could park and watch unseen for the

Buick in case Roberto decided to make a run to the grocery store, did he dial his phone again.

"I found them," he told Karin.

CHAPTER THIRTEEN

BRUCE HAD MADE the decision to move a team into place around the perimeter of the single-wide mobile home, but otherwise to wait until Roberto emerged to go to the store or do another errand. Hell, if he'd just take a few steps from the front door while having his smoke they might be able to bring him down. Bruce wanted him to be separated from the children when they attempted to make the arrest. A man as cold-blooded and egocentric as he was wouldn't hesitate to use the children to evade capture.

One by one, black-suited SWAT-team members slipped across the field and took up their stances behind the hulks of cars, trucks and tractors that studded the yard. A couple eased up to the single-wide itself, where they flattened themselves against the exterior walls so they couldn't be seen through the windows.

They'd considered trying to get in through one of the windows to the children, perhaps passing them through, but given the children's ages, the consensus was that they couldn't be trusted not to cry out. And the windows were small. Even an adult Molly's size, say, would have a hell of a time squeezing in. It wasn't going to happen without alerting Escobar, whose frequent, restless appearances at the front door suggested that he was hypervigilant.

A couple of snipers were in place, as well, and Bruce knew they were itching to take that shot, but until Escobar threatened one of the kids, killing him wasn't justified.

The girl's face appeared a couple more times. Bruce, sitting behind a pickup truck that had no axles or wheels, wondered what she was looking for.

The afternoon and early evening passed with no indication Roberto had any intention of going anywhere. Every cop in hiding tensed when he walked out once. Were they going to have a go? But, whatever he'd planned, he wheeled and went inside.

Back in the trees, they started holding a discussion. Did they camp out here all night? Hope for a chance tomorrow? Bruce didn't like the odds in a confrontation.

Bruce talked to Karin and Lenora a couple of times as the excruciating hours crawled by. He knew that Lenora's anguish must be a thousand times his own.

The decision of whether or not to wait was snatched out of his hands.

Bruce was sitting with his back to the rusting door of his chosen cover, when he heard a crash followed by the scream of tortured metal, a shout and an even louder crash. It sounded like a goddamn car accident, right there in the yard.

Growling an obscenity, he rose to a crouch.

One of the cars had fallen off its blocks. A cop lay half beneath. He was trying to sit up, but was pinned.

His face was twisted in agony, his teeth gritted. As if not screaming now would make any difference.

The door to the trailer snapped open. Roberto stared across the yard, let out a single expletive and disappeared within.

Bruce's earbud crackled. "What do we do? What do we do?" asked a couple of difference voices.

"The damn thing fell right on Fulton's *legs*," someone else said.

A second SWAT-team member was now crouched beside him. Someone else ran forward, and the two cops strained to lift the rusting heap to free their colleague.

The door to the mobile home opened again, and Roberto reappeared, his little girl in his arms and the barrel of a handgun pressed to her head. Most of his body was obscured by the door and by her. He wasn't taking any chances.

"Show yourselves!" he yelled in Spanish. "Show yourselves now!"

"Not everyone," Bruce murmured, then stood, holding his hands up.

Four other officers stood, as well, all doing the same. *See? We're harmless.*

"I'll kill her!" Roberto Escobar's face was that of a madman. Sweat dripped from him, and his eyes were wild. When Anna kept struggling, his arm snapped tight abruptly, viciously. She retched. "If you try to come in, I will shoot you, and I will kill them both."

Still holding the gun on his own daughter, he backed inside and yanked the door shut behind him.

More men ran forward to lift the car, finally dragging Fulton out.

A window scraped open. Their heads lifted. The barrel of a rifle slid into sight, and they all flung themselves to each side as it cracked. Bullets banged off the metal.

Men crawled, belly to the ground, a couple dragging their injured officer. Dirt and grass spat into the air when shots hit nearby. Then the barrel disappeared and the window closed.

Bruce began to swear again. This was his worst nightmare. Even Escobar hadn't had any idea how to get out of this. A man of limited education and experience, born paranoid—what was he going to ask for? A helicopter to carry him away? A Hummer?

No. Escobar knew he was trapped, knew they wouldn't, couldn't, let him go. Another man might have meditated, realized he was done and released his children. Maybe killed himself, but not the kids. Roberto would *want* to kill them, especially if he'd found out his wife had survived. Right this second, he'd be dreaming up an ugly, newsworthy end.

Would he do it right away? Did they have time?

A calm voice spoke at his side. "Did we get a phone number?"

Jerry Gullick, one of the top negotiators in the Northwest.

Bruce shook his head. "Phone company says there isn't one in there."

"I've got my bullhorn." He brandished it.

"I doubt he'll talk," Bruce said grimly. "But do your best."

They'd discussed earlier, if this moment came, what leverage Gullick might have with Roberto. They all knew that Lenora might be his one weakness. Bruce hated the idea of playing that card. Roberto wouldn't be persuaded by his wife; he'd want her here only so he could take pleasure in knowing she was watching as he murdered Anna and Enrico.

"Roberto," the negotiator called, stepping into sight. "There is no way out. Let's talk. Open a window so you can hear me and I can hear you."

Bruce dropped back for a consultation.

"We could lob in a canister of gas," someone suggested.

A captain shook his head. "He'd hear the window breaking. Even a couple seconds' warning is too much."

"And do we know the effect on a baby?" asked Bruce.

"They're his own *children*." More incredulity from a lieutenant.

Bruce tried to remember what it was that the uncle had said about Escobar.

He thought it was his right. As if he were God inside his own house.

Bruce said flatly, "He's incapable of loving them. They're *his*. A statement."

If a man can't be king in his own castle...

Not comparable, Bruce thought. His father, whatever his sins, would have run into a burning building to save one of his sons. He was a son of a bitch who believed he had a right to indulge his temper, but he wasn't a monster.

Not like Roberto Escobar.

Bruce left the huddle of men, walked a few feet and turned his back. He flipped open his cell phone.

Karin was waiting at the hospital with Lenora. She answered on the first ring.

"We screwed up," Bruce told her bluntly.

Her breath hissed in.

"The kids are fine still. I think they're fine," he added conscientiously, not wanting to lie. He told her about the car collapsing from its cinder blocks, presumably because someone had been leaning against it without realizing it was precariously balanced. The injured officer, the shots, Escobar's appearance with a gun to his daughter's head, the controlled hysteria.

"Our negotiator's talking to him right now, but Escobar isn't answering."

"Do you need me to bring Lenora?"

God. He wanted to say no, keep her far, far away. But he knew she was their only hope of luring Escobar out. And he knew, as well, that she wouldn't hesitate to sacrifice herself for the sake of her children.

He hated to think she might have to, but right this minute he didn't have any other ideas.

"Yeah. I'm sending someone to pick you up. You need to get here quick."

Karin said only, calmly, "We're ready."

He made another call, getting a uniform to fetch them and haul ass down here.

After grabbing a pair of binoculars, he studied the mobile home again. It was a relic of the sixties, at his guess; metal siding, once white, was scabbed with rust and curled up at the seams. He could imagine the floors were rotting. They could get under it, see if there was an easy place to punch up.

Same problem as going in the window. Short of teleporting, there was no way in without giving warning.

When he returned to Gullick's side, the negotiator murmured, "He cracked a window. He's listening."

"Good. What are you promising?"

"I'm not promising. I'm asking him what we can do. I'm reminding him that his children depend on him for protection, that their papa is a great man to them."

"Uh-huh."

Gullick returned to the bullhorn, his voice as magic as the highest paid DJ's, smooth and soothing. Right now, he was Escobar's best friend, his salvation. Thank God he spoke fluent Spanish.

Maybe instead of lobbing a gas canister in a window, they could quietly pop a hole in the floor. Insert it that way.

Bruce remembered the photo taken at Christmas of little Anna and Enrico and cursed under his breath.

The front door opened again, just a crack. Anna, held in her father's arms, appeared. He was no more than a dark shadow behind her.

Through the crack he shouted, "I will kill one of the children if you don't go away. You have five minutes." The door snapped shut again.

Swearing, Bruce grabbed the bullhorn. "Roberto, your wife is on her way. She wants to talk to you. We can't let her come if we aren't here to protect her."

There was a pause. Then, through the window, he called, "If she wants to talk, she must walk up to the steps alone. No one with her."

"No. You talk from this distance."

Silence.

"Do I have your promise to wait for her? You won't hurt Anna or Enrico?"

His voice, disembodied and less angry than earlier, was more disturbing devoid of rage. "When she comes." The window slid shut.

Behind him, Bruce heard someone say, "What the hell does *that* mean?"

But they all knew. Roberto wanted his wife to suffer.

This wait was more agonizing than all the previous hours put together. Nothing and no one could be seen moving inside the single-wide. Out here, every idea presented was shot down as fast.

"Goddamn tin can," Bruce's father used to call mobile homes. In this case, he was right. The windows were tiny, the door next to impossible to break down, the metal siding as good as a soup can at protecting its contents. Bruce tried to picture what Roberto was doing inside. Had he forced the children to lie down? Were they huddled in a corner? Why was neither crying? Were they that terrified of their father, even at their tender age? Or was Enrico already dead?

Bruce swore aloud, earning him a sidelong look from Gullick and from Marston, his captain. Neither commented.

The squad car carrying the two women pulled

partway up the dirt driveway before rolling to a stop. Why not? Roberto knew his wife was coming. Surprise wasn't a realistic goal here.

The two got out and walked to Bruce, Karin half supporting Lenora, who moved slowly and with difficulty. Her face was as white as those damn hospital sheets, the underlying bones stark without the softening effect of hair. Her eyes, despairing, dominated it.

Bruce tore his gaze away long enough to meet Karin's. She looked little better than Lenora. He hated seeing her so afraid, so aware that she was helpless to change what was to come.

"I'm sorry," he said, taking Lenora's hand. "It shouldn't have ended up like this."

"Perhaps it had to." The small Hispanic woman gave a shrug. Her voice was soft and somehow fatalistic. "It's me he wants to hurt."

Releasing her hand, he said, "I thought we could get the children out of this."

"I will offer myself." Despite the determination in her tone, her glance at the mobile home betrayed her terror. "But he must let Anna and Enrico go. Do you think he'll do that?"

"We want him to *think* he'll get you in exchange. We can't let him get his hands on you."

She bit her lip so hard blood smeared it. "I won't risk them. Only they matter. He will know if you try to trick him." She hesitated. "Have you seen them?"

"Only Anna," he admitted. "Earlier, I thought I heard two children crying, but that was hours ago."

Tears welled in her eyes, but she brushed impatiently at them. "He knows I'm here now."

"Yes."

If Roberto was looking out the window, what did he feel? Was he angry that his wife still lived? Did he feel even a pang of regret, perhaps remember slowly unbraiding her glossy dark hair, back when it hung nearly to her waist and when she would have gazed up at him trustingly?

Bruce issued instructions to her without any expectation they could be followed. Eyes trained on his face, she nodded.

Finally, Gullick asked, "Are we ready?"

Ready? Realistically, they weren't going to be tricking Roberto Escobar. They had only the hope of sacrificing this brave woman for the two young children she loved so much that she faced death without hesitation.

Inside, Bruce raged, but he gave a curt nod.

Gullick lifted the bullhorn. "Roberto, Lenora is here."

The front door opened. They all waited, breathless, none more than Lenora, who pressed her hand to her breast as if to still her heart. Karin held her closer, if possible.

Again, it was Anna he held up. Even from this distance, they could all see that one side of her face was bruised and swollen. Her eyes found her mother, and her mouth formed the silent, desperate cry *Mama.* Lenora's breath hissed in. Bruce fought to hold on to his cool.

"If you don't want to watch her die, you will come by yourself to the door."

"We told you she'd talk from this distance," the negotiator said.

"Then I'll kill Anna right now."

He must have rammed the barrel tighter against his daughter's head. Her eyes widened and she began to struggle.

"No!" Lenora called, and wrenched herself free from Karin's encircling arm. "I'll come if you will let Anna and Enrico both go."

"You lie!" he bellowed.

"No." She walked forward a few steps.

Bruce's every instinct was to snatch her back. It took everything he had in him to let her do what she must.

"Where is Enrico?" she asked. "Bring him out. I want to see him."

After a moment, the little girl was pulled back from the opening. A toddler was lifted instead. He wore no diaper, only a T-shirt. His face was soaked with tears that must have been shed silently, an extraordinary feat for a child that age.

Lenora's whole body jerked. "Let them walk out to meet me." Her voice was now eerily calm. "You can shoot them if I don't keep coming."

The silence was absolute. They all knew he might pull the trigger right now, throw the boy's body out for his horrified wife to see. That might be all he wanted, to kill their children in front of her, then himself. To leave her shattered.

Bruce reached out and gripped Karin's hand. She held on as tightly, her fear palpable in the connection.

After a moment, the door opened wider, just enough to allow the little girl to slip out.

She wore a dress; a pretty one, red, with white lace and a puffy skirt below which her legs were skinny and bare. That dress was so incongruous it struck a bizarre note. She raced to her mother, her hair flying behind her, tears streaming down her face now.

Lenora ran forward to meet her and fell to her knees. Their bodies met, and the weeping little girl vanished in her mother's enfolding arms. She held her and rocked her for a moment that was heartbreakingly brief, then lifted her head and said clearly, "Now Enrico."

"I want you closer first."

She bowed her head and spoke to the little girl. Lenora's hands lifted and smoothed her child's hair lovingly, lingeringly. Anna might never know that touch again, but she wouldn't forget it. Then Lenora stood, looked toward Karin and gave her daughter a gentle push.

Karin dropped Bruce's hand and stepped forward, kneeling with her arms out. The girl came to her, but with many backward glances. Once, she stumbled and fell. Finally, she let Karin in turn enfold her, but swiveled in her arms to stare yearningly back at her mother.

Steadily, Lenora walked forward. She wasn't five feet from the rickety steps when Enrico emerged. He scrambled down them on his short legs and raced in turn to his mother. Again, she crouched and held him. Not a single cop watching could tear his gaze from the reunion.

Finally, she sent him on his way, as well. He might not have been willing had he not had his sister in his sights. He ran to her, and the two seemed to meld, so closely did they cling.

Without a backward glance, Lenora climbed the steps. She never glanced toward the cops flattened against the wall, one perhaps ten feet to her left, another at the corner.

"Do you have a shot?" Marston was demanding. "Goddamn it, do you have a shot?"

In their headsets, they heard the sniper in the best position saying urgently, "I can't make him out. Damn it, she's in the way. Now she's in the way."

This was the moment for her to fling herself to one side. Roberto would have a shot, but only one. Instead, his arm snaked out and snatched her inside. She seemed to go meekly, her head bent. Incredulous, Bruce realized she'd never intended to avoid her fate.

But the door didn't shut. Something was happening inside. A scuffle, a clatter. A howl of rage.

The two closest SWAT-team members flung themselves up the steps. Bruce was running before his brain ordered, *Move!* What was happening? Why no shot?

It was over by the time he threw himself up the steps and inside. Roberto Escobar was facedown on the floor, writhing, cuffs being snapped on his wrists. He was screaming obscenities.

Lenora had backed away, hand to her mouth, staring at him. Huge shudders shook her. Bruce assessed the scene with a lightning glance. The handgun lay ten feet away, as if it had been kicked across the filthy, carpeted floor.

He took her in his arms, turning her away from the monster who had fathered her children and would have killed them rather than let her leave him. "What happened?" Bruce asked over her head.

One of the cops shook his head. "Somehow she brought him down. He was on the floor when I got in the door."

Lenora pushed away from Bruce and swung around to stare venomously at the man being hauled to his feet. "He thought I couldn't fight back. But somehow I knew what I should do. I chopped, like this—" she demonstrated a vicious snap of her hand "—and the gun fell to the ground. And then I kneed him, there."

Bruce had never in his life seen a look like the one Roberto Escobar gave his wife over his shoulder as he was shoved out the door. Baffled hatred and incredulity.

She was right. It had never occurred to him that she would fight back.

Bruce found himself grinning. Maybe it was inappropriate. This minute, he didn't care.

"It was the self-defense workshop," he realized. "We talked about those things. A chop of the hand and run. And where a man's most vulnerable."

"That," she said with an odd primness, "I already knew." Then, suddenly, her eyes filled with tears. "Anna! Enrico!"

She flew out the door and down the steps, then ran, lurching, across the field, passing her husband now surrounded by half a dozen cops. Karin let the kids go and they raced to their mother, both crying, "Mama, Mama, Mama!" the whole way.

Bruce watched both them and Karin, standing directly behind them. Once again, her fingers were pressed to her mouth, but now tears streamed down her face, too. She lifted her gaze to meet Bruce's, and hers was filled with joy so transcendent, he felt it like a blow.

No, like a caress.

I can't live without her.

And then, without the slightest difficulty, he thought, *I love her.*

THE CHILDREN WERE SKINNY and dirty and traumatized. Both stuck to their mother like leeches. Bruce guessed it would be several years before they would be pried loose for any length of time. But Lenora held them with extraordinary tenderness, speaking softly, pressing kisses to their cheeks and the tops of their heads. It was as if no one else existed.

Bruce felt something like envy. He had never seriously considered having children of his own before. But watching Lenora with her two children, watching Karin hovering over them, he felt like an idiot. Yeah, of course he was in love. And he couldn't imagine anything better than to have kids with her.

He wanted to be alone with her. Right now. He wanted to drag her into his arms and kiss her. He wanted to make passionate love to her, before or after he went down on bended knee and asked her to marry him.

Adrenaline kept pumping through him. His chest felt bruised, after hours of despair and the heart-wrenching sight of a mother reassuring her young children and then saying goodbye to them, in a way they might not have recognized but that every adult had. How had he gotten to his age *without* seeing how powerful love could be?

Of course, it was hours before he had a chance to exchange more than a few words with Karin.

Lenora and the kids went to the hospital, where her family enveloped them. Bruce's last sight of Roberto for the night was in the back of a squad car, his face a blur as he stared with dark, angry eyes.

Karin finally went home, but not before pausing at Bruce's side and saying, "Will you come when you can?"

"Yeah." He touched her face. Didn't trust himself to kiss her. He might not be able to stop.

He didn't get away for hours.

It was just after two in the morning when he knocked on her door. The porch light was on, and at least one lamp in the living room. Nonetheless, he barely tapped, in case she'd fallen asleep.

The door opened and she stepped forward as he did the same. His arms closed convulsively around her. For a moment he just held her. Why did he feel this way? he wondered. Neither of them had had a near-death experience today, or even been in danger. But he felt as if they had, as if they needed to grab and hold on to each other.

Karin pulled back. "Did you *see* her? Wasn't she amazing?"

"Yeah." His voice was rough. "She was amazing."

"You taught her to do that."

"She doesn't remember the class."

"But somehow she did. When she needed to."

Okay, damn it, that did feel good. He'd done something worthwhile. Knowing that helped a little, because his heart hadn't been the only thing bruised today. His ego had been, too. He'd be rethinking every damn decision he'd made for a long time to come. They'd been a blink of the eye from tragedy today, and he would have blamed himself. In the end, he hadn't been able to help Lenora. She'd had to rescue herself. The cop in him didn't like knowing that, even as the man marveled at her extraordinary courage.

"We're standing here for the whole world to see." Karin suddenly sounded self-conscious. She hugged herself and stepped back. Probably she'd just remembered that she wore only a camisole with spaghetti straps and a pair of low-slung pants that looked like sweats but thinner. Yoga pants, maybe. Her nipples showed through the thin knit fabric of the top, clear enough that he hardened at the sight. "Will you stay tonight?"

"Yeah." Gruff again. "I'll stay."

"Good." Her teeth worried her lip. "I think I need you."

"I need you, too."

Her smile warmed. "I'm glad." She shut the door behind him and turned the dead bolt, then moved naturally into his arms again.

The opening was perfect. Bruce suffered a momentary hitch. It reminded him of having to speak for the first time in a foreign language to a group of native speakers. You felt as if you were making an ass of yourself.

So? Be an ass.

Looking down into her face, glowing up at him, he took the leap. "I love you."

Her entire body went still. The smile vanished. Only her eyes were vividly, intensely alive, searching his. "You mean that?" she whispered.

"Yeah." He slid a hand around the back of her neck, reveling in the silk of her skin, the tension and strength and fragility that made up a woman who'd captivated him from the beginning. "I mean it."

"Oh." It was as much a sigh as an exclamation. "I love you, too. You know that, don't you?"

He hadn't expected to feel as if his heart had just been cleaved in half. Excruciating, and weirdly pleasurable. His heart would never be whole again. He imagined himself handing her a chunk of it, bloody and still beating, the wound in his chest open.

Bruce cleared his throat. "I...hoped." With his free hand, he brushed hair back from her forehead, loving the curve of it. "I think, today..." Why was this so hard to say? "We saw love. A different kind, but...indomitable." Not a word he could ever remember using, but it seemed right. "I thought, if he'd had that gun to your head..."

"You would have done anything."

He nodded. "Meeting you changed me."

She actually laughed, a soft sound, and shook her head. "You've always had the capacity to love someone. You do love Trevor."

"I want kids." The words seemed torn from him. "I want you."

Her lips parted in surprise.

"Will you marry me?"

She gave a cry and rose on tiptoe to press her mouth against his. The kiss was long and sweet, shared wonder more than physical hunger, although he felt that, too.

"Yes," Karin murmured against his mouth. "Oh, yes."

"Cops make lousy husbands."

"But you'll understand when I'm immersed in some poor woman's horror, or I have nightmares about a ten-year-old who's been raped by her grandpa."

Yeah, he'd understand. She'd get what he did, too. She was that woman in a million who'd be able to *handle* marriage to a cop.

"I love you," he said again, as if those three simple words summed up every one of the thousand emotions that swelled in his chest.

The amazing thing was, they did. And they got easier to say, too.

Tears sparkled on her lashes, and she murmured, "Now, make love to me."

That part, he'd already learned to do. He and she—they'd never just had sex, he realized sometime later, as he touched her and was touched, as they alternated passion and tenderness. They'd always made love.

Maybe she was right. He hadn't needed therapy to alter some vital part of him so he was able to feel love.

He'd just needed Karin.

* * * * *

THE SINGLE DAD'S VIRGIN WIFE

BY
SUSAN CROSBY

Susan Crosby believes in the value of setting goals, but also in the magic of making wishes, which often do come true – as long as she works hard enough. Along life's journey she's done a lot of the usual things – married, had children, attended college a little later than the average co-ed and earned a BA in English, then she dived off the deep end into a full-time writing career – a wish come true.

Susan enjoys writing about people who take a chance on love, sometimes against all odds. She loves warm, strong heroes and good-hearted, self-reliant heroines, and will always believe in happily ever after.

More can be learned about her at www.susancrosby. com.

To Renée Garcia, mom and home-school teacher
extraordinaire. Your value is beyond measure.
And to April Bastress, Education Specialist,
for the passion you bring to your valuable work.

Chapter One

Tricia McBride came to a quick stop a few feet from the interview room of At Your Service, a prestigious Sacramento domestic-and-clerical-help agency. She stared in disbelief at the owner, Denise Watson, who'd been filling her in on the details of a job opening.

"Hold on a second," Tricia said. "Let me get this straight. I'm not being interviewed by the person I would be working for, this Noah Falcon? I would be taking the job, boss unseen?"

"That sums it up," Denise replied. "It happens all the time, Tricia."

"It does?"

"Remember, I screen all my potential employers, just as I do my employees. If you find yourself in an impossible situation, you'll leave, but I don't think that'll be the case. Noah's a successful business owner, a widower with four children. Pillar of the community."

"Yet he's not doing the interviewing." Tricia didn't like how two and two were adding up. "There's something you're not telling me."

Denise hesitated. "Well, to be honest, he doesn't know his current employee is quitting. She told Noah's brother in confidence, and he decided to take matters into his own hands and do the hiring himself."

"Why's that?"

"You can ask him yourself." Denise opened the door, leaving Tricia no choice but to follow her inside.

An attractive man about her own age stood. Denise made the introductions. "Tricia McBride, this is David Falcon."

Greetings were exchanged, then Denise left them alone.

"Your résumé is impressive," David said, taking his seat at the conference table again.

It is? Tricia thought, but she said thank you then sat. "Why me, Mr. Falcon?"

He raised his brows at her directness. "Why not you, Ms. McBride?"

"I'm sure Denise told you I'll be leaving Sacramento in January to move to San Diego to start a new job. I would be in your brother's employ less than three months. That seems unfair to the family."

"And you're absolutely committed to this other job?"

"Yes, absolutely, unequivocally. I've given my word."

"Just checking," he said with a smile. "You know, it's obviously not the ideal situation for us. But the important thing is that we'll have that three-month cushion to find someone perfect, someone who *will* stay. Who knows, it could happen next week, and you'd be on your way. We're not guaranteeing the job for the whole three months, either. But in the past Noah has been forced into making expedient choices. You'll be giving him the luxury of time to find just the right person."

"By that you mean he loses employees frequently?"

David hesitated. "My brother tends to hire people fresh out of college who don't have a clue about life yet, not to mention how to handle four children. You were a kindergarten teacher, which leads me to believe that you like children, certainly a necessity for the job, plus you have actual experience working with them. You're thirty-four, so you have life skills, as well. Denise has done a thorough background check on you, and I feel comfortable that you'll be an asset."

She eyed him directly, not easily fooled. "And what's the real reason you're doing this behind his back?"

He half smiled. "Truth? Noah's children are in need of a woman like you, even if it's only for a few months. Their mother died three years ago. The house is…quiet. They need laughter. And someone who will stand toe-to-toe with Noah."

"Why?"

"He needs help, but he usually resists suggestions. Noah is still grieving. He doesn't know how to deal with his children."

"*Deal* with them?"

"Wrong word, I guess. He loves them. He just doesn't know how to show it."

He sounded to Tricia like a man out of his element and on the edge. "When Denise called me yesterday to talk about the job she made it seem like a nanny position, but after the details she gave me today, I'd say it's beyond that."

"It's more teacher than nanny. The kids are homeschooled, so your teaching background is important."

"Homeschooling four children is a far cry from being a nanny."

"Which is why the salary is so high. But the kids are bright and eager to learn."

"How old are they?"

"The boys are nine and the girls are twelve."

"Twins? As in two sets?"

He gave her a dry, apologetic smile. "Which is the other reason the salary is high. Yes, two sets of twins, who aren't nearly as intimidating as you might imagine. Just the idea of them tends to scare off the prospective help, which is why I asked Denise not to mention it."

"I'm really not sure about this…."

"I understand your reservations, but if you'll just give it a chance…" He leaned forward. "Denise is good at what she does, finding the right person for the job. In fact, she's downright uncanny at it. Why don't I just take you to Noah's house now, while he's at the office? You can meet the children and see the environment."

The children. Tricia pictured them, sad, and lonely for a father who didn't know how to show he loved them. She blew out a breath, trying to dispatch the heart-tugging image. "Where does he live?"

"About an hour's drive north of Sacramento, a little town called Chance City, although not within the town itself."

"You mean it's in the *country?*" Tricia couldn't contain her horror at the idea. She'd spent her entire life in the city. She liked concrete and grocery stores and fast-food restaurants.

"Depends on what you mean by country. It's in the Sierra foothills," David said. "His home is large and comfortable, on ten acres of property."

"As in no neighbors for ten acres?" This was getting worse and worse.

"Or thereabouts."

"So, I'd have to live in? What about my house? I'm getting it ready to put on the market."

"You could get Saturdays and Sundays off. He can hire weekend help locally, if he wants to," David said.

Silence blanketed the room. Living in, with weekends off. Not exactly what she'd signed up for. Or expected. Then again, it was only for three months, and her mantra of the past year kept repeating in her head: *Life is short. Make it an adventure.* She just needed to keep her usual safety net in place, too.

"Okay," she said at last. "Let's go check it out."

Claws of tension dug into Noah Falcon's shoulders as he turned into his driveway and followed it to the back of his property. He drove into the garage, shut off the engine and sat, trying to shift out of work mode and into parent mode. The demands of owning a company were a breeze compared to being with his children each night. Somehow during the past three years they'd become almost strangers to each other.

Lately he'd found himself coming home later and later, knowing they would be ready for bed, if not already asleep, thus avoiding contact beyond a query about how their day had gone and what they'd learned. When he did manage to make it home for dinner, he tried to carry on a conversation at the table, but unless he continually asked questions, they were almost silent. He didn't know how to breach that silence, to get them to open up on their own.

And this was Friday, which meant another whole weekend with them.

At least tonight he didn't have to worry about what to do, since it was past their bedtime. But as he walked toward the house he saw his daughters' bedroom light on and realized he'd come home too early, after all. The rest of the second-floor rooms visible from the back side of the house were dark—the master suite and the bedroom the boys shared. Although there was a bedroom for each child, both sets of twins remained doubled up, choosing not to be separated.

He understood their need to be together and hadn't pushed them to split up, even though he remembered having to share with his middle brother, Gideon, when they were young, and begging to have his own space, not getting it until he was a teenager.

But twins were different. Closer. At least *his* twins were. And Adam and Zach were only nine, so they probably wouldn't be ready for individual rooms for a while yet. Maybe Ashley and Zoe never would.

Noah let himself into the kitchen through the back door. As usual, a plastic-wrap-covered dinner plate was in the refrigerator, along with instructions on how long to heat it in the microwave. He peered through the clear wrap and saw meat loaf, mashed potatoes and green beans. His stomach growled. He shoved the plate into the microwave, set it and headed upstairs to say good-night.

As he neared the landing he heard a woman speaking, her voice dramatic. The girls must be watching a movie, because it wasn't their nanny, Jessica.

He'd almost reached the doorway to the girls' room when he spotted all four of his children reflected in Ashley's floor-to-ceiling ballet mirror on the bedroom wall. They wore pajamas. The boys were nestled in beanbag chairs they'd dragged into the room from their own. The girls were lying on their stomachs on Ashley's bed, chins resting on their hands. All of them were focused on a woman standing off to the side a little, an open book in her hand.

She was tall. He was six-four, and he figured she was five-ten, maybe taller. Her hair was a wild mass of golden-blond curls that bounced as she dramatized the story. She used a different voice for each character and put her whole body into the performance—her whole very nice body. Blue jeans clung to long legs; her breasts strained against a form-fitting sweater. Incredible breasts.

She would look magnificent naked, like some kind of Amazon. A warrior woman—

Noah scattered the image. She was a stranger in his house, in his children's bedroom. Who the hell was she? And where was Jessica?

He moved into the room. The children turned and stared but said nothing, just looked back and forth between the woman and him.

"Good evening," he said to them.

"Good evening, Father," they answered almost in unison.

He saw the woman frown for a moment, then she came forward, her hand out. Brilliant green eyes took his measure. "Hi. You must be Noah Falcon. I'm Tricia McBride, your new schoolmarm."

Chapter Two

"My new…schoolmarm?" he repeated as he shook her hand. "But, where's Jessica?"

"Watching television in her bedroom. We can do an official changing of the guard on Monday." Tricia leaned close to him, sympathetic to his shock. "You need to call your brother David."

His mouth hardened. "In the meantime, may I speak to you in the hall?" he said, more a command than question, then he left the room without waiting for a response.

Tricia steeled herself for the discussion. She'd expected surprise and resistance, based on David's comments, as well as Jessica's. But having spent the afternoon and evening with his children, she'd decided she would make him hire her. They needed her. Period.

She set down the book and smiled at the children. "I'll be back to finish it with you. Why don't you have a pillow fight or something in the meantime?" She grinned as they looked at each other in astonishment.

She crashed straight into her new boss as she left the room.

"What took you so long?" he asked.

"Ten seconds is long? I was assuring your children that I'd be back to finish reading the story."

"Aren't they kind of old for bedtime stories? They do know how to read."

She was definitely going to have more problems with the father than the children. And, really, someone should've told her how incredibly attractive the man was, with his rich dark brown hair and eyes, and all that height and broad chest and shoulders. Too bad he didn't have a funny bone.

"Personally, I still love a good bedtime story," she said, realizing he was waiting for her to answer.

He shoved his hands in his pockets. "I take it Jessica is quitting."

"That's the scoop."

"And my brother found out and intervened and hired you."

"Yes. I imagine he's waiting to hear from you."

"Oh, he'll hear from me, all right."

She wouldn't want to be on the other end of *that* call.

"What's your background?" he asked.

"Kindergarten teacher." She figured he didn't need to know yet that she hadn't taught for five years. "Jessica showed me the curriculum. It looks doable." Just needed a little shaking up to add some fun to the program.

He angled away from her. "I'm going to talk to Jessica, then call David. Please come to my office when you're done reading to the children. Do you know where it is?"

"Jessica gave me a tour." Seven bedrooms, seven bathrooms, three stories. The tour lasted half an hour.

"Good." He started to walk away.

"I'm sorry. I must have interrupted your saying good-night to your children," she said cheerfully.

He gave her a long look then sidestepped around her and went back into the room. She followed, wanting to watch them interact.

No pillow fight going on, but that wasn't a surprise.

"So. Another change," Noah said, standing in the middle of the room between the boys and girls. "I'm sorry."

"It's okay," Ashley said with a smile.

"No, it's not okay," Noah said after a long moment. "I'll fix it."

The girls were sitting cross-legged on the bed. He ruffled their long, strawberry-blond hair and said good-night, then did the same with the boys, who were so similar in coloring to their father, dark hair and eyes. They each said, "Good night, Father," in return. He nodded at Tricia as he left the room.

She picked up the book again. She only had three pages remaining to finish the story and figured he would need some time to take care of his business. She started reading, noted that the children got caught up in the story again instantly, their expressions rapt.

Ashley applauded at the end. She was easy to distinguish from her twin, Zoe, because Ashley almost always smiled, while Zoe rarely did.

"I guess it's time for bed?" Tricia asked them, thinking it was early for twelve-year-olds, but they didn't complain.

The boys grabbed their beanbag chairs and headed for the door.

"I'll come say good-night," she said to them.

They looked at each other. "Why?" Adam asked. Tricia had noticed that Adam often spoke for Zachary, too, after exchanging a look. But Adam and his sister Zoe were also similar in that they were constantly moving. Even if they were sitting, their feet were rarely still.

"Because I like to," Tricia said to Adam. "I think it's a nice way to end the day."

Again the boys looked at each other. The overly quiet Zachary shrugged and left. Adam followed.

"You'll be here on Monday, right?" Ashley asked as she climbed under her blankets.

"Your dad will make the final decision, but I sure hope so. I'm looking forward to it."

"Why?" Zoe asked from her side of the room.

Zoe was easily the most intense of the four, the one to question why.

"Because I like you," Tricia answered.

"You don't even know us," Zoë scoffed.

Ah, yes. Definitely not one to just go along. "That's true, Zoe. And you don't know me yet, either, but I really like what I've seen already." She tucked Ashley's blankets around her. "Good night. Sleep tight."

Ashley clung to Tricia's arms for a moment, smiling sweetly. Zoe was resistant to being tucked in, so Tricia didn't try.

"Do you leave your door open or closed?" she asked. She'd already noted a nightlight on in their adjoining bathroom.

"Closed," Ashley said, quickly adding, "but not the bathroom door."

The slight tremor in her voice told Tricia all she needed to know. "Okay. Good night."

She went down the hall to the boys' room. The door was already shut, no slit of light under it. She smiled. They had a lot to learn about Tricia McBride.

She knocked. No answer. She opened the door wide, letting the hall light guide her way. Neither boy spoke. The lumps in their beds remained motionless. In the dark she couldn't differentiate between the boys and didn't know which one slept in which bed, either. She took her cue from what surrounded them. One side of the room was military neat. The other was a maze of sports equipment. She headed there first, tripping over a basketball.

"Good night, Adam," she said, rubbing his shoulder for a second. He lifted his head in a hurry.

"How'd you know it was me?"

"You are one of a kind, young man."

A moment of silence, then, "I am?"

"You sure are. Sleep tight."

"Will you be coming back?"

"I hope so."

She moved to Zachary's bed and repeated her good-night and quick touch to his shoulder. He didn't say anything until she'd reached the door.

"I don't remember your name," he said in the darkness.

"Tricia McBride. 'Night."

After shutting the door, she leaned against it for a moment, grateful she'd been able to tell them apart, hoping that impressed them in some way.

Then she headed downstairs to beard the lion in his den.

Noah drummed his fingers on his desktop, phone to his ear, as he listened to his brother defend his decision to do the hiring this time around.

"Doesn't hurt that she's easy on the eyes, either," David said, a wink in his voice.

"That's about the dumbest thing you've said. I've never gotten involved with an employee, nor do I intend to start."

"You should take a page out of my book. Worked for me."

"You took a huge risk by getting involved with your house-keeper. She could've quit, or filed a lawsuit, or—"

"Get engaged to me," David interrupted. "Turned out great."

"You were lucky."

"Damn straight."

"I didn't mean it in a good way, David."

David laughed. Noah settled into his chair. Actually, he was glad not to have to deal with interviewing and hiring yet another nanny, but he didn't want David to think he had free rein to interfere.

"The kids seem to like her," Noah said. "They've had to adapt way too many times. I hope this one sticks."

David was quiet for a few seconds, then, "That's my hope, as well."

Noah heard someone coming down the stairs and assumed it was Tricia. "I have to go. We'll talk more at the office on Monday."

"I guess I can wait until then for my thank-you gift."

Noah shook his head as he hung up. David wanted everyone to be as happy as he was, now that he'd found the right woman. Noah had already found and married the right woman, once upon a time.

A knock came at his door. "It's Tricia," she announced.

"Come in." He tried to take in her tall, curvy body again without her noticing his interest. Easy on the eyes, indeed, he thought, remembering David's comment. He indicated the chair across from his desk.

"They're all tucked in," she said, crossing her legs, her foot bouncing. "They are sweethearts."

He leaned back. "Thanks. It's been hard on them since losing their mother."

"I'm sure it has. That was three years ago, right?"

"Right, but don't give me any pop psychology about how they should be over it by now." He was so damn tired of hearing that.

Her foot stopped bouncing. "In some ways it gets even tougher as time goes by. They're probably not able to bring up her face so easily now, and I imagine that bothers them a lot. It's scary when the images fade, and you want so much to keep them near."

Her observation struck home hard with him. He was going through the same thing, even with pictures as reminders. He couldn't hear Margie's voice anymore, except that Ashley and Zoe laughed like her. "You sound like you've had experience with it yourself."

"My father died when I was eleven, so I do understand their loss."

He appreciated that she had that in common with the children. It could only help.

"Shall we discuss the job?" she asked. "Did David fill you in on me?"

"He said you want weekends off and would live in during the week. Cora, the woman who cooks and cleans for us, also only works Monday through Friday. That leaves me without anyone on the weekend."

She smiled in a way that said she wasn't biting. "Since you don't need the house cleaned or the children schooled on the weekend, you only have to feed and play with them. I assume they make their own beds? And you must be able to cook by now."

Apparently she was going to be difficult. "Is there a particular reason why you can't live here full time?"

Her brows went up. "Do I have the job description wrong? David said I was mostly to be your children's teacher. That's a Monday through Friday job, as far as I'm concerned. And everyone is entitled to time off, you know."

"The rather lucrative salary I pay," he said, "has always included the general care of the children. A nanny as much as a teacher. That means weekends, too."

"Then you'll have to cut my salary proportionately, because I don't want to live here 24/7. I live in Sacramento. Is there some reason why you can't parent your children on the weekend?"

She'd touched a nerve. He was already aware he was failing as a father. He didn't need someone who didn't know anything about him or his history telling him that, too. "Sometimes I have work to do," he said.

"Then we're at an impasse. If you can't watch your children yourself, you'll need to hire weekend help. David must have told you I'm fixing up my mother's house to sell it." She cocked her head. "And I don't mean to be presumptuous, but you seem to be in a good position financially. You could hire a full-time, live-in staff."

"I haven't always been in that position. It's made me careful. Too careful, David tells me. I do what I feel is right for me, my family and my business." He had children to provide for now and in the future. He also had employees who depended on him, on the business he brought in and the solvency of the company. He lived up to his own personal standards, was proud that he did.

"Father?"

All four of his children stood in the doorway, crammed shoulder to shoulder.

"What are you doing out of bed?" Noah asked.

Ashley took a step into the room, her hands clasped. The others huddled around her. "We want Miss Tricia to be our new teacher."

He leaned back and steepled his fingers in front of his mouth. "I see. Well, I can't say for sure yet that she will be. Miss Tricia and I are still in negotiations."

"What's that mean?" Adam piped up.

"It means we're trying to figure out what would work best for all of us."

"The best is for her to live here," Zach stated, his voice quiet but strong.

Silence filled the room as the least talkative of the bunch announced his wishes.

"You just need to pay her a lot of money," Ashley said.

"It's not about the money," Tricia said, looking pleased at the children's insistence. "Your father pays a very good salary. The issue is that I need weekends off."

The children all looked at each other. Ashley seemed to take a silent vote. "We're not little kids anymore, Father. We don't need to have a nanny all the time."

"I'll take it into consideration. Right now you all need to go back to bed and let us discuss it."

Zach went up to Tricia and shook her hand, one big up-and-down shake, his expression serious. Adam followed suit, grinning.

Zoe came next. "Do you know how to play soccer?"

"I sure do."

"Okay." Zoe stuck out her hand for a shake, then left the room bouncing an imaginary ball from knee to knee.

Ashley finally approached. "Please say yes, Miss Tricia," she said, then gave Tricia a quick hug before she hurried out.

Noah saw how the children affected her. If she could become that attached after just a few hours, she was definitely the right one for the job. It would be a great weight lifted from his shoulders, too.

"So," Noah said after a long, quiet moment. "Saturday morning to Sunday evening off. And you'll be here this Sunday night."

She smiled. "Jessica's not leaving until Monday."

"Jessica will be gone by Sunday afternoon."

"I see." Tricia nodded. "Is five o'clock okay with you, Mr. Falcon?"

He stood. "Noah. And yes, that's fine."

She stood, as well. "I'm curious why you don't send them to public school."

"I made a promise that I would continue what my late wife started." He paused. "I'll walk you to your car. Where is your car, by the way?"

"Next to your garage. You didn't notice it?"

"I was preoccupied. Let me go tell the children that you've agreed to take the job. They won't go to sleep until they know. I'll be back in just a couple of minutes." He extended his hand, as his children had. "Thank you."

"I'm very happy we came to an agreement."

Her handshake was firm, one sign of her character. She seemed straightforward. She obviously could and would speak her mind.

The Falcon household was about to change.

As Tricia stepped outside with Noah ten minutes later, the chilly late October evening cooled her warm face and cleared her eyes and mind.

So. It was official. She was employed. She would have enough money to tide her over until she started her new job.

Peace settled over her at the thought, then the quiet around her struck her. Country life. It was going to take some getting used to. No. A *lot* of getting used to. But she was probably noticing the quiet even more because Noah hadn't spoken since they'd left the house.

"Have your children always called you Father?" she asked.

"Yes. Why?"

"You just don't hear it much these days. Did you call your father that?"

"No. Most of the time I called him a son of a bitch."

Tricia stumbled. He reached for her, caught her. She grabbed hold, steadying herself, then looked at his face, as he held her upright by her arms. At odds with the coldness in his eyes, his hands were warm, his heat leeching through her sweater. "Thank you," she said quietly, sorry when he let go. There was something comforting about his large and gentle hands. "Your words caught me off guard."

"No sense hiding the truth. I made it my goal to live as differently from him as possible."

"And you called him Dad, so you don't want your kids to call you that?"

They'd reached her SUV. She pressed the alarm button to unlock it.

"You haven't been here long enough to criticize," he said coolly. "Or analyze. I grew up in total chaos. It's not what I want for my children."

She opened her car door, wanting to escape. He was right. She should mind her own business. "I apologize, Noah. I was just curious. Everything seems kind of formal between you and your children." She didn't add what she wanted to—that they were all distant from him, physically and emotionally. And that they were starving for his affection. *Anyone's* affection, which was probably why they'd latched on to her so easily.

"Is there anything you'll need to start the job?" he asked, very directly changing the subject.

She sensed in him deep, unrelenting pain, and she wondered if he would ever break through it to embrace life again. Or maybe he never had. She shouldn't presume what she didn't know. Maybe she could carefully ask other people how he was before his wife died.

"If I think of something, I'll let you know or just go ahead and buy it in Sacramento," she said, getting into the car and sliding the key into the ignition. "I'll review their classroom work Sunday night so that I'm ready to go on Monday."

"You have my phone numbers?"

"Yes, thank you." She started the engine then glanced up at him as he rested an arm on the top of her door and leaned toward her a little. He really was an extraordinarily attractive man, even tightly wound as he was. She wanted to tell him that things would get better, that his life was going to change, that she would see to it, especially for his children. But did he want to hear that?

"Do you space out often?" he asked, his voice laced with surprising humor. "Should I worry for my children's safety?"

Her eyes were dry from not blinking. "You won't regret that your brother hired me," she said, wondering if it was true.

"David may have done the prelims, but I hired you. And my children. If any one of us had objected, you wouldn't be coming back."

"Of course," she said, then shifted into reverse. "Until Sunday."

He backed away, but he was still standing in the driveway when she looked in her rearview mirror before she turned onto the road. Maybe she'd been lying when she'd told him he wouldn't regret hiring her, because he may well be sorry. She was pretty sure she was different from any other teacher he'd hired before.

And she knew he was different from any boss she'd had.

Chapter Three

Standing in the kitchen, Noah watched his children say goodbye to Jessica, who had been their nanny for several months. Usually a changing of the guard, as Tricia had called it, was cause for moping and silent recrimination from the kids, but not this time. This time they said their goodbyes and let her leave, rather than following her outside to wave to her as her car pulled away.

They always liked their nannies. That was never the issue. The problem was that the nannies didn't usually like *him*. It hadn't been any different with Jessica, apparently, although she'd never indicated any problem before quitting. Even then she'd told his brother, not him, that she was leaving.

Noah knew he had a problem dealing with his help. He'd been giving it a lot of thought the past couple of days, analyzing the situation, trying to figure out how not to lose another nan—teacher. He should get used to calling Tricia that, since she seemed to prefer it.

He wondered why none of the other nannies had said anything about the job title. Maybe because they'd just graduated from college and hadn't taught in a classroom yet. He liked that Tricia had classroom experience. If she could handle twenty kids at one time, she must be able to handle four. Especially four, quiet, easygoing, uniformly bright children.

Not that he was biased or anything....

Margie would've liked her. Probably would've been a little intimidated by her, too, but his late wife would've liked Tricia's easy way with the kids and her refusal to back down—something he wasn't sure *he* liked. He was used to being in charge, at work and at home. There was room for only one boss in any situation. He didn't tolerate clashes of authority.

"She's gone," Adam announced, looking out the window as the car disappeared, then he glanced at Noah. "When will Miss Tricia be here, Father?"

Father jarred Noah now, since Tricia had brought it up. "She said five o'clock."

Which meant he had to figure out what to do with his children until then. Well, technically after then, too, since she wouldn't be on the clock. He hadn't even planned dinner.

He realized all four children were watching him, waiting. "Did you have something to say?" he asked, his gaze sweeping across them then landing on Ashley.

"We would like to have a family meeting," she said, her expression serious.

He shifted into head-of-the-family mode. "All right. Why don't we go into the family room?"

Their footsteps sounded behind him, seeming loud in their conversation-free trek. Even Adam was quiet, a rarity.

Noah sat in what was considered his chair, an oversize lounger that faced the television he rarely had time to watch. Each child took his or her usual seat on the sofa and other chairs.

"What's on your mind?" he asked the room at large.

"We think it's time for some changes around here," Ashley answered, all business.

"What kind of changes?"

"We counted up the nannies we've had. Seven."

That many? He knew there'd been a lot. And that didn't include his mother-in-law coming to stay for the first few months after Margie died.

"We're kind of tired of figuring out someone new all the time," Ashley said.

"I understand that. What do you think can be done about it?"

"We think you should smile more," she said without smiling.

"Smile more?" he repeated, confused.

"Not at us, Father. At Miss Tricia. Miss Jessica was scared of you."

Scared? Really? He liked order but was surprised he was feared. "I'll try," he said, adding it to his mental list of things to be aware of if he didn't want to lose Tricia as an employee. "What else?"

Ashley continued. "We want Miss Tricia to eat dinner with us, not in her room like Miss Jessica and the others."

Noah was fascinated with this new, mature daughter of his. "Why?"

"Because we think if she feels like she's part of our family, she'll be happier."

"You like her that much?"

"She seems okay. We just don't want another change."

"Yes, I know you're tired of it all."

Her hands folded in her lap, Ashley sat up a little straighter. "We also don't think you should argue with Miss Tricia about anything."

An improvisation, he decided, trying not to smile. "I can't

guarantee that. We are bound to disagree on some things. And you are *my* children, not hers. I know what's best for you."

They all looked at each other. Had they always done that or was it something recent? They seemed to be more attuned than before. Each set of twins shared a connection that had always been obvious, but not in combination with the other set. He figured they must be desperate, to face him like this, presenting a united front.

"Then please be nice *and* smile at her when you argue," Zach said, fixing Noah with a stare.

Laughter rose inside his chest. He couldn't let it escape or they wouldn't believe he was taking their concerns seriously. "I'll be nice."

"Thank you."

Noah leaned his arms on his thighs and looked at each of them until they each looked back. "Now. Is there something you'd like different for yourselves, not for Miss Tricia?"

Zoe raised her hand. "I want a swimming pool."

"Basketball court," Adam added.

Noah did smile then. How easily their focus changed. "Nice try."

Zach jumped out of his chair and raced to the window at the sound of a car coming down the driveway. "She's— Nope. It's Uncle David."

"Alone?"

"No. Valerie and Hannah, too."

Three of the children raced off to greet their uncle, his fiancée and her eight-year-old daughter, Hannah. Ashley lingered, moving more slowly with Noah toward the kitchen.

"Something else on your mind?" he asked.

She shrugged.

"Talk to me," he said, stopping just outside the kitchen door, his hand on her arm to keep her there, too.

"Can we watch the videos of Mom again sometime soon?"

"You know where they are. You're welcome to watch them anytime."

"I mean as a family."

He didn't know if he wanted to bring back all that pain. He'd stopped watching the videos when he realized they hurt more than helped. "Do the others want to watch, too?"

"Not Zach."

Which didn't surprise Noah. Zach kept the most inside.

"Okay. We'll do it tonight."

"Not tonight," she said in a hurry as the kitchen door opened and everyone came in, talking and laughing. "I'll tell you when, okay?"

"Sure." He was grateful for the reprieve.

Suddenly the kitchen teemed with people, then the kids all took off upstairs with their cousin-to-be Hannah in tow.

"We brought dinner," Valerie said, as David set a covered casserole in the oven and a bowl in the refrigerator.

"I chauffeured. *Valerie* brought dinner," David said. "She made everything."

"Thanks," Noah said, surprised. "But why?"

"To welcome your new nanny," Valerie said.

"Teacher," he corrected, looking over David's head to try to see what was in the bowl, guessing it was salad. David had lucked out when he'd hired Valerie through At Your Service. She was the calm, competent woman Noah had been looking for, too. He didn't think that description applied to Tricia. Well, competent, maybe. But calm? Probably not. *Lively.* That was a better word. "I hope you're staying for dinner, too," Noah said.

David made clucking sounds.

"What's that for?" Noah asked. "I'm not a chicken."

"You don't want to make small talk with your help."

"So? I've never liked to. It's no different with Tricia."

David stood. "She's just your type."

"She's on the other side of the world from being my type."

"Leave him alone," Valerie said to her fiancé, slipping her hand into his, firing a heat-seeking caution look with her eyes. "Yes, we'll stay for dinner. That was our goal, although David was supposed to call and alert you. I want to meet Tricia myself. I expect we'll become friends."

"She's here!" came a shout from upstairs, followed by the rush of footfalls scurrying down the staircase. As a group they ran through the kitchen and out the back door, Hannah grinning as she came last—following just to follow, Noah supposed.

"That's quite a reception," David commented, wandering to the window to watch.

Noah went to take a look. Ashley and Zach got up close to her. Tricia hugged Ashley, her face alight with pleasure, and said something to Zach that caused him to smile then look down at the ground. Adam and Zoe didn't allow her close enough to hug. She held out a hand to Hannah, an outgoing, happy girl who was just as caught up in Tricia's arrival as the rest of them.

Tricia opened the back of her SUV and started passing things to each child, then they marched toward the house like safari porters, carrying bags, boxes and garments on hangers, with Tricia bringing up the rear with the largest box.

"Aren't either of you big, strong men going to help her?" Valerie asked as the back door flew open and the children tramped through.

Criticized into action, Noah met Tricia at the back door and took the box from her.

"A welcoming committee. How fun," she said. "Hi, Noah. I'm glad to see you again, David."

"I'm more glad to see you," he said with a grin. "Tricia McBride, this is my fiancée, Valerie Sinclair."

The women shook hands. "Hannah must be yours. She looks just like you. She's darling."

"Thank you, yes, she's mine."

"They brought dinner," Noah said, balancing the box on the edge of the counter.

"Oh, how nice of you. And since you're not running off, would you mind if I excuse myself for a few minutes and go make sure the children haven't just heaped all my clothes on the floor?"

David and Valerie encouraged Tricia to go.

"Be right back," Noah said, then trailed her up the stairs. As he eyed her from behind he started to rethink the idea of putting in a pool, as Zoe requested. Getting a chance to see the teacher in a skimpy bikini—

"Maybe you should just come up beside me," Tricia said, stopping and turning around.

He kept his expression blank. Okay, she'd caught him. He was a healthy male who'd been without female companionship for three years. So sue him for admiring her very sexy body.

"I got it!" a child yelled from down the hall.

"I brought it up here!"

"I think the troops need a mediator," Noah said, hiding his surprise at the fact any of them were yelling, something that almost never happened. They all got along eerily well.

Tricia's mouth tightened, but she continued up the stairs again, and he allowed himself the pleasure of watching her hips sway until they reached the landing.

She stopped there instead of heading toward the yelling down the hall. "Do we need to have a discussion?" she asked him.

"About what?"

"Appropriate employer/employee behavior."

"I'm familiar with the laws," he said. "But why do you ask?"

"You know why."

"Enlighten me." He figured she was only speculating that he'd been eyeing her rear as she climbed the stairs. He'd painted her into a corner. Either she had an accusation to make or she didn't.

"I'm telling Father!" Zoe came charging out of the room. "Ashley won't let anyone help."

Noah moved past Tricia and Zoe. When he reached Tricia's bedroom, he set the box on the floor and looked around. The closet door was open. Clothes hung neatly on the racks, with shoes lined up like little soldiers on the floor below. Ashley and Adam were elbowing each other trying to put books onto shelves. Zach was perched on the bed, thumbing through a photo album. Hannah sat cross-legged on the floor, out of the way, wide-eyed. As an only child, she hadn't been exposed to sibling rivalry.

The tension was abnormally high, each child intending to make Tricia feel at home, but being pushy about it.

"Miss Tricia can put away her own things, and, in fact, probably prefers to. Everybody out," Noah said.

"But thank you for your help," Tricia added from the doorway.

Zach hadn't lifted his head. Noah slid the photo album out of his son's hands and pointed toward the door. Before Noah closed the album, he caught a glimpse of a photo of Tricia and a man wearing an army uniform, their arms around each other. She looked young and in love.

He set the album on the dresser. "I apologize for my children," he said to her. "They're trying to help. Obviously they went a little overboard."

"It's no problem."

"It is as far as I'm concerned."

She waited a beat. "You're the boss."

He remembered how Zach had told him to be nice, and how Ashley said he needed to smile. He wasn't doing what he'd promised his children he would. And none of them could afford to lose Tricia.

"I apologize," he said, purposely relaxing his shoulders,

trying to seem more accessible. "I wanted them to be on their best behavior for you. All of us, actually. Myself included."

"Why?"

"It's your first day. We didn't want to scare you off."

She laughed. Her face lit up when she smiled. Green eyes sparkled. "I'm not easily intimidated."

"Good. Is the room okay? Big enough?"

"It's beautiful. Since my time here will be limited, it'll do just fine." She hitched a thumb toward the door. "The children have put most of my things away, so we can get back to your guests. How long has your brother been engaged?" she asked as they left the room.

"Less than a week. He hired Valerie through At Your Service as his housekeeper and administrative assistant about two months ago. He's also adopting her daughter."

"How nice for all of them."

"Yes."

She cocked her head. "I hear a *but*...."

Should he voice his concerns out loud to someone he barely knew? Would she keep quiet about his reservations or tell David? Something about her invited trust. "They haven't known each other long, that's all. And David has said forever he wouldn't get married, so it's hard to feel comfortable about his decision."

They'd almost reached the bottom of the stairs. Tricia leaned close to say, "But they're just engaged, right? They'll have more time before the wedding to learn more about each other. They could change their minds."

He'd been prepared to hear her say the opposite—something about him being too jaded, or not a romantic or something. Instead she'd seen his point about how little David and Valerie knew about each other. He liked that she seemed practical.

He also liked how her hair smelled....

"We've been waiting for you," David said as they came into

the kitchen, a hubbub of conversation. Everyone held a glass of something pale and bubbly. David passed Noah and Tricia champagne flutes. Noah assumed the children's flutes held sparkling cider.

"What's going on?" Noah asked.

"I'm making a toast." David lifted his glass toward Valerie. "To my beautiful bride-to-be—for agreeing to marry me, and for not making me wait. You're all invited to our wedding, two weeks from yesterday."

Chapter Four

Tricia exchanged a look with Noah as they sipped the cele-
bratory champagne. After a moment, he shrugged, apparently
accepting the inevitable. She decided to make it a point to get
to know Valerie and see for herself that Noah could relax about
the quick marriage. She considered herself a pretty good judge
of character.

Valerie shooed the men and children off to the family room
while dinner was reheated.

"It's a good thing they're not depending on me to cook,"
Tricia said as Valerie opened a couple of loaves of buttered
sourdough bread and put them on a baking sheet.

"You don't enjoy it?"

"My mom and I opened cans exceptionally well. And I
make a mean PB and J sandwich." She smiled at Valerie, who
smiled back.

"The reverse is true for me. My mother was a housekeeper

and cook for a family in Palm Springs," Valerie said. "She taught me everything."

"Does Hannah cook?"

"She's not quite as into it as I was, but yes. But, you know, I couldn't do what you do, Tricia. Teachers amaze me." She gestured to a cupboard. "Plates are up there."

Tricia grabbed plates, salad bowls, glasses and silverware and carried them into the dining room. "Tablecloth or place mats?" she called out to Valerie.

"Take your pick. They're in the hutch."

As Tricia set the table, she could hear the men and children playing video games in the family room. "They're having a good time," she said to Valerie, who was grating fresh parmesan cheese. Tricia leaned against the kitchen counter. "Can I ask you some questions about Noah?"

"You can ask, but I don't know a whole lot. I haven't spent much time around him."

"Do you know if he's always so serious?"

"I think I can safely say yes to that. According to David, Noah's a workaholic. He never takes a vacation. He's pretty much in charge and in control at all times. Doesn't have a great deal of patience. Very action oriented. And he doesn't like change."

"Yet I heard he's had a whole lot of nannies for the children. That's change."

"That's where the lack of patience comes in, I think. The whole interviewing and hiring process is too tedious, so he takes the quickest route."

"Does he date?"

"Not that I've heard." Valerie had just taken the salad out of the refrigerator and set it on the counter. She half smiled at Tricia. "These Falcon men are hard to resist, aren't they?"

Tricia straightened. "What do you mean?"

Valerie peeked around the doorway, making sure they

were alone. "I started falling for David the first day I worked for him, too."

"'Too'? Oh, no. Not me. Uh-uh." Tricia held up both hands. "I'm out of here in three months."

Valerie frowned. "What do you mean?"

"I'm temporary. David hired me to buy time for Noah to find someone who *will* be permanent."

"Does Noah know that?"

"I'm sure David told him." And she'd mentioned she was selling her house, and that her room here was fine for the short term. He hadn't flinched at either point. "So, tell me. What's this about you falling for David on the first day?"

"I didn't want to, but there it was. He makes me very happy. My daughter, too."

"Why the rush to get married?"

Valerie took out the fragrant, bubbling lasagna and slid the bread under the broiler. Almost immediately the pungent scent of garlic filled the air. "Why wait? It's right, and we both know it. Plus I won't move into his bedroom until we're married. I want to set a good example."

"You mean, you haven't slept together?" Tricia couldn't keep the surprise out of her voice.

Valerie laughed. "Well...David often works from home. And Hannah does go off to school."

"Oh. Okay. Good."

"Good?"

Tricia nodded. "I'll tell you why some other time."

"I hope you'll come to the wedding."

"I'm not going to be here on the weekends."

"Make an exception, please? I don't have many girlfriends here. I'd like for us to become that. I'll introduce you to my friend Dixie, too. She's my maid of honor. You'll love her. And there's the bachelorette party, of course. You have to come to that." She poured dressing on the salad. "Maybe you could tell the gang that dinner's on? I'm sure it'll take them five minutes to actually get to the table."

Tricia stopped just outside the family room door and observed the activity. Noah sat with his back to her, watching David and Adam play a video game, complete with hoots and hollers and threats of maiming. Ashley and Hannah were intent on a second television, but Tricia couldn't see the screen, so she didn't know what held their interest. Zoe bounced a soccer ball from knee to knee, not an indoor activity, but Noah wasn't objecting, which seemed odd.

Then there was Zach, who sat cross-legged at his father's feet, not communicating with any of them, but taking in everything.

He spotted her and smiled. She smiled back. "Dinner is served," she said to the room at large.

"You're doomed!" Adam shouted to his uncle, who shouted back, "Not yet, I'm not!"

Noah got up. Ashley stood right away, too, and turned off the television. She and Hannah made their way to the door, grabbing Zoe by the arm and pulling her along. Zach held back, putting himself between Tricia and Noah.

"Dinner smells *good*," Zach said.

"Looks like your uncle got himself a chef in the bargain. Do you like lasagna, Zach?" Tricia asked.

He nodded.

"We eat a lot of pasta dishes and casseroles," Noah said. "It's an easy thing for Cora to fix that will keep and reheat well. Sometimes my other brother, Gideon, comes over on the weekend and we barbecue."

They came into the dining room. It was obvious Noah sat at the head of the table, with David at the other end for tonight. Zach found his place farther down. Which left one empty seat, next to Noah.

Tricia expected at least a small amount of chaos with so many people, but it was all very…civilized. As an only child, Tricia had craved the noisy family dinner table she observed at some friends' houses. Here there were five children and four adults and little conversation. David asked questions, and the children answered, but no one took it further.

After the dishes were done, Tricia excused herself to put away her things and then to look over the children's past work. The third-floor classroom was huge. Each child had a desk. A computer workstation held two computers, but only one was connected to the Internet and was password protected so that the children couldn't log on privately. Areas were set aside for art and music, and worktables for science projects or other messier tasks. The room was tidy and spotless.

The view was spectacular, as the room was made up almost entirely of windows that faced the surrounding woodlands, and no neighbors in sight.

After a while, Ashley came up the stairs, dressed in her pajamas.

"We're going to bed," she said. "If you'd like to say goodnight," she added hesitantly.

"Yes, I would, thank you." She put an arm around the girl's shoulders and walked down the stairs with her. "I'm looking forward to starting class tomorrow. Do you enjoy your schooling?"

"Sometimes. It kind of depends on the teacher."

"I'll do my best to make it interesting and fun, Ashley."

"I know you will," she said with a smile as they walked into her bedroom. Zoe emerged from the bathroom, her strawberry-blond hair damp and tousled, a dab of toothpaste above her lip. She hopped right into bed and pulled the blankets up to her nose.

"What time do you get up in the morning?" Tricia asked Zoe.

"When Ashley pulls the covers off and won't let me have them back."

Tricia smiled. "Who wakes you up?" she asked Ashley.

"My head. I wake up early on my own around seven. Then I wake up everyone else. We go to the classroom at eight. Zoe's usually the last one there."

"Do you make your own breakfast?" Tricia knew that Cora didn't come until eleven-thirty.

"I don't like breakfast," Zoe said. "It makes me sick to my stomach."

Ashley rolled her eyes. "We eat cereal or peanut butter on toast. And a banana or apple. We fix our own."

"What time does your father leave for work?"

"He's gone before we get up." Ashley climbed into bed and settled the bedding over her.

Tricia leaned down for a hug from her, then moved on to Zoe, whose body language said, "Don't come too close," so Tricia just smoothed back her hair and said good-night.

She encountered the same situation with the boys. Adam hugged her. Zack retreated from contact. She wondered where Noah was. She couldn't hear any sounds within the house.

How did he spend his evenings? Working? Watching television? Should she track him down and find out?

She decided to return to the classroom and finish reviewing the children's previous work. Thank goodness none of them were in high school yet and taking chemistry or something else she hadn't studied in years.

After a while she heard someone coming up the stairs, the footsteps heavy enough to be only Noah's. He called her name, alerting her that he was about to enter the room.

"How's it going?" he asked, standing at the top of the staircase, his hands shoved into his pockets.

She leaned back in her chair. "I'm making headway. At least it's early in the school year. They seem to stick to a fairly rigid schedule."

"That's my preference."

So, it *was* his doing that the children's class work was so highly structured. "I'll make an appointment to see their— What is the title of the person who oversees the children's schooling?"

"Educational Specialist, but everyone calls her an E.S. Cynthia Madras is her name."

"Thanks. I've read the rules and regulations on homeschooling, but I'd like her input on the children individually."

He dragged a chair closer to her desk and sat. "She'll tell you that Ashley is a visual learner who studies more than the others and worries if she doesn't do very well on tests. Zoe and Adam are kinetic learners who have a hard time sitting still and like to have a noisy environment, which drives Ashley crazy. And Zach is an auditory learner with an exceptional memory. He studies the least and absorbs the most."

Tricia liked that he knew so much about his children's learning styles. "I appreciate the summary."

"I keep a close watch on their education. I meet with each of them individually every evening to—" He stopped, hesitated. "I *used* to meet with each of them. I've been working so late the past year that I haven't gotten home in time most nights to have one-on-one time with them."

"So, you're not home for dinner?"

"Rarely."

"I see. Well, maybe you'll be able to incorporate the individual time into your schedule again soon."

"Maybe."

A long pause ensued. She knew she needed to change the subject. "Who cleans up the dishes at night?"

"No one. Cora takes care of it when she comes in."

"Do the children have any chores to do?"

"School is their job."

She decided not to start an argument with him on the value of responsibility through chores. Not yet, anyway. "Your future sister-in-law and I had a nice talk," she said instead.

He was obviously happy about the change in subject, because his expression smoothed out. "What do you think?"

"I think Valerie is head over heels about your brother, and yet very down to earth. I like her a lot. I expect I'll learn even more about her when I attend her bachelorette party."

His brows went up. "I'm sure you will. I guess as his best man I need to figure out a bachelor-party plan myself."

"Definitely. Next weekend. You don't want to have the party the night before the wedding. Saturday night, since Friday is Halloween."

"Right." He stood. "You're all set here, then?"

"Yes, thanks." A little nervous, but excited. "Are you ever gone overnight? For work," she added, realizing he might think she was wondering if he had a girlfriend or someone he visited when he had…needs.

"Not for the past few years."

"Good."

"Why?"

"I've always lived in the city. Being so isolated out here is kind of creeping me out."

He watched her for a few long seconds. "Come with me," he said, then he went down the stairs.

She followed because he gave her no choice. He waited at the foot of the last staircase, then they walked into the dining room, through the kitchen, into the utility room. He grabbed two jackets from the rack there, passed one to her, then he held the door open. She went down the stairs, putting on the jacket as she went. *His* jacket; she could tell from how the cuffs hung past her fingers.

The night was quiet and dark. Moonless. She couldn't see

the lights of another house or building, just stars. Millions of stars. She hadn't paid attention to them Friday night, hadn't paid attention to anything but him, and how he talked about his father.

Gravel crunched beneath their feet as they walked down the driveway to the four-car garage. She'd seen him drive a fancy black sports car, but had no idea of the brand. She figured it was his commute car. A large SUV was also parked in the building, a Cadillac.

"I'll give you a garage door opener," he said. "You can park in the garage. I want you to use the Caddy to drive the kids around."

"Okay." She tugged her collar up against her neck. "I don't even know what you do for a living, except that you and David are in business together."

"We own Falcon Motorcars, custom-made automobiles. We've been strongly in the European market for a long time but are moving more toward American business now. It's a big transition for us—David's brainchild, so that he can stay stateside more."

"So that shiny sports car you drive is one of your own?"

"The latest model. At this point we only produce the two-seater sports car, a four-door sedan, and made-to-spec limos. I'd like to incorporate an SUV, but that'll be a few years down the road, I think. We're headed to the American LeMans circuit first."

"You'll be making race cars?"

He nodded, then cocked his head as they heard a noise. "That's an owl."

"I'm not a complete idiot," she said with a smile. "What else is around?"

"Deer. Dogs and cats, wild and tame. Raccoons, fox, skunks, all the usual small wild animals. A variety of birds. Early in the morning you can sit at the kitchen table and see quail. There are grouse and mourning doves and hawks. None of them is your enemy, Tricia, although the deer eat the vegetation, which is annoying sometimes. And if threatened, any animal will protect itself. You really shouldn't worry about them."

At the moment she wasn't worried at all, because he was there with her. But on her own? She really, really hated the great outdoors.

"Is that why you don't have a garden?" she asked. "Because of the deer?"

He glanced toward the open space. "We used to have a garden. It was Margie's thing. She was into organics."

"Margie is your late wife?"

"Yes."

"How long were you married?"

"Eleven years. We met in college."

"You were happy," she said, hearing it in his voice, even layered with grief.

"Yes. Very."

"How did she die?"

"Pancreatic cancer. Very quick. Very painful."

His brief answers indicated he was done talking about it. "I'm so sorry."

"Thanks." He touched the small of Tricia's back, urging her toward the house.

That touch, that single, glancing touch through the layers of the jacket, rattled her. She was already worried about falling in love with the children and not wanting to leave in January. She didn't want to be worried about falling for the father, too.

It's just hormones, she decided. Long-repressed hormones coming out of years of hibernation, something she'd been hoping would happen—just not with her boss.

Inside the house, she slipped out of the jacket before he could help her, not wanting his fingers to accidentally graze her skin.

"Any questions?" he asked as they moved through the rooms to the staircase.

"Am I free to call you at work if I have any problems? Even ones that aren't an emergency?"

"Of course. My assistant's name is Mae. She'll know to put you through. Better yet, just call my cell. I'll always answer if it's you."

"Okay. I think that's all for now. We'll probably have things to talk about tomorrow. I would appreciate your letting me know if you're joining us for dinner, so I know whether or not to wait for you."

He looked annoyed. "I have business in many time zones. Sometimes I have to stay late for a call. I'll try to be here. That's all I can say."

Based on what David had told her, and on her own observations so far, Tricia knew Noah did his best to avoid being at home. That needed to change. "Your children miss you, Noah."

He looked about to fire back then smiled instead. Sort of. As if someone was making him. "I will try," he said quietly but resolutely. The boss, after all.

She didn't like his answer, but took it no further. However, she wouldn't hesitate in a week to remind him again of his responsibility to his children.

Tricia waited to be dismissed. Since she hadn't held this kind of position before, she wasn't sure of protocol, but she figured he would be the one to end the discussion.

"All your questions are answered?" he asked.

"For now."

"Then I'll say good-night. I hope you'll be happy here, Tricia."

"I'm sure we'll have a lot of fun together. The children and I, I mean."

"I know you're used to kindergarteners, who mostly just play."

"Please don't insult me," she responded. "You won't find their education lacking because of my teaching skills."

"I didn't mean—" He stopped, took a step back. "Good night."

As she climbed the stairs, she watched him walk toward his

office. Sympathy rose inside her. For all that he was successful in his work and had four beautiful children, he was not a
happy man. And not just because he still grieved for his wife,
she decided. Maybe he'd never been happy. Obviously his
childhood hadn't been good, his father no kind of role model,
although Noah didn't seem to be anything like his own father.

Tricia shut her bedroom door and leaned against it. She was
in a tough spot. Three months to help them as a family—
because that had become her primary goal now that she'd met
them—and still be able to walk away.

Get out now, she told herself.

The shouting in her head got louder and louder. She should
heed it. She knew she should. But superimposed over it were
the faces of the children, who needed her.

And Noah. Who perhaps needed her even more.

Life's short. Make it an adventure. Her brand-new mantra
began shouting even louder, reminding her of her own needs,
which she'd promised herself she wouldn't forget. *She* was
entitled, too.

But for the moment, she needed to be here, with this family.

Having an adventure.

Chapter Five

Noah pulled into the driveway the next night at six-thirty. He hadn't called when he left the office, and he could've called from his cell phone at any time, yet he hadn't.

He didn't know why. He wasn't rude, generally. Oblivious, maybe at times, but not intentionally rude. And it hadn't slipped his mind, because *she* hadn't slipped his mind. Tricia. He hadn't even been working, but reading trade magazines so that he wouldn't get home until a half hour after the usual dinnertime, although it was two hours earlier than his norm for the past year.

If he really wanted to figure out why he'd deliberately stalled, he could call his brother Gideon, who wasn't a psychologist but understood human nature better than most people.

Noah didn't want to know why.

He made the long walk from the garage to the house. No one opened the back door to greet him, although the dining room lights were on, and they all would've seen his car turn into the driveway, his headlights arcing across the window. Maybe they were done eating.

Margie would have had the kids racing to the back door to greet him.

He reached for the door handle, then stopped and reminded himself that his world had changed forever. There was no Margie. No wife. Even though the At Your Service agency where David had found Tricia was nicknamed "Wives for Hire," Tricia wasn't his wife. Except she was doing an admirable job of filling many of Margie's roles....

But no sex, of course. That was in the contract they both signed, although he wouldn't have gotten involved with an employee, anyway. It hadn't been an issue with any of the other nannies, contract or not. Tricia was the first one to even tempt him.

Noah entered the kitchen just as they were carrying their dirty dishes in, Ashley leading the way. Accusation and disappointment hit him full force from her expression alone. Why? He hadn't made it home on time for at least a year.

"Hi," he said, setting his briefcase on the counter.

"Hello." She turned on the faucet and rinsed her plate. She opened the dishwasher and slid her dishes inside then left the room.

"Dinner was good," Adam said. He put his dishes in the dishwasher without rinsing.

Zoe followed suit. "Beef stew," she said in way of greeting.

Then Zach, whose expression was even more accusatory than Ashley's. Why? What had he done?

Zach took his time rinsing his plate, using a cloth to get every bit off the plate and silverware, then loaded them. Finally he looked at Noah. "You promised to be nice," he said, then left.

Ah. So part of being nice was being home for dinner. Okay. Noah understood now.

"Hello, Noah. Did you have a good day?" Tricia said as she brought her own dishes in.

He was not in the mood to be chastised, directly or indirectly, and her tone indicated she was doing exactly that. He was especially annoyed because she'd been intruding into his thoughts all day already. "This is your doing, I assume."

"My *doing?*" She rinsed her dishes, avoiding looking at him. "Your children seemed to think things were going to change. I have no idea what or why. All I know is, you didn't call to say you were on your way home, so we ate without you. What's wrong with that?"

"I meant having the children doing dishes."

She looked startled. "*That's* what you're mad about?"

No. He was angry that his children were barely speaking to him, but he couldn't blame Tricia for that. "I don't want them doing chores."

"Why not?" She propped a hip against the counter and crossed her arms.

"Because you only get to be kids once."

"Home is where we are prepared for life. Doing chores is part of life."

"Not in my house."

"Noah," she said quietly, "the children want chores. They want responsibility."

"How do you know that?"

"They told me."

He didn't know what to say to that. He'd only meant to save them from the kind of childhood he'd had—babysitting his two younger brothers while his father and one stepmother, then another, worked full time. He was ten years old when he was first put in charge of seven-year-old Gideon and three-year-old David. As the years passed, Noah had supervised homework and cleaned the house, including doing laundry. The only way he'd gotten out of cooking duty was to be really bad at it, on purpose.

"I assume they didn't tell you without prompting?" he asked, heading to the dining room to eat.

She followed. "Not exactly." She made a move to grab the pot of stew. "I can heat this for you."

"It's fine." He served himself the remainder of the salad, rolls and stew, then glanced up as she hovered. "Not exactly?" he repeated.

"One of the things we did today was discuss their schedules, not just their academics but extracurricular activities. In the grand scheme of things, we talked about responsibility. I sort of tossed out the idea that they could make their own beds and do their own dishes rather than letting them sit in the sink all night."

He gestured she should sit. "And they jumped at the chance to assume that responsibility?"

She hesitated. "Not all of them."

"Let me guess. Ashley and Zach were gung ho. Zoe got huffy. And Adam…"

"Said they'd be putting Cora out of work, and how could we live with that?"

Noah laughed, which made Tricia laugh, too. "That's my boy."

"Is he the most like you, out of all of them?"

The stew was lukewarm but tasty, the salad lukewarm and wilted, and the rolls cold but still crunchy. "I think Zach's the most like me. How'd your day go?"

"Great," she said. "They're certainly all individual, and yet the twin thing is strongly at work."

"They used to have secret languages when they were very young, but not anymore."

"Maybe not spoken, but they know how the other feels. I've never had a sibling, so I have nothing to compare it to."

"And I only know my brothers and I didn't have it. So, everyone got all their work done?"

"Yes. If you'd like to see it, I can bring it to your office later. Or I can meet you in the classroom."

"I'd like a summary, but I don't need to see the actual work. If you can come to my office right after the children go to bed, that would be great. I won't take up much of your time."

"All right." She stood. "For now I'd like to go to my room. I've been on duty for almost twelve hours."

He hadn't considered how long she worked. No wonder he lost nannies all the time. But Cora was supposed to keep an eye on the kids during lunch, giving the nan—teacher a break before afternoon activities. "Cora didn't relieve you for a while?" he asked.

"She offered, but I didn't want to interrupt the flow of the day. I'll let her from now on. I hadn't realized how tired I would be without a break."

"Good."

With a quick goodbye, she left. She hadn't looked tired. Her blond hair still held its curl, her eyes were as clear as ever. She wasn't slouching. In fact, her posture was perfect, her shoulders back, her breasts a tempting sight he tried to ignore, which was hard to do since her form-fitting T-shirt showed off every curve.

Noah usually ate dinner alone, which was fine with him. Tonight it bothered him. Maybe because he was sitting at the dining room table instead of standing at the kitchen counter. He finished up in a hurry, then debated what to do about the dishes. There were no leftovers. He should've left some stew so he could just put some foil on top and stick it in the refrigerator.

In the end, he put his dishes in the dishwasher but left the pot soaking in the sink.

He wandered into the family room. Zoe was playing a soccer video game on the small television. Adam was intent on his handheld Game Boy. Zach and Ashley were watching something on the Disney Channel, a movie about teenagers and basketball, with a lot of singing and dancing involved.

Noah sat on the couch next to Ashley, who moved a few inches away, her lips pinched. He didn't know what to do with her. It seemed like everything he did these days was wrong, and she was so quick to judge him. And vocal. That was new. Before, he could guess by her expression when she was upset with him. Now she told him, as well. He should be grateful not to have to guess anymore, but it left him confused, too.

"When this is over, would you come to my office, please?" he asked her.

She waited a few seconds, then nodded.

He wanted to escape, but he made himself sit there, trying to be part of their world. He didn't have a clue how they usually spent their evenings after dinner. Like this? Watching TV, playing games?

What did they used to do, as a family?

Well, really, did the past have any bearing on now? They were older. Life had changed.

"Where's Miss Tricia?" Zach asked during a commercial.

"In her room," Noah answered.

"Why?"

"I guess she had things to do."

Zach eyed Noah like he was responsible, like he'd ordered her to her room, or something.

"Oh," Zach said glumly. "Will she come down later?"

"I don't know. She's off duty as soon as I get home."

All four of the children turned and looked at him for a few long seconds before they went back to watching television and playing video games without uttering their opinion.

"Would you like to play a game?" he asked the room at large. He knew the cabinet held tons of board games.

"Why?" Adam asked, not looking away from his Game Boy.

"To spend some time together as a family. Having fun." He tried not to sound defensive.

"It's too close to bedtime," Ashley said. "We probably couldn't finish."

No one else commented. No one made a move to play a game. So he sat and watched the rest of the movie with Ashley and Zach, trying to seem interested.

"I'm ready now, Father," Ashley said, getting up and heading out.

"What's she ready for?" Adam asked.

"I want to talk to each of you individually," Noah answered, including all of them in the answer. "It's nothing bad. I just want to know about your day and what you learned."

"Like you used to," Zoe said, not taking her eyes off her video match.

"Yes." So they remembered. Guilt came to sit on his shoulder.

"Are you going to test us?" Adam asked.

Noah almost sighed. "No. Just talk."

"For how long?"

"For as long as it takes. Ashley's coming first."

"Ashley always goes first," Zach muttered.

What happened to his agreeable, obedient children? When had he lost control? Or maybe it wasn't a matter of control but that they felt he'd abandoned them.

And wasn't it interesting to note that their newly found out-spokenness had coincided with Tricia's arrival?

"Tomorrow you can go first," Noah said to Zach.

Ashley was already seated in a chair opposite his desk, waiting. As he sat, he glanced at a photograph of Margie on his desktop. His daughters looked so much like her.

"Have I done something wrong?" Ashley asked.

He shook his head. "I just wanted a report on your first day with Miss Tricia."

"It was fine."

"Is she a good teacher?"

"Yes."

He didn't know whether to laugh or sigh at her succinct responses. "Would you elaborate a little?"

"She told us she would demand a lot of us because we're all very smart."

He liked that. "That's it?"

"Well, she said the room was too…orderly, I think. That we could start leaving our art and science projects out instead of putting them away each night."

Since that was a rule Noah had created, he wasn't happy about it. Children needed order, not chaos, to learn. "Anything else? I'm interested in your impression of how she teaches and how she relates to you."

"She's…I like her. I don't know what else to say about her. She's my favorite teacher, so far."

"She's been here for a day and she's your favorite?" What did that say about the seven who preceded her?

"You can tell she really likes us. She doesn't pretend."

Was that why the other teachers had left? Not because of him, after all, but because they hadn't liked his children? "You have good judgment about such things. Thank you for telling me."

She beamed. It had been a while since she'd smiled like that at him.

"Zach wants to be next," he said. "I'll be up to say goodnight later."

"Okay, Father."

She left the room, her footsteps not even registering. In the silence, her words seemed to echo—*Father*. It did sound formal. *Had* he done what Tricia had suggested? Made them call him Father instead of Dad because of his own painful reminders?

Zach appeared in the doorway looking like a child sent to the principal's office. He didn't take a step inside.

"Come in, son."

"Miss Tricia doesn't sit behind her desk. She says it's like a wall between us."

Noah was already tired of hearing how perfect Miss Tricia was. "Where would you like me to sit, Zach?"

"On the couch."

"Will you sit there, too?"

He nodded.

Noah walked around his desk and took a seat at one end of the couch. Zach sat, as well, then smiled shyly.

"How was your day?" Noah asked.

"Good."

"Anything in particular you enjoyed?"

"Miss Tricia showed me a new game on the computer where I can practice math during my free time."

They all had good computer skills for their ages, but Zach was by far the most advanced and ambitious. "Do you have any complaints?"

He thought about it for a minute then said, "No," decisively, his expression open.

"Any comments to add, Zach?"

"No, I'm good."

"Okay. Send either Zoe or Adam in, will you please? I'll be up to say good-night later."

He hurried off. After a minute Zoe popped in. He was still sitting on the couch and gestured to her that she should sit there, too. She eyed the chair in front of the desk for a moment, sighed, then plopped onto the sofa but didn't look at him. She was the most openly hostile to him, rarely hiding her feelings about anything. He counted on her to keep him aware of any unhappiness among them.

"How was your day?" he asked.

"It was okay."

"Did you like Miss Tricia as your teacher?"

"She's fine. So far."

He rested his arms on his thighs and leaned toward her a little, trying to get her to look at him. "Do you expect she'll change?"

She shrugged. "Most of them do."

That surprised him. "Why didn't you tell me about that?"

"Guess it didn't matter so much." She kicked her feet, still not looking at him. "They're supposed to give us our lessons, then we do them. That's it. Doesn't make much difference who's in charge, does it?"

He thought it made a huge difference, but it was a topic for another time, when life had settled down again for all of them. "If you think Miss Tricia changes, Zoe, if she isn't being a good teacher, or a good person, I want you to tell me, okay?"

"Sure. Can I go now?"

He needed to make eye contact with her. It occurred to him how little she looked at him. Why hadn't he seen that before? "Look at me, please."

After a minute she did.

"Promise you'll tell me, Zoe."

"I said I would. *Now* can I go?"

He wanted to hug her. He knew she would resist, because at some point he'd stopped hugging them. He didn't even know why.

"Send Adam in, please."

She dashed out. Adam came through the door immediately, making an imaginary jump shot as he entered, then he vaulted over the sofa arm and landed in the seat with a whoosh.

"You got here fast," Noah commented.

"I was outside listen—I mean, waiting my turn." He grinned, obviously not contrite.

Noah decided not to have the it's-rude-to-eavesdrop talk

with his son tonight. Zoe would've seen him right outside the door. If she'd cared, she would've said something.

"So, I guess you want to know what I think of Miss Tricia," Adam said. Like Zoe, he fidgeted. "She's cool. She said she'd get me signed up for basketball next week. And she promised to bring her guitar next time she goes home. She said it wasn't practical to ask for a guitar and lessons until I saw I was really interested. She's gonna give me a few lessons first."

Was there anything Miss Tricia couldn't do? Noah wondered. "I didn't know you wanted to play guitar. I thought you liked the clarinet."

"Come on, Father. That's so last year."

Father. There it was again. It sounded especially formal they way he'd used it.

"Can I go now?" Adam asked.

Noah made a goodbye gesture, trying not to sigh. He shouldn't expect miracles with his children. Obviously he'd ignored them for too long—plus they'd done some growing up. He had to make some adjustments.

He returned to his desk, pulled a folder from his briefcase and wondered if Tricia hadn't come along when she had if he ever would've seen the light.

She had come along, however, and if he smiled and was nice to her, according to his children, he wouldn't ever have to look for another teacher.

That was a goal worth making changes for.

Chapter Six

Tricia sat in the chair opposite Noah's desk, waiting for him, her notepad listing all her questions on her lap. She'd said her good-nights to the children, bumping into Noah as she left the girls' room and he was going in. She was glad he was tucking them in. They needed him to be more involved. Plus he would reap benefits himself from a closer relationship.

Noah breezed into the office. He stopped, hesitated, then sat behind his desk.

"You've made a big impression on my children already," he said.

"They're terrific kids."

"They've been through hell."

She nodded, understanding. "You said Zach was most like you. Is one of the girls like Margie?"

"Ashley."

"In what way?"

He leaned back. "Attention to detail. Not wanting to make waves. Needing peace between everyone. And yet she was also sure of herself and stubborn."

"What kinds of vacations did you take?"

"Vacations? As a family?" He frowned thoughtfully. "We did Disneyland and Disney World."

"Camping?"

"Margie wanted to. I didn't. We stayed home a lot. Probably because I was gone half the month to Europe—most months, anyway. I just wanted to hang out here."

Tricia wondered if Margie was okay with that or if she'd just never protested it, figuring there would be plenty of trips as the kids got older.

"She and the children would go to her parents' house in San Luis Obispo several times a year," he said. "The kids still do. In fact, they'll be gone Thanksgiving week." He gestured toward her notepad. "You have questions?"

"Did I pass first-day muster with them?"

"Is that a question on your list?"

She smiled at his teasing, almost not seeing the twinkle in his eyes. So, he did have a sense of humor. She'd been wondering.

"It's the first question," she said, flashing the pad toward him too fast for him to read.

"You got major thumbs-up," he said. "Major. Adam even proclaimed you to be 'cool.'"

"Awesome." She was more than pleased. After a minute she tapped a finger on the first real question she'd written. "Halloween."

"Friday, October thirty-first. I'm a little sketchy on the details, but I think it's been a tradition in this country since early in the last century."

She liked this playful side of him. "I'm trying to picture you trick-or-treating. I'll bet you were a pirate."

His good mood disappeared. "Nope. Never did trick-or-treat. We didn't live in a neighborhood, but out in the country, like this."

"Do your kids dress up in costume? Do I need to take care of that?"

He shuffled through some papers on his desktop. "Here." He passed her an invitation with a ghost flying across the cover for a party on Friday night.

"Did you RSVP?" she asked, noticing it had come from their education specialist, Cynthia Madras.

"I forgot."

And of course the requested RSVP date had come and gone. "Do the children want to go?"

"I haven't asked them."

Implied in his tone of voice was that it wasn't his job. Apparently the previous teachers had taken care of those kinds of matters. "I'll ask them in the morning," she said. "Cynthia is coming tomorrow anyway, so I'll talk to her, make sure it's not too late to RSVP. If you're okay with them going to the party?"

"Sure. She puts on a Halloween party every year for the students she oversees. She does a haunted house. Next year Ashley and Zoe will be thirteen, and Cynthia lets the teens become ghouls for the party."

"She sounds like a lot of fun. I'm looking forward to meeting her." She glanced at her list again. "Zoe says she has a soccer match on Saturday at noon. Do you and the family go to those?"

"Not usually. Someone picks her up and brings her home."

She could tell by his body language that she shouldn't take the discussion any further, but she only had three months to help this family. She had to speak up. "Zoe needs you to pay attention to her, Noah. All of you should be supporting each other in your endeavors. It's good for the other kids to be there to cheer her on, too. Same for Adam when basketball starts."

"Yes, teacher."

That annoyed her. "Sarcasm? Really? Your family is fractured, Noah. I'm trying to help."

He stiffened. "I don't think we're fractured. They're good kids. Everything's been fine."

Until you came along. The unspoken words reminded Tricia of her place. She could effect change in this family, good change, but she needed to do so without upsetting Noah. She just had to be patient, make a difference gradually. Then they would all adapt together. She had so little time to help them find each other again.

She also felt a strong need to help him lighten up. Everything didn't have to be so serious. She'd learned that the hard way, herself.

"Okay, maybe everything hasn't been exactly fine," he said after she'd been silent for too long. "But I'm working on it."

Tricia turned her notepad over. She wouldn't broach the other topics yet, especially since he was in denial about other issues anyway. One day at a time. One change at a time. "That's all I have for now." She waited to be dismissed.

"I have a question for you," he said. "Ashley told me you want them to leave their projects out instead of putting them away. Before you make big changes like that, you need to talk to me. In this particular instance, it's my belief that they need a clean and orderly place to study. Tomorrow you'll go back to having them put their things away at the end of the school day."

He was telling her how to run her class? She counted to five, silently. "Would you come up to the classroom with me, please?" she asked, standing, not really giving him a choice but making it seem like it.

He followed her. Once again she felt his gaze on her rear as she climbed the stairs. Just the idea of it aroused her—which she resented as much as appreciated. He was the wrong man at the wrong time. When she settled into her new job and her new life, she would be thrilled to have such attention from a man. But not now.

She stopped halfway up the staircase and turned around. He ended up eye level with her chest. His gaze rose slowly until it connected with hers.

"Did you forget something?" he asked.

My common sense. But she didn't say it out loud. After a few seconds, he smiled slightly, knowingly, and moved around her, continuing up the stairs, passing her by, even though he could have walked beside her, the staircase being wide enough for two. She had no choice but to follow.

It was a nice view. A very nice view. She wondered if he worked out. Since he seemed to have so little free time, she didn't see how he could fit it into his schedule. Maybe at lunchtime? He looked like he exercised. His rear was firm and molded. Her hands would curve perfectly over them....

Noah looked over his shoulder as he reached the first landing. "Are we even now?" he said, when what he wanted to say was, "Look, I'm not serious every second of the day."

She dared to look confused.

He refused to smile at her innocent expression, knowing she was toying with him. Women had flirted with him a lot in the past three years, since he'd been widowed. Tricia didn't seem to be flirting, but instead teasing. He'd never crossed any barriers with any teacher in the past, never even joked. Was teasing the way to hold on to her? Smiling and being nice, as the children said? Keeping things businesslike certainly hadn't amounted to success.

The problem was—what was teasing and what was flirting? That not-crystal-clear issue of sexual harassment always lurked in a business relationship between opposite genders.

She came up beside him on the landing then. "Even?" she repeated. "I don't know. Are we?"

"I'm even," he said. "You, on the other hand, may be a little odd."

She grinned, which relaxed him. So the kids were right? Smile. Be more approachable. Less of a…boss, the easier role for him.

They walked side by side until they reached the single-wide staircase to the schoolroom. They stopped at the same time and looked at each other.

Noah reached into his pocket and pulled out a quarter. "Call it," he said.

"Heads, I…you go first."

He didn't miss her carefully worded pronouncement.

Noah flipped the coin, caught it then slapped it on the back on his hand. Tails. He won. He followed her up the stairs as she exaggerated the sway of her hips, making a game of it, as if to make him laugh. He didn't, nor was it a game to him. He wanted to put her hands on her, feel the movement, pull himself up close and wrap her in his arms….

Arousal hit him, hard and fast, a situation he had no way of hiding before they reached the classroom. He'd already flipped the light switch at the bottom of the stairs. No chance to stall, not even for a second.

She reached the top first and turned around, smiling, then her expression froze. He had no idea what to say, if he should even say anything at all. She was apparently having the same dilemma—in both respects. She wasn't saying anything, and her nipples had hardened, drawing his attention.

They stared at each other for long seconds, then he continued up the stairs until he stood in front of her. It was all he could do to keep from touching her. She had incredible breasts, high and firm, and she didn't wear loose clothing, but tops that molded, although not low cut at all.

Damn.

By unspoken agreement, they ignored the moment of attraction and moved into the classroom.

Neatness reigned on one end of the room, chaos on the other.

"This is exactly what I mean," he said. "No one can learn in this environment."

"You mean *you* couldn't learn in this environment."

He crossed his arms.

"See the first table on the left, Noah? That's Adam's."

The table was littered with Legos, none in containers but scattered, some kind of structure rising from the pile.

"Are you sure? It looks like Zach's handiwork."

She smiled. "They're supposed to do something outside their comfort zone. Adam is having to sit still and create something, which is what Zach likes to do."

"What's he building, do you know?"

"I'm not sure *he* does, yet. Maybe tomorrow it will take form enough for him to see." They moved to the next table, on which was a small stack of paper printed from the computer. "Zach is designing a putting green that they'll all work on starting tomorrow. Group project."

"Zach likes to work alone."

"Exactly."

"That one must be Zoe's," he said pointing to a small construction zone.

"Ashley's. She's using slats, nails and a hammer to build a crate bed for her stuffed dog, Harry. By process of elimination, you can see that Zoe is painting."

"Modern art, obviously," he said, eyeing the painting on the easel.

Tricia laughed. "Doesn't matter. She's doing it, even though Ashley's driving her crazy, giving advice. And Zach's happy because he gets to research putting greens on the computer, but his discomfort will come when we start the actual work and he has to be outdoors, digging in dirt."

"Not his favorite thing to do."

"Right. But my point is, you can see how long they would stall each day before tackling the work if they have to get it out and set it up every day."

"They would take their time. Run out the clock." Had they learned the art of the stall from him, the way he stalled about coming home?

"Probably so. This way there's no downtime. They come back from lunch and work on their projects for a half hour, and then we head outside to do something physical or whatever's on the agenda. I look at this part of the room and I don't see a mess. I see busy minds creating, testing themselves. What's wrong with that?"

He would sound ridiculous arguing her point, which was valid. "I'll give you that. As long as the rest of the workspace remains organized."

"Ahh. A compromise." She stuck out her hand. "Deal."

He shook her hand. She pulled free first, tucked both her hands in her pockets.

"Where are you thinking about building the putting green?" he asked.

"To the right of your deck, if that's okay."

"The lawn's dead."

"I thought we could pick up some sod."

"You think it's as easy as that?" He tried to remember when they'd moved into the house five years ago what Margie had done with the garden. He hadn't really paid attention. "I have a friend who's a landscaper, Joseph McCoy. Let me call him in the morning and have him stop by tomorrow, if he can. It can still be a learning experience, but you might as well put in a lawn that's going to live."

"That would be great, thanks. As long as he knows the kids are all going to be involved in it."

"I'll let him know. Maybe you could talk to him about doing a whole new garden. It's looking bad these days."

"Sure. I'll ask him to draw up some plans. Although I have to warn you, I know little about gardening."

They'd run out of topics. He stalled, not wanting to go work in his office, as he needed to. "So, you said Cynthia will be here tomorrow?"

"All morning, apparently. She's required to spend an hour per child each month. I'm glad she's coming when everything is new for me. I can make adjustments before something becomes routine." She covered her mouth as she yawned. "I'm sorry. I need to go to bed. I've been out of teaching for a while. It'll take a little getting used to."

"You know, I never saw a resume on you. Maybe tomorrow after dinner we could talk about your background."

"That's a plan. I'll see you tomorrow, then." She started to walk away, then turned back. "You'll make an effort to be here for dinner? Or call?"

After the cool greeting he'd gotten tonight? Did he have a choice? "Yes, on both counts."

"Great. Good night."

He watched her until she disappeared down the staircase, then he took a closer look at each child's project. He liked that Tricia was making them do something out of their comfort zones. She was innovative, unlike most of the other teachers, who had a plan and followed it. "Teaching to standards," it was called, which they all had done, but not much beyond. Most homeschoolers were taught by their own parents, who'd made that choice for a reason, and put a lot of effort into the job.

Hiring a teacher was different. It became a job then, although Tricia wasn't making it seem like that.

Early in the game, though, Noah reminded himself.

He picked up Ashley's crate-in-progress. Her slats were nailed at precise intervals, as he would have expected. So…out of her comfort zone but still with the exactness she always demanded of herself.

Ashley had changed the most recently. Well, Zach, too, a little. His was probably infatuation for the teacher, but Ashley was asserting herself as a leader more than ever. Maybe she'd completed the grief process. It was hard to tell with any of them, because they really didn't talk about their mother much at all. Even when he mentioned her, they didn't carry the conversation forward.

Noah opened the top drawer of each child's desk and pulled out folders, reviewing their weekly assignments. Adam really needed to work on his penmanship. The others were legible. A portable filing system sat on Tricia's desk. He was entitled to look through it but decided against it. Too soon. He would talk to Cynthia after her visit and get her opinion, but he had a feeling his search was over. He'd found the right person.

Now he just had the simple task of keeping her happy.

Chapter Seven

The next day, the children were crammed around the computer looking at Halloween costume possibilities as Tricia and Cynthia talked. Tricia tried to guess how old the petite, athletic-looking, redheaded Cynthia was. Thirty, maybe? They'd discussed the academics and requirements, but Cynthia hadn't made a move to leave yet. And although she'd been warm with the children, she'd been cool with Tricia.

"If Jessica had told me she was leaving," Cynthia said, "I would've gotten myself involved in the search for a replacement. They've had too many teachers, too much disruption. I hope you intend to stay for a long time."

Guilt hammered Tricia. Should she tell Cynthia about how she was staying only until January? Tricia didn't want the kids to overhear news that should come from their father, but maybe Cynthia *could* help find a permanent replacement.

Or Tricia could talk to Noah about it, suggest the best way to find someone permanent, someone right for all—

"You wore that last Halloween," Zoe said to one of her siblings, exasperation in her raised voice. "*And* the year before."

"So?" Adam replied, belligerent.

"So, think outside the box," Zoe countered.

"What does that mean, stupidhead?"

Cynthia leaned toward Tricia. "Adam has dressed up as a basketball player, two years running,"

"Gee, what a surprise," Tricia said, tongue in cheek.

"Will you be coming to the haunted house?" Cynthia asked.

"No." Tricia was going to force Noah to interact with his children by staying at his house and keeping to her off-duty schedule, especially since she wasn't going to go to Sacramento until after the bachelorette party Saturday night. "Noah will bring them."

"Well, there's a first."

Tricia couldn't decide if Cynthia was surprised or being sarcastic. "Sarcastic" didn't jibe with what Tricia had been told about the woman. Noah and Jessica had sung her praises, and the children were comfortable with her.

So, it must be something personal. Maybe Cynthia didn't like clutter, either.

The thought made her smile.

"I should get going," Cynthia said, gathering her briefcase. She had looked at all the work from the past month, regraded homework and tests, and taken samples for a portfolio she put together yearly on each child. "I'll take care of your purchase orders and drop by your supplies when they arrive, so I'll probably see you next week with those. I tend to make deliveries once a week. Bye."

She walked over to say goodbye to the children. Ashley hugged her. The others barely acknowledged her, including

Zach, but they were intent on their task to come up with costume possibilities. Tricia was secretively happy that Zach didn't hug her, which was really small of her. But there was something about Cynthia that bothered Tricia, like she'd have to watch her back.

Most people took to her. Kids liked her. Dogs adored her. Salespeople remembered her. She didn't think she'd done anything to offend Cynthia Madras, but...

Adam marched over to Tricia's desk and plopped there on his elbows. "If I want to be a basketball player, I can be one, right?" he asked, challenging her.

"Yes."

"See?" he shouted at Zoe, who rolled her eyes.

"I don't want to hear any more name-calling, Adam," Tricia said quietly.

"I didn't—"

"Yes, you did."

He frowned. "You mean 'stupidhead'?"

She nodded.

"That's just my nickname for her. It means I like her."

It was all Tricia could do not to laugh at his innocent expression. "Well, come up with a nicer one."

He walked away, muttering, "Everyone's picking on me." He plunked himself down at his activity table and started fiddling with Lego pieces.

The intercom crackled. "Tricia?" came Cora's voice. "Joseph McCoy is here to talk about the yard. And your lunches are ready."

Tricia punched a button. "Thanks. Be right down." Then to the children, she said, "Zach, please bring your plans for the putting green. Then as soon as we've consulted with Mr. McCoy, we're going on a picnic."

"All right!" Adam said.

"Isn't it a little cold?" Ashley asked.

Zach frowned.

Zoe didn't react at all.

"The sun's out, Ashley. It's really nice. Everyone grab a backpack and a sweatshirt, then hurry downstairs," Tricia said, heading down, then hearing arguing as she got closer to the kitchen.

"You stay out of my kitchen, Joseph McCoy," Tricia heard Cora almost shout.

"What? It's just a little dirt, Cora. It'll clean right up."

"Yes, by *me*. You can wait outside."

"Is everything okay?" Tricia asked as she stepped into the kitchen. "Do I have to send you to your corners?"

Joseph raised a hand in greeting. "Hey. You must be Tricia. Noah sent me."

Late twenties, Tricia decided. He was about her height and built like a man who worked hard all day, sturdy and toned. He had a long brown ponytail and wore shorts, a T-shirt and mud-caked boots.

"You're prompt," she said. "The kids will be down in a minute. They need to be involved in this project."

"No problem."

"So, you know Joseph?" Tricia said to Cora, whom Tricia had guessed to be in her early fifties.

"It's a small town. And he's always been obnoxious." She wielded her mop at him, and he laughed.

The kids came scurrying down the stairs then, making a race of it, jostling each other as they rushed through the dining room, coming to an abrupt halt when she gave them a look meant to stop them.

"Hey, kids!" Joseph shouted. "Let's go. Time's a wastin'."

They all sneaked past her, only Zach giving her a little smile.

"Thanks for packing the lunches," Tricia said as she passed by Cora.

"Happy to."

Tricia went outdoors and into the backyard. The kids were hanging around Joseph, barely giving him room to walk—except for Zach, who followed more slowly, his design clutched in his hands. Was he nervous? Unsure?

Joseph climbed the steps to the deck and looked out at the property. "Be quiet a minute," he said to the noisy children. "Let me think."

Tricia could hear the silence, that is, the slight breeze in the air, some rustling of leaves—from the breeze or an animal? She scoped the terrain, wondering. She would rather be hearing car horns and sirens, which would block sounds she wasn't comfortable with. Ignorance is bliss.

"All right. Zachary, let me see your design, please." Joseph held out a hand.

Zach dropped it in Joseph's hands like a surgical nurse handing over a scalpel, then he stepped back and looked away.

Unsure, Tricia decided. Testing new waters.

"I didn't know you were a golfer, Zach," Joseph said while studying the design.

"I'm not."

"No? You want this built for Adam, then, I guess?"

"No. I just thought it would be something fun to do. As a family."

Surprisingly, all the children stayed silent, but they looked at each other in a moment that was so telling to Tricia, it almost broke her heart. They desperately wanted their father involved in their lives.

"Does your father play golf?" Tricia asked Zach.

"He used to."

Tricia traded looks with Joseph, who seemed to have gotten a clear picture himself. "Okay, crew, let's go scout out the turf.

Zachary, my man, you did an amazing job of research and design. Let's go see how we can make it come to life."

Tricia hung back, letting Joseph be the boss. Instead of going on a picnic, they all ate their lunches on the deck, with Cora bringing one for Joseph, as well. He talked to them for a long time about the process of getting the space ready for sod, and why it was important. They calculated how much sod they would need, then they discussed a design for the rest of the yard, as Noah had requested.

Adam asked that Joseph include an estimate for a full basketball court, not just the backboard and hoop on the garage. Zoe wanted a pool included. Ashley wanted a rose garden. Zach made no request. The putting green seemed to be enough for him.

They were wrapping things up when the sound of a car turning into the driveway reached them. Noah. And it was only three o'clock. Zach headed toward the garage, at first walking, then picking up his pace. Ashley went next. Adam and Zoe not only stayed where they were but studiously avoided looking at him.

"Go greet your father," she said softly to them. They seemed relieved to be told to do so, as if they'd wanted to but didn't know how to change a habit.

Tricia caught Joseph studying the scene but also gathering his paperwork and rolling it into a tube. She moved to the deck railing and waited, enjoying hearing Zach so excited and talkative as he told Noah about the project. And Ashley was holding her father's hand, while Adam carried his briefcase. Zoe lingered at the fringes. Tricia would've said Ashley was trying the hardest to connect with Noah, if Zach hadn't made his need known himself.

Noah set a hand on Zach's head, quieting his steady stream of dialogue, as he described the plans in detail. "Am I early enough?" he asked Tricia as he approached.

He looked happy. The children mostly looked happy, maybe a little intense, too, but, for the most part, smiling.

She didn't want to crack a joke in front of them, so she just smiled and nodded.

"Joseph," Noah said, holding out a hand. "Thanks for coming so fast."

"It sounded important. If you've got time, I'd like your input before I run an estimate for you."

"Sure. Come in to my office."

Joseph winked at Tricia. "I just have to take my boots off first."

"Okay, kids," she said. "I need to take Zoe to soccer practice and Adam to karate. Zach and Ashley? You can stay here or tag along. Which do you want?"

"I want to stay," Zach said, eyeing his father. "Can I come to your meeting with Joseph?"

"For a little while, then Joseph and I will finish up alone."

"Okay."

"Ashley?" Tricia asked.

"I'll go with Adam."

"Really? Okay." Tricia glanced at Noah, surprised.

"Her *boyfriend*'s in my karate class," Adam said.

Ashley reacted like any sister. She denied, denied, denied until an argument ensued. Tricia waited for Noah to step in. When he didn't, she did, sending Adam off to change into his uniform, his *gi,* and Zoe to get into her own gear.

"Did you have a good day?" Noah asked her as Joseph sat to take off his boots.

"We did, thanks."

"You, Tricia. Did *you* have a good day?"

She didn't understand the difference, but answered yes, then added, "Cynthia was here."

"She called me."

There was something in his voice… Is that why he was home early? Because of something Cynthia told him? "Did she have a complaint?"

He hesitated. "We'll talk tonight, after the children go to bed."

Great. Now she had to spend the rest of the day worrying. Then she changed her thinking. She was a good teacher, and the children were responding well to her. She had nothing to be concerned about.

"Okay. Tonight, then," she said. "Excuse me."

Tricia moved away from him. She didn't like keeping things locked up inside, had given that up during the past year. But she couldn't get insistent with Noah now, not with Joseph's obvious curiosity about the family dynamics.

So, until tonight, long after dinner, even, she was stuck having to live with anticipation. It wasn't a good feeling.

Noah decided Zach was right. Sitting on the couch instead of behind his desk created a different environment. Each child had been more open during their how-I-spent-my-day conversation with him, even Zoe. So when Tricia came in his office after the kids had been tucked into bed, Noah indicated she should sit on the couch, then he sat at the other end.

"I take it Cynthia was critical," she said, her voice a little on edge, not even waiting for him to start the conversation.

"She said their class work was excellent."

Tricia's hands were folded primly in her lap. "Which I had nothing to do with, having been their teacher for only one day."

"Why do you assume she criticized you, Tricia?"

"She was very warm to the children, and they obviously like her. But she was very cool to me. I didn't say or do anything I thought would be considered rude or presumptuous."

Noah stretched his arm along the back of the sofa. If he moved over a few inches, he could touch her—and she seemed to need some kind of consoling. Touching her, however, broke all the rules.

"Cynthia expressed some concern," he said, "about the way you were structuring the class."

"What does that mean? I'm following the schedule that Jessica used. Academics in the morning. Then after lunch, hands-on work, physical activity, lessons, play dates with friends. I've got some field trips planned, too. It's no different at all, except a little more adventurous, maybe." She frowned then. "Or do you mean she agreed with you about the kids leaving their projects out? Did she think that made me look lazy? That I wasn't encouraging the children toward neatness?"

"I don't know for sure, although she does know what rules I have in place. We are going to meet later in the week to discuss it. For the record, Tricia, I'm happy with what you're doing, so far."

"How can you even judge that at this point?"

"The children judge it. I take my cues from them."

That made her relax into the cushions again, her hair bouncing with the movement. He wanted to wrap a long curl around his finger and pull her closer.

Instead he clenched his fist. "So, we were going to talk about your work experience tonight."

"David really did leave you in the dark, didn't he? Has your brother always been so pushy?"

"He's always been assertive, but not usually aggressive, except in business. As the oldest, I've always been the dominant one, especially since our father died."

"You haven't mentioned your mother."

"My mother lives in New York." He was aware of the harshness seeping into his own voice, but didn't try to soften it. "My parents were divorced when I was two, and my father got sole custody. He married again the next year, and they had Gideon a year later. That marriage lasted three years, and he got sole custody of Gid. Then my father married David's mother the same year—she was already pregnant. That marriage lasted a surprising eleven years—eleven years of screaming, yelling and throwing things at each other. They divorced the year I escaped to go to college. Again, he got sole custody."

Her eyes had gone wide. "Do you see your mother?"

"She came for Margie's funeral. I hadn't seen her for five years before that."

"She ignores her grandchildren, too?"

"Pretty much. I'm grateful to Margie's parents, who are very involved." He was done with the topic. "How about you?"

It took her a few seconds to catch up with the abrupt change of subject. "My father died when I was eleven, as I told you. My mother died almost a year ago. I had stopped teaching to take care of her after a severe stroke. She hung in there for four years. I have one grandfather living. He's a spry old guy. Lives in Arizona. Golfs almost every day. He married a woman twenty years younger. They seem very happy."

"How long did you teach kindergarten?"

"Six years. I'm thirty-four, in case you've been wondering, but I haven't taught in the classroom since my mother got sick five years ago."

"What'd you do the past year?"

"Healed."

He leaned forward, resting his arms on his thighs. "How?"

"I have to backtrack a little to answer that. While I was in college I met a man, Darrell, and fell in love. We got engaged. He went into the army while I was in the credential program. We planned our wedding for right after I finished school, then he was killed in a helicopter training accident before the wedding. I buried myself in my work, ignoring the grief, then my mom got sick. She outlived all predictions by at least three years."

Noah was grateful for the eleven years and four children

before he'd lost Margie, but he was sympathetic to Tricia's losses, too. "I'm sorry."

"Thank you. Anyway, you asked how I healed." Her expression opened. She smiled. "I saw America. I drove all over the country, stopping whenever something interested me, talking to people in all walks of life. I stayed overnight one place and two weeks at the next, depending on my whims. I learned to laugh again. I decided to shake up my life."

He wondered what that would be like—shaking up his life. He had too many commitments, too many people counting on him. He couldn't make much in the way of change. Not that he wanted to remove himself from the business or the children he loved, but having no options sometimes felt overwhelming. Sometimes he even missed all the European travel he used to do.

"Maybe you could try shaking up your life a little," she suggested.

"How?"

"Do something different. Start small, like going to Zoe's soccer game, then take the kids out for pizza. Whatever you've been doing, change it up."

"That sounds chaotic to me."

She smiled. "It will be. Until it's normal. Your new normal."

Normal. Well, what did he have to lose?

Chapter Eight

Chaos, Noah thought, listening to the children run around upstairs. Absolute chaos.

"You're really going to abandon me to this?" he asked Tricia, who sat in the living room casually flipping through a magazine like a woman who was off the clock. Which she was.

"They're just excited," Tricia said, humor lacing the words. "It's Halloween."

"How much candy have they already had?"

She laughed. "None."

"Are you sure I can't just drop them off at the party and go back and get them later?"

"You could, but they'd be very disappointed. You'll have a good time, Noah. There's something so fun about kids dressing up in costumes. Seems to take away their inhibitions."

"That's a good thing?"

She grinned.

Noah paced at the bottom of the stairs. The past few days had been great—except for his argument with Tricia about a hike she'd taken the kids on. He didn't feel she knew the area well enough to go off exploring. She'd said she had a great sense of direction. And they hadn't gotten lost, had they? Not for a second.

Still. What if something had happened to her? How would they have known how to get home?

"Cell phone and my portable GPS locator?" she'd replied, her eyebrows arching high. "Noah, they need to experiment and get experience. If there's no risk, there's no growth. I'm not talking about physical risks or danger, but testing limits and taking chances, things necessary to really living life, not just observing it. I was getting over my own fears, too, about whatever unseen creatures are around."

He'd spent a lot of time considering her words. He knew he was overly cautious. In theory he agreed with Tricia, but he had a hard time putting it into practice. He wanted his children safe.

Noah looked at his watch then hollered up the stairs, "Party started fifteen minutes ago." He eyed Tricia. "How are you going to spend your evening?"

"Watch a video. Eat popcorn. Take a bubble bath." She smiled serenely.

The image of her amid a mound of bubbles held fast in his mind. "You know we'll only be gone a couple of hours."

"Since the movie I want to watch isn't appropriate for the kids, I'll do that first, and take my bath after you get back, so I know someone else is around."

Great. He'd be at home when she was in the bathtub, naked and wet. "You're still afraid of being here alone?"

"One trip into the woods isn't going to change that. I hear every sound, especially at night."

"Does it keep you awake?"

"Sometimes."

If you come to bed with me, you'll sleep easier. He didn't say the words, of course, but the enticing thought added to his arousal, something that no longer surprised him.

The kids finally came flying down the stairs. As expected, Adam wore a Sacramento Kings jersey and carried a basketball. Zach wore a white lab coat and wire-rimmed glasses, and his hair was spiked with gel, giving him a mad-scientist look. Ashley had donned a delicate costume from last spring's ballet production, but had added wings. As for Zoe, she wore a bathing suit over tights and a long-sleeve T-shirt. She carried a mask, snorkel and flippers, with a handmade scuba tank on her back, its original shape probably an empty oatmeal container covered in foil. Yet another hint for a swimming pool.

He had a big surprise for her, come Christmas.

They made a half circle around him, apparently awaiting his approval.

"Don't you all look fabulous!" Tricia exclaimed, coming to stand beside him. "Zach, your hair is perfect. Nice touch."

"Zoe did it, since I helped her design her scuba tank."

"You mean you didn't help them make their costumes?" Noah asked Tricia.

"Miss Tricia had to approve our choice, but we had to make them," Ashley said. "I didn't make my tutu, but I added the angel wings. Zach designed them, and Adam helped put them together."

"You're all very clever," Noah said. "Where'd you get the lab coat, Zach?"

"From the costume trunk. Mom put a whole bunch of stuff in there, remember?"

Mom. Noah made a decision. "I've been thinking maybe you all should call me Dad instead of Father."

"How come?" Zoe asked.

He shrugged.

They all looked at each other for a few seconds.

"It's okay with me," Adam said.

"Me, too. Dad," Zach said with a quick grin.

Noah looked at Zoe. "Sure," she said. "If that's what you want. Gonna seem a little weird at first."

"I know. Just try it out. If you don't like it, you don't have to. Ashley?" He figured she would be his toughest sell, since she had the most problem with change.

"I'll think about it," she said.

"Can we go now?" Adam asked.

"Sure. Tell Miss Tricia goodbye."

"Have fun," she called out. "You, too," she added to Noah when the kids had raced toward the kitchen.

"No comment on the *Father/Dad* thing?"

"I think you made the right decision."

He appreciated that she didn't say I-told-you-so. "Sometimes you can be so diplomatic."

"Sometimes." She gestured toward the kitchen. "They're probably buckled in by now and starting to wonder where you are."

He gave her a long look. "Enjoy your evening."

"I intend to, thank you."

He didn't want to leave. Or rather, he wanted her to go with him. He hadn't had much experience being the parent who hauled the children, not alone, anyway. He realized what a disservice he'd done to them by not being involved. It had taken Tricia's honesty to give him a kick in the pants.

"Thank you," he said, remembering it was his job to be nice to her so that she would stay.

"You're welcome. For what?"

"I think you know. See you later."

She was right. They were all buckled in and raring to go. The drive to Cynthia's took less than twenty minutes. It was the perfect place for a haunted house—a two-story Victorian, probably built around the turn of the twentieth century and restored a couple of times through the years. It looked in need of some TLC now.

The kids ran ahead of him. Howls penetrated the night, and clashes of thunder and lightning.

"Hurry up, Dad," Zach called, having adapted immediately, apparently, to the change in title.

Noah liked the sound of it, like he was a more hip father or something. He picked up his pace and joined the kids at the front door, which was open. Spooky sounds came from within.

"You can stay here," Adam said, apparently deciding that having Dad by his side made him a sissy or something. "We've done this before, you know. We're not scared."

"Should I wait outside?"

"The parents wait in the living room. Over there."

A child shrieked then laughed nervously. Noah headed to the uncool lounge with the other parents. He didn't know any of them, and he silently cursed Tricia for leaving him to this torture on his own.

He nodded to a few people, grabbed a couple of jack-o'-lantern cookies and headed for the front door. He'd give the kids some time then return to the room, and grin and bear it. Small talk with strangers had never been his strong suit, unless they were ordering a Falcon car.

"Noah, hi!" Cynthia caught him just as he was about to step outside.

"Hey. The place looks great," he said. "Sufficiently scary."

"Thanks. I'm glad you came."

Like he had any choice. "Listen, I'm sorry I had to cancel our meeting yesterday. We had a long conference call with some people overseas. The time difference often ruins my best-laid plans."

"No problem. I really would like to meet with you soon,

however. As I said, I have some concerns. Maybe instead of me coming all the way to your office, we could just meet for dessert and coffee somewhere around here after dinner one night next week?"

Was she hitting on him? She'd moved in a little closer, but there was a lot of noise, too, making it hard to hear and be heard. "I could probably manage that," he said, almost stumbling as he backed up a little, bumping into the threshold.

She grabbed his arm. "Careful."

She didn't let go, so he knew without a doubt that she *was* hitting on him. "I'm fine, thanks."

He wondered what movie Tricia was watching. Something the kids couldn't watch, she'd said. Nudity? Love scenes? He'd learned to avoid those movies, didn't need to be reminded of what he was missing.

"What night are you free?" Cynthia asked.

She drew closer as someone wanted to get by them. Her breast pressed into his arm. The rest of her body, too, for a few seconds, then she stepped back, although not too far. She was a petite woman. Maybe five-three, maybe a hundred pounds. Still, she had curves in all the right places. Nothing like Tricia's, but—

"Noah?"

"I'm free every night, I think," he said, focusing on her again.

"How about Tuesday, then? Would you like to meet at the Lode?" which was the locals' term for the Take a Lode Off Diner, a play on words since Chance City was in the heart of California's Mother Lode region.

"Sure," he said. "How about eight o'clock?"

"Perfect. Tuesday at eight, then." She gave him a quick hug, startling him, then she disappeared into the manufactured-fog-filled room where his children had first gone.

What was going on? She'd always been so professional with him.

Maybe he was reading too much into it. He had sex on the brain now that Tricia had come into his life.

Noah returned to the parents' room in time to see Cynthia giving a big hug to a couple about to leave, and then their two children.

Okay, he thought. She's just a hugger. No problem. Except... she'd never hugged him before.

After a while his children came charging into the room, laughing. He stared at them, thinking how beautiful they all were. How perfect. And how empty his world would be when they left to pursue their own lives one day.

Zach came at him full force and wrapped his arms around Noah's waist. Noah hugged him back and smiled at the others. The moment didn't last, however, as Adam looked away quickly and Zoe soon after. They both went to the tables and picked up a juice box and cookies. Ashley didn't take her eyes off Noah until he let Zach go. She looked just like Margie then. Exactly like her.

An eerie feeling swept through him, especially when her smile widened, as if it were Margie standing there, giving her approval of what was happening between them as a family.

"Did you thank Miss Cynthia?" he asked the group at large.

They went together to thank her. She gave them all hugs, although Zach tucked his arms in close and moved back right away. She looked at Noah over the top of Zach's head.

"Thanks," Noah mouthed, then waved. He gathered his brood, and they walked to the car, talking excitedly, reliving some of the scariest moments. Apparently Adam had jumped the highest when a ghoul had leaped at him. Tough-guy Adam was going to have to live it down, which was not something siblings let slide too easily.

At home they found Tricia in the family room. She'd lit a fire, set two huge bowls full of popcorn on the coffee table, and two thermal carafes of hot cocoa. She'd rented *Bedknobs and Broomsticks*, a movie as old as she and Noah.

Noah sent the kids up to change into pajamas. He sat next to Tricia on the couch.

"Did you have a good time?" she asked.

How could he tell her he was pretty sure Cynthia has been flirting with him? "It was fine." He made a broad gesture. "This was nice of you."

"I had fun."

He slid his arm along the couch. His fingers grazed her sweater. She didn't react, so either she hadn't felt it or was ignoring it. "Why didn't you go home to Sacramento tonight, since we were going out, anyway?"

She looked surprised. "I promised the children I wouldn't leave until Saturday mornings, but I also decided it's kind of crazy for me to go home tomorrow for a few hours then drive back for the bachelorette party at night. I'll go either right after the party or very early on Sunday. I've got some old wallpaper to remove and some woodwork to prep so that my painter can come in during the week while I'm gone."

"How soon are you putting it on the market?"

"As soon as it's ready to show. It was hopelessly outdated. I've been working on it since I got back into town, but some things I'd rather pay to have done. I'd like to remodel the kitchen and bathroom, but I'm settling for some upgrades. I can't delay too long. The way real estate is going, I'll be lucky to sell it by January. Not the best time of year."

Adam bounced into the room, leaped over the arm of the recliner, landed, then grinned at them. The patter of other feet followed. In a minute the room looked like a small theater.

Tricia stood and said good-night.

All of the kids except Zoe protested, so Noah ended up not having to. Giving in to the pressure, Tricia took her seat again.

Zach sat on the floor between them, his shoulders resting against Tricia's left leg and Noah's right. Popcorn and mugs of hot chocolate were passed around, then Ashley climbed over Zach and snuggled between Noah and Tricia. They started the movie.

"This is baby stuff," Adam complained after watching a few minutes.

Ashley shushed him.

Adam entertained himself by tossing popcorn into the air and catching it in his mouth. Agreeing with Adam's assessment of the movie, Noah threw a fluffy kernel into the air himself and caught it, then winked at Adam, who grinned back. Ashley got prickly and vocal. Zach was engrossed in the movie, apparently hearing nothing going on around him. Zoe ignored them all—pointedly.

The popcorn competition continued. Ashley put her arm through Tricia's and leaned her head against her shoulder. Noah caught Zoe glancing their way now and then.

He considered how life had changed in the Falcon household. The children had blossomed in such a short period of time. Ashley becoming outspoken, instead of always trying to please. Zach opening up, speaking for himself, finally. And hugging. As for Adam, he'd always been a busy kid, the least complicated, but now he was more vocal, too. Zoe was the toughest to identify change in. She was the only one who seemed to have taken a step backward—but maybe that would lead to changes in other ways.

Tricia McBride was one magical woman.

After the movie ended, Noah waited at the top of the stairs until Tricia had said her good-nights to the kids, then he stopped her on her way to her bedroom.

"Thank you for setting up the movie night," he said. "They— we all enjoyed it."

"Who won the popcorn contest?"

He smiled. "Adam. Or at least he had fewer pieces on the floor than I did. You know, for all that he said it was a movie for babies, he seemed to get pretty interested along the way."

"I was glad to see it. He gets bored so fast."

"All his life." Noah didn't know what else to say, but he didn't want to stop talking. He'd thought it would be hard to do what his children had asked of him, being nice to the teacher so she would want to stay. He was finding it way too easy.

She yawned. "Sorry. I'll say good-night now."

"You still going to take a bubble bath?" Why the hell had he asked that? It was none of his busi—

"That's my plan. Hope I don't doze off in the tub."

She gave him a sleepy smile that seemed incredibly sexy to him. He wanted to drag her into his arms and kiss her, pull her body against his so that they touched all the way down.

Her eyes went serious. She lifted a hand, almost touched his chest. "Noah—"

"Dad!"

Noah closed his eyes for a moment then turned his head toward his son's bedroom. "Coming, Zach."

When he looked back, he spotted Tricia hurrying to her bedroom. Now he'd never know what she would've said next. He would go to bed picturing her in a hot bubble bath, remember the anticipation of her hand almost touching him, and not wonder for a minute why he didn't get to sleep for hours.

Chapter Nine

Saturday night—date night—and the dateless Noah leaned his elbows on the bar behind him and surveyed the scene before him. Being the designated driver at a bachelor party stunk. He'd had one beer hours ago at Gideon's house, where they'd barbecued steaks and played poker until all four of the other bachelor-party-goers declared the evening the dullest in history.

"Where's the stripper?" David had asked, not meaning it, but definitely meaning the party needed to pick up some steam. So he announced that they were moving it to the Stompin' Grounds, a local watering hole. Noah hadn't been there in years.

It hadn't changed a bit. The walls were dark and paneled. The tables had history carved into their tops, initials and dates, hearts and Xs through them, added later. The jukebox still played tunes about good dogs, great trucks and cheating women.

Noah scanned the room. David and Gideon were being

competitive and noisy over a game of pool. Joseph and his brother Jake stood nearby, waiting to take their place.

Noah hadn't seen Tricia before he left—she'd still been getting ready—so he didn't know where the bachelorettes were going to party. It had been the subject of speculation all evening, the possibilities becoming increasingly creative, with Joseph saying he hoped they were having private lessons in the art of stripping. The image of Tricia peeling off her clothes had stuck in Noah's head and refused to budge.

A woman he didn't recognize headed his way then. She had to be old enough to drink legally, but she didn't look it. Her hair was black, her eyes bright blue. Her body was compact, one that would've appealed to him if Tricia hadn't come into his life.

"Hi, there. I'm Melanie." She rattled the ice in her empty glass. "Buy a thirsty girl a refill?"

"Sure." He figured if she was brave enough to ask, he could at least treat her. He signaled the bartender.

"How come you're all by your lonesome?" she asked.

"I'm not. My friends are over there. Bachelor party."

She checked them out. "Which one's the groom?"

"The one lining up the shot."

"Cute butt," Melanie said.

Noah grinned.

"Yours, too," she said. "Makes me want to grab ahold. What's your name?"

"Noah."

"Yeah? Biblical cool. Do you have pairs of everything?"

"Sort of. Two sets of twins, nine and twelve."

Her mouth dropped open. She pointedly looked at his left hand, which bore no ring. "Seriously? Wow. You really look good for your age."

"How old do you think I am?" he asked.

The bartender set her drink on the counter. She scooped it

up and took a sip, giving Noah a long, measuring look. "I'm thinking forty. Like my dad."

Ouch. Double insult. Four years older than his actual age.

"Not quite," he said, not knowing whether to laugh or start asking around about Botox. He caught Gideon looking his way. Gid could read him—or anyone—like a neon sign. He'd won the most at poker tonight, too, able to pick up on tells that no one else would notice.

Noah gestured toward him with his glass. "See the tall guy in the dark blue shirt, Melanie?"

"Uh-huh."

"He's not old enough to be your father. Tell him I sent you." Noah sat on a stool to watch the fun. Gid spotted her heading toward him, gave Noah an I'll-get-you-for-this look, then made his shot while Melanie hovered, talking to him the whole time.

Noah laughed. Then Gideon said something to the girl that made her face turn bright red, and off she went, back to a table with her girlfriends, where she leaned close and said something that made the others cover their mouths with their hands and look at Gid.

Noah wandered over to his brother. "What'd you say to her?"

"I asked if she'd like to try out my new whip. Brand-new. Never before used."

"You took a chance there. What if she was into that stuff?"

Gid gave him a cool look.

"Oh, yeah," Noah said. "Sometimes I forget you can read people's minds."

The front door opened. Raucous laughter spilled into the already noisy bar, followed by five bachelorettes who appeared to be having a helluva lot more fun than the five bachelors.

Valerie came first, wearing a gaudy gem-encrusted tiara with a short, pink veil attached to the back. Noah had never seen her look so uninhibited or carefree. Laura Bannister, attorney, former Miss Universe contestant and former girlfriend of David, came through next—or rather, danced through, as if in a conga line.

Dixie, Joseph's on-again, off-again fiancée—burst in. Joe had proposed recently, and she'd accepted, then gave the ring back because he wouldn't set a date. They'd been together since they were fourteen—off and on.

Next came a very attractive brunette he'd never met, but since he knew the rest of the women, it had to be Denise Watson, the owner of At Your Service.

Then finally Tricia, who wore boots, jeans, a white blouse with blue pin stripes, and a tan suede jacket. She'd added long, silver earrings and a pendant that hung low enough to almost rest between her breasts. It was the first time she'd worn anything that showed cleavage.

The arrival of the women changed the tone of the evening. Valerie ran into David's arms and was kissed for so long that Noah had to turn away. He'd forgotten what that felt like, but the need for it hit him hard. Loneliness hit him even harder.

Dixie pointedly ignored Joseph, who eyed her with longing. No one had any doubt that they would reconcile, but Joe had to step up to the plate and name a wedding date. They were it for each other.

"Thanks for sending Tricia our way," Noah said to Denise.

"She sounds happy to be there, too. I'm glad it's working out."

Tricia came up beside him and smiled. A slightly woozy smile, like she'd had a drink—or two—too many. "You all having a good time?" she asked.

"Depends on who you talk to," Noah said. She smelled good, was wearing some kind of perfume, although mingled with the scent of champagne. "Your timing was perfect. How about you?"

"Oh, yeah." She laughed girlishly. "Good time. Definitely."

"Who drove?"

"Denise arranged for a limo. No need for a designated driver that way. Plus she'll be able to go home to Sacramento tonight. I would've liked to have hitched a ride with her so I could get busy on my house first thing tomorrow morning, but I wouldn't have my car to get back tomorrow night." She flattened a hand on his chest. "Did you know your children have never been inside a limo? Your company *makes* limos. What's with that?"

He was distracted by the touch of her hand, even through his shirt. "Let's dance," he said, moving her onto the tiny dance floor, not waiting for an answer.

She didn't protest, even though it was a slow dance. He figured he was taking advantage of her having a few drinks, which had undoubtedly clouded her ability to think too clearly. The dance floor filled quickly, forcing them closer together, although they weren't touching all the way down their bodies…. It had been a long time since he'd held a woman that close.

"What'd you do tonight?" he asked.

She smiled leisurely. "What happens at bachelorette parties stays at bachelorette parties."

"That good, huh?" Now she really had his curiosity up. "No hints at all?"

She got close and whispered dramatically, "I can only say it involved champagne and a pole."

A pole? Had they learned how to pole dance? He could picture Laura and Dixie doing that, but not Valerie—obviously he didn't know his future sister-in-law well. He didn't know anything about Denise except that she ran a successful business.

As for Tricia, he could picture her dancing seductively, enticingly, using the pole for all it was worth. Could picture it too well. But the only possibility he had of seeing it would be if she left his employ. It couldn't happen while she worked for him—and that was his goal, to get her to stay.

He couldn't win either way, but he could enjoy this moment, this night. He danced her around in a tight circle, showing off his moves. Dancing was something he did well. But the moment he started around a second time, she said, "Whoa, there, Fred Astaire. My stomach doesn't like that move."

"Serves you right." He slowed everything down to accommodate her, hoping the slightly green tinge on her face was from the strange lighting in the bar. "Okay?"

"Yeah. Thanks." Her smile was…adorable. He was sure he'd never used that word before.

David and Valerie bumped into them.

"Thanks for letting Hannah stay over tonight," David said to Noah. "I think I'll take my blushing, slightly drunk, almost-bride home and have some fun. You don't mind if we sleep in, do you? Pick her up later in the morning?"

Noah was envious as hell. He wanted to go home to his big bed and have someone in it with him. A certain someone who felt really good in his arms. "No, that's fine. I'll take you home."

"Denise offered the limo driver, since he's just hanging around waiting for us, anyway," Valerie said. The music stopped, so they all did, too. "You stay and have fun. I'm going to say my thanks and goodbyes." She hugged Tricia. "It was great getting to know you."

"I had a blast," Tricia said. "Thanks for including me." As soon as they left, Tricia turned to Noah. "How much longer do you plan to stay? I might as well go home with you. It'll save Fabian a stop."

"Fabian?"

"Our driver. Fabian Kowalski." She leaned close and whispered, "Our Pole."

Pole? Not a dance pole—a Pole. Noah started to laugh, then laughed so hard he began coughing. Tricia pounded him on the back. Gideon came over, concerned.

"I'm fine," Noah said, choking a little.

Denise joined them. "I'd like to get going. Tricia, are you ready or do you want to go home with Noah?"

"Actually," Noah answered before Tricia could. "Tricia, why don't you let Denise drop you off at your house in Sacramento? The kids and I will come pick you up tomorrow afternoon."

"Really? Are you sure that's not too much trouble?"

As much as Noah would've liked to have continued the evening with her, she'd been drinking, and his babysitter was spending the night. No privacy, which was probably a good thing. No moral dilemmas to contemplate.

"I'm going to take the kids on a field trip to my shop," he said, "and show them the cars in production, something I haven't done in years. We've got a limo ready for its owner. I think a test drive is in order."

Tricia beamed. "Good for you. Sounds like a great plan to me. I'll see you tomorrow, then."

Farewells were made, with Dixie still ignoring Joseph, then the women left. Joseph and Jake wanted to finish their match at the pool table, so Noah and Gideon wandered off a little to wait.

"Are you out of your mind?" Gideon asked the minute they sat at a table.

"Hey, I was just having a little fun with you. She may have been young, but she seemed—"

"Hell. I'm not talking about the girl you sicced on me. I'm talking about slow-dancing with your nanny. You, who gave David such grief about getting involved with his housekeeper. Are you crazy?"

Or something. "Teacher, not nanny. And we didn't get too close."

"She was toying with your collar and looking at you like you were her next meal."

"She was?"

Gideon dropped his head into his hands. "You can't be that dense. She's totally into you."

"I know there's a certain…*attraction* between us, but I haven't seen more than that."

"You're not looking."

"I noticed when Cynthia Madras was hitting on me last night."

"Yeah? Cynthia? She's very attractive."

"I hadn't really noticed until last night." But in comparison to Tricia?

"You should ask her out."

"Cynthia?"

"Are we talking about anyone else? It's time to date, Noah. And maybe it'll put the skids on your attraction to Tricia." Gideon's expression turned intense. "I can't believe you're willing to risk losing her. She seems perfect for the kids."

"No 'seems' about it. She *is* perfect."

"Then ask Cynthia out," Gid repeated, more emphatic this time.

"I'll think about it. We're meeting for coffee on Tuesday night to talk about the kids. But you know who would be better for me? Denise."

Gid's gaze sharpened. "Why?"

"She doesn't live here, for one thing. Makes it easier if things don't work out. Plus, she doesn't know the kids, so no potential problems there."

"She's not right for you."

It took a few seconds for his words to sink in. "How would you know that? Did you spend a lot of time with her?"

"Actually, I did. While you were dancing." He spun his empty glass around slowly, looking at it then finally raised his gaze. "Trust me. She's not the one for you."

"Why's that, Gid?"

"Because she's the one for me."

Chapter Ten

It took Tricia a minute to adjust to waking up in her own bed again the next morning. No sunrise greeted her through a big picture window like at Noah's. Here her room was small, although not oppressive by any means. She'd grown up in this house and hadn't thought much about its size until she'd moved into Noah's huge place.

Her house was an early-1900s, two-bedroom, one-bath craftsman, with shingled siding and a wide front porch. His was built in the past decade and was a mansion—the only word that could describe it, even with its rustic wood-and-rock exterior.

She loved her cozy home and all its wonderful memories, would miss it when she moved away.

But change is good, she reminded herself. The new adventure would lead her to an entirely new environment, close to the ocean, a different, more laid-back lifestyle, yet still in a city, where she felt most comfortable. She would buy a bicycle and explore. Maybe get a dog. She hadn't had a dog since she was a kid.

Tricia made her way to the kitchen to brew some coffee, her head aching from her champagne overindulgence. Caffeine would help. Normally she sat at the kitchen table with her coffee and newspaper on Sunday morning, but she'd canceled the paper, being home only one morning a week now. Since she had no car, she couldn't go get a paper, so she showered away last night's party instead, then dressed in old jeans and a T-shirt and started peeling wallpaper from her mother's bedroom walls.

She'd been avoiding thinking about Noah, but doing a few hours of the mindless work left her thoughts free to wander. Seeing him last night at the bar, away from his normal environment, gave her a new look at him. He'd been more relaxed, had even laughed out loud. He'd been dressed similarly to her—in boots, jeans and a white shirt. The boots added height to his already tall frame, but since her heels were just as high, they were still well matched on the dance floor.

The dance floor. Being held by him. Her pulse pounded at the memory. He was a stunning, imposing man to start with, and the feel of him close to her had made her tingle everywhere. Heat up everywhere. Sizzle…

Oh, yeah, he'd dressed down well.

She was pleased, too, that he'd responded to her shock that his kids hadn't ridden in a limo, even though his company built them, an oversight of Noah's she'd discovered as the kids had streamed out of the house when the party limo arrived to get her. The children were wide-eyed, even the usually unimpressed Zoe.

Yes, Noah was coming around to his role as father, getting more involved, seeing the light. Tricia was proud to have had something to do with that. Just think what more time would do. She could leave happy, knowing that she'd done what she could to bring them together as a family again.

Happy. Tricia ran her scraper up the wall, peeling away a strip of wallpaper. *Would* she be happy? Maybe not that, exactly, but satisfied that she'd been able to help.

Oh, who was she kidding? It was going to be hard to leave. Horribly hard, even moving on to a new, exciting job in a new, stimulating city.

At least he hadn't been trying to convince her to stay on. That would've made things even harder. There was no way she couldn't show up for her new job. She was committed.

Which reminded Tricia that she hadn't heard from her friend Jennifer, whose job she was taking, since Tricia had left a message last week about her new phone number. Tricia hoped Jennifer was all right. She'd had an easy pregnancy so far.

The phone rang. It was only two o'clock. Too early—

"It's Noah," he said, like she wouldn't recognize his voice. "How's it going?"

"It's going." She was hours from being ready to be picked up. "What's up?"

"The Falcon family would like to come help you. It was Zach's idea, but we all agreed. We can sand, strip paper, whatever you need. Then we'll spring for pizza before we head up the hill. What do you think?"

Touched, Tricia sank to the floor. "It would be wonderful of you to help. I could really use it. Thanks."

"Good. Go open your front door and let us in."

She laughed and hung up. Pretty sure of yourself, Noah Falcon.

She wanted to take a minute to clean up a little, but she went straight to the front door. Noah stood in the middle, his brood gathered around him.

"Hi, Miss Tricia," Zach said, grinning ear to ear. "We came to help!"

"And I am so grateful to you. All of you. Please come in."

Zach hugged her, as did Ashley. Adam flew past. Zoe

followed more slowly, looking in every direction, taking it all in. Then Tricia finally let herself look at Noah.

"Bit of a headache this morning?" he asked, his eyes shining.

"A tiny one. The questionable reward of not being the designated driver. Please, come in." She almost reached for him, almost hugged him hello, but caught herself just in time. He was in jeans again, and a T-shirt that showed off his chest and shoulders.

"Nice," he said, looking around then focusing squarely on her. "Good bones. Great architecture."

"It's a mess at the moment."

"Oh, we're talking about the *house,*" he said lightly, surprising her.

Was he flirting? she wondered.

"Renovating is messy," he said. "So, what can we do?"

Everyone took jobs based on their skills and interests. Zoe worked with Noah on the kitchen cabinets, using a small hand sander to rough up the old paint to accept new. Adam used sandpaper to do the crevices that the flat sander couldn't reach. Zach helped Tricia strip wallpaper. And Ashley was everywhere, cleaning up after everyone. She gathered old wallpaper to put in the trash and vacuumed sandpaper dust constantly, so much, in fact, that a frustrated Zoe yelled at her to stop getting in the way.

Tricia peeked into the kitchen at the surprising outburst. Ashley started to cry. Zoe looked miserable. Adam kept sanding away, music blasting through his earbuds, keeping him unaware. Zach had stayed in the bedroom.

Tricia exchanged a glance with Noah. That was all. Just one glance.

"What do you think, Miss Tricia?" Noah said, reading her exactly. "Time to break for dinner?"

"Absolutely. I'm starving. I'll call in the pizza order. What does everyone like?"

They settled on two different kinds. The kids went into the backyard to play and unwind while Tricia and Noah finished the cabinets and cleaned up, getting everything ready for the painter to come the next day.

"This helped so much," she said when they were done.

"Zach's idea, as I said. It's interesting seeing where you live."

"How did they like the limo ride?"

"Adam insists I bring one home and hire a chauffeur. He says the family should be the official product testers. Where'd he come up with that phrase, do you suppose?"

"Your kids are smart, Noah. Good luck when they hit their teens."

"That's only a couple of months away for the girls."

She smiled sympathetically.

"How do you do it?" he asked.

"Do what?"

"Be so at ease with them. I don't know how to talk to them."

She figured it was a huge admission for him to make. "You seem to be doing okay."

"They're stiff with me. They don't say much in our nightly talks in my office, although it's better than it used to be."

Tricia shoved the last box out of the way, the kitchen finally straightened up. "Take them on dates."

"What?"

"Do something one-on-one with each of them, something they like. They'll open up." She wandered over to where he stood watching them play tag in the backyard.

"It's that simple?"

"It's a start. Just keep at it." Their arms were almost touching. She felt heat, tempting, exciting.

"I probably wasn't the most interactive dad to start with, but since Margie died, I pulled away more. It should've drawn us together. Closer."

"There was a disconnect with my mom and me, too, when my dad died. Losing someone you love so much isn't something you can prepare for. No one knows how they'll react. What matters is what's happening now." She put her hand on his back, needing to touch him, to offer comfort, but also to just connect with him.

He faced her, his gaze intense, his jaw set. "You're very wise."

"It's easy to give advice to someone else." She rubbed his back. He closed his eyes and made a soft, low sound. After a minute, he turned his head and looked at her, his gaze intense, his jaw taut. A second later he eased away and went outside to join his children.

The pizza arrived. Everyone crowded around her dining room table, elbowing each other, shoveling pizza down as if they hadn't eaten in years.

"Who's that, Miss Tricia?" Zach asked, pointing to a framed photo inside a box of others she'd taken down.

"That's my mother and father."

Adam scrutinized it. "They're too young."

She smiled. "That picture was taken twenty-three years ago."

"Where do they live?" Zach asked.

"My mom passed away last year. My dad died when I was eleven."

Silence filled the room, then finally Zach said, "You're all alone?"

"I have a grandpa and some aunts and uncles and cousins, but none of them live around here."

"And you have us," Ashley said, patting her hand.

The simple gesture and surety of her words touched Tricia's heart. Why hadn't Noah told them she was leaving? They needed not to be so invested emotionally in her—nor she in them.

"You don't have any brothers or sisters?" Zoe asked, the first time she'd gotten personal with Tricia.

"No. I always wished I did. You're all very lucky to have

each other." She hadn't looked at Noah during the exchange, but she felt his interest, his sympathy.

"How come you're fixing up your house?" Adam asked, trying to stuff a long string of cheese in his mouth.

"It was time for a spruce-up."

"She's going to sell it," Zoe said, challenging Tricia with her eyes. "I saw the papers."

"Snooping's wrong," Ashley said, chiding her sister.

"I didn't snoop. They were on the dining room table, right out in the open. Miss Tricia put them away."

"Are you coming to live with us all the time?" Zach asked. Every gaze trained on her.

"No, I'm still going to have weekends off."

Noah stood. "It's time to head up the hill. Do you have everything you need?" he asked Tricia.

"Everything except my guitar." She looked at Adam. "It's in my bedroom. Do you want to get it?"

Adam raced off, and the girls followed, then Noah left, after throwing out the trash. Tricia grabbed a couple of things from her closet. She double-checked that the windows were closed and locked. Zach was waiting by the front door for her.

"Did you forget something?" she asked.

"No. I wanted to give you a hug."

"You did?" She knelt. He went into her arms and squeezed her tight. Her eyes welled. "Thank you so much, Zach. How did you know I needed a hug?"

"I miss my mom a whole lot, but you don't have a mom *or* a dad."

He really was the kindest, sweetest little boy she'd ever met. She framed his face with her hands and kissed his cheek. "Thank you," she managed to say.

"I have lots of hugs. Whenever you want one, just tell me, okay?"

"Deal. You do the same. I wish I'd met your mom, Zach."

"Me, too."

They walked hand-in-hand to the car. Noah looked curiously at them but didn't ask any questions until they got home and the kids all took off to the family room.

"Everything okay with you and Zach?" Noah asked before she could head up to her own room. She intended to take a long, hot bath in the spa tub, then go to bed early.

"He's a sweetheart. It really bothers him that I don't have a mom or dad." She'd found a special bond with all of the children today because of their shared losses, a bond she wished they didn't have, but a fact of life.

Noah stared at her oddly, intently.

"What's wrong?" she asked.

"That's my question."

"What do you mean?"

"What's wrong with you, Tricia McBride? How can anyone be so perfect?"

"You're crazy. I'm not perfect. Far from it."

"Really?" He leaned an arm on the newel post and smiled at her. "What do you think your flaws are?"

She ticked them off on her fingers. "I can barely cook. I'm not diplomatic all the time. I used to be comfortable with routine, then when I decided to shake things up, I swung too far the other way, so now I'm impatient."

"Not with the kids."

"No. With myself. If you'd known me before, you would see the change in me."

"What do you think my flaws are?" he asked.

"Oh, no. Uh-uh. You have to say them yourself."

"But I'm interested in what you see."

She smiled. "I wouldn't presume to say. You're my boss."

"I don't feel like your boss."

The discussion was getting way too serious for her. "That's *your* problem," she said with a grin.

"Not necessarily. You don't let me be boss."

"Life's short—"

"Dad!" Zach came running from the family room, skidding to a halt next to Noah. "Tell them *everyone* has to say yes."

"To what?"

"They all want to watch the video of Mom. I don't. Tell them no."

Tricia could see how torn Noah was—and she was partly responsible for the problem. Talking about her parents' deaths had probably spurred the interest. "If it's all right with you, Noah," she said, "Zach and I could do something else for now."

Relief settled in Noah's eyes. "Works for me. How about you, Zachary?"

He nodded.

"Come on," Tricia said, holding out her hand to the boy. "What would you like to do?"

Noah mouthed a thank you as they started up the stairs. She smiled back.

"I want to play chess," Zach said.

Great. "I've never played chess."

"I meant on the computer."

Nine years old and a chess aficionado already. Tricia wondered if Zach would be the one to cure cancer or something else equally significant. He seemed destined for greatness.

Tricia sat next to him and was given a lesson in the game of chess. It amazed her how he could look three moves ahead.

"Miss Tricia?" he said when the match ended. "Do you remember your dad?"

She laid an arm on the back of his chair. "Yes."

"Like what kinds of things?"

"He smoked a pipe, so I remember how that smelled. When

I'm out someplace and I smell pipe tobacco, I always think of my dad. And he wore plaid shorts, a white undershirt and hiking boots when he mowed the lawn. Always the same thing. And he kept his car spotless. Oh, and he loved fried chicken. It's one of the few things I can cook well."

"Was he nice?"

"Very nice." She paused to let him direct the conversation.

"My dad used to go to Europe a lot. Mom would let us all get in bed with her sometimes and watch television and eat popcorn. And she made the best chocolate cake in the whole world."

Jealousy nipped at Tricia. Noah had been married to a saint. No wonder he was still grieving. He probably found flaws in every woman he met.

Except you, she reminded herself. He thought she was perfect, which was dangerous thinking. She didn't want to be put on anyone's pedestal.

The sound of him climbing the staircase stopped further conversation. He appeared at the top. He seemed to have aged years in the past hour.

"Time for bed, son."

"Okay," Zach said, moving toward the stairs.

"You doing okay?" Noah asked him.

"I won."

Noah didn't say anything for a few seconds, then he squeezed Zach's shoulder. "Good for you."

"Will you tuck us in?"

"Be there in ten minutes."

"You, too, Miss Tricia?"

"Sure thing. Thanks for the lesson."

"You're welcome." He hurried off.

Noah came all the way into the room. He slipped his hands in his pockets. "Thanks. I know you should be off duty."

"This was more important." She met him midway. "How'd the kids do?"

"Ashley cried. Zoe never said anything. Adam was surprising. He was the only one to laugh." The lines on his face deepened.

Sympathetic, she laid her hands on his shoulders. He stiffened, then settled a little—just a little. Like earlier today, she had no business touching him, but their shared losses were a bond she couldn't ignore. "I'm so sorry, Noah. I know how much you must miss her."

After a long, emotion-escalating moment, he drew her into his arms and held her. She held him back, hard, then he completely enfolded her, pressing his face into her shoulder, a quiet moan escaping him.

Oh, but it felt wonderful to be held again, especially by this man. She'd been drawn to him from the moment she'd seen him walk into the girls' bedroom. The initial part of his appeal was physical, then had grown from there, way too fast. She was walking a tightrope, had thrown away her own safety net by touching him, holding him.

She made no effort to move away, enjoying his heat and scent and need.

Finally he straightened. He cupped her head, his fingers threading through her curls to lie against her scalp. Would he kiss her? Could she let him?

He defused the situation himself, dropping his hands, moving back. He looked bewildered.

"Thanks. I needed that," she said lightly, making it seem like she was the only one in need. "Talking about my parents today was hard."

"Sure. No problem." He glanced at his watch, then hitched a thumb toward the stairs. "Time to tuck them in."

"You take the boys first and I'll take the girls?"

He nodded.

They passed each other in the hall as they changed rooms, then met in the middle again in a few minutes.

"Thanks again for all the help today," she said. "One more thing I can cross off my list. Now comes the big, brave moment when I actually put the For Sale sign up. Talk about shaking up my life. Although not as big a shake-up as taking the job in San Diego, I guess."

"When did you work in San Diego?"

Tricia stared at him. She put a hand to her mouth as awareness sank in. "He didn't tell you."

"Who didn't tell me what?"

"David. He didn't tell you my plans."

"What plans?"

"Noah, I've accepted a job in San Diego that starts in January. My dream job. Working for you is only temporary, has always been temporary, to give you time to hire the right person this time. Someone who'll stay."

Her throat burned at the look on his face—shock, then anger, escalating to fury.

"I had no idea you didn't know. I'm so sorry, Noah."

"You never talked about leaving." His jaw seemed locked.

"And I kept wondering why you never brought it up. I never hid it. You knew from the beginning that I was selling my house and never questioned me about it."

He tunneled his fingers through his hair. "I assumed you had your own place, that you were just selling your mother's house."

"I'd been taking care of her for four years, then traveled for a year," she said gently, seeing how staggered he was. "Why would I have lived someplace else?"

"I don't know. I didn't think about it."

"The night I moved in here you asked if my room was okay, and I said it was fine, that my time here would be limited, anyway."

He blew out a breath. "I thought you meant because you wouldn't be here on weekends."

She admired the way he pulled himself together, could see the CEO, man-in-charge in him. She wondered what would change now. He would have to tell the children. She didn't want to think about how that would change things between them, too.

"I need to go out," he said. "You'll watch the kids?"

"Of course. Noah…" She put a hand on his arm, which was as rigid as steel. "I'm so sorry," she said again.

He nodded then turned away.

All she could do was wait.

Chapter Eleven

Fifteen minutes later, Noah pulled into David's driveway. He hadn't cooled down by even one degree. He'd made the drive to David's, forcing himself to go the speed limit, gripping the wheel so hard his hands cramped.

He climbed the back stairs and rapped on the kitchen door.

"Hey!"

Noah turned around at the sound of David's voice coming from behind him.

"We're in the cottage. Come join us."

"I need to talk to you. Alone."

"Okay. I'll tell Valerie and be right there. It's unlocked."

Noah went into the house and headed for the living room. He had to walk past a wall of photos on his way, so he stopped there, knowing he couldn't sit. There were several shots of the three brothers at various ages. Pictures of David's mother, June, whom Noah remembered more than his own.

And one of their father, alone, in front of the first car he'd designed and built.

Falcon Motorcars may have been created by Aaron Falcon, but it was the successful company it was today because of David and Noah. Gideon had bowed out of the business a long time ago.

"I had a talk with him the other night," David said from behind him. "Dad, I mean. Told him how much he'd messed me up. Didn't forgive him, either, just chalked it up to experience and moved forward."

"You've got some of his traits."

"Like hell I do."

The brothers squared off. "Everything he did that hurt us in some way, he'd justify it by saying it was for our own good," Noah said.

"I remember. What's that got to do with me?"

"What's that got—? You didn't think it was important that I knew Tricia was only temporary?"

"Ah. She told you."

"It came up in conversation. She thought I knew. What the hell were you thinking, controlling my life like that? Controlling my children's lives. Once again, they're set up to be hurt. This time even more, probably, because they've already bonded with her. Having her leave is going to destroy them."

"Then you need to do something about it."

The volcano of Noah's anger roiled, ready to spew. "Who are you to—"

"Your brother," David interrupted before Noah could get going. "Which gives me rights."

"Not when it causes pain for my children, it doesn't."

"I'm their uncle. I love them. What I did, I did for them as much as you." He set a hand on Noah's shoulder. "Let's sit down. Have a beer."

He shrugged off David's hand. "I'll pass."

David sighed. "Okay, then. Here's what I did and why. When Jessica told Valerie she was going to quit, I knew you'd handle it the way you always do—hire someone fresh out of college who doesn't really understand what she's getting into. Like how isolated she would be. How you would expect her to be a nanny, not just a teacher, available all the time. Someone who wouldn't stand up to you. So, I got busy. I found you the best person I could in the short amount of time I had."

"Who already has another job lined up," Noah said. "And who also hates the country, by the way."

"All you have to do is convince her to stay."

"Oh, sure, simple. She called the job she's going to her dream job."

"Noah, the woman already adores your children. I could tell when we were there for dinner, and she'd barely had a chance to know them yet. Your kids are doing *their* part just by being themselves. It's up to you to do your part."

Noah was completely bewildered. "Which is what?"

"Woo her."

"She's my employee." Should he admit he'd imagined her in his bed? Had dreamed about her naked and rolling around with him, her hands and mouth touching him everywhere? Him touching her everywhere?

"Valerie was my employee," David said. "Worked out just fine."

"I'm not looking for a wife. I just want a teacher who'll stay. I want my children to have stability."

"They get their stability from you, Noah, because you are the one thing in their lives that never changes. And, just so we're clear, I wasn't looking for a wife, either. Anyway, I'm talking about being good to Tricia, receptive to her ideas, open to debate, giving her time off when she wants it. I'm talking about wooing her as an employee. Although if something else should happen…"

"If by 'something else' you mean have a physical relationship with her, you know I can't. I can't keep her as the children's teacher *and* be sleeping with her. That's certain disaster." He walked away, needing to move. "And I'm not getting married again. At least not until the kids are grown. I won't put them through that kind of potential loss again. It's been too hard. A second time? Can't do it."

His tension ebbed slightly. David's idea was good. Do whatever it takes to keep Tricia.

Get her to see that being their teacher was her dream job. The idea presented itself in neon in his mind.

"Keep your eye on the prize," David said. "You especially need to be open to change, which you know is one of your problems. Status quo makes you very happy."

"There's nothing wrong with status quo."

David only laughed.

"Why didn't you tell me?" Noah asked.

"Because you would've dismissed her out of hand. I knew she was the right one." David cocked his head. "Didn't take too long for you to see that, either. And you're welcome, by the way."

"You've totally complicated my life, and I'm supposed to thank you? I may never speak to you again."

David only smiled. "That could make my life at work a whole lot easier."

Reluctantly, so did Noah. "I think I'll take you up on that beer now."

"Everyone needs to shake their lives up now and then, you know." David took a couple of steps backward. "I'll let Valerie know I won't be back tonight, get my good-night kiss."

"You don't sleep together?"

"Not until we're married—at night anyway," he added with a wink. "Hannah may only be eight, but she notices everything. We can wait a few more days. Be right back."

Shake up your life. It seemed to have become his life quote—according to everyone else.

Noah wandered back to the wall of photos. There were a few things he wanted to say to their father, too. If he were alive, Noah would make him stand there and take it like a man. He'd bullied all three of his sons, had gotten sole custody of each of them by bullying their mothers, effectively destroying the mother/son relationships, too. Only Gideon had reconnected well as an adult.

Status quo makes you very happy. David's words rang in his head. Status quo had not been his father's contentment barometer. He'd needed the adrenaline rush of risk, and also constant change. Maybe Noah *had* gone to extremes to be unlike his father. Demanded too much of others, especially his children.

Tricia had forced changes there. The children had responded well.

Noah heard the kitchen door open and close. He couldn't figure out everything in one night. For now, he would toss back a beer with his brother and forget for an hour or two that he was CEO of a thriving international corporation and single father of four.

And a man tempted by a woman he didn't dare touch.

Tricia's bedroom window faced the front of the house, so the only way she would know that Noah had come home was to watch the road through a small forest of trees for his car to approach. She'd pulled up a chair and was waiting. She didn't know where he'd gone. She only knew he was furious. No one should drive anywhere furious.

She didn't want him to fire her. She didn't even want him to find a replacement for her until January. They needed her to stay for a while and continue to help them rediscover each other as a family.

That was a lie. Yes, it was. They could do fine without her. They'd had a good foundation and were on their way again. It hadn't taken much time at all, just someone to help them look at things differently. Noah had been ready for it, without knowing he was ready.

Yes, they would do fine. She, on the other hand, might not, especially as she found herself drawn to Noah more and more.

Finally, at close to midnight, she spotted headlights. She tugged her sweater down, pressed her hands against her stomach and went downstairs. If she were wise, she would probably give him until after work tomorrow, let him think things through. But she couldn't wait that long for her stomach to settle down from the worry.

She encountered him when she reached the bottom stair. He came to a quick halt.

"You waited up?" he asked.

"You know that old adage about not going to bed worried."

"I thought it was never go to sleep angry."

She shrugged. He seemed calm, not furious at all. She wondered where he'd gone and how he'd settled down. A girlfriend, maybe?

"Safe and sound, as you can see," he said. "But thanks for the concern."

She figured she might as well ask the question that would either keep her up all night or let her sleep. "You're okay with me staying on?"

"Yes."

That was it? *Yes?* She would've liked more than that, but she guessed she couldn't push at this point. "Okay, good. I'm glad. See you tomorrow."

She turned to head back upstairs. He cupped her elbow, stopping her, turning her toward him again. "I don't want the kids to know yet. I'll tell them when the time is right."

She had mixed feelings about that. "I don't want to drop a bomb on them right before I leave."

"I won't wait that long."

She wanted to kiss him, ached to kiss him. And be held by him, her head against his broad shoulder, his strong arms wrapped around her. It'd been so long. So very long…

He rubbed his thumb above her elbow. On purpose? Now that he knew she was temporary, was it going to change their relationship? Would he act on the attraction she could see was mutual?

"Good night, Tricia."

She forced a smile. "'Night." She headed up the stairs, knowing he was watching her, not swaying her hips as she had once, but aware of the fact he hadn't moved.

She made it to her room then dropped onto her bed, covering her eyes with her hands. She hadn't felt that kind of pull toward a man since…since Darrell, and he'd died more than ten years ago. She'd been attracted to a few men since then, but nothing like this.

Now what?

Maybe she should leave, after all. Maybe she should tell him to find her replacement right now, and she could go back to Sacramento, finish up the work on the house and take off for San Diego as soon as it sold. She would have a little money to live on from the sale, could find a place to rent and get to know the area before she reported for work. Spend extra time with Jennifer, whose job Tricia would be taking. The learning curve would be huge.

Although when Tricia had finally reconnected with Jennifer, her friend hadn't encouraged Tricia to come to San Diego early.

Except for Jennifer, she'd let most of her friendships die since she put her life on hold to care for her mother and then take the time to travel and heal. It wasn't as if she had reasons to stay on in Sacramento for any length of time.

Tricia dragged a pillow onto her chest and hugged it. She'd lived with regrets for a long time. She was done with living with regrets, had promised herself never to pass up an opportunity again, to take the road to adventure whenever it presented itself.

She wanted to stay for the time she'd agreed to. Wanted to be with Noah and his children. Wanted to see them come full circle.

That was it, then. Decision made. She would stay for now. If Noah hired a new teacher next week, she wouldn't be leaving out of her choice but his, so she wouldn't have anything to feel guilty about.

Hugely relieved at having made her decision, Tricia got ready for bed, turned out the light and climbed under the blankets. Knowing Noah was doing the same thing at the other end of the long hall comforted her—and excited her.

Tomorrow things would return to normal. Whatever happened, happened. For now, she had a plan.

Chapter Twelve

Noah didn't like to be kept waiting. Cynthia was supposed to meet him at the Lode at eight o'clock, and it was now ten minutes after.

It was Tuesday, two nights since he'd held Tricia in his arms. Since he'd learned she planned to leave.

Two nights since he hadn't corrected her when she said she knew how much Noah missed Margie. Guilt ate at him for not telling her the truth.

He'd watched the clips of his late wife with Ashley clinging to him, squeezing painfully now and then. He'd kept an eye on Zoe, who was too quiet, too controlled. Adam had been fully engaged, but then he'd been six when Margie died. His memories weren't as strong or detailed as his sisters'—or Noah's.

And seeing Margie talking and walking and laughing, holding the children as babies, playing with them as toddlers, and all the events that followed, hadn't crushed him like they used to. He missed her, but not with the day-to-day ache hovering over him like a black cloud, the way it used to.

How much of that was because of Tricia? He figured he'd been inching toward recovery, but the embrace he'd shared with her had seemed to catapult him further.

She'd felt amazing in his arms, fitting perfectly, her body as strong and curvy as he'd imagined. She'd also tried to make it seem as if she'd been the only one to need the hug, when they both knew his need was as powerful as hers, maybe even more so.

Noah spun the salt and pepper shakers on the tabletop, flipped through the song list on the mini jukebox.

The diner door opened, and Cynthia hurried in. Not counting Halloween, the only times he'd seen her away from his house had been for business reasons, so he was surprised to see her wearing a definitely unbusinesslike low-cut sweater and second-skin jeans.

He stood to greet her.

"I'm so sorry I'm late," she said, her long red hair down and flowing, curls drifting over her breasts, which seemed to be pushed up and in. "I'm meeting someone after this, and my last evaluation with a family ran over. I tried to call and let you know but my cell had died."

She hugged him, as if that was something they always did. Her perfume transferred to him, clinging, filling his head, even when they sat on opposite sides of the table.

Having just watched the video of Margie, he realized how much Cynthia resembled her. Red hair, although a different shade, quick smile, and a petite but sexy body.

"Am I forgiven?" she asked when he didn't say anything.

"No problem. I hadn't ordered yet. What would you like?"

"They make wonderful hot fudge sundaes here. Of course they're way too big. Maybe you'd like to split one?"

That seemed too intimate. "I'd decided on lemon pie, but thanks."

She ended up ordering apple pie.

"So, you said you have some concerns," he said, wanting to get the business going.

She leaned her elbows on the table. "I've noticed some changes in the children for a while now. I'm a little worried about them."

"In what way?"

"They stopped pushing themselves to excel. They seem to do the bare-bones requirements but nothing more."

"Even Ashley and Zach?"

"Yes."

He was annoyed that she hadn't said anything until now.

"I had been working more closely with Jessica to improve the situation," she said. "I was stunned when she left. She didn't tell me she was quitting."

"Me, either. She told my brother David. He hired Tricia for me." The waitress brought their pies and coffees, which forced Cynthia to sit up straight, for which Noah was grateful. "What do you think is the problem with my children?"

"Boredom. Sameness. Getting older, especially the girls, which brings about personality changes. Frankly, Noah, none of the teachers you've hired have inspired the children very much. They were competent, and the children liked them, but that was all."

He knew that. As David had explained, they hadn't had enough experience, being fresh out of college. And they weren't happy in the remote location. Or with him. He was doing his best to change that now. "Tricia has experience."

"Only with kindergarteners, and that was six years ago."

"Does that matter?"

"It can. That's why I decided to work very closely with her, rather than it getting away from us this time. We can make adjustments early on."

"That sounds like a good idea." He took a bite of pie, enjoying the tangy lemon flavor balanced by the sweet meringue.

"I'm glad you agree. Would you talk to Tricia about getting on the same page with me, then?"

"You mean you talked to her, and she isn't cooperating?" He had a hard time picturing her being uncooperative about anything to do with the kids. "Did she tell you why?"

"She wants to see what she can do first."

"That makes sense to me, Cynthia."

"She's new at being a homeschool teacher. I've had eight years of experience in the field. She should listen to me, don't you think?"

Noah would have openly agreed with Tricia that she be allowed the opportunity to find her own path to success with the kids, except that she didn't intend to stay—unless he could convince her otherwise. And time was wasting on that front.

"What I've observed," he said instead, "is that the kids have become very engaged with their studies under Tricia's tutelage. She's making them stretch. She gets them outdoors a lot more than any of the other teachers did. Maybe you should reserve judgment until the next time you come. Let her settle in."

She mulled that over for a minute. "I'll do whatever you say, of course."

"Don't think I don't appreciate your concern or suggestions, Cynthia. Or that I don't value your expertise. I realize we've been through a lot of teachers, but I've also come to realize why, so I'm trying to make adjustments myself. I want consistency for my children, too."

"So, you think she'll be the one who'll stay?"

"I'm doing my best to assure that happens." Noah eyed her curiously. So far, they hadn't discussed anything they couldn't have dealt with over the phone.

She set her fork down and picked up her coffee mug. Before

she took a sip, she said, "I know this is going to sound strange coming from me, but maybe it's time you seriously consider public school."

Strange wasn't the word. Shocking, maybe. "Why?"

"We both know it was Margie's passion to homeschool them, not yours. It's been very difficult for you to continue. I understand why you wanted to keep the status quo for them in the beginning, but given the problems you've come up against, I think you'd find more consistency for them in public school. Or even in private schools, if you'd prefer, although they'd have a longer commute each day." She reached across the table and covered his hand with hers. "You've made an incredible effort, Noah. But maybe enough's enough."

He pulled his hand free. Her words had the opposite effect from what she'd intended. It made him dig his heels in further to convince Tricia to stay. He wanted Margie's legacy continued. He believed she would've approved of Tricia and her approach to education. He knew his children already did.

He picked up his mug. "I'm not ready to do that."

"I just wanted to plant the idea. I apologize if I overstepped."

They ate in silence for a little while. He liked Cynthia, always had. He thought she had a good head on her shoulders, and stayed focused on the goal. *Had* she overstepped? She was a critical part of his children's success. If she couldn't talk to him honestly, who could?

"I do appreciate your input," he said to her. "I'll keep a closer eye on what's happening at home. If I see a problem before you're due for their monthly evaluation, I'll have you come sooner. We can revisit this at another time."

"That's fine." She glanced at her watch. "I need to get going."

"I'll walk you to your car." He dropped some bills on the table and followed her out the door. She drove a van large enough to be a mobile office. "Do you like your work?" he asked.

"I love my work. I love children. If I weren't doing this, I'd be teaching." She cocked her head. "Do you like *your* work?"

He nodded. "Everything about it."

She glanced at the Falcon sports car he'd driven, parked ahead of hers. It was too cold to have the top down, which always made him feel hemmed in.

"So, when is Falcon Motorcars going to make a van that doesn't make a thirty-two-year-old single woman look like a soccer mom?" Cynthia asked. "If anyone can redesign the van to appeal to that market, it would be you."

"I'll pass along the idea, but don't hold your breath."

She grinned, then did just that, drawing in a deep breath, making her breasts seem ready to pop out of her sweater.

"We'll be in touch," he said then headed for his car. He waited until she'd pulled away, then he pulled out his cell phone, hit a speed-dial number.

"You free?" Noah asked.

"No, but I'm reasonable."

Noah laughed. "I'll be there in ten."

The house was quiet when Noah got home, not surprising, since it was midnight. He turned off the pendant light over the kitchen sink, which Tricia must have left on for him, then he followed a light trail through the dining room to the staircase. He stopped whistling when he heard the sound echo in the house. He hadn't been aware he *was* whistling.

He felt better than he had in a while, more sure of what he must do in order to keep his life moving in an orderly fashion and his children happy.

He climbed two steps at a time, got halfway up the staircase, then looked down and spotted Tricia curled up in an oversize chair in the living room. She hadn't said a word. Hadn't alerted him in any way that she was there. Guilt snaked through him that he hadn't called to let her know he would be later than he'd expected. She was supposed to be off the clock, after all, yet he'd needed her to watch the kids so that he could meet with Cynthia.

Then he'd taken advantage by going elsewhere and staying late, figuring the kids would be asleep anyway.

He went back down the stairs and approached Tricia.

"Hi," she said. "How did your meeting go?"

"It was fine. What's going on? Why are you down here?" She wasn't dressed for bed but wore jeans and a sweater.

"I heard a wolf. Or a coyote. How do you tell the difference? And then I saw something large and black. It raced across the driveway." Fear made her voice tight, raising it an octave.

He noted how tightly she hugged herself. He was pretty sure if he turned on a light, her face would be ashen. For a woman who otherwise always seemed in control, it was strange to see her fear. And kind of endearing. "We don't have wolves, and rarely a coyote. Plus, you're indoors, Tricia."

"It wasn't the only noise I heard."

He put his hands on her arms and rubbed them. "What else did you hear?"

"I don't know. Something below my bedroom window. Banging." She closed her eyes. "I hate that you're seeing me like this."

He wasn't sorry. He could use all the insight he could get so that he knew how to deal with her. "Fear can be irrational, Tricia, and your particular fear is closer to a phobia. Give yourself a break."

"I feel so childish."

"When was the last time you heard the banging?" he asked, diverting the conversation.

"An hour ago, when I was getting ready for bed."

He held out his hand. "I'll go to your room with you and check it out. If we can identify it, will you be able to sleep?"

"I'll sleep now anyway, because you're home."

He liked that. "Humor me."

He wondered if she would accept his hand, accept his help. She did, not letting go until they reached her room.

They stood just inside the door, listening.

"That?" he asked.

"No, I recognize that. It's branches from the tree outside. I've already asked Joseph to trim— There. That."

He couldn't identify it, either. "I'll check it out. Do you want to stay or come?"

She hesitated. "I'll go with you."

He didn't take her hand again until they'd put on jackets and he'd grabbed a flashlight. They had to walk down the driveway, around the back of the house, across where Joseph had tilled the land for the putting green. As they made the turn along the side of the house, she pulled herself closer to him.

Was it totally chauvinistic of him to be enjoying her fear? To be feeling protective of her? It really should just have been a reminder that she wasn't cut out for living here, for staying on. Conquering that much fear seemed like a big, uphill climb.

Something banged against the rock trim that lined the lower six feet of the house. Tricia not only squeezed his hand harder, she grabbed his arm, as well. He turned his flashlight toward the sound. A large crate the kids used to store their outdoor equipment was turned upside down, sporting gear scattered around it. Something was inside, trying to get out.

"What *is* that?" Tricia asked.

"Skunk, probably."

She let out a small shriek and took off backward. He laughed. "I'm kidding. A skunk couldn't move a crate that size."

She heaved a breath. "You brat."

"Sue me." He knelt, shining his light inside. The crate began to move again, accompanied by grunts. "Bear."

"A bear? You have bears?" Fear shifted to panic in her voice.

"No. Sorry. Bear is the name of a dog from up the road. He does a lot of night traveling. He also howls. It's eerie. That's probably what you heard."

"Why haven't I heard him before now?"

"His owners try to keep him penned up at night, but he's a regular Houdini." Noah grabbed hold of the temporary prison. Bear jumped and wriggled, making the crate move. As soon as he was freed, he took off, almost knocking both of them down on his way.

"Not much of a people dog," Noah said as he righted the crate.

They dumped the equipment back in. Tricia found the lid propped against the house and eyed it thoughtfully.

"What?" Noah asked.

"Doesn't it seem odd that the lid is way over here?" She asked for the flashlight and started searching the ground.

"What are you looking for?"

"I'll know it when I see it. Ah-ha!" She picked up a slat of wood and groaned. "Adam."

Noah took the slat, noted the small vee-notch carved into one end—the better to keep the crate up. "Why would Adam do this?"

"His science project. They had to do something that involved the outdoors. I gave them a list of possibilities. Obviously Adam chose a project not on the list."

"I doubt he'd expected to trap Bear."

"No, but maybe he *had* intended to lure a skunk. And notice where he put his trap—right under my window."

That didn't make sense to Noah. "Adam likes you."

"Does he? I can't read him well. He seems to go with the flow more than the others, but I'm not sure he isn't hiding his feelings from us, maybe even from himself."

"I'll talk to him tomorrow morning," Noah said.

"How did your meeting with Cynthia go?" she asked as they made their way back into the house.

"It was fine."

"So, what are her concerns?"

"The same as mine. That you're a little unconventional."

A long pause ensued. "Well, you can always hire someone conventional for my replacement."

There was an edge to her voice he hadn't heard before.

"How's that search going, by the way?" she asked.

He felt her gaze bore into him. "I just found out two days ago, you know." His goal to keep her had been reinforced tonight during a long conversation—after watching the Kings game—with Gideon. Noah hadn't wanted to involve him, but David had clued Gid in.

He'd given good advice: "You want the teacher to stay, you have to keep your hands off her."

More than just good advice—solid advice.

It had even seemed feasible—until he'd come home and found her scared and vulnerable. Hell, who was he kidding? He just had to be in the same room for her to have impact.

But the biggest realization he'd come to tonight was that if he didn't do something to distract himself from his attraction to his children's teacher he was going to make a big mistake with her, and she would quit for sure. Maybe sooner than January.

So. Invite someone out to dinner, that was the plan. Not this weekend because of the wedding, but the following one.

Which gave him plenty of time to plan.

Or change his mind.

Chapter Thirteen

The exquisite setting for David and Valerie's wedding was a white clapboard hotel that had survived since the gold-rush days, and recently renovated to all its mid-nineteenth-century glory. All the tables and chairs in the dining room were pushed to the perimeter, forming a circle, then the whole place was decorated with purple and yellow flower arrangements—tabletop centerpieces, garlands, and an arch of yellow roses and tiny purple orchids under which the bride and groom would take their vows.

Tricia admired the simplicity. Even though David could afford big and lavish, he and Valerie had chosen exquisite—and simple—beauty.

Because Noah was best man, Tricia was in charge of the children, who were uncharacteristically quiet. In fact, they'd been quiet for several days. Also polite and cooperative. She missed their little moments of rebellion or glee or antagonizing a sibling.

She wanted to talk to Noah about it, but every night when they sat in his office to discuss the school day, there never seemed to be a good time to bring it up. Because, really, what could she say? Your children behaved too well today? He would laugh.

And then there was the other issue she hadn't dared ask him about—why he'd been gone until midnight after meeting with Cynthia. He'd been completely relaxed when he got home— very un-Noah-like, had even been whistling when he came through the back door. Did he have a woman on the side? Someone his family didn't know about?

Like any other red-blooded male, he must have needs—

"Hi, Tricia. Is there room at your table for me?" Denise Watson, dressed to the nines in a stunning burnt orange silk gown, perched on the chair next to Tricia. "I don't see place cards, and I don't know anyone else here."

"Of course. I don't even know if Noah is supposed to sit here or at a table with the wedding party. Either way, we can make room for you." She introduced Denise to the children, who were sitting quietly, driving her crazy.

"What well-behaved kids," Denise whispered to her. "Are they always this good?"

"Pretty much." She knew she couldn't complain. No one else would understand.

"Really? I must admit I hadn't totally believed David when he said the children weren't a problem for the nannies. Usually you'd think: Four kids? The problem has to be them."

"They're wonderful."

"So, Noah is that difficult?"

"I don't know what he was like before, but he hasn't been difficult with me. In fact, I think he bends over backward to be nice." The lights dimmed. A man sat at a piano. He was the epitome of tall, dark and gorgeous. And brooding. He started to play. Tricia couldn't have identified Mozart from Mendelssohn, but she recognized beauty when she heard it.

After a minute, when the room had settled into silence, he switched seamlessly to another piece as the adorable junior bridesmaid Hannah walked with groomsman Gideon into the center of the circle, followed by maid of honor Dixie and best man Noah. The judge performing the ceremony came in and took his place, followed by David, who stood under the floral arch. All the men looked gorgeous in their tuxes, but especially Noah, whose height and build really filled out the suit, an imposing sight.

He looked like he could save the world single-handedly. She hadn't realized she'd needed—or wanted—a man to protect her, not until he'd been there for her.

And she'd greatly appreciated how he hadn't teased her about her fears, except to lighten the mood when they were outdoors seeking the source of the strange noise. Since then he hadn't brought it up.

The music segued into something Tricia did recognize, the traditional wedding march. Valerie emerged at the edge of the crowd, dressed in a stunning, simple white gown, her mother beside her. They moved into the open circle, then David took a few steps to meet his bride. The ceremony began.

Tricia had been to a few weddings since Darrell died all those years ago. Each time pain and regret had overwhelmed her so that she hadn't heard the vows or the music. This time was different. This time she heard Valerie's nervousness and David's assuredness. She saw the love reflected in their eyes, in the way they touched, and how they leaned toward each other as if pulled together magnetically.

She let her gaze slide over to Noah, whose expression was blank, and then to Gideon, who looked her way. Why? Then she realized he was focused on Denise, who looked right back.

Tricia glanced around the table at each child. Ashley was enraptured. No surprise there. Zoe, surprisingly, sat still, no fidgeting, no rolling her eyes. Zach yawned. As for Adam, he was carrying on a flirtation with a little girl at the next table.

Adam had owned up to setting the trap to try to catch a wild animal, any wild animal, so that they all could study it up close before they let it go. He said he hadn't realized it was under Tricia's window. He'd only meant to put the trap out of sight from the back windows, creating more of a temptation for an animal to explore and find the steak he'd left as a lure. He'd apologized again and again.

Tricia would've preferred he flash his impish grin instead, as if he were only sorry he got caught, which she believed was closer to the truth.

Magical wedding words drew Tricia back to the ceremony: "You may kiss your bride." They were introduced as husband and wife to a huge round of applause from the hundred or so guests. Formal photographs were taken. Food was served.

Gideon came over to say hello, while Noah stayed behind, although each of the children went up to talk to him on their own, which made Tricia happy.

"I think I'll slip out," Denise said after the toasts were made and the cake served. "I'll try to catch David and Valerie to say goodbye."

Tricia didn't want to be left alone. "Would you mind dropping me off at Noah's? I've had enough, too, and he can keep an eye on his children now that the ceremony is over. They're having fun with their friends, anyway."

"I'd be glad to."

Just then the piano player sat down, and Joseph, the official emcee for the evening, picked up a microphone. The entertainment part of the program was about to begin.

"Guess we can't leave during the couple's first dance," Denise said.

Both women sat again, waiting through announcements and introductions—the pianist was Joseph's brother Donovan, who'd come all the way from London to play at David's wedding—then the first dance. Before it ended, Gideon was there, asking Denise to dance.

"I was just leaving," she said, her protest going unheeded as he took her by the hand and headed toward the dance floor.

Tricia smiled at her gesture of helplessness and settled back to wait. Noah invited Ashley to dance, then tried to include Zoe, who shook her head. Tricia wondered if she knew how. A memory of her own father dancing with her snuck in. He'd been such a sweet man, such a kind father.

She let go of the memory and watched Denise and Gideon instead. She was keeping a little distance from him, but the trade-off was that they had to look at each other. Gideon didn't seem to mind. Actually, neither did Denise.

The song changed and so did a lot of the partners, but not Gideon and Denise. Tricia figured she wasn't going to be leaving anytime soon, after all.

Joseph's brother Jake approached her. "I know we only met briefly at the Stompin' Grounds last week, but if I promise not to step on your feet, will you dance with me?"

She smiled and stood. "Are you taking pity on the wallflower?"

"Nope. I've been admiring you all evening."

They got onto the dance floor just as the song changed from fast to slow. It felt strange to Tricia, being in the arms of a man she barely knew. He was taller than Joseph, and more lanky. Contrary to his opening line, he danced very well. "I hear the man who's playing the piano is your brother. I guess I hadn't realized how big your family is," she said.

"Five girls and three boys. The girls are all married, the boys have escaped, so far. The town has begun to call it the McCoy family curse—subtitled, 'The men who don't commit.'"

"Is that why Joseph won't set a date with Dixie?"

"Only Joe can answer that. He sure is unhappy today, though. And she's gotten really good at ignoring him and seeming to have a good time without him."

"It seems to me a relationship that volatile isn't destined for happiness," she said, then regretting she'd opened her mouth.

"In most cases, I would agree. But they're meant for each other. Everyone knows it." He looked past Tricia to something that caught his attention. "Looks like I've stirred up a hornet's nest by asking you to dance."

"What do you mean?"

"Noah's none too happy with me."

Tricia turned around to look. He was dancing with Dixie, but looking at Tricia.

"We have a history," Jake said. "Goes back to high school, when we were always in competition."

"In sports?"

"That, for sure. But academics, too. School politics. Girls."

"And it continues even now? After all these years?"

"Obviously, since here he comes, ready to cut in. You're not…involved with him, are you?"

"Absolutely not." *Just in my dreams,* she thought.

"Could I call you sometime?"

Tricia had the feeling that it was the competition that piqued his interest, since he asked loudly enough that Noah couldn't miss hearing it.

He clamped a hand on Jake's shoulder. "Dixie wants to talk to you. It's important."

Jake gave Tricia a slight smile. "I'll track you down later, if you don't mind."

"I don't mind." The words had barely been spoken before

she was in Noah's arms. This time he pulled her closer than he had at the party last weekend.

"He's a ladies' man," Noah said. "Be careful."

And exactly who were you with until midnight Tuesday? She wondered. Who exactly *is* the ladies man? "I'm not looking for someone for the long haul. Not in Chance City."

His hold on her tightened. Where was the relaxed Noah she'd seen all week? Was his competition with Jake that fierce?

"I'm no one's pawn, Noah. Don't put me in the middle of your feud. And if you continue to hold me like this, everyone is going to jump to conclusions about us."

He loosened his grip. "So, he told you."

"Not in any detail, but enough that I know there is a game of one-upsmanship between you that should've ended in high school but continues almost twenty years later."

"Maybe you shouldn't be so quick to criticize when you don't know the whole story."

"What does that mean, Noah?"

The piano equivalent of a drum roll resounded, then Joseph spoke. "Okay, all you single ladies. Time to catch the bouquet. Gather over here, please."

No one came forward.

"Don't be shy now."

Still no one.

"Why aren't you going over there?" Noah asked.

"I don't want to be the next one to get married. I've got some things to accomplish first."

"You mean you believe in the myth of the bouquet catch?"

"Of course I do."

He smiled and shook his head. "Every time I think I have a handle on you, you throw me for a loop."

"Is that bad?"

"Could be."

"Okay," Joseph said, "I see I have to take charge. Hometown beauty queen and fearsome lawyer Laura Bannister, get up here."

"Don't want to get leg-shackled, Joseph!" she called back.

"Tricia McBride!"

"No ticking clock here!" she shouted back—a lie, since she did want to get married and have a family, but she wasn't about to stand up there by herself. She was an outsider.

"Denise Watson!"

"I'd sooner swim across Lake Tahoe in the winter."

He named all the single women except Dixie, the exclusion blatant. It took Valerie pretending to cry to get the women huddled on the floor, without Dixie, who Tricia believed would ordinarily have put herself front and center.

Valerie turned around. Quiet descended. She tossed the bouquet in the air but not at the women waiting. Instead she fired it at Dixie, who caught it reflexively, then, as if it were on fire, pitched it at the group of women, hitting Tricia in the face.

She held on tight as people hooted and hollered, although just as much at Dixie as at her.

Tricia buried her face in the white-rose-and-orchid bouquet, inhaling the sweet scent, the fragrance a sudden, sharp reminder of her own lost love. They'd decided on white roses, too.

Regret laid her low in an instant. If Darrell had lived, she would've had her own family now, a husband to sleep beside, to lean on, like she'd leaned on Noah the other night. It was the first time she'd revealed that layer of herself to anyone. Not even Darrell had been witness to it. But then, they'd lived in the city, where those irrational fears didn't exist for her.

When she'd taken the children on the big hike, she'd been testing herself, and she had passed with flying colors. But that had been during the day. It was what she couldn't see that got to her— what was inside the darkness. She wanted so much for that fear to go away, to feel strong and capable in all aspects of her life.

"You aiming to catch the garter, too?" Noah asked, humor in his voice.

"What?"

He gestured to the small group of men encircling her as David knelt in front of Valerie to remove her garter.

Tricia forced a smile and left. Instead of returning to the table, she found her way to the back patio. She just needed some air.

Regrets, she thought again. She thought she'd banished them. She'd created her mantra as a way of eliminating regrets. And certainly she did believe that life was short, and she'd done a good job the past year of making it an adventure. So, why were regrets taking center stage again? Been there, done that. *Over* that. Or so she'd thought.

She inhaled her bouquet again. A little backsliding was probably realistic, especially at a wedding, where emotions ran a little higher.

"Tricia?" Noah's voice came soft in the darkness.

She moved into his line of sight. "I'm here."

"Are you okay?"

"I'm fine, thanks. Just needed a break."

"I'll leave you alone, then."

"Noah, wait. You don't need to go. The cool air feels good, doesn't it?"

He came up beside her. He'd taken off his jacket and tie long ago, and rolled up his shirt sleeves a few turns. He had incredible arms, amazing hands. Watching him put his hands on one of his children always made her smile, and sometimes made her feel like weeping. Feeling his hands on her had a whole different response—and he'd barely touched her, aside from dancing.

"Who caught the garter?" she asked.

"David slung it at Joseph."

"Did it make a difference? Did Joseph go talk to Dixie?"

"I don't know. I came looking for you."

"Why?"

"To apologize for my behavior during the dance. You're right. I should've buried the issues with Jake long ago."

"So, will you now?"

He gave her an enigmatic look. "Maybe."

Tricia laughed. At least he was trying. He seemed to be doing a lot of trying lately—with his children, with her, with life in general. So, an old dog could learn new tricks, after all.

"Obviously, you're free to date whomever you want," he added.

"I appreciate that you're concerned," she said, grateful for his candor.

"Why did you take this job?" he asked, looking up, eyeing the stars that were out in full force. "Why did you even look for a job if you only had until January?"

"I like having a safety net, for one thing, but I also needed the money. Plus I have to keep busy."

"Won't you have enough from the sale of the house?"

"After my mother's savings ran out, we had to refinance the house a couple of times to cover her medical expenses, so there's not a whole lot of equity there. She had a small life insurance policy that financed my travels and should be enough for a down payment on a condo."

She wrapped her arms around herself, the chill of the night finally seeping through her dress into her skin. "I'd gone to Denise's agency hoping to get a job to tide me over, certainly never expecting she would have a position like yours. My understanding is that she mostly places clerical or domestic help. Lucky timing for me."

"And for my family," Noah said.

"You may want to reserve judgment on that."

He touched her shoulder. "You're cold. I wish I had my jacket to put around you."

"I won't stay out here much longer. Neither should you, since the kids are on their own."

"Gid's keeping an eye on them, but so will everyone else. It's a close community."

"I noticed." She shivered, but she didn't want to go back inside yet.

Without asking he put his arms around her and held her close to his body. "Warmer?"

"Yes, thanks."

Conversation stopped. She closed her eyes. Scent from the roses drifted from the bouquet she held behind him, adding to the emotion of the moment, reminding her of the wedding that never happened, the regrets that haunted her. Noah's hands were splayed over her back, twin spots of heat.

"Are weddings hard on you?" he asked close to her ear.

"They've always brought out the what-ifs. But then after my mother died, I vowed not to have regrets again, and I haven't. Not so far, anyway. But a few from the past still linger. Still have impact."

She didn't want to regret this moment with him, either, even though she knew it would change everything if she did what she wanted to do. The fact he'd taken her in his arms told her a whole lot. He wouldn't have done that for just anyone. He wanted to be close to her.

"How long do you think we have until someone comes looking for us?" she asked.

"Probably not much longer. Why?"

She'd never been the aggressor before. But then, she'd rarely wanted something as much as this. She would only regret it if she didn't try. "Because I need to do this."

She pulled his head down and kissed him, and after a moment of surprise, he kissed her back—no tender, explora-tory caress but a powerful action, his tongue seeking and finding, lips molding, breath mingling, hot and arousing. He groaned into her mouth, clasped her head with those big, beautiful hands and kissed her deeper than she remembered it was possible to do.

Tricia dropped her hands to his waist and pulled him even closer, feeling his need pressing into her. He slid a hand down her neck, dragged his fingertips along her heated skin then under the neckline of her dress. She sucked in a deep breath as he found her nipple, already aching for his touch.

"You're incredible," he whispered, his voice shaky, as he caressed her.

"So are you."

"We shouldn't—"

"Shh. No shouldn'ts. No regrets. No complications."

"I was going to say we shouldn't be standing right here where anyone can see." He moved her backward, out of sight of the door, and urged her against a post. "I've had dreams about you," he said, curving both hands over her breasts, thumbing both nipples, nipping at her mouth again and again.

"Same here." He felt wonderful. Exciting and arousing. Exotic and yet familiar somehow, too.

He took the kiss deep again, wedging a leg between hers, drawing his thigh up to press into her where she ached and throbbed. Not a single sound made it through the pleasure that had taken over her mind. She dug her fingers into his shirt and arched her back as his tongue made a hot, wet trail down her neck.

There! Don't stop. Please…

He stopped. Jerked back.

"Sorry," she heard someone say, then retreat, footsteps fading.

"Who was that?" she whispered, frantic.

"Gideon." Noah took a step back, looking around. He tucked his shirt in.

She hadn't realized she'd pulled it out.

"Regrets?" he asked.

"Well, yeah."

"I'm sorry, Tricia. I don't know why I let it get out of control. I know better."

She set her fingers on his lips. "I regret being interrupted."

He pulled her in for a last kiss. "I don't know what this means for us."

"I don't, either. We'll talk about it, I guess." She finger-combed her hair, then picked up the bouquet from where it had fallen on the ground. "I'll go first." Tricia went inside and slipped into the nearest restroom to put herself back together. She stared at her reflection and wondered if anyone else would see changes in her. She hadn't reached the ultimate point of satisfaction physically, and her hunger for it did more than linger now. She could see it in her own face, in the brightness of her eyes.

"Now what?" she asked aloud. The question echoed, in the room and in her head. She ran her fingers over her tender, well-kissed lips.

She wanted to finish what they started, to know what it felt like. What *he* felt like. No guessing. No wondering.

She didn't know how to make it happen. She only knew she wasn't done with him yet.

"I'm done," Noah said. "Won't happen again."

"Why don't I believe you?" Gideon asked. They were waiting outside the hotel for the limo coming to take David and Valerie to the airport for their honeymoon trip to Hawaii, the place she wanted most to see. "You told me the other night that you were going to keep your hands off her."

"She started it."

"What?"

"It's true. She kissed me first."

Gideon eyed him, making a point without words.

"I know," Noah said. "What can I say? I'm trying to verify the rumor that it is like riding a bicycle."

Gid laughed. "I guarantee you, you won't have forgotten how to do it."

"I know. You're right." Noah knew he'd made a mistake. He should've walked away once he found out she was okay. But he *had* forgotten how good it felt to kiss a woman. And caress her body. And taste her perfumed skin—especially *this* woman who'd been living in his house, driving him crazy just by existing.

"What are you going to do?" Gideon asked.

"Remember my priorities. I need her as the kids' teacher. I can't do anything to jeopardize that. They would never forgive me." Especially since he'd just seemed to finally start to connect again with them. He couldn't risk doing anything to ruin that. But he sure as hell wanted to strip Tricia naked and have his way with her just once.

"What's going on with your plan to start dating?" Gideon asked.

"I haven't asked anyone out yet, but I will. For Saturday night, when Tricia will be in Sacramento."

"Maybe it's best if she knows you're dating."

"I don't know if all the advice you're doling out so freely is all that great, Gid. You haven't exactly made the best choices in relationships yourself."

"Which is why you should pay attention to me. I've learned."

The limo pulled up, the Falcon Limited he'd taken the kids out in last weekend. On Monday it would be on its way to its new owner in Las Vegas. Noah directed the driver to a parking place they'd blocked off for him, then walked over with Gideon to make sure the champagne and food they'd ordered was in place.

"You know," Gid said thoughtfully, "maybe I'm all wrong

about this thing, this attraction. Maybe Tricia's someone you're thinking about marrying. You could have compromised your reputation and hers tonight if someone other than me had come across you, and, frankly, I've never known you to make that kind of misstep. You've always needed a complete picture of the outcome and consequences before you act."

Marrying? The idea was so far off Noah's radar, he barely paid attention to it. Noah knew exactly what was driving his irrational behavior. "Consider that I haven't had sex for three years, then rethink your comment."

Gid laughed. "Point taken."

"What about you? You spent most of the evening with Denise."

"She intrigues me."

Noah eyed him curiously.

"There's something about her," Gid said with a shrug. "Did you know she's blond?"

"Looks like a brunette to me."

"Nope. I find it curious that she dyes her hair brown. Do many blondes do that? I need to know why."

They went into the hotel to announce the limo had arrived. In the flurry of sending David and Valerie off, checking to make sure everyone who'd been drinking had a sober driver to take them home, and corralling the children, who were completely wound up from the punch and cake, Noah didn't even make eye contact with Tricia.

Finally they all climbed into the SUV for the drive home. She sat in the front seat beside him, her hands in her lap, a small smile on her face, looking sweet and innocent.

He liked that he knew she was a contradiction, that she could be sweet and did look innocent—if you didn't look below her neck—but he also knew how hot she was. How soft her lips were. How demanding her mouth was. How she wasn't afraid to be bold, to give as much as she gave.

Yeah, he was glad he knew that. And now that this new knowledge of her would be melding with his fantasies, his dreams would become more complex, more detailed.

What would happen next was anyone's guess.

Chapter Fourteen

Tricia stepped into her Sacramento house the next morning and was greeted with a sparkling fresh interior. Almost every surface had been painted or restained, giving her a fresh palette, and also a lot of work. She spent the morning moving furniture into place, trying different arrangements, but mostly trying to keep herself too busy to think.

No such luck.

She was bombarded with thoughts about Noah, had barely slept because of it. Need had arisen after a long period of dormancy. And in the light of day, she'd pretty much determined there was nothing she could do about it.

Even if they had wanted to risk taking things further last night with the kids in the house, Zach had complained of a stomachache, then had run to the bathroom and thrown up.

He didn't have a fever, so she guessed it was all the cake, mints, peanuts and other treats he'd overindulged in.

Tricia had been conflicted over what to do about him. Her instinct was to step in and take over, but it was past time that Noah learned to deal with a sick child instead of leaving it to the help.

Ultimately, Zach resolved the dilemma on his own when he asked Noah if he could sleep with him.

Noah had been so stunned that Tricia had almost laughed. He'd looked at her as if she would rescue him. She didn't accommodate him.

"Mom would've let me," Zach said, as Noah remained silent.

"Okay," Noah said, defeated by a nine-year-old's creative coercion. "Go get your pajamas on."

"Me, too," Adam said, his hand on his stomach. "I don't feel so good, either."

Tricia understood that the boys had never spent a night apart, so that on its own would've been hard for Adam. But factoring in the privilege of sleeping with Dad? Well, Adam could never allow himself to be trumped by Zach about that.

"Just keep an empty bucket handy," she'd said, patting the bewildered Noah on the arm as she went off to her own room, her body humming with anticipation that would find no satisfaction tonight—or maybe any night, once he had a chance to think it over.

"Deserter," he'd called to her as she reached her room, grinning.

Frustrated at not sleeping, Tricia had gotten up at four-thirty and headed for home, so she didn't know how Noah and the boys had done through the night.

She hated that she didn't know, but decided not to call and ask. Whatever she and Noah had to say to each other should be in person, not over the phone, where she couldn't see his expression or body language. Would he decide they'd made a mistake? Would he—rightly—blame her? He may have been an enthusiastic participant, but she'd definitely been the pursuer.

Oh, for heaven's sake. It was just a kiss. Why was she making such a big deal out of it, anyway? Just a kiss.

Right.

When the phone rang close to noon, she was headfirst into her refrigerator, giving it a good cleaning. She hoped it wasn't Noah. She needed space from him for one day, but she also needed to finish getting the house in order.

"Hi, Tricia."

She recognized the golden voice of Rudy Wiley, Realtor, and a dear and trusted friend of her mother. As a second career, he did voiceovers for local radio and television programs. He could make disasters seem okay with that smooth voice of his.

"Hey, Rudy. What's up?"

"I met a young couple at an open house yesterday. Told them about your house. They're interested."

Already? "But…it's not on the market yet. I'm not finished getting it ready."

"I explained that, and it doesn't matter to them. Can I bring them by today?"

She looked around her kitchen.

"Tricia." His voice soothed. "You know what the market's like. To have a buyer lined up before the For Sale sign goes up is almost unheard of."

She knew that. It was just that now it had become real. She would be leaving her childhood home, leaving the tangible memories of her parents, replacing them with only the visuals in her head, and photographs. She would be leaving her hometown for parts and people unknown.

"Okay," she said finally. "How about three o'clock?" She would have time to finish up and take a shower.

"Great. See you then."

She hung up, then sat on the floor and leaned against the door frame. Was she doing the right thing, selling the house, moving to San Diego? Starting over? She'd been so sure before.

Probably just seller's blues. She would get over it.

By the time Rudy and the couple showed up, everything looked shipshape. While they toured, she went outside and sat on the front porch swing, waving now and then at a neighbor. The neighborhood had undergone a change in the past few years, with several young families moving in, changing the landscape in that lots of children now played outdoors, and houses were now fixed up, looking fresh again. A new era. Revitalization. Cities depended on it for survival.

When the front door opened, she stood. The woman smiled and the man nodded, then they took off without a word. Tricia went inside to talk to Rudy. He passed her a sheet of paper.

"Here's their offer."

Tricia's eyes opened wide. "This is more than what you and I talked about for a starting point."

"I told them your asking price. They don't want it to go to market."

"But I thought this was a buyer's market."

"They love the house, Tricia. They want it. As is. You don't have to do anything else to it. There's a hitch, however."

She blew out the breath she realized she was holding. "Isn't there always?"

"They haven't qualified for a loan yet. In fact, they just decided yesterday to start looking. So, they'll put in loan apps tomorrow. You should hear sometime later in the week. It was part of their decision to offer you a little more, because they don't want you to entertain offers from someone else until they've got an answer on financing."

"Do you think it'll be an issue?"

"I don't know. It's a tight market for getting mortgages, too. So. What do you want to do? I've got a deposit check right here."

She liked the idea that a young couple just starting out would be living in her house, maybe even have their first baby there, bring new life to it. "I'm game."

"They'd want a thirty-day escrow. Would that be a problem?"

"I have a place to stay," she said, considering it, knowing for sure she could stay with Noah and the kids. But maybe she could ask a friend if she could spend weekends in Sacramento. Or perhaps Denise. They had something in common now—Falcon men. At least Denise had a chance for a normal relationship.

"All right then, thanks," Rudy said. "I'll be in touch. You did a great job fixing up the place. Your mom would've been pleased."

She hugged him, happy to be with someone who remembered her mother, and who also reminded her that she was making the right decisions for herself. She just needed to stay on track, follow her dream, reach the goal. It was all there, within reach.

An hour later she pulled into Noah's garage. The SUV was gone. Her mind swam with possibilities. Zach had gotten sicker. Or it'd been his appendix, not overindulgence. Or one of them had gotten hurt. Adam caught another animal and it'd bit him. They were all at the hospital.

She pulled out her cell phone just as the big black Caddy turned into the driveway. All the kids except Zoe waved at her. Everyone looked to be safe and sound.

"Miss Tricia! Miss Tricia!" Zach shouted as soon as the car door opened. "We went to the Railroad Museum in Old Sacramento. It was awesome. We could go inside the trains and everything. They were humongous."

The children all piled out. Zoe headed toward the house without saying hello. Adam waved and took off after her. Ashley and Zach brought up the rear. Tricia looked at Noah. He looked back in a way she couldn't describe but could feel.

"How was your day?" he asked as they all trooped up to the house.

Her roaming thoughts were jarred back into the moment. "It

was fine. I got a lot of work done." She decided not to tell him about the offer until the sale went through. *If* it went through. "Sounds like you all had fun."

"I think everyone enjoyed it. I know Ashley liked the restaurant where we ate lunch. And they all went a little wild in one of the candy stores."

He was driving her crazy. No hints at all about how he felt? No, "we'll talk later," or something like that? Just keep her on pins and needles, instead?

"How was your sleepover?" she asked.

"Not a whole lot of sleep involved. Adam and Zach are huge bed hogs."

"Used to having their beds to themselves," she said.

"As am I."

"Me, too." An image of them sleeping together blinked once then disappeared. "What's in the grocery bag?"

He hefted it. "Dinner. All the fixings for ice cream sundaes. We had a really healthy lunch," he added as reasoning.

He was different today. Looser, livelier. Why?

"Something wrong with Zoe?" she asked.

"Apparently, but I don't know what. She was sulking all day."

Adam stuck his head out the back door. "Dad! Miss Tricia! Come watch the movie."

"I made the mistake of leaving him in charge of the video camera," Noah said. "I apologize in advance for what's bound to make us all seasick to watch."

She was just happy that they'd done something as a family, something she hadn't even recommended or urged them to.

And she also felt a little left out. She wanted her cake and to eat it, too.

After she tucked the children into bed, Tricia headed for Noah's office. She hadn't rehearsed what to say to him. She figured it would just evolve, based on what he had to say. But when she got there, he was on the phone.

"Overseas," he whispered, covering the mouthpiece. "I'll be a while."

Tricia didn't go back to her room but grabbed a jacket from the utility room peg, went outdoors and sat on the stairs, close enough for a quick retreat into the house, if necessary, but needing to face her fears, needing to feel strong about something.

Because she was weak about Noah. Now that they'd kissed, she felt different. Kind of irresistible, even. Would it lead to more? Should it? She wasn't going to be there forever. Would it be so bad if they gave in to the attraction. Who could it hurt?

She wondered which scenario had the potential for the most regrets—sleeping with him, then moving on, or not sleeping with him, then moving on? Which could cause the most regrets for *him?*

Did it matter? If the point was not to have regrets at all, she needed an option three. What could that possibly be?

Tricia jumped as something emerged from the trees. She hunched, making herself small, then realized it was Bear. Was he friendly? He'd hightailed it away the other night, happy to be free of his trap, and Noah said Bear didn't like people.

"Bear," she called softly. He went perfectly still, looked her way. "C'mere, boy."

He came cautiously, stopping a few feet away and sniffing the air. He inched closer. She waited, not moving. "Hey, boy. How are you?"

He raised his muzzle, as if answering.

"Do you like your ears scratched? C'mere."

He got within a few inches, then took a quick step back when she reached to touch him. "It's okay. I'm a friend."

He closed the gap, setting his head on her knees. She rubbed him gently, his fur long and soft. After a few seconds he whipped around and took off, probably hearing something outside her range.

Yes, she was definitely going to get a dog after she got situated in San Diego. Someone to talk to, a buddy to go for walks with, to pet while they watched television on the sofa together. He'd have a great dog name and be so well behaved that everyone would welcome him into their homes. She wouldn't be alone.

Tricia made herself walk down the driveway to the end of the house. She hovered there, straining to peer into the darkness. She'd seen wet paw prints across the deck a few times. Noah identified them as a raccoon once, then a fox. She didn't want to encounter either one, even with assurances that they were more afraid of her than she of them.

She made herself stand there until she counted to sixty, then hurried back to the house, making as little noise as possible. As she headed toward his office, she saw the office door was closed, a sliver of light indicating he was inside.

Closed? So, he didn't want to talk to her? Was that what that meant?

An image of throwing open his office door, barging in, swiping his desktop clean with her arm and having her way with him grabbed hold and wouldn't shake loose. Maybe the option three she was looking for was just to do it and then worry about it later.

It was so unlike her. She liked being safe, even as she searched for adventure. She didn't have much practice in being a femme fatale. Would he notice? Would he care?

What are you doing? He's your boss.

The loud voice in her head would talk her out of it, if she let it, so she gave it an equally loud answer: *Trying not to have regrets. You know he won't make a move unless he knows it's what you want, too. Maybe not even then.*

She waited. No other sound came to her. No pro and con list. No admonitions of any kind.

Should she dare? Could she pull it off?

Tricia put her shoulders back and knocked on his door.

"Come in."

She did, shutting the door behind him. He sat back, eyeing her with interest.

"I thought we should talk," she said.

"About what?"

"Last night." Gathering every bit of nerve she owned, she moseyed around to his side of the desk then leaned against it, bracing herself with her hands behind her. Could she sweep his desk clean in one swoop or just end up looking like an idiot? She picked up a letter opener and toyed with it, enjoying the way he watched her, his brows raised. She was showing him a new Tricia McBride, one completely out of character. She figured he was as shocked by that as she was.

He plucked the letter opener from her before she poked a hole in the paper she was twirling it into. "You're cold." He took her hand between his to warm it, then gathered the other one, too.

"I've been outdoors for a while."

"Really? Why?"

"Facing fears."

"Good for you."

"I didn't go far. Bear came to visit, though. He was friendly."

After a few beats, he said, "You wanted to talk about last night?"

It's time, she decided. *You're not going to be here forever. Go ahead. Take a chance. No regrets.*

Fly without your safety net....

Noah waited, fascinated. She looked both nervous and, well, sexy.

"Is everything okay between us now?" she asked. "You said last night that you didn't know what it meant for us. The kiss," she added, as if he didn't remember.

He remembered—how she tasted, how she felt. "It's been on my mind."

"Does it change anything?"

His stomach tightened at the possibilities. "That's a loaded question. I'm male. I'm human. I want. But…"

"But I'm your employee."

"In part."

"Short-term employee," she said, looking unsure suddenly.

"Why does that make a difference?" He wasn't being as honest as she was. He knew he was trying to get her to stay. She didn't know that.

Silence rang in the room. "Okay, then," she said finally, as if it didn't matter. "Good night." She left the room.

Noah leaned back and shut his eyes. He'd convinced himself the kiss had been an anomaly last night. He thought she felt the same. And he needed to keep on track—his children needed her to stay. So did *he*. He had to convince her this job was more important than her other one.

What now?

According to Gideon, there was only one way to get Tricia off his mind, to deflect his attraction, and that was to start dating. On the other hand, he'd promised his children there would be no more changes.

He had to think this through, as he would a business problem.

Okay. Option one: Give up on the possibility of keeping her and hire someone else, taking the time he needed to find exactly the right person.

Option two: Ignore his attraction to her and try and get her to stay.

Option three: Was there one? The only thing left was to marry her.

The consequences of option one meant he could sleep with her, since she would be leaving. He liked that possibility, except it had an end date attached to it, and it meant his children would lose her.

Consequences of option two meant not sleeping with her, but his household would run smoothly, and his children would be loved and cared for and taught well, which would make his life easier. Easier for what? He couldn't answer that yet. He'd just come out of a black pit that had lasted three years. He didn't know what would happen next.

And the consequences of option three meant he'd be married. Good consequence in terms of sleeping with her and his children being happy, but long term? They hadn't known each other long, hadn't fallen in love, making option three only a back-burner possibility down the road.

His goal was to keep his children happy. They were connecting again, laughing together, playing together. He needed that to continue, and Tricia was a key element in that happening. So. Option number two: He would need to ignore his attraction and get her to stay, even if that was the hardest personal choice.

Noah shoved his hands through his hair. He hadn't asked a woman out in about fourteen years, but the process couldn't have changed much. He flipped through his Rolodex, located the phone number he wanted, then dialed.

"Hello?"

"Cynthia, it's Noah. I hope it's not too late to call."

"Not at all. Is everything okay?"

"Yes, fine, thanks." He plowed on, no small talk, no building up to it. "I was wondering if you'd like to go to dinner with me on Saturday night."

A stretch of silence followed. Obviously he'd really caught her off guard.

"Would it be too awkward, since you work with my children? I understand if that would be an issue for you."

"No, I— Noah, I'd love to go to dinner with you."

"Great. I'll pick you up around seven?"

"Sure. Okay."

"See you then." He hung up. He was moving forward.

A moment later Tricia appeared in his doorway again. Had she overheard? He waited for her to speak first.

"I'm sorry," she said, taking a few tentative steps in. "I just need to clarify that we are just going on as if nothing happened, right? I know it was just a kiss, but it mattered to me."

His options and consequences ran through his head again. When he said nothing in return, she headed out the door.

"Sorry I bothered you. I won't again, I assure you."

He watched her disappear around the corner. Option two flew out the door behind her, disappearing, vetoed by the consequences of option one: He could sleep with her.

He didn't wait a second more but raced from the room to catch up with her. He beat her to the staircase, put himself in front of her.

"You are one tempting woman," he said, the words dragging along his throat. Then he kissed her, not tenderly, not teasingly, but as a man with a fierce desire, no matter how many reasons he had for not acting on it.

"Are you sure?" he asked, his voice gruff.

"Yes. Oh, yes."

It was enough permission for him. This was human need after a three-year drought with a consenting adult who wanted him, too.

Noah slid his hands down to her thighs, picked her up and carried her back to his office, her legs wrapped around him, their mouths still fused. She was a whole armful of woman, all curves and temptation. Deep, arousing sounds transferred from her mouth to his, vibrating down his throat.

He locked the door behind them, then lowered her to the

couch, moving back only long enough to pull his shirt over his head and toss it aside. His jaw felt locked, his skin hot, his breath hard to catch, especially when she touched his chest, dragging her fingertips from his collarbone to his waist, lingering there.

He needed to be skin to skin with her. He peeled her sweater over her head, tossing it toward his. She sat up as he reached behind her to unhook her bra, sliding it off her, then he cradled her breasts with his hands. Her amazing breasts.

"So, you thought about me today?" he asked, his hands in constant motion, his fingers stroking her nipples. He dragged his lips along her jaw, then moved low to take a nipple into his mouth. Ah the glorious feel of her puckered skin, surrounded by smooth, firm flesh. The stuff of dreams.

She arched up. Goose bumps rose on her skin as his tongue made a trail then retraced it, over curves, into valleys, onto peaks.

"I thought about you *some* of the time," she finally answered, her breath catching as he tugged lightly at a nipple with his teeth, not wanting to rush so much, but knowing he couldn't hold out for long.

"You're not very flattering." She felt incredible to him. Perfect. Everything he'd thought she would be, and more.

"You have a big enough ego," she said, a smile in her voice.

She moaned as he cupped her between her legs, rotating his thumb, pleased at her reaction. All sense of playfulness stopped. She writhed beneath his touch, giving herself up to what he offered.

The couch was small for two people so tall. He considered taking her upstairs to his bedroom, but he figured that might give them both too much time to think about the consequences....

Consequences be damned. She wanted it as much as he did. He wasn't taking advantage. There would be equal satisfaction, and equal blame, if it came to that.

He slipped to his knees alongside the sofa, giving himself

space to undress her the rest of the way. She was having as much trouble breathing as he was. Anywhere he touched her he could feel her pulse pounding.

"I wonder whose heart is beating faster?" he said, laying his hand over her heart.

"Mine. Definitely mine. And I'm going to explode if you don't keep things moving along."

He laughed, soft and low, at her demands. "Yes, ma'am."

The snap of her jeans popped open easily. He kissed the skin revealed, moving down as he pulled on the zipper, his head filling with her heat and her scent. She lifted her hips as he tugged at her jeans.

"You're on the pill, right?" he asked, some amount of sense surfacing for a moment.

"The pill? What— Oh." She let her hips drop. "No."

He sat back on his heels slowly. His chest heaved. He dragged a hand over his mouth, forced himself to meet her gaze, seeing confusion there. Well, this created a big problem, because he didn't have any condoms. Hadn't needed any.

"Um, maybe this would be a good time to tell you something else," she said, sitting up, using her arms to partly cover her breasts. "I, uh, this is the first, uh— I'm a virgin."

For a long moment he couldn't say anything. Think anything.

"Say something," she said.

"You can't be."

Her eyes went wide. "Your disbelief doesn't change the fact that I am."

"I'm sorry. I—I don't know what to say." And he didn't. He was just…shocked. "This changes things."

"Why?" She looked bewildered.

He ran his hand down her hair, wanting to soothe. She pulled back, clearly hurt.

"This isn't the way to lose your virginity, Tricia. On a couch, in my office? It's not right." He picked up her bra and sweater and passed them to her, then he grabbed up his shirt, turning away, giving her privacy to dress, talking so that she would be less uncomfortable, as if anything could erase the discomfort of the moment. "You don't have birth control. I don't have birth control. More than one reason to stop."

"I'm dressed. You can turn around now." Her voice sounded strong and sure, not embarrassed. She sat primly, her hands locked in her lap, her eyes vacant. "I agree we didn't really think this through. I mean, the whole birth control business. You'll have to forgive me, since I don't have a lot of experience at this sort of thing. It was kind of a spur-of-the-moment, heat-of-the-moment thing."

What did one say at a time like this? He had no idea, didn't even want to continue the conversation, although he was curious how she could make it to age thirty-four and still be a virgin.

"I apologize, Tricia. I seem to lose control when I'm with you," he said, telling her more than he probably should, but not wanting her to be hurt too much.

"I'm sorry, too, Noah. But you don't need to worry. I won't let it happen again. Back to business for both of us." She smiled in a way that said she was confident and okay, then it faltered a bit, just enough to know she was hurt, and nothing he could say or do would change that. Only time would.

"That would be for the best," he said. "Business."

She walked out the door, shutting it with a quiet click behind her.

He sat behind his desk, not even sure where to begin focusing his thoughts. He hated that she'd been hurt, but it was impossible to take steps back, to alter time. They had to live with it.

And he had to make sure it stayed that way. His children needed her.

But now, recalling the look in her eyes as she'd left the room, he wondered if it wasn't too late. They'd crossed a bridge that had blown up behind them, leaving them no choice but to find another path.

Chapter Fifteen

Tricia stood with Joseph on the back deck, supervising the children as they raked the tilled ground. The putting-green sod would be installed in a few days, much to Zach's delight.

A few days had passed since her disastrous encounter with Noah in his office. She hadn't let herself cry about it. They'd agreed. Business only. It was a good decision, she kept reminding herself, but she wanted to be sure the kids didn't pick up on any tension, so she went out of her way to be friendly with him. He seemed to be doing the same in return—when he was home. He hadn't come home in time for dinner Monday and Tuesday, had barely made it in time for their individual meetings in his office. Her own meetings in his office were brief. He stayed behind his desk, keeping the division between them.

Without him at the dinner table, tension hung in the air as the children stared at his empty chair now and then, even though conversation continued, something they'd gotten good at, whether or not Noah was there.

Was he avoiding her? If so, he needed to stop, because the kids were being hurt by it.

"Jake asked about you," Joseph said, leaning on the railing, giving Tricia a quick look. "He said that *you* said he could call."

She'd completely forgotten that, not exactly a compliment to Jake. "I did say that."

"So, I should give him your cell number?"

Should he? Would dating someone else help? "All you McCoy men are interesting, Joseph."

"I hear a *but* coming."

"*But,* I'm at a point in life where I'm looking to settle down, and I hear you all have a problem with commitment."

He straightened, crossed his arms. "I don't need another speech about Dixie."

"I don't plan on giving one." Although she wished she could say something that would make him act. Dixie was miserable without him. It didn't take a psychic to see that.

She stopped the thought from going further. Obviously she'd gotten in too deep already with this community if she was overly concerned with whether two people she barely knew would reconcile. "I'm just telling you, Joseph, that I'm done with dating for the sake of dating. I want a home and family."

"What makes you think Jake doesn't want the same thing? Why not give him a shot?"

She was human enough to consider that dating Jake might prompt a little jealousy from Noah, but to what purpose? What would it change? And what an adolescent idea, anyway.

"Miss Tricia?"

Startled, Tricia turned around. Ashley offered up two glasses of iced tea. She'd gotten good at avoiding the dirtier work in the yard, plus she'd suddenly started hovering around Tricia now that her father wasn't home much.

"You both looked thirsty," Ashley said, her smile irresistible, as always.

"Thank you." Tricia took a sip. Ashley had said she'd left her gloves in the utility room, then had stalled a good ten minutes before coming back. "Did you find your gloves?"

She pulled them from her pocket. "I think I should just supervise today. I'm getting a blister."

"Let me see," Joseph said.

She stuck out her hand. He examined it closely. "Where? Here? This tiny spot?"

She looked herself then nodded.

"No sweat," Joseph said dismissively. "Best thing for it? Hold that finger away from the rake. Don't let it have contact."

It wasn't the answer Ashley wanted. With a little toss of her head, she tugged on the gloves and joined her siblings as a van came down the driveway. Cynthia Madras climbed out and headed over. Something was different about her, Tricia thought, not putting her finger on what it was, except for the fact she looked friendlier than the first time they met.

"I'm sorry it took so long for me to bring your supplies," she said, climbing onto the deck. "Several items were on back order."

"Can I get anything out of your van for you?" Joseph asked.

"Would you? That would be great, thanks. The three boxes behind the driver's seat. If you could just put them inside the house, please? Tricia and I don't need to go through them. They're self-explanatory." She came up to the railing as Joseph left. "Hi, kids!"

They acknowledged her with waves. Ashley said she'd get Cynthia a glass of iced tea and hurried off.

"Busy bees," she commented to Tricia, after they'd stood and watched for a while.

"They're having a good time, I think. Even Zach, who's not big on being outdoors, and Ashley, who's 'really not into manual labor,' as she puts it." Tricia smiled at the memory of Ashley making that announcement. "It's been a good project for them as a family."

Adam took that moment to hurl a dirt clod at Zoe's feet, splattering it over her shoes. She retaliated, and a war began.

"Aren't you going to stop them?" Cynthia asked.

Tricia heard the disapproval in her voice. "Not unless they start hurting each other. They're just having fun."

"I wonder if Noah would approve."

Killjoy. Tricia decided it was a good thing that Cynthia supervised, not taught. What a dull classroom that would be.

"I think Noah likes what I'm doing with his children," Tricia said. "I'm sure he'd tell me if he wasn't happy."

"I've known Noah a *lot* longer than you, and I can tell that he keeps quite a bit to himself. Tell you what, I'll see what I can find out at dinner Saturday night, then let you know."

Tricia felt swept in a tornado that swirled her violently around and around. Dinner? Saturday? He had a *date?*

All she could do was look at Cynthia. Words stuck in her throat, where her heart had lodged. Her mind was busy, however. *Well, you idiot. Business only. What'd you expect?*

"Can you keep a secret?" Cynthia asked, unaware of the emotions warring inside Tricia.

After a moment, Tricia nodded. When had he made the date? After their disastrous encounter? Before? Which was worse?

"If Jessica had told me she was quitting, I would've given up my job to be their teacher. I would've done anything to get Noah to notice me. As a woman, I mean. But now you're here, and he seems much more relaxed, much less worried about things in general, and he finally asked me out. So, thank you."

The tornado dropped Tricia back on the ground, feet first, hard. She wanted to wipe that gloating smile off Cynthia's face. That was what was different about her today. She looked…smug.

"Miss Cynthia?" Ashley said from behind them. "Here's your tea."

"Thank you, sweetie."

"You're welcome." Without being ordered to, she went back to work, Joseph having intervened in the dirt fight as it had escalated.

Tricia continued to say nothing to Cynthia, who rattled on in a gratingly endless monologue, like fingernails on a chalkboard.

"You don't come across a lot of men like Noah," Cynthia said with a sigh. "You know, financially secure, someone you wouldn't have to worry about straying."

And he's kind, Tricia thought. Well intentioned. A loving father who was getting better at it all the time. Handsome. Sexy…

Tricia spent the rest of the day brooding. Then Noah made the mistake of coming home late again, long after dinner.

She didn't even try to be friendly this time, but went to her room and stayed there until Ashley knocked, telling her they were ready for bed.

"Are you okay?" Ashley asked as they walked to her room.

Tricia put her arm around the girl's shoulders. "I'm a little tired today. Nothing to be worried about."

"Are you mad at Dad?"

Obviously she needed to maintain better control of her emotions in front of the kids. "Why do you think that?"

"Because he's been late every night, which means you have to hang out with us longer."

"Oh, honey. That's not it at all. I love being with you." She hugged Ashley a little tighter.

"But we wear you out."

Tricia laughed. "Sometimes, yes, but in a good way. You bring me a whole lot of joy."

"We like you, too."

Tricia knew that was true of Ashley, Adam and Zach. As for Zoe? Tricia wasn't too sure. She seemed to get more distant, more…surly, every day, the only one who hadn't warmed up to her.

On the other hand, Zoe wasn't treating Noah any better.

After Tricia told them all good-night, she went downstairs to Noah's office. He looked up from his paperwork when she knocked on his open door. She shut the door before she took a seat across the desk from him.

"Do we have a problem?" he asked.

"You are undoing everything good that's happened in the past few weeks. Everything."

He leaned back. "In what way?"

"You know exactly."

"Probably, but why don't you tell me, in case I'm missing anything."

"Don't be condescending."

He put down his pen and dragged a hand down his face. "I apologize. You're right. I'm making you pay for my mistakes. Please. Go ahead and tell me what's wrong."

"First of all, Noah, we both made a mistake. Equal blame, okay? But more importantly, you need to be home for dinner. They've come to count on it. It hurts their feelings, especially since you haven't explained why. What *is* the reason, anyway?"

"It's work related."

She didn't believe him. "Work *created,* it looks to me. You're avoiding me, for the obvious reasons, I think, but the upshot is that it's hurting the children."

He was quiet for a while. "Again, you're right. I was avoiding you. I lost control the other night. I don't lose control. Ever. I didn't know how to handle it."

"The same way I'm handling it. By forgetting it happened." Which was so far from the truth, it was pitiful. It was all she thought about—how it had felt to be in his arms, to kiss and be kissed, to touch and be touched. To be desired. "Now. Change of subject. What can I do to help you find my replacement?"

His expression never changed. "I'm taking care of it."

"Fine. If that's all?" She started to stand.

"No. Please." He gestured for her to sit. "In all that's happened, I haven't asked you about the job you've taken. I'd like to know what makes it your dream job."

She set her hands in her lap. "It's as director of curriculum for a chain of private girls' schools, grades kindergarten through eighth. The corporate office is in San Diego. They have twelve locations in the western U.S."

"What qualifies you?"

"While I was taking care of my mom, I got my master's with a concentration in curriculum. I've always been interested in *what* we teach, how it affects overall education."

"But you don't have actual work experience in the field?"

"No."

He frowned.

"I know, I know," she said. "How'd I get the job without experience?"

"Can't help but wonder."

"My closest friend from college holds the position now. She's pregnant and wants to take off a year, maybe longer, to spend with her baby. She also doesn't want to lose her job. So she convinced the board to take me on in the interim."

He sat up straighter. "You mean the job is temporary?"

"Yes. But a very good addition to my resume."

"You're going to sell your house, pull up roots altogether, for a temporary job?"

What good had roots done her? she thought. "Lots of people do that for their careers."

"I never would have pegged you as being that career oriented."

She opened her mouth to argue his chauvinistic point.

He put up a hand. "No need to get huffy, Tricia. Obviously you're an exceptional teacher, but I just don't see you as someone who would ever put career above family."

"The only immediate family I have is a grandfather who's living it up in retirement with his new young wife." He'd struck a deep nerve, though. She wouldn't have anyone special to care for when she left his employ, and it was fine with her. Just fine. She'd done her share.

"On the subject of family," he said, after some time passed. "I got a call from the children's grandparents today. They usually have the kids for Thanksgiving week, but they need to bump it up. My mother-in-law is going to have foot surgery. She wants the kids while she's still mobile."

"So, what's the plan?"

"I'll drive them to San Luis Obispo on Sunday."

"Will you stay over?"

"No. I need to be in the office on Monday."

"That's a long drive in one day, there and back."

"Can't be helped."

"I guess you'd better not stay out too late with Cynthia Saturday night, then, hmm?" she said with a bright smile. "Do you have a sitter lined up?"

His jaw turned to marble. "Not yet."

"I'll stay here, then. Since they're leaving on Sunday and I won't see them for a week, I'd like to stay until you all take off."

A beat passed. "Okay. Thanks."

"You're welcome," she said with forced lightness. "Are we done?"

His mouth tightened. "Looks like it."

"You'll be here for dinner tomorrow night?"

"Yes."

"Thank you. Good night." Her knees were shaking as she left. She shouldn't have done that, shouldn't have mentioned the date. Big mistake. Bad move. Her jealousy was obvious.

She got to her bedroom and sat on the bed. What now? He'd apparently made a clean break of his attraction to her and was moving on.

She should do the same. In fact, she could call Joseph's brother, Jake, and line up a date. She didn't know why she'd told Joseph she wasn't looking to date for the sake of dating anymore. She was temporary. Jake would be temporary. So, why not? No chance to become dependent on him and have him go away, like everyone else.

Like everyone else?

Tricia moved to look out the window. "Since when have you become so cynical?" she asked aloud. There was a big difference between someone dying and someone leaving.

"But the end result's the same," she said, her breath fogging the window a little. She dragged a finger through it, then realized she'd drawn a heart with a crack down the middle.

Noah retreated to his bedroom, even though it was only nine o'clock. He flipped on the television, stretched out on his bed with the remote, channel surfed, then left it on a Kings' game, catching the score before tuning it out. He just needed background noise. Too much quiet resulted in too much thinking.

But thoughts intruded anyway. He'd actually forgotten about the date he'd made with Cynthia. He didn't have to look too far as to why it had slipped his mind. Nor did he have to look too far for an answer to the question of how Tricia found out about his date. Ashley told him Cynthia had stopped by earlier.

He didn't know why he'd expected her to stay quiet about it. Why should she? And in a small town like Chance City, news would travel.

Now that Tricia knew, it would hover between them, an issue that was personal, not open to discussion.

He was surprised she'd brought it up. But then she'd never been a normal employee, had rarely deferred to him. The way she'd spoken to him about being home to have dinner with the kids? No one else would've dared to tell how to run his life.

Even Margie, he thought. She'd been stubborn at times, but she was very traditional, especially about roles and the division of labor. He'd been the head of the household. After a mutual discussion, she would've let him make what decision needed making. She never would've told him what to do.

You like Tricia because she does tell you, he admitted to himself.

His life with Margie had been good, very good, with few bumps in the road. Maybe a tiny bit of resentment on her part now and then for them never doing anything out of the ordinary, for the way he'd always wanted to just stay home with her and the kids. The resentment cropped up every once in a while then would go away.

His business was much more stable now. If she'd lived, their lives would've been different.

Well, maybe not. Maybe they'd been too entrenched in routine for many changes to be made. Tricia had forced changes.

After another minute Noah left his room, walked to the opposite end of the hall and knocked on her door. He could hear the television on, then the sound stopped. She opened the door. She hadn't changed into whatever she wore to bed.

She didn't say a word, but he saw worry in her eyes while she waited for him to speak.

"I just want to tell you thank you."

Her brows drew together. "For what?"

"For everything you've done for us. All of us. No one else has had anywhere near the impact as you. We all appreciate it."

She swallowed. Her voice got soft. "Thank you."

He nodded then started to turn away.

"Noah?"

"Yes?"

"I think it's good you're dating. And Cynthia is very nice."

Nice. He'd had that once before with Margie, and it was good. Fine. But Tricia's more in-your-face approach left him…energized. Involved.

"Good night, Noah."

She closed the door slowly, as if giving him an opportunity to say something. Then when it was shut tight it seemed like she'd just closed an even bigger, heavier door between them, one that locked from the inside, leaving him no way to get in, even if he wanted to.

Chapter Sixteen

Noah was true to his word, coming home for dinner the rest of the week, spending time with them. He and Tricia never talked about his date again. Not one word. They'd lost their communication skills together, asking and answering questions but nothing more. Small talk.

On Saturday they all went to Zoe's last soccer game for the year, then to a pizza party with the whole team for a presentation of awards.

Tricia thought Noah would burst his buttons when Zoe was given a trophy for most goals scored and a special award voted by her teammates as the most helpful player.

Tricia had never seen Zoe so happy. All the little girls gathered around her, squealing and laughing, hugging her. Tricia didn't know *that* Zoe at all. How could she be so different away from home?

"We need to talk about Zoe," Tricia said to Noah when they

arrived home, keeping him back by the car while the kids went ahead. He'd told her he would be leaving the house at six-forty-five. She had two hours to get through, two hours to keep up the appearance that she wasn't dying inside at the thought of him holding another woman's hand, kissing her, embracing her.

"What about Zoe?" he asked.

"About what's wrong with her."

He looked baffled. "I don't know what you mean."

"You haven't noticed how withdrawn she's become? How little she's actually eating? Except for at the pizza parlor, when was the last time you saw her smile?"

"She's always been serious."

"Noah, this isn't her being serious. She's got a problem. It's eating away at her."

"Did you ask her about it?"

"We had a one-sided conversation this morning. I let her know she could come to me anytime, tell me anything. She said okay and off she went."

"I'll talk to her."

"Good. While you do that, I think I'll go for a drive." She didn't need to hang around the house, waiting for him to go. "I'll be back before you leave. Since they just had pizza, I know they'll be okay to eat dinner a little later. Cora left plenty of spaghetti for me to reheat. See you in a bit," she said, not giving him options. She got in her car and left, watching in her rearview mirror as he walked up the driveway.

She didn't know where to go. Valerie was still on her honeymoon. She liked Dixie but didn't know her well enough to just drop in. Denise lived in Sacramento, so no time to make a connection there.

Tricia had gotten used to being alone. Her mother hadn't been very communicative during the last year of her life, and Tricia had been mostly alone since then. Oh, she'd talked to a lot of people, but it wasn't the same as having someone along for the ride, someone to share a gorgeous sunrise or sunset, or even a meal, except at diner counters in various towns across the country. The healing process had necessitated her finding out who she was at that point in her life.

But now? Now she'd been living with five people, had gotten used to the noise and activity, and the fact that someone was always around to talk to, or laugh with, or share a meal. She'd put down roots already, although not deeply set ones, just tentacles dipping into the surface soil of their community.

When she moved, those roots would be pulled up, and new seeds planted in San Diego, only to be torn up again and tossed away when she had to leave that job. Wasn't there a good compromise between independence and deep roots?

Tricia drove into the tiny downtown, deciding to window-shop. As she wandered, people waved and nodded. She didn't know any of them, but she smiled and was happy to be acknowledged.

"Tricia?" Jake McCoy came up beside her. "Hi. Doing a little shopping?"

"Killing time," she answered.

"Me, too. Want to kill it together at the Lode? Can I buy you a cup of coffee?"

She pictured Noah and Cynthia at dinner, gazing at each other over candlelight. "Thank you. I'd like that."

He took her arm as they crossed the street. She glanced at her watch.

"Do you have an appointment?"

"I need to get back to the house by six-thirty."

"Tell you what. I'll keep an eye on the time, if you'll just sit back and relax."

She smiled, appreciating his desire to spend time with her. "You've got yourself a deal."

They'd no sooner taken seats in the diner when her cell

phone rang. She saw it was Rudy, her Realtor, and went outside to take the call.

"You're in the money," he said. "They got the loan."

"That's…great," she said, finding it hard to breathe.

"Tricia?"

"What?"

"Everything's going to be fine. It's a big change, but it'll be good. Your mother would be so proud of you." He talked more about the deal and paperwork and closing, but she heard little of it. "I think maybe we should talk tomorrow or Monday," he said.

"That would be better. Bye, Rudy. Thanks."

"Everything okay?" Jake asked, coming up beside her.

She couldn't get a word out. She looked at him, helpless, devastated, feeling like her memory had been wiped free of her history, good and bad. She didn't want to start over. She didn't want to give up her house, her roots. What had she done?

Tears spilled down her cheeks.

Her car. She needed to get to her car. She ran up the street. Just as she reached her goal, Jake caught up with her, turned her to face him, then pulled her into his arms and held her tight.

He didn't ask any questions. She told him nothing. She just wanted to go home.

And now she had no home.

Noah paced. If Tricia wasn't home in five minutes he would be late to Cynthia's, but more than his being late, he was bothered by the fact that Tricia was. She was a responsible person. If she could have called, she would have.

The phone rang. His "Hello" sounded harsh even to him.

"What's going on?" Gideon said. "What's wrong?"

Noah shoved his fingers through his hair. "Nothing. I don't know. Maybe something. Tricia was supposed to be here by now or I'm going to be late—" He spotted her car headed down the driveway. Relief and anger dueled in his mind, neither and both coming up the winner. "Here she is."

"Where are you headed?"

"Dinner date with Cynthia. I don't have time to talk, Gid."

"All right. All right. I'd been wondering if you'd worked up the nerve to ask her out, then I spotted Tricia and Jake hugging downtown today. Figured you'd backed away from her. That's good, Noah."

What? Tricia and Jake? *What?* How long had that been going on?

"I gotta go." He hung up the phone as Tricia rushed in.

"I'm so sorry, Noah. I'm never late—"

He grabbed her by the arms, holding her still, staring at her. "What's wrong? What happened?"

"Nothing. I—"

"You've been crying."

"It's nothing. Really. I'm fine." She wriggled free. "You need to go."

He studied her for another long moment. She was panting from running up the driveway. She looked nothing like her normal self. He would push harder later for some answers, not only to why she'd been crying, but what it had to do with Jake.

He made a quick trip into the family room to say goodbye. The boys waved. The girls barely acknowledged him. He'd hoped he would have a couple more years before they took on the rite of passage called adolescent unpredictability. No such luck.

"Did you talk to Zoe?" Tricia asked as he headed out the door.

"Yeah. I couldn't get anything out of her, either. I'm clueless."

She smiled. "Well, I could've told you that."

He was glad to see her smile, glad to have her joke with him, although it didn't change the fact she *had* been crying. She didn't seem like a woman who cried easily.

"Go. Have fun," she said.

He took his time walking to his car and backing out. The night was beautiful, crystal clear. When he hit the open road, he stayed at the speed limit, not in a hurry for what was ahead.

He pulled up in front of Cynthia's house, rang her bell. She opened the door, smiling, looking very nice, all dressed up.

Nice. There was that word again.

"Hello, Noah. Would you like to come in for a few minutes first? I don't know when our reservations are, but, if there's time…?"

He stepped inside and shut the door. Before she could lead the way, he stopped her. "I'm sorry, Cynthia. I can't do this. I came to tell you and to apologize. I realized I'm just not ready to date."

Her eyes went cool. "It's Tricia, isn't it?"

"Pardon me?"

"She told you what I said to her. About—"

"Stop. Please. Tricia didn't say a word to me about you except that she thinks you're very nice." *Nice.* "And she's right about that. It's just me. I'm sorry."

It took her a moment to respond. "Well, so am I, Noah. But at least you did prove me right about you. I haven't met many men who've had the class to deal with a relationship issue face-to-face. I appreciate it."

Although her words were civilized, her tone really wasn't. He didn't blame her. He never should've asked her out in the first place, had been reacting to his own frustration even after making a sensible plan. Yeah, he'd done some damage there. He wouldn't make that kind of mistake again.

When it came down to it, he was happy with the current status quo, especially if he could convince Tricia to stay. It was hard to believe that one woman could make such a difference in his life. *Their* lives.

One beautiful, sexy woman.

* * *

Tricia kept herself busy all evening. After dinner she supervised the children's packing of their suitcases to take to their grandparents' house the next day. Adam spent the least amount of time at it but packed the most, filling a second duffle bag with all his portable electronics.

"Where did our dad go tonight, Miss Tricia?" Zach asked as they had cookies and hot chocolate late in the evening.

"He told you. Out to dinner with a friend."

"Who?"

"You'll have to ask him that."

"Don't you know?"

Wasn't this a strange turn of events, Tricia thought. An interrogation. She might have expected it from Ashley, but not from Zach.

"You can ask him yourself, Zach."

"He's with Miss Cynthia," Zoe said, her words icy.

Stunned, Tricia took a bite of cookie, trying to look nonchalant. How did Zoe know that?

"Miss *Cynthia?*" Adam repeated, for once paying attention to the conversation. "You mean, like on a date?"

They all looked at Tricia. She raised her hands in surrender.

"That's stupid," Adam said. "If he wants to date somebody, it should be you. You're cool." He smiled and took a huge bite of cookie at the same time.

Tricia didn't know whether to laugh or cry. "Thank you for the compliment, Adam. I appreciate it."

"You're welcome. Can I go play a game?"

"Sure. Half an hour until bedtime, guys, okay? You've got to be up and on the road early."

They each carried their own mugs and napkins to the kitchen and took care of them, without her asking. She contemplated asking Zoe how she knew about Cynthia then decided against it, not wanting to give it too much significance.

Would one of them bring it up in the morning? Blindside Noah with it?

As soon as the kids were in bed and the house was quiet, she took a second mug of cocoa with her to her room. She changed into her bedtime T-shirt and pajama bottoms, turned on the television, found an old Cary Grant and Deborah Kerr movie she'd always loved, then snuggled into bed. But another couple took center screen in Tricia's mind.

Where were they now? Were they laughing over dessert? Holding hands across the table? Would he kiss her good-night?

This is ridiculous, she thought.

Tricia threw back the covers and went across the room. From the bookshelf she took down a photo album, a kind of life-summary album she'd put together recently, her own highlight reel, but in photographs. From the top of her dresser she grabbed a picture of Noah and the kids that she'd taken at the soccer party then printed on the computer.

She flipped through the album, stopping occasionally to recall a moment. One picture made her pause longer, a snapshot of her with Darrell as he was leaving for what became his last assignment. They'd been so young and so in love. She could look at him now and remember the fun they had and what he'd brought to her life, not the devastation of the loss. She'd clung to that loss for a lot longer than was healthy.

Tricia slid the Falcon family photo into a clear square at the back of the album. She ran her finger across it, smiling at the memory of the day. She loved those kids so much, even the belligerent Zoe, maybe even especially the belligerent Zoe, who was doing her best to be difficult, which only made Tricia love her more. She'd always rooted for the underdog.

Her finger landed on Noah. She ran it back and forth over his image, then stopped, her fingertip over his heart.

She loved *him,* too.

The revelation didn't come as a shout but a whisper, not as some flash of recognition but a sigh of acknowledgment. She'd been falling for him from the moment she watched him respond to his children come into his office when he and Tricia had been in negotiations. She'd seen strength of character there. Everything else had come slowly, day by day.

She was in love with him. And he was on a date.

She didn't want to leave, but staying meant she'd only have a family on loan until something changed—the kids grew up and went to college, or he fell in love and got married again.

Nor was she getting any younger. She didn't believe that love conquered all. Loving him was easy, but love itself was complicated and messy.

She shut the album, flattened her hands on it, bringing herself back to the present reality. What was wrong with her? She couldn't even think about staying. She'd made a commitment to her friend, who was counting on her. She was obligated for at least a year. By then the new teacher would be entrenched. Tricia couldn't even stay in touch. It would be unfair to the teacher, to all of them.

She needed to stop fantasizing about possibilities that didn't, couldn't exist. And really, it was a good thing she had somewhere else to go, something else to do. It was bound to save her from major heartbreak down the road.

Tricia heard a noise. She still hated the dark unknown of her surroundings. She crept to her door, opened it slightly…

Noah was home. She shut the door and picked up her watch from her dresser. Not even ten o'clock. Why was he back so early? A drive to Sacramento and back, plus dinner, should've taken at the very least an hour more.

She pressed her ear to her door, heard his shut, then absolute quiet descended on the house.

She had to see him. Tonight. She'd finally let herself accept that she loved him. She needed to see him, to see how it felt to look at him through new eyes.

Tricia pulled her flannel robe over her T-shirt and pajama bottoms, not bothering with slippers. She made her way down the hall and knocked lightly on his door.

He opened it as if he'd been standing there, waiting for her. His shirt was untucked and his shoes off. His hair looked like he'd run his hands through it a few times. Love swept through her, warming her, enveloping her.

"Everything okay?" he asked, ducking a little, capturing her gaze, pulling her out of her wonderment.

"I thought I should warn you," she said.

"Okay. About?"

"The kids know you went on a date with Cynthia. I don't know how, but they do."

"What was their reaction?"

She made herself smile. "Adam thought if you should be dating anyone, it should be me, because I'm cool."

He didn't smile at that. Big mistake sharing that bit of information, she decided.

"And the others?" he asked.

"Hard to say." She couldn't tell him how cold Zoe had been. That was something they had to work out themselves. "We were having cookies and hot chocolate, so they were busy with that. Anyway, I just wanted you to be forewarned, so you can figure out what you want to say to them."

"You think they'll ask?"

"Oh, yeah, they'll ask."

"Thanks. I appreciate the heads-up."

"Okay." Her hands found her pockets and plunged deep. "Good night." *I love you.*

"Tricia, I'd like to ask you something."

"Sure."

"Maybe you could come in for a few minutes? It seems ridiculous to have you stand in the hallway."

She'd never been in his bedroom before, had peeked in from the doorway but hadn't ever stepped inside. She did remember seeing a framed photograph of Margie on his dresser that wasn't there now. He'd put away the one in his office, too. She wanted to know what that meant.

He pointed to a sofa in a sitting area. She tightened her sash and sat, curling her legs and bare feet under her.

"Are you cold?" he asked, then without waiting for an answer, he picked up a remote and started the fireplace.

She shook her head.

"What?" he asked.

"This is something out of a James Bond movie to me. Gadgets galore. No more building a fire. Click. Instant heat." *Instant heat.* She wished she could get close enough to feel the heat she knew he radiated.

"If I had to build one, I'd rarely have one." He sat down. A few feet of space separated them. "If I'm being too personal, tell me. I'll understand."

"All right." She knew exactly what he was going to ask.

"Why are you a virgin?"

Bingo. "Because Darrell and I made a pledge to wait until our wedding night. Then he died, and I was in mourning for a very long time. Just about the time I was finding my place in the world again, my mother had the stroke, and I ended up quitting my job—and my life, in a way—to care for her. I let life-long friendships die. My world closed in. No one else came along who I wanted intimacy with. And that's it, in a nutshell."

"Do you regret it?"

"What? Not making love with Darrell?"

He nodded.

"Oh, yes. Biggest regret of my life. That, plus my parents dying so young, changed the way I look at life. My dad was only thirty-two, my mom barely fifty-three. My goal now, as I've said, is not to regret anything. I think it's why I'm able to take more risks than I used to, even though I seem to still need my safety net in place. I know that's a contradiction." She loved that they could sit and talk like, well, friends. They hadn't had a whole lot of relaxed conversation, she realized, that didn't pertain to the children.

He leaned an elbow on the back of the couch, angling toward her more, bringing a leg up so that he faced her directly. "Why were you crying?" he asked.

She linked her fingers in her lap. "While I was out for my drive, my Realtor called to say my house sold. It hit me kind of hard. Kind of like a guillotine cutting off all the years before, all the memories. I pretty much fell apart, right there on Main Street. Jake McCoy happened along right at that moment and let me cry on his shoulder."

"I'll bet he did."

She laughed. "I thought you'd decided to grow up and leave that feud behind."

"Yeah, well, I know Jake. Damsels in distress are his specialty."

"You sound jealous." She didn't dare let herself feel flattered.

He didn't say anything for a few seconds. "I just wish I'd been the one you turned to. My shoulder you cried on. You've taken care of all of us, Tricia. It would've felt good to take care of you in return."

She decided she didn't want to examine that. Or talk about

Jake anymore. He didn't matter. So she invited trouble instead. "How was your date?"

"I've been wondering if you would ask."

"When have I not interfered in your personal life?" she asked, which wasn't an entirely true statement. There was so much she wanted to know about him. Those horrible years with his father, and how he overcame it. The wonderful years with his wife. Tricia didn't have a bone of jealousy about Margie. She was glad he'd had a good marriage, and four beautiful children because of that marriage.

He nodded, all serious, except for sparkling eyes. "That's true. You are kind of in my face a lot."

"You need it."

"I'll reserve judgment on that."

She waited for him to answer as he stared across the room. And then she waited some more. "You don't have to tell me, of course," she said finally, uncomfortable with the silence.

"I didn't go on the date." He met her gaze. "I realized I wasn't ready. She was gracious."

Tricia didn't know how to react. Relief and joy swept through her that he hadn't held Cynthia's hand or kissed her good-night. On the other hand, he'd acknowledged anew that he was still grieving, still not ready for a woman in his life. His work and kids were enough.

"Do you think that's going to complicate your professional relationship with her now?" she asked, the only thing she could think of that wasn't too personal.

"Probably. I can live with it." He reached over and touched her hand. "This has been good. Thank you."

"Yes, it has." She stood. "I'm sure you need to get to bed. You'll be on the road for what, ten, twelve hours?"

He walked with her to the door. "I'll grab a couple hours of sleep before I head back."

"Would you call me when you get in? I'd like to know, you know, that you're home." Had she gone too far? That was a girl-friend kind of thing she was asking of him.

"You're going home, I take it."

"Yes, of course. No reason for me to be here, right?" She didn't expect an answer, so she hurried on. "I need to start boxing up my things. Having this week off is perfect timing for that."

He opened the door, held it as she passed by him. "Good night," she said. *I love you.*

"Sweet dreams," he answered.

But she didn't sleep, much less dream. After tossing and turning for an hour, she put her sneakers on and went outside. It seemed like the right time to conquer her worst fear.

Tricia grabbed a flashlight on her way out, then headed for the backyard. She didn't know if the noises she heard were real or her imagination, but she felt surrounded by sounds—dry leaves crackling, trees limbs creaking, fleeting footsteps. Her pulse thundered, her stomach churned. Still she remained planted in place.

A small animal zipped across the yard, twenty feet or so away. Dog? Cat? Fox? Large rat? Tricia didn't move. An owl startled her, taking off from a branch, its wings noisy. She ducked, but she didn't run.

She didn't know how long she stood there. Maybe fifteen minutes. Her bones were cold, her mind clear. Not that she wasn't afraid, but she could handle it now, not let it win, although she wouldn't walk beyond the buildings. She wasn't crazy. Then something approached from behind and nudged her. She jumped, raised her flashlight—

"Bear!" She exhaled the word on a relieved laugh as he shoved his muzzle against her hip, asking to be scratched. She dropped to her knees and accommodated him, relaxing more every second. Then he took off running, off to wherever he went next on his nightly route.

She hugged herself, looked up at the sky to see the stars she'd discovered her first night here. Then as she lowered her gaze she saw Noah framed in his bedroom window, watching her.

She smiled and waved, happy that she'd managed to tame some of her fear. He lifted a hand, left it on the window like a permanent greeting. It was too dark to see his face. She hoped he was smiling.

Her bed felt good this time, the down comforter creating warmth in short order. Peace descended on her. She could sleep now and dream of the man she loved.

Chapter Seventeen

Tricia's heartstrings were being tugged in four different directions by four wound-up, raring-to-go children at seven o'clock the next morning. Well, three raring-to-go children, anyway, Zoe having retreated into her own silent world. She'd started to scare Tricia with the intensity of her anger, or whatever it was. When they got back from their trip, Tricia would try to talk Noah into getting a counselor for her, since she didn't seem inclined to talk to either of them.

Tricia didn't want them to go, didn't want to spend a week apart from them. She had a hard time not telling them that.

Finally breakfast was done, the car packed. They were ready to go.

They gathered in the kitchen. "I hope you all have a wonderful time," she said, looking at each of them. "I love going to the beach, even in November."

Ashley gave her a big hug. Then Adam, who made it brief,

but who was grinning ear to ear. Zach came up next and squeezed her.

"Will you be here when we get back, Miss Tricia?"

"Yes, I will."

"Will you *always* be here?"

The world came to a halt. Tricia fired a look at Noah. How could she possibly answer that?

"Go ahead, Miss Tricia," Zoe said, harsh and cold. "Tell him you'll always be here. Lie to him. You're good at that."

"Zoe!" Ashley grabbed her sister by the arm and tried to pull her away.

"No. I'm sick of all the lies," Zoe said. "From you, too, *Father.*"

"Lies?" Adam repeated, looking back and forth between Noah and Tricia. "Who's lying?"

Zoe pointed at Tricia. "*She's* only going to be here until she moves away for another job. A *better* job." She angled her finger toward Noah then. "*He* knows it. Big, fat liars."

Tricia automatically reached for the angry girl. This was the burden she'd been carrying? Zoe wouldn't let her near. "I'm so sorry, Zoe. I—"

"Don't blame Miss Tricia," Noah interrupted, giving Tricia a look that said "I'm sorry" and "I'm in charge here" at the same time. "She wanted to tell you. It was my choice. My decision. There are reasons I didn't involve you, any of you. This is grown-up business."

"Oh, brother." Zoe threw up her hands. "Like you've been doing such a great job of being a grown-up. How many nannies have we had? How much time did you spend with us before Miss Tricia came and made you? What's going to happen when she leaves? Back to having no father again. What does that matter? You can't even tell the truth to your own children."

The other children had gone silent and still.

Tricia was handcuffed, unable to say or do anything. Noah had to handle it without interference.

"We *picked* her for you, me and Ashley," Zoe said, pounding her fist against her chest. "You promised you would be nice. But she's leaving anyway, aren't you, Miss Tricia? You're selling your house, and you're leaving."

She couldn't be anything less than honest. "Yes," she said.

"When?"

"I don't have an exact date. Maybe in a month." She dared a glance at Noah, who didn't look back.

"What do you mean you picked her for me?" Noah asked Zoe.

She let out a huge sigh. Ashley took over. "When we heard Miss Jessica tell someone on the phone that she was leaving, we talked to Uncle David. We asked him to find somebody good this time. Somebody who wouldn't go away just when we got them figured out. Somebody as old as you, Dad. You know, so she would be a friend, too. Uncle David found Miss Tricia. He said she could only take the job for a little while, but she was the best. He said everyone else was..." She looked to Zoe to fill in the blank.

"Frivolous," Zoe said.

"What does that mean?" Adam asked.

"Silly and stupid."

"Right," Ashley said. "Uncle David told us we had three months to get her to change her mind about her other job and stay with us." She put her arm around Zoe's waist. "We tried our best, Dad. And you promised to try. But it wasn't good enough."

"You're going away?" Zach asked Tricia, seeming to finally understand what was happening.

"I made a promise to someone, Zach. It's not like I have a choice. She's counting on me." She looked at Noah helplessly.

"*We're* counting on you!" Tears filled Zach's eyes. He looked accusingly at Noah, who had gone more rigid by the second—internalizing his emotions, Tricia figured. She wished he would just let go of them, open up. His children would not only understand but appreciate him for it.

"I have been trying to change her mind," Noah said. "Like you, I thought if I was nice enough, good enough, she would give up the other job and stay with us. But she has an obligation. Do you understand what that means, to have an obligation to someone?"

"We had her first," Zach said. "It's only fair."

"I made the commitment before I knew you," Tricia said, her heart breaking at their suffering. "I promise we'll find you someone wonderful. Your father's working on it. It'll be someone who can be here for you for a long time, someone you'll love."

"But I love *you*," Zach said. "I don't want to love someone else."

Silence hung thickly in the air until Noah took over. "Okay, everyone out to the car. We have to go."

A cheery goodbye was impossible now. They left with their heads down, shoulders slumped.

Noah held back after the door closed. "I guess we know what's bothering Zoe now," he said.

"Poor kid. I feel so guilty."

"Don't, Tricia. You're always willing to cut me a break. This time I don't deserve it. We both know it's my fault. I should have discussed this with them the moment I knew your plans. My fault. My problem. I'll fix it."

She wished she could hug him, kiss him goodbye. "Call me, please."

"Yeah."

She decided not to go outside to wave them off, afraid they wouldn't wave in return, which would hurt too much.

She guessed that having them know everything now would

bring about some changes. They wouldn't feel required to be nice to her—if that was what they had been doing all along—and they wouldn't hide their feelings. She admitted to wanting that honesty between them.

She also knew that it was going to be easier in some ways, too, since they had no expectation of her staying, although they would put distance between her and them, keep her at arm's length. The closeness they had would be a thing of the past. She was going to miss that more than she could say.

And then there was Noah. In her goal to keep her life safe and adventurous at the same time, things had gotten complicated—and yet simple.

She loved him, which was simple to do, complicated to undo, and not safe at all.

Noah glanced at his dashboard clock, saw it was close to ten-thirty. He was as tired as he could ever remember being. The drive itself had taken a lot out of him, but the emotional upheaval wore him out the most.

One good thing to come out of the day was that Zoe had finally purged herself of everything she'd been holding in. He'd taken her for a walk on the beach, and they'd sat and talked for more than an hour. All her fears had come spilling out—how much she missed her mother, how much she'd missed him when he wasn't around. How she worried about growing up and boys and the changes in her body and didn't know how to talk to him about it.

They talked about it, and everything else. He was as honest with her as he could be. At the end, she'd inched over and leaned against him. He'd put his arm around her, and she'd started to cry. His eyes had burned, too, hearing her sob. He finally pulled her into his lap and held her tight, her pretty hair, so like Margie's, smelling like strawberries.

The other good thing was an open discussion he had with the kids—about life in general and expectations in particular. It had become a full-blown brainstorming session, the longest, most productive family meeting they'd ever had.

As for Tricia, Zach had summed it up best when he'd said, "Well, she isn't gone yet!"

But Noah knew differently. He'd finally accepted that she had another obligation. That was that.

Noah was coming up to the freeway exit that would take him to Tricia's house. He had a couple of minutes to make up his mind, needed to settle on a plan. He did better with a plan, always had. When he acted hastily, like during that spontaneous liaison in his office with Tricia, it was disastrous.

So. A plan. He'd been thinking about it for most of the drive.

Option one: He could leave her alone for the week, not having any contact at all.

Option two: He could go see her now, even though he was exhausted and wouldn't be at his most logical.

Consequences of option one meant he wouldn't see her for a week. That wasn't an option.

Consequences of option two meant they could just talk, get things squared away, or they might make love.

Consequences of making love? Satisfaction…

He smiled at the understatement.

Other possible outcomes? Her first time. His first time in three years. He could end up being way too fast and she not enjoy it.

He laughed at that, knowing he was letting his concerns go a little far afield and was avoiding the real issues.

So. Real issues. He shows up at her place. She welcomes him. They end up in bed. It's great. Fabulous. Life-altering.

Then what? Do they agree to a week of sex? A week only? There didn't seem to be an option beyond that. A long-distance relationship had little chance of working. And a year from now, when she would be free to come back, another teacher would be in place. He couldn't do that to the children.

So, when are you going to put some value on yourself? Don't you deserve it?

Noah took the next exit and headed where he wanted to be most.

Wrapped in her robe, Tricia sat on her sofa, her legs tucked under her, the television off. She clung to her portable phone. It had been a very…long…day.

She should've been packing. Instead she'd been paralyzed. She had no safety net in this situation. She didn't know how the children felt. She didn't know how Noah felt. Being out of the loop had been slowly driving her out of her mind. She needed him to call, tell her what happened, what was going to happen now.

Headlights swept across her living room window, someone making a U-turn in front of her house. Then the sound of a car door shutting. Footsteps up her walkway.

She hurried to the door, looked out the peephole. Noah.

She waited for him to knock, giving herself a moment to collect herself, then opened the door.

He was framed in the doorway, an image captured in her mind as powerfully as a photograph. He presented her with a single yellow mum.

"You stole that from my neighbor's yard."

"In my defense, I tried to buy you roses. But it's Sunday night, so…"

She loved that he'd tried. "Come in."

"The house looks great," he said, looking around.

"Check out the kitchen. See how your handiwork came out."

He eyed her steadily and smiled. "Maybe later." He slipped his hand in his jacket pocket, pulled out something, handed it to her. A perfect little shell, orange and conical. "Zoe sent you this. She said to say she was sorry."

Tricia cradled it in her hand, then closed her fingers over it. Without a word she went into his arms, tears flowing fast and hot. "I was so scared they would hate me now."

He stroked her hair, her back, her arms. Soon, he wrapped her tighter, and let her cry herself out. Finally, he kissed her, tenderly, eloquently, if a kiss could be called that. It seemed to say more than words, anyway.

"We have a week," he said against her mouth.

She nodded. Her pulse picked up pace.

"You need to think about it," he said. "I have. It's what I want, even though I know it could complicate everything."

"I've *been* thinking about it. For weeks. It's what I want, too."

"Okay." He kissed her forehead, his breath rushing out against her skin. "One more gift." He dug into his jacket pocket again. "I couldn't find a place to sell me roses, but it was incredibly easy to find these."

He held up a package of condoms. She laughed, relaxing a little. "Brilliant minds think alike."

"You got some, too?"

She smiled. "I was hopeful."

"I know you're probably curious about what happened with the kids," he said. "But can I just sum it up and say everything is okay for now? We have more important things to do."

"Thank you for that." Happy, she took his hand and led him to her bedroom. She perched on the edge of the bed.

"I don't want to kiss you until we're both naked," he said. "If I kiss you now, I'll get tangled up in getting undressed. I want this to be slow and easy for you."

She reached for her sash. He stopped her. "I'd like to do that. Just give me a second to catch up to you."

She didn't mind a bit. Watching him undress was like a live-action Christmas present, her gift unwrapped a layer at a time. And, oh, what was underneath the packaging was rare, unique and memorable.

He took her hand, bringing her to her feet. "You're going to have to let me be in charge this first time," he said with a soft insistence. "Let me do the touching. Later, you can do whatever you want."

She didn't have any issues with his request except for wanting to touch him everywhere, to be close enough to him to taste his skin, and feel all the planes and ridges of his body. But then he untied her robe and let it fall to the floor, and her mind went blank—except for an awareness only of him. How he took a step back and looked at her, more than approval in his eyes—appreciation and arousal, too, although that was in full evidence already.

He pulled her in for a kiss, lips to lips, skin to skin, heart to heart. Heat to heat.

"I've wanted you for so long." He brushed his lips against hers again and again, her breathing more and more labored. "I dreamed about you, about this, but never expected it."

"Me, too. Exactly the same."

He took the kiss deep finally, groaned into her mouth. His tongue swirled, discovered, treasured. She savored the sounds and flavors of him, then he started on a slow path down her body, tempting her with lazy flicks, long strokes, intense explorations. She tipped her head back as he went lower still, his fingers busy, his mouth busier.

"You are a warrior woman," he said, kneeling. "Strong and smart and sexy."

His words upped the ante of arousal. She couldn't manage a single word in return, just threaded her fingers through his hair and pressed his scalp. Her strength disappeared as all her nerve endings seemed to narrow, gathering in one place. Her knees went weak. He moved her onto the bed, blanketed her body, settled between her legs, and kissed her long and deep and endlessly, urgency building, second by second.

She could hardly breathe. Her heart thundered so hard, she couldn't hear. Finally he nudged her legs apart. She'd waited for this moment for so long. So very long.

The tip of him felt scorching hot inside her as her body opened to his, welcoming him. He wasn't all the way inside her before the climax hit her full force, full measure, full glory. His mouth came down on hers, blocking the uncontrollable sounds bursting from her. He moved all the way up into her, bringing pressure that added to the eruption happening inside her, but no pain. No pain.

Then his body went rigid, moved more urgently, more rhythmically, and he followed her into the incredible oblivion that suspended time and sustained life.

Neither spoke, not for a long time, yet a sense of joy and satisfaction danced around them. She clung to him, treasured him, appreciated him.

"You are magnificent," she said finally.

He drew a deep, relaxed breath. "I bet you say that to all the guys."

She laughed and kissed him.

He rolled to his side, taking her along, tucking her close. "Do you need a blanket?" he asked.

"No. You're like a furnace."

"How are you?" His hands, his amazing hands, comforted, protected, soothed.

"Happy."

"No regrets?"

"No regrets at all. How about you?"

He sort of laughed, as if the idea was ridiculous. "No."

"How about tomorrow morning?"

"Ask me tomorrow," he said, teasing her, as he rubbed her back. "Thank you. I know it was a gift."

"I'm glad it was you."

He yawned and closed his eyes. Sleep came instantly. She wasn't surprised, considering the day he'd had.

She figured she'd give him a few hours, then take him at his word that she could do whatever she wanted to him.

She mentally rubbed her hands together. She had a lot of years to catch up on. Oh, yeah. He would never know what hit him.

Chapter Eighteen

Nerves wrapped around Tricia like a boa constrictor, slithering and squeezing. It was Sunday. She hadn't seen the children in a week. They were due home with Noah at any minute. She had no idea how they were going to react to her.

And she didn't know how she was going to stand not sleeping with him, hadn't truly understood how hard it was going to be to give him up. He'd spent the workweek at her house, then they'd come back to his house Friday night. There were a number of rooms that held fond memories for her.

She smiled at the thought, especially about the time she'd cleared his desktop and had her way with him, a fantasy come true—except she'd had to help him sort out his papers afterward, which he made her do naked.

Yes, memories. Great memories. Ones that had to sustain her.

That morning, before he left for San Luis Obispo, he told her he'd been in touch with Denise to start the search process for a new teacher. The kids had given him a list of what they wanted. He'd promised them they could be involved in the hiring. They were not just a family now, but a team.

He didn't shy away from talking honestly about his relationship with Tricia, either. That this was the end of it, this morning, in his big bed with the view of forested hills and the glorious sunrise.

She got it. She'd gotten it since he'd come home from his nondate with Cynthia. He wasn't ready to date, but an affair worked for him.

She had no right to be angry about that. He'd been honest from the beginning. A week only. Fantasies fulfilled. Questions answered. Curiosities satisfied. They couldn't let on to the children that anything was different.

So why was she angry? Anger was unfamiliar territory. It generally took a lot to rile her.

She acknowledged the worst of it—she'd hoped he would fall in love with her. And while the sex was great, and the conversations amazing and endless, it hadn't happened for him. She'd wanted him to come to a big revelation and wake up this morning, their last morning, and tell her he loved her. It hadn't happened. He just talked of being careful, of not letting on there was anything between them.

And if he'd said he loved you? What then?

She would've found a way to deal with the other job. No question about it.

She saw the car approach. A chunk of hot lead lodged in her stomach. Should she go outside to greet them?

She stayed put. Before too long the door opened. Adam popped in, a duffle bag in each hand.

"Yo," he said with a toss of his head.

"How are you?" she asked, nerves hitting her hard. *I missed you. I missed you so much....*

"Pretty good." He kept moving.

Ashley followed. She smiled, but it wasn't her sparkling-eyes, flashing-teeth smile of the past. And she didn't hug Tricia. "Hi, Miss Tricia," she said as she walked through.

"Did you have a good time?" *I missed you....*

"Yes. My grandparents are a lot of fun." Then she was gone.

Zach came in, struggling with a suitcase way too big for him. He didn't hug her, either, which hurt more than with the others. Should she call in his marker and ask for one of those hugs he said he had plenty of? No. She couldn't force the issue. It would only make things harder.

"How was the ocean?" she asked. *I missed you....*

"Kinda cold. And a wave knocked me down. It hurt, and I got sand in my underwear."

She wanted to talk to him some more but he kept going.

Zoe finally walked in. She stood in the doorway staring at Tricia.

"I missed you," Tricia said without stopping to think about it.

Zoe dropped her bag and threw herself into Tricia's arms. "I missed you, too."

"Thank you for the shell, Zoe. It's the most special present anyone has ever given me."

"I'm sorry, Miss Tricia. Did my dad tell you?"

"Yes." Tricia looked up as Noah joined them. He smiled at her, then his gaze went all tender as he looked at Zoe. "You don't have anything to be sorry about, sweetie. I understood completely. I'm sorry, too."

Tricia wanted to pull Noah into the hug, too. Group hug, she wanted to shout, and have all of them come running, entwining arms and bodies until they laughed.

Zoe's face shone when she looked up at Tricia. Then she took off at top speed.

Noah took a couple of steps, stopping short of her.

"Looks like everyone had a good time," she said, linking her fingers.

"Yes. The week apart was a good way to start fresh, all of us. I feel like I've been given a new life."

"That's wonderful, Noah."

He came closer, close enough to touch, but he didn't. "It's all because of you."

"No. You would've found your way—"

"It's all because of you, Tricia. We'll never forget you. None of us."

She laughed nervously. "No need to throw me a farewell party yet."

His smile was bittersweet. "I'm going to check on them, then go to bed."

"Should I tuck them in, too, do you think? I'm at a loss here."

"I think you should do what feels right. They may not be quite as open or receptive as they were. Just so you're prepared."

Zoe will be, though. And that was a triumph in itself.

Noah lay in bed that night trying to sleep. He should have been exhausted. Hell, he *was* exhausted. The drive alone was enough to be its own kind of sleep aid. Factor in he was sleeping alone for the first time in seven days, and it changed everything.

He missed her. Missed the feel of her in his arms. The sound of her voice as they talked well into the night. Her playfulness when they showered together, her body sleek with soap. It had been a long time since he'd laughed so much, if he'd ever laughed so much.

When he stretched out his arm now, he felt only a cool sheet over a flat mattress, not a warm, curvy body that molded to his. She'd greeted him at the front door every night after work like he was the only man on earth.

Like she loved him.

But if she loved him, she would've said so. Or figured out a way to stay with them instead of taking the other job. She didn't offer to do that. She didn't say she loved him.

He hadn't set out to seduce her into staying, but during their week together, he'd seen it as a possibility.

But she never had. She had an obligation. He wouldn't have admired her as much if she didn't take her commitments seriously. He'd tried to make sure the children understood that as they talked during the drive home, using the example as a way of getting them to see the importance of keeping your word. It was a good life lesson, he'd decided, even if the outcome wasn't the desired one.

The kids adjusted easier than he'd expected, almost shrugging it off.

Which led him to believe they had a plan.

Noah had no intention of interfering. If his only chance for success was a little deviousness from his children, who was he to spoil their fun? What had Tricia told him her mantra was? *Life is short. Make it an adventure.*

Maybe there was still a chance.

Chapter Nineteen

November gave up its amber glow to the blues and whites of early December morning frosts. Tricia had started getting up earlier in the morning and going for a walk, watching her breath cloud around her, the chill biting, invigorating, renewing. She tried not to think so hard while she walked but just enjoy the beauty. Before too long, escrow would close on her house. She had assumed she would leave Noah's house at the same time, when the moving van was loaded and gone.

There was a hitch in the plans, however. No new teacher was in place yet.

It wasn't like they hadn't been looking. They'd interviewed several applicants. No one was right. They were too old, too young, too strict, too lenient. One liked bending the rules. Another enforced every one. Balance. They were missing balance.

Then the inevitable day when Ms. Right came along, or

rather Ms. Megan Wright. When she came to the door for her interview, Tricia thought she was looking in a mirror. Well, okay, maybe not *that* close a match, but an uncanny one. She was as tall, as blond, as friendly. Competent, progressive, forward-thinking. Fun. And she was willing to live in 24/7.

They held a family meeting after she left, then Noah tracked Tricia down and told her the offer would be made tomorrow. Tricia was free to leave.

Time to pull up roots.

She thought she saw a bit of sympathy in his eyes after he delivered the news. They'd danced around each other for two weeks, surrounded by crystal-clear memories of the week of exquisite intimacy they'd shared, in and out of bed. She'd come so close so many times to knocking on his door in the middle of the night. And she'd seen the hunger in his eyes for her, too— and the restraint.

Evenings were the hardest, when she met with him in his office to report on the day with the children. He'd kept the desk between them, had never once alluded to their relationship.

As for the children, they were different, too, but in a wonderful way. They were sweet to her and to each other, but they bickered a little more, which she saw as healthy. They didn't let things build up to a breaking point. A normal household with a loving father and four well-loved children, learning how to function well in the world later because of what they learned about relationships at home.

And tomorrow someone else would take her place, and be well loved by these beautiful children.

Would she be Ms. Wright for Noah, too?

"I think this is the longest you've gone without speaking," he said, having waited for her to respond.

She didn't know what to say. "I'm sorry."

"It's what you wanted, right?"

No. But she nodded. "You expect she'll accept the job offer?"

"According to Denise, yes."

He seemed to be waiting for something. "She seems great," she said. "The kids took to her right away." Did you, too? she wanted to ask.

"It's good that they were part of the process this time. Should make for a smooth transition."

"That's important."

"Yes."

He still seemed to be waiting for something. *What do you want, Noah?*

A few more seconds passed without conversation. "I'm going to join the kids in the family room," he said. "Want to come along?"

No. She needed to go somewhere and cry. It hit her so hard, she couldn't wait to get away.

Zach came into the living room and tugged on her sweater. "Miss Tricia?"

She swallowed the lump in her throat, set a hand on his shoulder. "Yes, Zachary?"

He placed a DVD in her hands. "Would you watch this with me?"

It was the video of his mother, the one he hadn't wanted to watch before.

She looked at Noah, who gave nothing away with his expression. Why wasn't he offering to watch it with his son?

Because Zach asked you. She could hear the words as clearly as if he'd said them aloud.

"Of course I would, Zach. Where should we go?" They couldn't use the family room, since everyone else was there.

"How about my room?" Noah said. "Would you like that, Zach?"

He nodded.

"Why don't you head up there?" Tricia said. "I'll be right behind you."

He trooped up the stairs. Tricia looked at Noah. "What's going on?"

"No idea."

"Are you okay with me doing this with him? Would you rather I talk him into letting you be there, instead—or both of us?"

"He wants you. I don't want to interfere with that, not about something this emotional. I guess the question is, are *you* okay with it?"

"Honestly? I've been curious about her."

His brows raised a little. "Question answered, then."

Oh, she wanted to kiss him. Hold him. Sleep curled against him. Wake to his handsome face in the morning and see his sleepy, sexy smile. She gave in to the ache for just a moment, put her hand on his chest and looked into his eyes. She saw the same temptation reflected back, his breath catching a little. She loved this man completely, infinitely.

"See you later," she said, hoping he would come to her after the children were asleep, for one last time.

Zach had the DVD in the machine when she got there. He'd pulled back the covers, piled pillows against the headboard and was stretched out there, the remote in hand. She climbed in bed with him, remembered the two nights she'd spent there in Noah's arms.

Zach snuggled close. Taking her cue from him, she put an arm around him, understanding that he needed her to be close, to feel emotionally safe. He started the video.

It was a professionally put together disc, set to music, with photographs of Margie as a baby, a child, a teenager, a college student, a bride. Twins in her arms. Another two babies later, with toddlers around her, too. Noah, looking tentative holding the girls, and then comfortable with the boys. Like Ashley,

Margie smiled a lot, obviously adored her children and her husband. Every image proved it.

There were snippets from their vacations in Disneyland and Disney World. Birthday parties. Halloweens. Christmases. Joyful times.

Zach didn't move, didn't comment. Occasionally he squeezed Tricia's hand, but that was all. Then when it was over, he was quiet for quite a while before he finally spoke.

"She sure loved us."

Tricia gathered him closer. "Oh, sweetie. She sure did."

"I love you, Miss Tricia," he whispered.

"I love you, too. So much."

"I don't want you to go."

Noah came into the room and saw them hugging. He walked toward them. She pressed her fingers to the corners of her eyes, trying to staunch a fresh flow of tears. Zach popped up, ran across the bed and leaped into Noah's arms. Tricia couldn't bear the tender scene. She hurried out of the room and went to her own.

Her own—for one more night.

Then after staring at her phone for a few long seconds, she picked it up and dialed.

Noah lay in his bed, the dark surrounding him, the scent of Tricia's perfume on his pillow. He'd been waiting two weeks for her to come to him, had slept fitfully every night, anticipation always on his mind. She never came. He never went to her. He knew that neither of them needed that complication, but it hadn't stopped him from hoping.

Now that they'd found a new teacher, she would leave. As early as tomorrow. Should he—could he—go to her tonight? Should he wait until she went back to Sacramento and see then if she wanted to continue what they'd started? They would have only until she left town.

Left town. Left their lives. His life.

He pushed himself up, his knees raised, his head tipped back, resting against the headboard.

The thought of her being gone from his life hit him like a gut punch, hard and out of the blue. Staggering. His hope that the kids had a plan hadn't turned out to be true. They hadn't interfered in the hiring process, hadn't delayed anything. And when a qualified person showed up today, they'd expressed their approval.

Weren't children supposed to be difficult when they weren't getting their way? He knew they wanted Tricia to stay.

He dragged the pillow she'd rested against earlier to press into his face, inhaling her scent, wishing for her, conjuring her up.

A quiet knock came at his door, then it opened just a crack.

"Noah?" she whispered.

"Come in," he said in a hurry. Was that all it took? Wishing for her? He reached over, turned on a bedside lamp, saw she was still dressed—at two in the morning.

"I'm sorry to bother you," she said.

He shook his head, not sure what to say until he knew why she was there. He patted the bed, inviting her to sit.

"I have to talk to you about something," she began, then stopped to take a breath, her hand pressed to her stomach.

"You're pregnant?" he asked, setting his hand on hers, waiting for the panic that should come but didn't.

"I— Pregnant?" She frowned. "No. Why would you think— Never mind. Here's the thing. I called my friend tonight, the one whose job I'm taking. I told her I couldn't take the job after all. She'd have to find someone else."

Couldn't do it? Wasn't leaving? "You backed out of the job? Out of your commitment?"

"What else could I do? I can't let just anyone teach your children. And, you know, the more I think about that Megan Wright, the more I think she's too good to be true."

He tried not to smile. If he wasn't mistaken, Miss Tricia was a little bit jealous. "I trust your instincts," he said. "If you don't think she's right, then we should rethink it."

"There's no rethinking about it. I'm staying. You have to keep me, because now I don't have a house or a job."

"I have to? Who's the boss here?"

"Technically, you are."

"Technically?"

She shrugged. He didn't buy the nonchalant act for a minute. "What did your friend say when you told her?"

"This is the funny part. She's been trying to figure out a way to tell me that her husband lost his job, and they decided he should be Mr. Mom for now. The school is offering me a teaching position, but I don't want it. I have a job here, a job I love."

A new kind of hope caught fire inside Noah, breaking down the wall he'd put up in order to survive her leaving. Because there were no barriers now, he heard something in her voice he hadn't heard before, or maybe she hadn't allowed him to hear it before. "There's going to be a problem with your plan," he said.

"You haven't offered her the job yet. You wouldn't have to renege."

He heard a bit of panic in her voice. It settled him like nothing else could have. He reached for her hands, feeling confident, and finally understood his jumbled emotions and sleepless nights.

"But, you see, Tricia, I can't continue to stay in the same house with you," he said, feeling her try to pull away, "and not be with you, in every sense of the word. You see, I've fallen in love with you."

After a moment, she threw herself into his arms, knocking him against the headboard. "I love you, too. Oh, Noah. I love you so much."

"You're not going to cry, are you?"

"I might." Her words were muffled by his shoulder. "Deal with it."

He laughed, and then he kissed her, tenderly at first, desperately after a minute. "I've missed you," he said.

"Not anywhere near as much as I've missed you."

"Well, we could spend a little time arguing about that, or I could go lock the door. You want to argue about that?"

"Who, me? Argue? Never."

By the time he'd walked to the door and back, she'd stripped and was kneeling in the middle of his bed waiting. He knelt in front of her. "I know this is fast. David's going to ride the hell out of me. But, here goes. I love you with all my heart. Will you marry me?"

She framed his face with her hands. "Yes."

"I hope you like children," he said with a grin.

She grinned back. "Pretty well, I guess. You know where I can get a couple of matched sets?"

Would she want more than that? A child with him? "Do you, that is, having more children, is it—"

"Yes," she said instantly. "One or two, if you're in agreement."

"Yes. Just not quadruplets, please." He kissed her, grateful and happy. "I've wondered for a long time if I would, or could, find someone who would love my children as if they were her own. I know you do. You were willing to stay on here, just as their teacher, weren't you? Without any promise from me? No declaration of love."

"Yes, although to be honest, it may have ended up being harder than I expected, being here, not being with you. In the end, the question I asked myself was, would I be happier with you or without you? I made my decision."

They fell into each other, made love this time knowing they loved, then slept a little while before she returned to her room, glowing and excited. In the morning they gathered the children in the family room.

"I have news," Noah said, eyeing each curious face. "I've asked Miss Tricia to marry me, and she said yes."

There was a long moment of silence, then smiles began to appear on their faces.

"It worked!" Adam shouted, jumping up. Zach did, too, high-fiving him.

Zoe and Ashley hugged.

"What worked?" Noah asked, glancing at Tricia, who shrugged.

"Our plan," Zach said, obviously proud of himself.

"I'm afraid to ask." So he'd been right. It made him happy to know he knew his children that well. He wouldn't let on to them, however. Not now, not ever. "What plan would that be, my plotting children?"

"We talked to Denise," Zoe said, "and told her to send a whole lot of people we wouldn't like, figuring Miss Tricia would get upset and say okay, okay, she'll stay. But that didn't work. So then Uncle David said, what if he sent someone that we all could say we liked. He bet Miss Tricia would be jealous and come to her senses."

"You mean if I offered Ms. Wright the job today, she would have declined?" Noah asked.

"She's got a job already," Ashley said, grinning. "She's big shot vice president of a bank or something. But she looks like Miss Tricia, and Uncle David said Miss Tricia wouldn't like that."

Tricia gasped, then started laughing, then bent over, she was laughing so hard. "Why you devious children," she said finally. "And can I say, I love Uncle David."

"We didn't want you to go," Adam said, a big admission for him.

"And now you can kind of be our mom," Zach said, coming up to her.

"I think Mom would be okay with that," Ashley said, looking at Noah.

"I think you're right. We won't ever forget her, I promise you."

Tricia was fighting tears. "When I first came here, I thought you all needed me. But the truth is, *I* needed all of you. And I sure could use one of those hugs now, if you don't mind," she said to Zach, opening her arms. He went straight into them. Pretty soon the others pushed their way in, bringing Noah into the circle as well.

He looked into Tricia's eyes over his children's heads. She looked back, her eyes shimmering, love shining from her, a beacon that lit up the whole room. He didn't know how he'd gotten lucky twice in his life. Maybe he was being rewarded for having survived childhood. Who knew?

All he knew for sure was that he was a happy man.

* * * * *

Don't miss Gideon's story,
The Millionaire's Christmas Wife,
on sale in December from Mills & Boon®
Special Moments™.

The Inherited Twins
by
Cathy Gillen Thacker

In most situations, twenty-nine-year-old Claire Olander had no problem standing her ground.

The only two Texans who could weaken her resolve ambled to a halt in front of her. In perfect synchronization, the "negotiators" turned their faces upward.

Her niece, Heidi, pushed the halo of short, baby-fine blond curls from her face and tucked her favorite baby doll under her arm, football-style, so the head faced front. "How come we have to clean up our toys now, Aunt Claire?" the preschooler demanded.

Her twin brother, Henry, adjusted his plastic yellow hard hat with one hand, then gave the small wooden bench he was "fixing" another twist with his toy wrench. His amber eyes darkened in protest as he pointed out with customary logic, "It's not dinnertime!"

Claire wished it was. Then the business meeting she had been dreading ever since the bank auditors left to tally their results, six weeks ago, would be history. Aware there was no use worrying her nearly four-year-old charges, she smiled and tidied the stacks of papers on her desk one last time.

Everything was going to be all right. She had to keep

remembering that. Just like her late sister, Liz-Beth, she was more than capable of mothering the twins and managing the family business they'd started. "We are cleaning up early, kiddos, because we have company coming this afternoon," she announced cheerfully. In fact, the Big Bad Wolf should be here at two o'clock.

Heidi sat down cross-legged on the floor, placed her doll, Sissy, carefully across her lap, and began stuffing building blocks ever so slowly into a plastic storage bin. "Who?"

Claire knelt down next to her, and began to help, albeit at a much quicker pace. "A man from the bank."

"Can he hammer stuff?" Henry demanded.

Claire surveyed the two children who were now hers to bring up, and shrugged. "I have no idea."

Heidi paused. "What *can* he do?" she asked, curiously.

"Manage a trust." *Destroy my hopes and dreams...*

Henry carefully fitted his wrench in the tool belt snapped around his waist, and sat down beside Heidi. "What's a trust?"

"The fund that's going to pay for your college education one day."

"Oh." He looked disappointed that it wasn't something he could "repair" with his tools.

"Is he our friend?" Heidi asked.

Claire fastened the lid on the building blocks bin, and put it on the shelf in her office reserved for the twins' playthings. "I've never met him, honey. He just moved here a couple of weeks ago." She'd heard a lot about him, though. The newest member of the Summit, Texas, business community was supposed to be thirty-three years old, to-die-for handsome and single, a fact that had the marriage-minded females in the community buzzing. Fortunately for Claire, she was not one of the group jockeying for attention. She had her hands full with her fledgling business and the twins she had inherited from her late sister and brother-in-law.

"Is he going to have good manners?" Henry, who'd lately become obsessed with what to do and what *not* to do, inquired.

"I'm sure Mr. H. R. McPherson is very polite," Claire said. Most bankers were.

Heidi put Sissy on her shoulder and gently patted her back, as if burping her. Her brow furrowed. "What's H. R. McDonald's?"

"H. R. McPherson, honey, and those are initials that stand for his first and middle names." Claire could not blame him for using them on business correspondence, even if it did make him sound a little like a human-resources department. "Although," she observed wryly, shelving the last of the toy train cars scattered about, "who would name their son Heathcliff *and* Rhett in this day and age, I don't know."

"As it happens," a low male voice drawled from the open doorway behind her, "the hopeless romantic who came up with that idea was my mother."

As the sexy voice filled the room, it was all Claire could do to suppress her embarrassment. Talk about bad timing! She'd just mouthed off about the man she could least afford to insult.

Slowly, she turned to face the interloper.

The ladies in town were right, she noted with an inward sigh. Tall, dark and handsome did not begin to do this man justice. He had to be at least six foot four inches tall, and buff the way guys who worked out regularly were. Nicely dressed, too, in a striking charcoal-gray business suit, navy-and-gray-striped shirt and sophisticated tie.

His midnight-blue eyes glimmering with amusement, he waited for her to say something.

Flushing, Claire flashed a smile. "This is awkward," she said.

"No kidding."

She took in the chiseled features beneath the thick black hair, the straight nose, the eminently kissable lips. "And you're early."

He shrugged and stepped closer, inundating her with the compelling mixture of soap, man and sun-drenched November air. "I wasn't sure how long it would take me to find the ranch." He extended his hand for the obligatory greeting, then assisted her to her feet. A tingle of awareness swept through her.

"I didn't think you'd mind," he added cordially.

Claire probably wouldn't have, had she not been down on the floor with the kids, speculating inappropriately about his lineage, at the exact moment he'd walked in.

Ever so slowly, he released her hand, and she felt her palm slide across the callused warmth of his. She stepped back, aware she was tingling all over from the press of skin to skin.

"You can call me Heath," he told her.

She swallowed nervously. "I'm Claire." Aware of the little ones taking refuge at her sides, she cupped her hands around their shoulders and drew them closer, conveying that they would always be safe with her. "And this is Heidi and Henry, the beneficiaries of the trust."

Heath shook their hands solemnly. "Pleased to meet you, Heidi. Henry, nice to meet you also."

"Pleased ta meet you!" the twins echoed, on cue.

Claire grinned, happy her lessons on manners were sinking in.

"So when do you want to get started?" Heath asked in a more businesslike tone.

"Just as soon as their sitter arrives," Claire declared, glad he was putting them on more solid ground.

© Cathy Gillen Thacker 2008